The Veiled
GARVEY

The Veiled

GARVEY

The Life & Times of

AMY JACQUES GARVEY

ULA YVETTE TAYLOR

The University of North Carolina Press

Chapel Hill and London

Manufactured in the United States of America
Set in Adobe Garamond and Trajan types
by Keystone Typesetting Inc.
The paper in this book meets the guidelines for
permanence and durability of the Committee on
Production Guidelines for Book Longevity of the
Council on Library Resources.

Library of Congress Cataloging-in-Publication Data
Taylor, Ula Y.
The veiled Garvey : the life and times of Amy Jacques
Garvey / Ula Yvette Taylor.
p. cm. — (Gender and American culture)
Includes bibliographical references and index.
ISBN 0-8078-2718-5 (cloth: alk. paper)
ISBN 0-8078-5386-0 (pbk.: alk. paper)
1. Garvey, Amy Jacques. 2. African American women
political activists—Biography. 3. Political activists—United
States—Biography. 4. Feminists—United States—
Biography. 5. Women intellectuals—United States—
Biography. 6. Garvey, Marcus, 1887–1940. 7. Black
nationalism—United States—History—20th century.
8. Pan-Africanism—History—20th century. 9. African
American women—Political activity—History—20th
century. 10. Feminism—United States—History—20th
century. I. Title. II. Gender & American culture
E185.97.G28 T39 2002
305.896'073'0092—dc21   2002018713
[B]

cloth 06 05 04 03 02 5 4 3 2 1
paper 06 05 04 03 02 5 4 3 2 1

For my first teachers, my parents,
William Taylor and Lillian Taylor,
and my lifelong friend,
Otis Campbell

In loving memory of
John Climmie Rogers, maternal grandfather
Thretha Jackson, paternal grandmother

CONTENTS

ACKNOWLEDGMENTS

This book emerges out of my sincere appreciation and love for Pan-African freedom fighters. It began as a dissertation, and similar to most long-term research projects, I have matured tremendously with this text. Each successive draft conjured up new intellectual challenges that paralleled both personal hardships and exciting triumphs. I cannot properly thank everyone in a few pages, so what follows is a modest attempt to express my gratitude to colleagues, friends, and family who offered support and encouragement.

Given that Amy Jacques Garvey represents the epitome of a diasporic subject, I conducted extensive research in New York City; Nashville, Tennessee; Cleveland, Ohio; Washington, D.C.; Kingston, Jamaica; Accra, Ghana; and London. Financial assistance from the Ford Foundation (dissertation and postdoctoral fellowships), the Schomburg Center for Research in Black Culture Residence Fellowship, and the University of California (UC), Berkeley (travel grants) was essential to completion of the archival research. I also appreciate the help I received from all of the archivists and reference librarians who pointed me in the proper direction. I am extremely grateful to Beth Howse and Ann Shockley at Fisk University, Nashville; Diana Latachenere and Jonathan Mason at the Schomburg Center in New York City; and Eppie D. Edwards at the National Library of Jamaica. They always met my numerous requests with total cooperation and patience.

At the University of North Carolina Press, my sponsoring editor, Sian Hunter, prodded me to rewrite when I lacked energy and focus. The anonymous readers offered valuable comments on how to improve the overall text. I am especially indebted to the perceptive critique offered by my dear friend, Chana Kai Lee. Her insightful suggestions and willingness to plow through a taxing rough draft have demonstrated not only her historical talents, intellectual sharpness, and, of course, endurance, but also how a close friend can be an extraordinarily generous and supportive colleague as well. Barbara Bair and Tera Hunter took time out from their work to give me valuable critical responses to earlier versions of various chapters. Kathy Checkvotich and Lynnéa Stephen provided editing advice that helped me to present a more polished manuscript. As a result of their collective criticism, my book has fewer errors and obscurities than it would otherwise have contained.

Many people guided me in preparing this book. During my graduate years at the University of California, Santa Barbara, Patricia Cohen, Douglas Daniels, Carl Harris, and Gerald Horne affirmed my passion for historical research. I found inspiration in the quality and intellectual breadth of their teaching and scholarship. I am especially indebted to Gerald Horne for the example of his own work and for his detailed commentary on mine. To Rupert Lewis, Tony Martin, Robert Hill, Barbara Bair, and Horace Campbell I am also deeply obligated. Their Garvey scholarship has been an indispensable foundation from which my own thought has proceeded.

Advice and encouragement have come from many quarters, but I take special note of the following family members and friends with whom I discussed many of the ideas in this book. My cousin, Lynnette Wooten, read several chapters and offered critical insight; I owe her more than I can express. My aunt, Mary Wooten, provided scrumptious Sunday meals, wake-up calls, and warm advice. Saidiya Hartman, my heartfelt sister, gave me gentle counsel and unconditional friendship when I needed it the most. My weekly lunches with my comrade, VèVè Clark, provided me with much-needed laughs and relaxation. My grandmother, Willie Rogers, and my aunt, Priscilla Venable, cheerfully asked about "the book." Both old and new friends—Otis Campbell, Venus Green, Kofi Hadjor, Marti Adams, Ralph Russell, Omar Garrett-Wray, Tamarra Lewis, Claudine Michel, Sharla Dundy-Millender, Kristy Bright, Shirley Burton, Jeffrey Baker, Terry Lindsey, Javanè Strong, and Lamont Toney—offered support at pivotal moments. A special thanks to all of my colleagues and the staff in the Department of African American Studies at UC Berkeley.

The final version of this book was actually written in the company of my nurturing father, William Taylor, and my beautiful sisters, Nan Taylor and Yolanda Taylor. Their willingness to listen to my "Amy" rambling and their questions regarding my work inspired me to write daily. I am blessed to have a loving "home."

For everything else, I am deeply grateful to God.

The Veiled
GARVEY

INTRODUCTION

The life and times of Amy Jacques Garvey challenge our understanding of Marcus Garvey and Garveyism and unveil the complicated reality of a black radical. Although Jacques Garvey was born in Jamaica on 31 December 1895, empowered by her father's teachings, she assumed her political identity in earnest in 1919, when she affiliated herself with the Universal Negro Improvement Association (UNIA) in Harlem, New York, as a private secretary to its leader, Marcus Garvey. As Garvey's personal secretary, confidante, and later second wife, she worked closely with him to keep the movement afloat, and as the archivist for the organization, she kept meticulous records of his speeches and the efforts of other activists determined to empower Africans at "home" and throughout the diaspora. Moreover, when Amy and Marcus married in 1922, she fully embraced the endeavor "to be conversant with subjects that would help in his career, and [to] try to make home a haven of rest and comfort for him."[1] This view of herself as a helpmate to Garvey would be transformed. As Jacques Garvey grew beyond the color and class boundaries that had permeated her world during her formative years, she became an independent Pan-African intellectual of stellar proportions.

As a political journalist, Jacques Garvey unfailingly wrote about the shortcomings of Jim Crow America, while simultaneously presenting the UNIA as a viable alternative, creating a refined discourse on the politics of race in the United States. In addition, her editorials on the woman's page in the UNIA's newspaper, the *Negro World*, destabilized masculinist discourse, offering a glimpse into the range and scope of feminism possible during the 1920s and a model of women as political beings who could change the world. In fact, Jacques Garvey's writings were a key component of early black feminism. She was adamant that men fulfill certain gender-specific roles; nor did she question the prevailing ideology that women should be self-sacrificing wives. Jacques Garvey did, however, challenge myopic gender politics. Her politically diverse articles encouraged women to navigate between both helpmate and leadership roles, and she was openly critical of black men who stifled options and choices for women.

Amy Jacques Garvey, along with other "race women" at the dawn of the twentieth century, mastered what I call "community feminism," a term that names the territory that Jacques Garvey was carving out—a territory that allowed her to join feminism and nationalism in a single coherent, consistent framework. At times, community feminism resembled a tug-of-war between feminist and nationalist paradigms, but it also provided a means of critiquing chauvinistic ideas of women as intellectually inferior. Essentially, community feminism permitted Jacques Garvey to balance her commitment to Garveyism and Pan-African ideas, and her commitment to her own personal development and feminist interests.

As a community feminist, Jacques Garvey encouraged women to educate themselves and to perform as both helpmates and leaders in their communities. By reading and discussing Pan-African materials, women, she believed, would be empowered not only to confront racism, colonialism, and imperialism, but to contest masculine dominance as well. In one of her last published articles, "The Role of Women in Liberation Struggles" (1972), she argued that women should use their "intelligence in a righteous cause" and that they were needed to "fill the breach, and fight as never before, for the masses need intelligent dedicated leadership."[2] Times changed, but Jacques Garvey never wavered from her belief that women should be given every opportunity for intellectual development.

Arguably representing the epitome of feminist agency, Jacques Garvey often suffered from the snubs of male comrades who believed that women should exclusively perform private, behind-the-scenes, domesticated roles within the movement. Her life reveals how one woman struggled to negotiate this highly masculine terrain. Unlike many of her female peers who refused to "air dirty laundry," Jacques Garvey defended herself both verbally and in print. Her personal relationship with Marcus Garvey (this book covers episodes from their private and public lives), as well as with other black men, generated ideas that rebuffed male dominance while still embracing aspects of patriarchy. Her stance was inconsistent in that she did not want men and women to be liberated from socially constructed gender-specific roles. For Jacques Garvey, "real men" were at the very least breadwinners, and "true race" women inhabited a consciousness that allowed them to celebrate their distinct culture and femininity without being delimited by it.

Jacques Garvey's burgeoning intellectualism blossomed into an authoritative tone and an expansive position in the UNIA. She was hailed as the Joan of Arc of helpmates by UNIA members, but to her frustration, this saintly moniker did not catapult her into real power within the organization. She resisted feeling powerlessness in a cauldron of patriarchy by never stifling her efforts, working sometimes up to eighteen hours a day to disseminate a Pan-Africanist political agenda. This heavy workload wreaked havoc on her physically, producing ailments and exacerbating already existing ones. Throughout her life she suffered from malaria, eye strain, arthritis, rheumatism, and excessive weight loss. In fact, she believed that her eventual cancer was a result of all the years she had compromised her health for the movement. Jacques Garvey's acts of self-subordination confirm her sincere commitment to the struggle and signal the complicated but very real life of a dedicated activist.

Over the years, Amy Jacques Garvey moved from simply perpetuating her husband's ideas to shaping and disseminating the philosophy of Garveyism. Most significantly, as editor of two volumes of *The Philosophy and Opinions of Marcus Garvey* (two of the most important primary collections in the field), she coalesced the scope of Garveyism and how it would be presented to the world. Defending Garvey the man and Garveyism as an ideology became the purpose of her existence until her death in 1973. For example, when publications explained Garveyism as a theoretical philosophy, she responded by underscoring that it was "not only a theoretical philosophy, but a working idealism, geared to the crying needs of an entire race."[3]

For the Garveys, addressing the concerns of people of African descent was paramount. In fact, they argued convincingly that black people were living internationally as second-class citizens, largely as a result of economic oppression. The Black Star Line Steamship Company was the UNIA's main venture to offset this injustice. Unfortunately, this capitalistic enterprise sowed the seeds of the organization's demise and Garvey's downfall. Mismanagement of the Black Star Line gave the U.S. government legal justification to entangle Garvey in a web of innuendo and fraud.

Since the early days of the organization, the federal government had targeted Garvey as an enemy. Special agents were assigned to monitor his every move with the goal of gathering incriminating evidence against him. Ironically, once the government incarcerated Garvey in a federal prison in 1925, Jacques Garvey was free to move beyond the strictures of wifehood and veiled helpmate, becoming a mature political thinker who frequently occupied the limelight. Although she often struggled to have her ideas taken seriously by male colleagues, who at times criticized her dominating personality, she never doubted her importance to the Pan-African cause in general and to the UNIA in particular.

After her husband's death in 1940, Amy Jacques Garvey experienced a political rebirth. For example, she began to deviate from her belief that the solution to black people's problems was linked to black capitalism, as she witnessed the suffering they endured in the backbreaking process of building a nation based on capitalist principles. Moreover, her private hardship as a single parent of two children encouraged her to think differently about the production, consumption, and distribution of resources. Clearly, she was not afraid to alter her thinking in response to a dynamic world. Her post-1940s articles thus emphasized the state's need to intervene and regulate the economy in order to benefit the majority of citizens. Evermore conscious of working-class issues, she moved from espousing community feminist ideas, which begin to fade from her political vocabulary, to championing the cause of exploited workers.

Jacques Garvey's private correspondence, largely written during the World War II period, reflects her intellectual evolution as a Pan-Africanist and explains how she moved the discourse to new heights with her call for "UNITY." By initiating dialogue with former enemies, she helped to facilitate an international network of thinkers working to achieve the goals of black self-government, self-reliance, and self-determination. Jacques Garvey argued that a redeemed Africa not only achieved decolonization but also offered strength and protection to New World Africans wherever they lived. Moreover, because she refused to let personal or petty differences disrupt her work, she metamorphosed from an isolated political woman to a group organizational woman for the Pan-African movement. It is interesting how her intimacy with the spirit of Marcus Garvey increased his emotional importance in her life and she became progressively aware of the need for collective input and approval. With the assistance of others, she completed major projects during the World War II period—among them her *Memorandum Correlative of Africa, the West Indies and the Americas*, a document addressed to United Nations representatives analyzing the loopholes in the Atlantic Charter and an appeal for an international African Freedom Charter and Council.

Jacques Garvey was a prolific writer, and her voluminous output testifies to her passion and selflessness for the Pan-African cause. She seldom relaxed, listening primarily to news on the radio and "read[ing] the newspapers and magazines with pen in hand."[4] She was a disciplined, arduous scholar whose objective was to fold Garveyism into existing progressive organizations, thus uniting a divergent Pan-African movement. Viewing herself as an authority on the Pan-African world, Jacques Garvey during the post–World War II period included among her comrades Nnamdi Azikiwe, W. E. B. Du Bois, Kwame Nkrumah, and George Padmore.

Amy Jacques Garvey's fifty-four years of activism demonstrate the complexity and conditions of a progressive female radical, as well as the limitations of conventional labels to describe her political participation. Her activism filled every aspect of her life, and when each historical moment brought new challenges, her supple mind adapted. Thus she could metamorphose from community feminist to organizational woman when conditions dictated yet another role in the struggle for liberation. Her political trajectory was vast, and she thought and wrote about many issues, always tying her ideas to a Pan-African theme, even when they were not in vogue or elicited ill will.

Jacques Garvey's skills were remarkable, and her grasp of international politics outclassed many renowned intellectuals of her day. Her theories about women as leaders and helpmates are noteworthy not only in the black radical tradition, but also in early twentieth-century feminist thought. As both a community feminist and an organizational leader, she served as journalist and editor, rallied support on behalf of Marcus Garvey, gave numerous public speeches, and managed UNIA affairs. As a female Pan-Africanist, she was not simply a symbol for the movement, but an active participant with fluid political ideas who refused to be silenced or manipulated.

Amy Jacques Garvey's activism represents the crossroads of many important historical moments in Europe, Jamaica, the United States, and West Africa, and her mind-set positioned her at the intersection of a distinctive type of feminism and nationalism. Her biography and her ideas remain impressive and important because they demonstrate how these historical movements rigorously critiqued racism, colonialism, and imperialism throughout the world.

L ittle is known about the early life of Amy Jacques Garvey—the woman who became not only the second wife of Marcus Garvey but also a prominent Pan-African activist and intellectual in her own right and, for a time, the unofficial leader of the worldwide Universal Negro Improvement Association and African (Imperial) Communities League (subsequently referred to as the UNIA). But the scant information available—especially in terms of racial/color attitudes and class—is important because these complex issues were crucial in Jamaican society and undoubtedly influenced Amy Jacques's formative years as a member of the "brown" middle/upper class. Two other factors seem to have also been significant but less typical: her formal schooling and her role in the family. Thus, though we do not have much information on Jacques's upbringing, it is important to underscore what we do know, since it gives us some thin threads that were woven into the tapestry of her later life, sometimes in surprising ways.

Amy Jacques never described the island of her birth, Jamaica, as a tourist paradise. She did not share memories of visiting the North Coast (Montego Bay), where the blue-green water is serene and hummingbirds abound. Nor did she write about the sun warming her "brown" face or describe walking through the countryside or playing in waterfalls. The girlhood recollections found in her essays and interviews are limited to a few vivid accounts of how her father, George Samuel Jacques, challenged her intellectually and prepared her for adult responsibilities. In hindsight, she gives the impression that her childhood was filled with serious duties; other than private piano lessons, her social engagements—whether festive or formal—were apparently so few that she elected not to mention them. And evidence to the contrary has not yet surfaced, despite the fact that the island offered a variety of amusements.[1] Though it is difficult to draw many conclusions from such sketchy remembrances, it is important to glean what we can from the record of Amy's early life in Jamaica, because it was there that she blossomed into a bright, cultured young woman—one in whom both her parents would take pride. What neither could have anticipated was that she would ultimately be transfigured, after living in the United States, from a typical debutante into a disciplined Pan-African thinker and leader.

Amy was born on 31 December 1895 in Jamaica's capital city of Kingston, the heart of the island's commercial, industrial, and professional life.[2] Horse-drawn wagons and carriages still roamed the poorly paved streets, but the loud cable cars gave this otherwise tranquil place a citified air. The geographic beauty and amply stocked stores attracted sophisticated urbanites to this seaport. The wealth of Kingston was largely generated by black workers, and, to some observers, women were the most visible laborers. Edgar Mayhem Bacon, who visited the island in 1890, reported that "women are the workers among the blacks in the neighborhood of Kingston. They carry the coal on the wharves, load and unload vessels, drive donkeys and mules with produce, break stones on the road, carry stone and other building material for house builders, wash, bake, dig in the fields."[3]

As was the case in most colonized communities, black labor overwhelmingly benefited elite Europeans, and Amy's own lineage was deeply rooted in an upper-class British heritage. Her great-great-grandfather, John Jaques or Jacques, had been the first mayor of Kingston.[4] (Only prosperous European men could participate in the political process and hold public office.)[5] As mayor, John Jaques was one of forty-seven members of the Jamaican House of Assembly. During his tenure, and well into the mid-nineteenth century, the assembly seems to have been shamelessly corrupt and controlled by privileged planters who lacked "fitness in character, education or morals."[6]

Mayor Jaques was not noted as an exceptional politician. For example, after much debate Britain abolished the trading of Africans in 1807 (though slavery remained legal for another thirty-one years), but apparently Jaques did not participate in this discussion and ultimately resigned his assembly seat in 1812 for health reasons.[7] Today, like many councillors, Jaques is celebrated in Kingston by his namesake, Jacques Road.

There are no records of what Amy's father, George, inherited in terms of material wealth from his great-grandfather, John Jaques. It is clear that he had the opportunity to receive a formal education and travel to the United States and Cuba before accepting a managerial position at the La

Paloma Cigar Factory. The tobacco trade was not a lucrative Jamaican industry, since there was insufficient profit to entice planters to manufacture cigars and cigarettes as compared to sugar, coffee, cocoa, and bananas. Planters also resisted tobacco production because it required large growers to employ "a special manager" who was familiar with the Cuban cultivation and curing process.[8] Further, it was generally conceded that Cubans grew a superior leaf. Nevertheless, by the early 1900s consumption of Jamaican cigars in England and Germany had begun to generate a greater demand for tobacco, and George's employment at the cigar factory must have seemed relatively secure.

Sometime in 1891, George married Charlotte Henrietta from the parish of St. Elizabeth. Charlotte's mother was a black woman named Jane, and her father, Frank South, was an English farmer. Like George, Charlotte was formally educated. With few exceptions, only members of the capitalist elite received a higher education during this period, and because of their class status it was incumbent on both George and Charlotte to socialize with, and ultimately marry, someone of comparable means. George demonstrated his financial security by purchasing seven acres of property on Long Mountain Avenue, located in the eastern section of Kingston where he built the family home. In addition, he bought real estate in the Windward Road area, a popular section for the "brown"/colored elite on the outskirts of the city.[9] Charlotte and George were married for five years before the birth of their first child. (George had fathered children prior to his marriage, but they did not count as "legitimate" heirs.)[10] They had prayed for a son but were blessed with Amy.

Though Amy was later to serve as the archivist for the UNIA, she provided little documentation of her personal life before migrating to the United States and meeting Marcus Garvey. Her reluctance to share the details of her earlier life may be accounted for in several ways. Perhaps she believed that it was not until she met Garvey that her life had profound meaning. Or her decision not to fully disclose her well-to-do Jamaican upbringing could have been tied to her need to maintain a public image of modesty and thrift in spite of her access to wealth. Nevertheless, a look at what it meant to be a part of the Jamaican middle/upper class in the early twentieth century provides some clues about her girlhood.

The middle/upper class is difficult to define precisely in any culture or community, because class is a relative term that is linked to the conditions of a particular situation. In Jamaica, level of formal schooling and training strongly influenced earning power and, therefore, class standing; however, skin color was another important variable in class divisions. Amy's family fell in the category of—and received all the privileges accorded to—formally educated "brown" Jamaicans.

The venomous seeds of the color/class system in Jamaica germinated in the course of slavery. During that time, inhabitants were legally divided into free (white), slave (African Caribbean), and freedmen/women (former slaves who lacked the full rights of a free person). In terms of legal rights, political power, wealth, and prestige, the whites of Jamaica were at the top of the hierarchy. Occupying the oppressive role of "masters," they had definite color preferences among the enslaved population; their obsession with pigmentation is evident by the color-coded records in all of the slave registration returns from the British Caribbean.[11] Skin color and physical features were just as important as gender and age. Phenotype functioned as a means to categorize enslaved people into specific occupations; later it determined treatment and labor expectations. A ranked order, based on a racial gradation between "African" and "European," was first established by the Spaniards but later adopted by the British, who used it crudely to label individuals and ultimately to create contested identities. Under this system, fluid racial classifications were divided, subdivided, and then diced into well-defined but confusing categories:

Negro—child of a Negro and Negro
Mulatto—child of a White and Negro
Sambo—child of a Mulatto and Negro
Quadroon—child of a White and Mulatto
Mustee—child of a White and Quadroon
Mustifino—child of a White and Mustee
Quintroon—child of a White and Mustifino
Octoroon—child of a White and Quintroon.[12]

In addition to bearing the labels that were assigned them by this classification system, members of the miscegenated population (largely produced by the bodies of black women) were collectively regarded as "colored" people. During slavery, coloreds far outnumbered Africans in skilled trades and were underrepresented in field gangs because they were generally regarded by planters as more intelligent. Clearly, the ability to think was linked to a lack of "color." Everywhere in the British Caribbean, the darkest Africans were relegated to the hardest field work because snide colonists linked their ancestry with savagery.

Not surprisingly, these racist and racialist attitudes toward the enslaved

coloreds and Africans were passed on to the freedmen/women's population. There is little doubt among Caribbean slave scholars that, by and
large, freedmen/women tended to share the dominant and damaging
European cultural precepts about race; economically, they were just as
committed to slave owning as the principal route to wealth. The majority of colored freedmen had inherited material wealth from their white
ancestors, and they owned "almost four times as many slaves as free
Blacks."[13] Freed coloreds lagged behind whites in terms of financial
wealth but were far ahead of freed blacks in terms of occupational skills,
financial wealth, formal education, and thereby status. When slavery was
legally abolished in 1838, the glaring vestiges of the institution remained
firmly intact. This color/class system continued to be reinforced throughout the nineteenth and well into the twentieth century.[14]

As a member of a well-to-do, middle-class family—and, more importantly, of a society in which race was intrinsically important to class formation—Amy Jacques was proud of her light brown hue, which granted
her an assumption of difference, or "superiority," when compared to the
black laboring classes of the island. She, like most Jamaican citizens of the
period, had no doubt internalized the Eurocentric, but very real connection between color and prestige fused during slavery. She had inherited
her mother's genetic makeup: light brown skin and a fine hair texture. In
contrast, her father was of a darker hue. Amy often credited him with her
intellectual development and apparently loved him dearly, but as the
product of an environment where individuals often prejudged others
based on appearance, she recalled how "she had been ashamed of her
father coming to school because of his dark color."[15] Her reaction was one
of self-preservation. Physical attributes (skin color, hair type, and facial
features) could work like radar in terms of detecting one's lineage and
evaluating that individual's presumed manner of living. George Jacques's
color, Amy thought, implied to her school peers that her pedigree was not
as "lightly-colored" as she wanted them to believe. And since women were
generally regarded as having less status than men, it was even harder for
them to escape color and class restrictions.[16]

Despite the fact that no legal color bar existed, scholars have documented color discrimination against dark-skinned people in employment, particularly in public service occupations. Unquestionably, class
and color were interwoven to an extent that class tensions often mani-
fested themselves as conflict over color.[17] It seems that color clouded
Amy's thinking in such a dramatic way that at times she felt uncomfort-

able sharing a public space (her school) with her own father—a man who clearly put energy into his parenting as well as providing for all of her material needs and desires.

Racial characteristics, such as color, thus had a powerful impact on everyday racial discourse in Jamaica; in this setting it would have been nearly impossible for Amy to discover and embrace her "blackness." But two other features of her early upbringing may have helped to put her on the path toward eventually becoming a Pan-African intellectual: her formal education—which confirmed standard ideas about race, but ironically, at the same time, gave her the intellectual tools to later challenge the imperialist myth of European superiority—and the fact that, as a child, she was treated "like a boy."[18]

Amy stated that she learned at an early age the significance of an education. Often her father would give her exercises to increase her knowledge and develop her literary skills. "On Sundays, after dinner, he would collect foreign newspapers, and I had to get a dictionary, and read the editorials and news items." Jacques would explain events and answer all of her questions. Sometimes he would give her an assignment to write an essay on a news item or article. This dialectical, intergenerational exchange provided a double-learning environment for Amy, causing her to "learn to think independently on world affairs and to analyze situations."[19]

While her father challenged and stimulated her intellect at home, Amy attended school at a time when compulsory elementary education was nonexistent in Jamaica. Her formal instruction began at St. Patrick's, then continued at one of the twelve Deaconess Home Schools for boys and girls. These Anglican schools were operated by nuns from London who geared the curriculum toward the Cambridge Local Examinations, which included instruction in religion, English language and literature, arithmetic and mathematics, history, geography, music, and drill. Given that the schools received a grant from the government, they were subject to examination and inspection. In addition to requiring that all candidates for admission submit testimonials of good character and conduct, Deaconess schools called for proof of vaccination and a medical certificate of good health. Tuition was mandatory for all pupils, and scholarships were few and extremely competitive. Deaconess was noted for preparing Jamaican women to be parochial workers, nurses, and teachers.

In Jamaica, education was touted as the most efficient way to secure and maintain wealth. No doubt, the pronounced inequalities of the stratified social order at the turn of the century were perpetuated by its educational system. While the European elites sent their children to be educated in Britain and the United States, a select few from the middle/upper stratum, many of whom were racially mixed people, sent their children to the local secondary schools on the island. After completing her primary schooling at the Deaconess Home School, Amy went on to the even more prestigious Wolmers Girls' School, which represented the essence of elite secondary education. At that time secondary instruction in Jamaica had a literary slant, including classes in Latin, English language and literature, and modern languages as well as bookkeeping and shorthand. Manual subjects were not a part of the curriculum, which prepared students for the Cambridge Local Examinations, the External Training College Examinations, and the Pupil Teachers' Examinations.[20]

Founded in 1729, Wolmers remains the oldest existing secondary school on the island. In 1911, while Amy was a student there, it was comparable to a "good Girls Day school in an English town." She and her sister Ethlin attended Wolmers from 1911 to 1913.[21] Because they were enrolled together, their parents paid a slightly reduced tuition, but even so, this fee (£8 to £6 annually) would have been affordable only for parents of the middle/upper class. The Jacques girls were undoubtedly distinguished from their peers since only a handful of "brown"/colored youth had the opportunity to receive a secondary education. In fact, in 1910 only about one-quarter of the colored population could read and write.[22]

In addition to providing academic skills, Wolmers acculturated its students to adopt the essentialized values and lifestyle of the British. Numerous testimonies by former pupils express how the school was not just an educational institution, but a way of life. In many ways, Wolmers provided a training ground not only for occupations but also for the social roles individuals were expected to play as adults. One former student stated that generations of girls had established an "unofficial code of behavior" that could only be slightly modified. She further observed, "No team of scientists can determine what the effect of that institution was on our personalities." It is impossible to accurately assess the full impact Wolmers had on Amy Jacques in particular, but we know that her classmates were from the upper class, and she most likely associated with similar peers outside of school.[23] Her best friend, Leila Tomlinson (the first woman to receive a Jamaican scholarship to attend a British university), also attended Wolmers. It would have been highly unusual for a young woman with Amy's pedigree not to think and act like the people around her—especially since, as Etienne Balibar points out, no identity is ever acquired in isolation even though "all identity is individual." Moreover, "there is no individual identity that is not historical or, in other words, constructed within a field of social values, norms of behavior and collective symbols."[24]

Skin color and formal education were key markers of the Jamaican middle class, but family structure was also important, particularly in terms of reinforcing gender-specific roles and "appropriate" behavior. Studies that highlight Jamaican family configurations are primarily anthropological and sociological in nature and center mostly on the post-1950s. These works generally document how financial wealth largely determined the roles each family member played out or at least was encouraged to accept. Though it would be ahistorical to apply these findings unhesitatingly to the early twentieth century, aspects of these studies enable scholars to reconstruct a "typical" Jamaican middle-class family structure for the time frame encompassing Amy Jacques's youth.

In contrast to the numerous working-class family studies, considerably less is known about the socialization and variations among middle-/upper-class families in the early twentieth century. It appears, though, that these families modeled themselves on their British and U.S. counterparts. This is why, as Stuart Hall puts it, "If you live, as I've lived, in Jamaica, in a lower-middle-class family that was trying to be a middle-class Jamaican family trying to be an upper-middle-class Jamaican family trying to be an English Victorian family," your identity was grounded in the notion of displacement.[25] Essentially, well-to-do Jamaicans attempted to replicate Victorian families, which were presumed to be "superior," by creating households that were patriarchal and nuclear.

The foundation of this household formation was based on the prevailing assumption that a middle-class Jamaican woman would marry a man with a secure economic and social position. The relationship of Amy Jacques's parents supports this generalized notion. George and Charlotte were compatible mates in that his status affirmed his ability to maintain a style of living that she was most likely accustomed to. Financial security ensured a nonimpoverished home and amplified familiar choices, but it also strengthened male dominance within the marriage. Most middle-/upper-class women were believed to defer to masculine authority to a greater degree than working-class women did because of their father's or husband's strong earning power.

Whereas many wives evaluated their husbands in terms of their ability to provide for the family financially, many husbands, in turn, judged their wives based on how well they functioned as helpmates and mothers. For young women in Jamaica, full adult status was achieved by the "rite of passage" of either marriage or the birth of a child. Once a woman became a mother, she was instrumental in the socialization of her children, particularly her daughters. Girls were feminized by following the patterns of their mothers and other women around them. Role training began by the age of five, primarily by learning "women's work." The major aim in the female socializing process was "the repression of aggression and independence." Charlotte Jacques could be identified as a woman who succeeded on these terms. In one of few statements about her, Amy describes her mother as "soft and a goody-goody, if you know what I mean."[26] Perhaps she meant that Charlotte was shy and expressed herself in a genteel fashion. Or, perhaps, as a housewife, she had internalized a specific type of behavior that was displayed as meek or humble. Amy never states that she wanted to emulate her mother's temperament, despite the fact that it was in keeping with an "appropriate," feminine, middle-class demeanor.

Amy's strong personality—presumably an antithesis to her mother's—was perhaps in part a reflection of her father's displacement of his wish for a son onto a desire to rear a strong daughter. The fact that he was active in raising his children put him in direct contrast with most middle-class fathers of the time. Men were believed to be inaccessible because their work and social activities took them away from home during a child's waking hours. These conditions ultimately produced offspring who had little "experience with their fathers' personality, values or behavioral traits."[27] George Jacques, on the other hand, took an atypical stance and was sincerely interested in child rearing after Amy's birth. In fact, Amy recalled that he trained her in the tradition "befitting" a male child. He exposed her not only to international affairs but also to "male responsibilities of handling [his] field hands and sternly keeping the property clear of stray cattle."[28] Understanding that her father viewed her as a substitute for a son, she explained that "I was brought up like a boy, you see." On another occasion she stated that "when I could walk around, he would put me on his shoulders and trot me around the place and talk to me as if I was a boy."[29] Her description of their interaction is noteworthy because Amy viewed her father's attitude toward her in socially constructed, gender-specific terms. Being treated as a boy seems to have brought an element of freedom and adventure to her young life.

But a "masculinized" daughter was charming only as long as she remained in a child's body. Adolescence marked the period when her parents, most likely at the urging of her mother, became more concerned about Amy's cultural refinement. They insisted that she study music. Amy tried to excel, but she had "no ear for music" and eventually convinced her father to let her take shorthand and typing instead. He reluctantly agreed, cautioning that these skills were to be used only to take notes when she entered nursing school in England. As Amy matured, it seems that her father backpedaled from his earlier instruction and began to reinforce more traditional ideas regarding cultural and social values. He now wanted to ensure that her decisions were appropriate for a lady. It was not controversial to expose a girl to boy activities, perhaps, but a "proper" young woman's place was very different from a young man's.

Although Jacques had socialized Amy to be self-confident and high-achieving, he "graciously declined" her first employment offer, a "beginner's post" in a law firm. As a protective patriarch, he later said, "I do not want any daughter of mine to be exposed to the wiles of men in an office." Thus, even though the first lessons that Amy learned from her father were to "stand on her own" and "never be afraid of men," as she came of age he did not want her to be in an unsupervised setting with mixed company. By her own report, she learned to negotiate her father's colliding messages to his satisfaction, and she proudly stated that "the biggest influence in my life was my father."[30]

Soon after Amy finished at Wolmers Girls' School, she and her family were forced to reckon with the tragic death of her father, who died from a stroke on 3 August 1913 at their residence, Jacques Villa, on Long Mountain Road. On 16 August, in keeping with middle-/upper-class etiquette, the Jacques publicly thanked family and friends in the *Daily Gleaner*—the newspaper read by all of high society—for the expressions of sympathy during their bereavement. And on 23 August, Charlotte began proceedings to file her husband's last will and testament with the local records office. He had bequeathed to all of his "lawful children," Amy Euphemia, Ethlin Maud, Cleveland Augustas, Ida Chole, and Joscelyn Samuel, "all of my properties real and personal: provided that all monies in the banks remaining with all interest accruing be divided by giving to each when twenty-one a quota of one fifth and each child after receiving its claims shall not have any further claim in any remaining divided."[31]

Jacques had added the stipulation that his wife serve as the "sole executrine" of his will and that all rents collected from the properties be "used by her for the maintenance of the children and to repair and build upon these premises as the executrine thinks fit and desirous (without the consent of the children)."[32] Perhaps he included this clause concerning his "lawful" children because he was aware of his wife's "soft" demeanor, as noted by both Amy and her sister Ida, and feared that the children would squabble and take liberties with the property. But however meek Charlotte appeared to her daughters, the will confirmed George's faith in her ability to oversee the household.

Though Charlotte was the legal executive, Amy took over as the head of the family. She continued to stress the importance of a formal education to her younger siblings and made sure that they all attended fine secondary schools. The following year her family's personal solicitor, T. R. MacMillian of Kingston, suggested to Charlotte that Amy work in his office as a clerk to better facilitate the management of their estate. Her mother may have had some reservations about her working outside the home, but she did not have the puissant influence over her daughter that her husband had had. No longer having a protective father to prohibit it, Amy accepted the offer. Her earlier private lessons in shorthand and typing enabled her to perform her duties quite well. In fact, MacMillian was so impressed that he encouraged Amy to become a lawyer, and her sister Ida believed that she could have been the first female attorney in Jamaica.

As she worked in MacMillian's chambers, Jacques suffered chronic health problems due to recurring bouts of malaria. All around the island undrained mosquito-breeding swamps generated the optimum conditions for transmission, which resulted in epidemics in spite of quinine treatments. There are many clinical variations of malarial fevers; uncomplicated malarial symptoms include headache, sudden chills, shivering, high fever, vomiting, shallow breathing, and muscle aches and pains. In Jamaica, however, a severer form, Plasmodium falciparum, was responsible for high malaria mortality. Ida recalled that Amy would "faint" in the MacMillian office due to her sickness. Fainting could have been a sign of comatose malaria, a form that resembled apoplexy or sunstroke. Also, "sudden collapse" could have been a reaction to a falciparum infection. Amy's physician no doubt informed her that malaria transmission did not occur at temperatures below 16 degrees centigrade and, more importantly, that every variety of malaria, with all of its consequences, "may be considered as cured after the patient has lived in a malaria-free country for some years."[33] Clearly, her condition dictated that she seek relief in a cooler climate.

After four years (1913–17) in the MacMillian office, Amy Jacques left the island of her birth. World War I prevented her from considering England as a destination, since most shipping lines were refusing women passengers due to submarine warfare.[34] These circumstances caused her to decide on Harlem, New York, where a well-established African Caribbean population existed.

Departing any Caribbean island legally could easily turn into a bureaucratic nightmare. The *Jamaican Gazette*, a popular newspaper that printed information on immigration procedures, indicated that all travelers would have to "convince the consular authorities of the necessity of taking such a journey before they were granted an American Visa." In addition, all Jamaicans had to "satisfy the requirements of the U.S. Consul at the port of departure." A legal sponsor in the United States also had to be identified. Charlotte Jacques had relatives in America, but Amy could not stay with them because "they all passed as white."[35] Although she offers no further comments on her relatives "passing," unquestionably her presence would have called into question their racial "purity," automatically disqualifying them to claims—and the economic, social, political, and legal privileges—of a white identity. She therefore had to look elsewhere for a sponsor. Since the legal process was so cumbersome, it was not unusual to have someone masquerade as a relative. Mrs. Lilly Francis, a resident of New York City, agreed to pose as Amy's "sister."[36] Finally, with all of her paperwork in order, Amy packed her bags and prepared for the voyage.

This was a very emotional time in the Jacques household. Amy's mother "was so upset that she had a conference with [their] minister and lawyer in hopes to dissuade [her]." They all agreed that America "was no place for [her] type." Although concerned about Amy's sickness, Charlotte resisted the trip partly because honorable women seldom traveled by themselves, and she did not even want to imagine Amy living alone in the United States. Indeed, her daughter's boldness frightened her. But Amy had the self-confidence needed to venture into another territory. As a young girl she had become empowered by her father's early teachings to look beyond prevailing gender-specific constraints. As a strong-willed young woman, she was convinced that she could take care of herself and maintain her respectability in New York City. Nevertheless, to appease her mother she promised to return home in "three months if conditions were unbearable."[37]

On 21 April 1917 Amy Jacques boarded the SS *Carrilo* in Kingston Harbor and set sail for New York City. The ticket cost at least $65, but the expense was not a major issue for her: at the age of twenty-one she had inherited money from her father's estate and had saved her earnings from her secretarial job over the previous four years.[1]

One of approximately 160 passengers, she sailed unaccompanied to a land that was, according to her father's description, "one mixed of opportunity and restrictions."[2] She was undoubtedly filled with anxiety about the trip itself, since at that time ship travel was very rough, and the accommodations were deplorable. Yet New York City would provide the cool climate and refuge that she so desperately needed to end her repeated bouts of malaria. Still, she must have felt nervous about living away from her nuclear family for the first time in her life.

After five days at sea, the ship docked safely. Though the sky was overcast and the air was cool, the dreariness of the day would not have tempered Jacques's excitement on arriving at Ellis Island. Here she faced her first hurdle as an immigrant. For years Ellis Island had been a symbol of opportunity, but the Immigration Act of 1917, the first in a series that favored national groups thought to be more "assimilable," had already stifled the hopes of many newcomers. Everyone over age sixteen had to pass a literacy test, and all had to undergo a stringent and too-often-humiliating medical examination to determine if they had a contagious disease. But Jacques met both requirements and was subsequently released to Mrs. Lilly Francis, who was posing as her sister. Francis gave officials her name and address and agreed to assume full financial responsibility for Jacques. Participating in this charade may have been easy for Francis, since she was well aware of Jacques's status in Jamaica and had to know about her resourcefulness. In addition to managing her family's financial affairs after her father died and working as a secretary, Jacques's take-charge personality no doubt affirmed to others that she could provide for herself.[3]

Although we can make these assumptions with reasonable confidence, Jacques said little about her life in America between 1917 and 1919. Several interviews report merely that she went to the United States for "additional education" or because she was "restless" and desired to travel (and Europe was not an option during wartime).[4] Moreover, although her bouts with malaria are well documented, Jacques herself never mentioned this as the reason for her move, nor did she indicate how or where she lived in New York before meeting Marcus Garvey. Locating Jacques is further complicated by the fact that racial and gender hierarchies placed her at the margins of organizational and normative structures. Cheryl Harris contends that any intervention by a black woman was "subject to be overlooked, misheard, misinterpreted, misrepresented and ultimately misappropriated."[5] Thus, what appears to be a deficiency of information about Jacques in particular was actually the case for most black women. That is, under these conditions it was difficult to be known via public records. Essentially, one can speculate about Jacques's life only by contextualizing and drawing conclusions from the few tidbits of information that she did share.

We do know that her arrival in the United States coincided with the peak period (1911–24) of black emigration from the English-speaking Caribbean islands.[6] Between 1899 and 1937 approximately 150,000 black immigrants were legally admitted, making them the largest group of black people who migrated voluntarily to the United States.[7] Poverty (a series of devastating hurricanes between 1910 and 1921 ravaged the agricultural economy of the islands), lack of access to postsecondary education, and limited professional opportunities in Jamaica all prompted migration. Generally, it was easier to secure a visa if one had access to financial resources; thus, the vast majority of immigrants were literate, skilled, and ambitious. Many of them were men (from 1911 to 1915, 126 males arrived for every 100 females, but the ratio dwindled to 96–100 from 1916 to 1920). They were young and unmarried (3 out of 4 were between 14 and 44 years old, and 2 out of 3 were unmarried), and, by and large, their fathers' occupations identified them as middle class.[8]

Jacques's first two years in the United States obviously changed the direction of her life—an experience shared by other black immigrants at the time. The entry of the United States into World War I had provided an opportunity for both American and Caribbean black people to leave their place of birth and move to northern cities. The war initially created an economic boom for the United States, and with the lessening of European immigration, black people were offered work to fill the void in the labor market.[9] Once they settled in the North, however, African American migrants and African Caribbean immigrants were restricted to low-wage occupations and were forced to live in segregated, overcrowded residential areas with high rents and poor sanitation. The newly emergent northern "ghettos" became characteristic of black life.

These stressful conditions radicalized many Caribbean immigrants who presumably would not have engaged in "race" or "class" activism in their native countries. For the first time, numerous African Caribbean people found themselves cast in the role of a "racial minority" and had to suffer the indignities that resulted from that status.[10] This spurred many to political action. Caribbean immigrants who became the forerunners of black reform during this period included W. A. Domingo, Hubert Harrison, Cyril Briggs, and, of course, Marcus Garvey.

It is impossible to ascertain the direct impact these historical events had on Amy Jacques, but her volunteer participation in the Universal Negro Improvement Association (UNIA) had to be the last stop in a series of adjustments, some of which we can only guess at. For example, it is unclear if she actually lived with Lilly Francis at her home on West 134th Street in the heart of black Harlem or if Francis simply identified herself as a sponsor for the immigration officials. Jacques's sister Ida, who was still in Jamaica at this time, recalls that Amy had actually arranged to stay with their cousins, the Graves. If Jacques did not live with Francis or the Grave family, she most likely resided with another African Caribbean family. It would have been highly unusual for her to live in an apartment on her own, since most single black people, whether Caribbean or American, stayed with a family or in a rooming house.[11]

Even though Jacques was not financially desperate, as were many European immigrants, and the foreign currency exchange rate favored the Jamaican/British pound over the dollar, her personal drive and intelligence would eventually have led her to find some form of employment. No doubt, her search quickly disclosed the harsh realities of racism in the United States. Black women were almost exclusively limited to menial jobs, regardless of their skills. Even college graduates often found themselves working in a service occupation at various times throughout the year. Essentially, "black women's work," regardless of whether one was native-born or from the Caribbean, "was synonymous with domestic service"; thus, Jacques would have been an exception if she had found a job that did not relegate her to domestic service or another low-paying occupation.[12] At best, she might have convinced a respected community member to vouch for her character, which could have paved the way for a black-owned business to hire her, since she could easily pass any typing test.

The majority of African Caribbean women who trekked to the United States in the early twentieth century sought work; only a smattering came specifically to study. In a 1964 interview Jacques reported that she had wanted to attend college, but she did not indicate that she ever enrolled, and the 1920 U.S. census confirms that she had not attended any school since September 1919.[13] For whatever reason, her desire to expand her formal education in an institutional setting was apparently never fulfilled.

Amy Jacques was fortunate that Harlem had a well-established Caribbean community; nonetheless, for recent immigrants there was no place like their homeland. Although the United States offered many material comforts, these could not replace the comradeship that the newcomers had previously known or eradicate their feelings of alienation. Joyce Toney points out that one adaptive mechanism for Caribbean immigrants was to "look for esteem in the societies they left behind."[14] Though Jacques makes no reference to an involvement in any social or political organization prior to the UNIA, she undoubtedly had access to a number of associations that would remind her of home.

Groups such as the West Indian Committee on America, Foreign-Born Citizens Alliance, West Indian Reform Association, British Jamaicans Benevolent Association, or American West Indian Ladies Aid Society—a likely group for Jacques, since Caribbean women "tend to flock to each other for their social life"—were all possible sites for fellowship. These benevolent organizations, with their elite underpinnings, provided both charitable services and social activities, and members often established lifelong friendships. Carol Boyce Davies has shown that societies are a response to the "exile" felt by migrants, who "demand the creation of new communities with new relationships to those homelands."[15] A longing to reconnect to home could have spurred Jacques to attend a function or a meeting, but if she did they seemingly had no lasting meaning for her, as she does not mention them in her writings.

Less formal interaction was more characteristic of Caribbean women's daily lives. For example, for Paule Marshall's mother, who migrated to

New York from Barbados following World War I, social life "consisted mainly of sitting around the kitchen table after their return from work each day and talking. Endlessly talking." Much of their talk centered around holding onto "the memories that defined them," the people and events at home. "It was clearly an effort on their part," Marshall points out, "to retain their cultural identity amidst the perplexing newness of America."[16]

The likelihood that Jacques established meaningful connections with African Americans is even harder to imagine. Cross-cultural friendships were difficult to forge because stereotypes and prejudices adversely affected social relations between African Americans and African Caribbean people. Economic competition and cultural differences produced obstacles between the two groups that too often resulted in mutual suspicion and tension.

African Americans often described islanders as overly aggressive, arrogant, and clannish; islanders identified native-born black people as lacking ambition and self-confidence and possessing a radical edge. As a child, Paule Marshall observed how "the West Indian woman" during this period "considered herself both different and somehow superior" to the African American woman. The distance that Caribbean women sought to place between themselves and African American women was reinforced by the dominant culture, "which often praised them [the Caribbean women] for being more reliable, trustworthy and hard working."[17] Cultural differences were so vast that people from the same island tended to associate only with one another; they often expressed an alienation from all African Americans and sought to escape any identification with them.[18]

Though it is tempting to speculate about Jacques's activities between the day she checked out of Ellis Island and the day she entered the UNIA, the fact is that she elected to keep her personal memories to herself. What is verifiable is that she was drawn to the UNIA when it was already a formidable organization. Jacques claims that she had heard conflicting reports about the organization and that its purpose was unclear. Nor did she understand what Marcus Garvey, whom she had first met in Jamaica in 1913, intended to do. Out of curiosity, she went one Sunday night in the summer of 1919 to the newly purchased Liberty Hall, a "low-roofed, hot, zinc-covered" former Baptist church that held six thousand people, at 138th Street in Harlem where the meetings took place.[19] The thirty-five-cent admission charge included not only speeches and debates but upscale musical performances and poetic renditions as well. After the session she approached Garvey to congratulate him on his inspiring talk and ask him about the many issues he had failed to explore. She told him that not only did she want to be convinced that he was correct, but also to have the opportunity to argue her convictions. His answers, however, generated more questions, so they agreed to meet at his office, where they would have more time to converse. At the office, he showed her around and asked her opinion of it. She frankly told him that he needed a daily reporting system so that he would be able to track the UNIA activities and calculate the amount of money they generated. Garvey was impressed with her suggestions and after much pleading on his part, she accepted a secretarial position.[20]

Amy Jacques's description of her initial meeting with Garvey is somewhat surprising if not downright hard to believe. She claims that at Liberty Hall that first night she was able to challenge him on points that he did not cover in his speech, implying that she was well versed on diasporic issues. She also opted to question Garvey afterward, face-to-face, instead of addressing her concerns to the entire audience.

Her account of their conversation raises many questions. For example, why would Garvey invite an unknown, inquisitive woman to his office, when there was a host of UNIA officers whom he could direct to answer her questions? Why would Jacques put so much energy into wanting to be convinced that Garvey's ideas were right when she believed that her own convictions were just as valid? We need to bear in mind that this is her account, not Garvey's, and that she gave it for public consumption twenty-six years after his death. Amy Jacques, like many individuals, chose to remember and emphasize what she felt was essential—and perhaps what showed her in the best light. She dwells on the fact that Garvey was captivated by her sharp mind, her efficiency, and her willingness to challenge and criticize his ideas. No feminine charms are hinted at; Garvey apparently admired her solely for her intelligence.

Another problematic version of how Jacques came both to learn about and to enter UNIA's headquarters is offered by Amy Ashwood. A cofounder of the UNIA, Ashwood claims that the two women were friends in Jamaica. It was in Jacques's birthplace, Kingston, that Ashwood and Garvey "planned a great Black Confraternity, under our own vine and fig tree in our own Africa" in early July 1914. The two were serious about their mission; Ashwood later described their commitment as a "bond of comradeship based upon a common ideal and belief, directed to a common goal."[21] The objectives of their new organization were:

To Establish a Universal Confraternity among the Race.
To Promote the Spirit of Race Pride and Love.
To Reclaim th[e] Fallen of the Race.
To Administer to, and help the Needy.
To Assist in Civilizing the Backward tribes of Africa.
To Strengthen the Imperialism of Bas[u]toland, Liberia, etc.
To Establish [C]ommissioners in the Principal Countries of the
    world, for the Protection of all Negroes, Irrespective of
    Nationality.
To Promote a Conscientious Christian Workshop among the Native
    Tribes of Africa.
To Establish Universities and Colleges and Secondary Schools for the
    Further Education and Culture of our Boys and Girls.[22]

Despite these published goals, the *Daily Gleaner* reported on 14 September 1914 that the object of this "New Society" was "to improve the elocutionary and literary tastes of the youth of our community," along with doing social and charitable work. UNIA meetings and activities in Jamaica thus resembled those of any other "society" at the turn of the century. They raised funds to feed the poor of Kingston on Christmas Day and distributed flowers at hospitals.[23]

Although she makes no mention of it in later interviews, Amy Jacques may have heard about the UNIA through the middle-class grapevine. Ashwood's father was a successful caterer, and seventeen-year-old Amy was a recent graduate of the prestigious Westwood High School. No doubt her public association with the likes of Marcus Garvey was considered scandalous. Ashwood's mother did not approve, and even Garvey admitted that he had "some terrible experience[s]" with Mrs. Ashwood.[24] To be sure, although Garvey was educated and had traveled abroad, he was already twenty-seven years old, and, though not a ruffian, he was poor. Despite the fact that Garvey had his eyes on the elites, Ashwood's parents might have been concerned that he was using their daughter to gain access to their respectable middle-class circle to further his schemes. Whatever their particular concerns, Garvey was far from a prime catch for any young woman outside the Jamaican working class.

Reports of UNIA activities in the *Gleaner* or the *Daily Chronicle*, where

Garvey appealed for elite support, may have also caught Jacques's eye. Garvey believed that "the intelligent must lead and assist the unfortunate of the people to rise." But most middle- and upper-class colored and "brown" Jamaicans were not interested in an organization that embraced and celebrated a black identity. Jacques, for example, was proud of her "brown" family and was financially well off herself; why would she want to be connected with a group that challenged the values of her own circle? Surely her mother would have disapproved of any organization that would arouse suspicion, and as an unmarried woman Jacques would not have wanted to be caught hobnobbing with "ordinary members of the association," men who closely resembled her father's former field hands.[25] She definitely would not have wanted to give anyone the impression that she undervalued her own worth.

Any affiliation with an organization that might question the foundation of her status would almost certainly have been shunned by Jacques and her peers. Financial wealth was the basis of this position, but "color" was at least as important a determinant of one's place in Jamaican society, as the contrast between Amy Jacques and Amy Ashwood illustrates. Ashwood's family was lower middle class, but her experiences were very different from Jacques's because Ashwood's genealogical roots were not colored. Ashwood's response to this was to take pride in her Ashanti heritage; her biographer, Lionel Yard, comments that "being dark" positioned Ashwood to be part of "the avant garde of a new social element that refused to accept the color lines of the older generation." This is undoubtedly at least part of the reason why Ashwood cofounded an association that, first and foremost, did not view dark skin as offensive but regarded it as an indication of an honorable lineage and beauty. The UNIA appealed to dark-skinned middle-class Jamaicans at a time when other comparable associations denied them membership. According to Ashwood, she moved to New York in October 1918, and it was in Harlem that she learned that Jacques needed lodging. Because of their prior friendship, Ashwood invited Jacques to move into the apartment that she shared with her father at 552 Lenox Avenue. Jacques accepted the offer, Ashwood claims, but did not develop an interest in any black movement.[26]

Meanwhile, Ashwood herself was continuing to raise funds for the UNIA, now headquartered in Harlem. Garvey had settled in New York in March 1916, and Ashwood reports that by the time he left the island, many individuals had visited the debates and enjoyed the musical performances, but only about one hundred people had become active members. Moreover, Garvey was swimming in debt, and his contributors were clamoring for an accounting of the organization's funds. In New York, however, the UNIA began a new course when Garvey became one of Harlem's most exciting step-ladder orators. His commanding voice could be heard several blocks away. More important, though, was his message, which struck a chord with disgruntled Harlemites who had been disappointed in black leadership. Garvey convincingly argued that it was not "humanity that was lynched, burned, jim-crowed and segregated, but Negro people." No longer was the UNIA a mere society pledged to uplift the poor and unrefined; it was now a political organization committed to a Pan-African nationalist ideology. In Harlem Ashwood and Garvey once again worked as a team to increase support for the UNIA.[27]

All of this activity left Ashwood feeling overwhelmed by her UNIA duties. On top of that, in November 1919 she and Garvey began planning an elaborate wedding for Christmas Day. In need of a personal assistant, Ashwood believed that she had now spent enough time with Jacques to know that she had good secretarial skills, so she offered her the position. Ashwood claims that she considered Jacques a good friend and anticipated that after the wedding she would be able to take over Ashwood's own role as one of the UNIA associate secretaries. According to Ashwood's biographer, at this point Amy Jacques was not knowledgeable about "the African past," nor was she a Garveyite, "but she was keen enough to sense the economic importance of the organization and the important segment of the power structure occupied" by Ashwood. Jacques was attractive and intelligent, he continued, "but [had] never had the opportunity to gain much recognition nor to wield the power which she saw with amazement was in the position for which Amy [Ashwood] was grooming her."[28]

There is something persuasive in the idea that Jacques entered the organization in a position of influence. Being a secretary for the headquarters would have been a comfortable role for her, giving her an opportunity to express a range of talents that were in keeping with her middle-class training. Further, the post would not challenge the class structure of her Caribbean upbringing, since she did not have to fraternize with the working-class rank-and-file membership. Instead, her secretarial duties gave her access to the privileged leadership, replicating, to a degree, the people with whom she expected to associate. And, since the New York branch of the UNIA had many West Indian members, Jacques might have initially believed that she was joining a basically West Indian nationalist organization, as opposed to a Pan-African movement.[29] This mind-set made her UNIA membership not a major leap but one that kept her tied to the class structure and cultural home of the Caribbean.

The precise conditions under which Amy Jacques initially became affiliated with the UNIA are now beyond retrieval. Jacques denied that she and Ashwood were acquaintances in Jamaica, and she gave the impression that Ashwood had no influence over her decision to attend a UNIA meeting. It is difficult to reconstruct the two women's early relationship because of the animosity that later developed between them; no doubt, their mutual ill feelings tainted their perceptions of earlier events. But their interaction, whatever its particulars, is significant, because it sets the stage for defining the social roles that were deemed suitable for women in the movement and the possible repercussions if one went against the grain.

There is no reliable evidence that Jacques actually lived with Ashwood before her first UNIA meeting.[30] However, though Jacques refused to acknowledge any prior friendship with her future foe, more than three thousand people witnessed her standing by Ashwood as the maid of honor at her wedding to Marcus Garvey on the evening of 25 December 1919 at Liberty Hall. Five ministers assisting at this grand Roman Catholic service, and the pageantry-filled event was the talk of Harlem.[31] One can easily imagine Garvey dressed in his ceremonial regalia—a dark military suit adorned with UNIA badges, brass buttons, and tassels, set off by his legendary plumed chapeau—and Ashwood cloaked in an elaborate white gown, her hair styled fashionably. Despite the fact that years later Jacques distanced herself from the possibility of any sisterly relationship with Ashwood, her role at the wedding substantiates the fact—or at least substantiates the *appearance*—that she and Ashwood were once close.

The Garveys' two-week honeymoon was not traditional in that they shared this intimate occasion with UNIA friends, including Jacques. The newlyweds' trip to Canada had a dual purpose: to celebrate the beginning of their life as husband and wife and to negotiate UNIA business in Montreal and Toronto. By January 1920 the UNIA had emerged as one of the largest black organizations in the United States, and its considerable international membership further distinguished it from others. Marcus Garvey was slowly becoming the king on a neoteric throne, largely because of his ability to capitalize on the broken promises and injustices of the post–World War I period in the United States. Countless black men and women had begun adopting a militant stance and demonstrating against racial injustices in an unprecedented fashion. The "New Negro" was symbolized by the overt expressions of self-defense and a deep frustra-

*Photograph of Marcus Garvey, founder of the Universal Negro Improvement
Association, taken on his wedding day in 1919. Photographer unknown. Schomburg
Center for Research in Black Culture.*

tion with the status quo. Between June and December 1919 there were at
least twenty-six race riots in urban cities. A life-affirming racial consciousness had taken hold, which in turn stimulated an optimal climate for a
Pan-African movement. Garvey responded by shifting the UNIA ideology
to include the "development of Independent Negro Nations and Communities."[32] He was the president-general of the organization, but his
new wife was a good fund-raiser and also in demand. Their Canada trip
was essentially a working honeymoon, and Amy Jacques was one of several traveling secretaries who accompanied them.

After the couple returned to New York, Garvey moved into his wife's apartment. Ashwood must not have had any reservations about Jacques at this point, because Amy continued to live there as well.[33] In addition, two men—Ashwood's brother Claudius and Alonso Roberts—also shared these living quarters. (Almost every household in this black working-class neighborhood had lodgers.)[34] Apparently these accommodations proved too cramped for Ashwood's father, who had moved out by January 1920.

The Garveys experienced only a few months of marital bliss. Ashwood writes: "In the full glare of the limelight the Marcus Garvey I knew receded into the shadows. The public figure Garvey took his place, and we found we were unable to continue the old partnership."[35] Certainly Garvey would not have been the first man to change under the pressure of leadership. It seems, though, that what happened was not so much a transformation of the man as a transformation of his expectations of Ashwood. It was one thing to be Garvey's cofounder and fiancée, but it was another to be his wife. He demanded that Ashwood function in a way that she had never done before their marriage—to subdue her public persona and support him in all of his undertakings, questioning neither his political nor his business decisions. Jacques recalls him saying that he "must have her [Ashwood's] sympathy and understanding of every action of mine."[36]

Despite his progressive political views, Marcus Garvey was in some respects very traditional, and his Jamaican upbringing stipulated that wives were to be compromising helpmates. He described his mother as a "soft and good" woman who "always returned a smile for a blow."[37] Although Garvey was critical of his father's maltreatment of his mother, he believed that women should be self-sacrificing and supportive, a standard he set for his own spouse and all UNIA wives. In fact, gender-specific roles have had a long history in black intellectual traditions. Paul Gilroy has pointed out that Martin Delany was the first black intellectual to argue that masculine power was fundamental to nationalist doctrine and that women were to be educated exclusively for motherhood. The idea that a "supreme patriarch" was needed for the "integrity of the race" has since become something of a mantra for black nationalist thought.[38] For his part, Garvey argued that his male-centered nation benefited women because it allowed them the opportunity to develop their God-given talents: making the home a haven of comfort and nurturing children, the future generation.

In theory, Ashwood did not oppose this premise and had been raised in a comparable environment, but she represented a new generation of black women and it was against her nature to submit totally. She had a mind of her own and refused to accommodate Garvey's every need. Ashwood was a free spirit, and her lifestyle resembled that of a few other women in America who were experiencing a taste of liberation during the Roaring Twenties. This wife frequently consumed alcohol in public and apparently never terminated her close friendships with other men.[39]

Because Garvey could not control his wife, he soon concluded that her behavior was detrimental to the UNIA. By March 1920 he had separated from her. According to Jacques, Garvey met with her and Henrietta Vinton Davis to explain the situation; "he said he wanted us to know before the reporters had it their own way. He had decided to separate from his wife and get a divorce afterwards." He told them that his "life can either be wrecked because of her [Ashwood's] conduct, or embellished by her deportment."[40]

Jacques's comments suggest that Garvey had previously discussed his reservations about his marriage with both her and Davis. When he left Ashwood's apartment and relocated to a flat on 129th Street, he wanted to keep both women near him. Davis had been elected international organizer of the UNIA in 1919, and Garvey trusted her immensely. Born in 1860, she was a dramatist who had toured the Caribbean islands in 1912 and 1913. Davis was well acquainted with global events and had a history of progressive activism. A loyal colleague, a good organizer, and a captivating speaker, she was well respected by the general membership. Jacques, on the other hand, was one of many secretaries. Her starting salary of twenty-three dollars a week eventually increased to forty dollars but was still less than half that of Gwendolyn Campbell, who was in charge of the stenographic force at UNIA headquarters. Her physical presence, however, may have reminded Garvey of the women who had shunned him at home because of his dark color and his poverty. Jacques was slight in stature—only five feet two inches tall and 110 pounds—and her mixed racial heritage was evident in her appearance. Jacques recalled: "My hair, let down, thrilled him. It was long and naturally wavy; he asked me to never cut it." Further, "the first time he saw it down, curiously he felt some strands and said, "Why, it is so soft." As I tossed my head, he exclaimed, "Oh, but it is so alive!"[41]

It is ironic that Garvey seemed to relish this most celebrated symbol of "mulatta" beauty—fine-textured, long hair—since he was pointedly critical of all products that aimed to "knock the kink" out of hair and lighten black skin, declaring that they "destroyed the racial pride and self-respect of the race." In his desire to foster racial consciousness, he welcomed anyone to the UNIA with "one-sixteenth or more black blood provided they work for the unity of the race."[42] But he remained openly skeptical of mixed-race people, particularly men, and wanted to "save the Negro race from extinction through miscegenation." Garvey believed that mulattoes were untrustworthy because their allegiance to the black race was precarious. So Jacques's heritage represented the colored privilege that repulsed him; yet he was clearly enamored of her and viewed his own attraction as somehow different from that of other "darker men" whom he indicted for their desire to marry the "lightest colored woman for special privilege and honor."[43]

Not only was Jacques beautiful, but she was intelligent as well—and Garvey was obviously attracted to smart women who were committed to his nationalist vision. Garvey immediately "offered Miss Davis and I [Jacques] a room to share there [the flat on 133 West 129th Street]; we accepted." Jacques may not have consciously flirted or enticed Garvey to take a personal interest in her, but she had to have understood the possible ramifications of living in his home. Nevertheless, she states only that she and Davis accepted because they "would be better protected at nights coming from meetings."[44] The idea that decent women should not walk alone at night was a serious issue that had nineteenth-century origins. For example, a black Philadelphia schoolteacher, Fannie Jackson, hired a "janitor to escort her home in order to avoid the appearance of impropriety."[45] Accepting lodging, however, was an altogether different issue. Jacques never admitted that she was attracted to Garvey or desired more than a professional relationship with him at that time. Years later she continued to maintain that she had married Garvey for the sake of the black nationalist movement and dismissed the idea that she would have married him for love. Admitting an intimate attraction would have tainted the political image that Jacques wanted to construct for the world and could have made her accountable for her role, if any, in the ultimate breakup of Garvey and Amy Ashwood.

It must have been painful for Ashwood to witness her husband and her former maid of honor living under the same roof without her. In fact, she specifically blamed Jacques for the demise of her marriage, claiming that Jacques had betrayed her and orchestrated a situation (suggestive of an affair) in which Garvey found her with another man, Sam Manning, a noted Trinidadian calypsonian.[46] Whether Jacques had had something to do with the breakup or not, she had to have felt some pressure from Ashwood over her decision to go with Garvey. It is unsettling to imagine Jacques not having some compassion for her former housemate. It is also unpleasant to visualize this scenario of two intelligent women reduced to squabbling over a man. Though on the surface all of their bickering seems to have been over Garvey, it is likely that there were other points of disagreement that never became a part of the public discourse. Ashwood and Jacques, like anyone else, were vulnerable to human emotions, and whatever the specific differences between them, their fractious interaction is evidence, sadly, of how fragile friendships can quickly spiral downward into an abyss of mudslinging. More significantly, their behavior also reveals the fallacy of a utopian black sisterhood. E. Frances White has warned against adopting the position that "accepts as unproblematic an Afro-centric sisterhood across class, time, and geography," because differences and tensions exist between and among black women, as they do among members of any other group.[47]

Whatever the state of Ashwood and Jacques's relationship, Ashwood and Garvey were far beyond reconciling their differences, and on 15 July 1920 he filed for an annulment of their marriage in the New York County Circuit Court. In addition to being the general secretary for the New York division of the UNIA, Amy Ashwood was one of the directors of the Black Star Steamship Line Company, and Garvey accused her of misappropriating the organization's funds to buy a house in Harlem. He vowed to "exercise every possible precaution to determine if one penny of the Association's funds had been expended for the purchase" of her personal property. Garvey also claimed that Ashwood had been an adulteress. Along with the Sam Manning incident, Garvey charged that she had consorted with a UNIA member, "a fashion plate in the employ of the Black Star Line." Finally, he identified her former Panamanian beau, Allan Cumberbatch, as another man with whom she had continued to correspond after their marriage.[48]

Ashwood responded to Garvey's legal charges by accusing him in an affidavit, dated 30 August 1920, of consorting with other women, one of whom was her presumed good friend, Amy Jacques. Ashwood had heard gossip that her husband and Jacques were becoming more than business associates. In a Federal Bureau of Investigation (FBI) report, filed on 31 August 1920, Special Agent F. B. Faulhaber stated that a Mr. Green, an employee of the Black Star Line, had been "informed by Mrs. Garvey" that she had information "on some of the trips made from Philadelphia to

New York in 1920 by Miss Jacques and Garvey." It was alleged that "they had both traveled in a pullman sleeper" and "slept together." Green "could furnish no definite information on the source of Mrs. Garvey's information."[49]

The FBI report was the result of an investigation spurred by the rapid growth of the UNIA's power and membership. The meteoric rise of the movement was a reaction to imperialism and the rape of Africa under the guise of Christianity and civilization, the horrific lynchings of black people in the United States, and the dehumanization of African peoples in the Caribbean and Central and South America. Essentially, the racial nationalism espoused by Garvey was a means to mobilize people to reclaim territory and resources for self-protection, self-government, and self-determination. The U.S. government, however, did not view this movement to build a united African homeland simply as an effort among people of African descent to find reconnection, especially those in the Americas who "were/are products of separations and dislocations and dismembering," as Carol Boyce Davies has shown. Nor did they interpret Garvey's attempt to remap boundaries as an attempt to unite people of African descent and create what Benedict Anderson has called an "imagined community" that Paul Gilroy locates within the lure of "romantic conceptions" of "race," "nation," and "people." Instead, governmental officials, fueled by "Red Scare" propaganda, believed that Garvey's efforts "to build a tradition of liberation in the African cultural roots of the masses" was a subversive activity. In fact, any organization that did not pledge loyalty to the United States was perceived to be allied with the Communist Party.[50]

Under the command of J. Edgar Hoover, the FBI had launched an attack against all "radical" and "racial" political activities, seeking incriminating evidence to provide grounds for Garvey's arrest and ultimate deportation. Special agents were assigned to trail him and send periodic reports back to the superintendent of the FBI's New York division. Hoover was so intent on disarming radicals that he pressured his agents to distort and falsify evidence in order to satisfy his official request.[51]

In the course of their "investigation," FBI agents instigated gossip, recorded rumors, and leaked their "findings" to the general UNIA membership. This may explain why Amy Ashwood was so soon convinced that her husband had been unfaithful to her. In her affidavit she maintains that she "felt near and dear to the said Amy Jacques and up to that time had not the slightest suspicion that any improper relations existed between the plaintiff and the said Amy Jacques." According to the affidavit, "the said Amy Jacques resides in the same apartment with the plaintiff herein and appears daily on the streets arms locked with him, the two being attended always by a body guard or two or three men." Ashwood concluded her sworn statement by denying "most emphatically, that she has ever had at any time since the date of her marriage, sexual intercourse with any man except" her husband.[52]

Not long after submitting the affidavit, Ashwood packed her belongings and left New York for Canada. In December 1920 W. E. B. Du Bois reported in the *Crisis* that Garvey had already "divorced the young wife whom he married with great fanfare of trumpets about a year ago," but in fact the couple was still legally married when Ashwood left.[53]

As the months passed, Garvey and Jacques were seen together more frequently, and she was often his only traveling secretary. Clusters of FBI reports continued to detail their alleged activities. A special agent who trailed them filed a report, dated 1 March 1921, stating that "Garvey was accompanied by a girl named Amy Jakes [*sic*], his secretary." Jacques was identified as "the woman who caused all Garvey's marital troubles, being the cause of separation from his wife and an impending divorce." This "girl Jakes is commonly known as the woman Garvey lives with." The report also noted that "they can always be seen walking arm in arm to and from the office. He takes her on all his trips over the country and his followers always entertain fears that some day he may be arrested [for] White slavery." UNIA officials "tried in vain to discourage this state of affairs, but for some unknown reason she exercises a wonderful influence over Garvey." The agent concluded that Jacques "travels with Garvey under the guise of private secretary to cover [for] him, but it is common knowledge that they live together as man and wife."[54]

The following month Garvey, Jacques, her brother Cleveland (who had arrived in the United States in May 1920 and served as a secretary for the UNIA's Negro Factory Corporation), and stenographer Enid Lamos caravanned to Cuba, Port Limon, Costa Rica, Panama, and Jamaica to sell Black Star Line stock and spread the message of Garveyism.[55] After they returned to the United States, another FBI report was filed by the same special agent, this one dated 1 July 1921, claiming that Garvey was married to Ashwood but "he left here in company of Amy Jacques, an unmarried woman negress. She is traveling as his wife by rail and his steamer KANAWHA over protest of all negroes he represents." By seizing on the fact that

Garvey had left the country with Jacques, the FBI was attempting to charge him under the 1910 White Slave Traffic Act, also known as the Mann Act. This statute made it a federal crime to "transport or aid or assist in obtaining transportation in interstate or foreign commerce any woman or girl for the purpose of prostitution or debauchery, or for any other immoral purpose, or with the intent and purpose to induce, entice, or compel such woman or girl to become a prostitute."[56] The Mann Act, one of the first "federal crimes" laws, was aggressively enforced by the nation's police—the FBI. By 1912 the charges made under the act were so numerous that the attorney general established the Office of the Special Commissioner for the Suppression of White Slave Traffic.

White slave officers became the custodians of American morality in a campaign to protect innocent, friendless young immigrant women and girls who were in danger of being trapped in a life of ill repute by their slavers. The law primarily aimed to jail incorrigible men, but women were also arrested "to induce them to testify against their male transporters." Marlene Beckman notes that the name "White Slave Traffic Act" is a misnomer, because "the Act makes no distinction as to the race or the color of the female whose transportation is a violation of the law." Beckman's study of 150 women who were convicted under the statute between 1927 and 1932, however, documents that 96 percent of the incarcerated women were white.[57]

It was highly unusual for a black woman to be prosecuted under the Mann Act because to do so all of the negative stereotypes surrounding black womanhood had to be subverted. Progressive Era reformers believed that white women were chaste and that "no woman became a whore unless she had first been raped, seduced, drugged, or deserted." On the other hand, black women throughout the diaspora struggled against a Jezebel/harlot image that had been constructed during slavery to justify the rape of them.[58] This damaging image continued to haunt all black women, no matter how virtuous they were. Nevertheless, FBI officials were so committed to arresting Garvey that they were willing to ignore their customary racist assumptions about black women in order to identify Jacques as a chaste, vulnerable victim. It was only under those circumstances that Garvey could be held liable.

As part of the FBI's attempt to frame Garvey, Special Agent Faulhaber tried to convince Jacques's brother Cleveland to provide information on Garvey's alleged violation of the Mann Act, but Cleveland Jacques refused "point-blank" to cooperate. In addition, it was customary in Mann Act cases to obtain a statement from the victim; thus, Agent Bremmann awaited advice as to whether he should proceed with "interviewing Amy Jacques."[59]

In the end, government officials decided not to pursue this avenue not only because Jacques was not a "whore," but also because they sensed that a legal charge of immoral impropriety against a UNIA woman could be catastrophic to their case against Garvey. Garveyites preached that their nation could rise no higher than their women, and an unsubstantiated attack against this foundation would be aggressively countered. In addition, since the 1890s black club women had organized and defended their womanhood against accusations that defamed their reputation. Conscientious African Americans, even those who opposed Garvey, were united in their belief that the protection of black women (which often translated into paternalistic privileges) was paramount to the moral uplifting of the race. The FBI wanted Garvey without the burden of battling black America on these grounds, so it continued to monitor him but changed its witch-hunt strategy.

The federal government was not the only enemy that Garvey had to contend with. By 1921 a cohort of black leaders—W. E. B. Du Bois, Cyril Briggs, Chandler Owen, and William Pickens—had grown critical of his approach and his unwillingness to cooperate with other black groups. They attacked Garvey on many fronts, and on one occasion his relationships with Jacques and Ashwood became fair game. Cyril Briggs, leader of the African Blood Brotherhood, a socialist organization, was careful not to name or malign these women with degrading details, but he did question Garvey's morality. As editor of the *Crusader*, Briggs favorably compared himself to Garvey, stating, "The editor of the Crusader has never left his wife, nor turned his wife out. The editor of the Crusader is not now living with a woman not his wife and never has so lived."[60] Although Garvey always fiercely defended himself against negative allegations, he was uncharacteristically silent in response to this disparaging remark.

While Garvey was under attack from every conceivable angle, Jacques made it her business to submit a declaration of intention on 19 August 1921 to become a naturalized citizen of the United States. In general, British West Indians did not enthusiastically acquire citizenship. A testament to this fact is revealed by the low number of naturalization records. In 1920 only 18 percent of all foreign-born black women and 14 percent of foreign-born black men were naturalized, as opposed to 53 percent of foreign-born white women and 49 percent of foreign-born white men.[61] Most Caribbean immigrants did not seek citizenship, and those who did were often scorned by their islander peers who remained loyal British subjects with access to legal protection from the British consul. Jacques never offered an explanation for her decision, but it does represent a process to negotiate her migratory subjectivity by becoming a U.S. citizen.

At last, on 15 June 1922, Garvey was able to remove his personal life from the glare of public scrutiny when he received his divorce decree. In his court testimony, he had convinced the judge and jury that Ashwood had been deceitful, offering a detailed description of how he had found her sitting by a man in a parlor. The court found that "the allegations in Plaintiff's [Marcus Garvey's] petition are true; that plaintiff is injured and [an] innocent party and entitled to the relief prayed."[62]

Rumors had circulated among the officers of the UNIA that Jacques and Garvey would marry, and they did, two months after his divorce became final.[63] Jacques described Garvey's motives for proposing this way: "He must have someone who had the right to be his personal representative— to act on his behalf, and on his instructions," especially since the FBI was trailing him. A "secretary," she claimed, "would only be brushed aside as an employee, and dismissed too. He must get a wife." Garvey wanted an African American "so as to please the people. The duty of sharing his turbulent life might have been requested of Miss Davis[,]" but she was "older than he, and he had hopes of having a son to carry on his name." Although there were "other eligible among the membership," they "lacked the sum total qualities of what he wanted for a wife now—a stand-in, in an emergency." Since he respected and valued her contributions to the UNIA, "he turned to me, and very adroitly put the onus on me, stating that it was in my power to help the organization in this crisis. He had already obtained a divorce, so we were married 27 July 1922."[64]

Ashwood, who by this time was living in England, became infuriated on learning that Garvey had divorced her and married Jacques. She immediately returned to the United States and filed a countersuit seeking to "invalidate the proceedings" and naming "Amy Jacques as correspondent."[65] On 24 August 1922 she had Garvey served, at Liberty Hall, a summons and complaint stating that no decree of divorce had been obtained in any court and that she demanded judgment against him, "severing the bonds of matrimony," given that she had "ever been true and faithful to her marriage vows." She also accused Garvey of bigamy and failure to pay support of twelve dollars a week ordered by the New York court.[66] It was in Ashwood's nature to stand up for herself, so it was not surprising that she was now demanding the right to be treated with respect and not be pushed aside. She had dedicated her life to the UNIA and refused to be denied her due. Despite Garvey's "mean-spirited" attitude toward her and the ultimate failure of her countersuit, she refused to accept the divorce and continued to refer to herself as Mrs. Marcus Garvey until her death in May 1969.

This time around there was no public wedding for Marcus Garvey—just Amy Jacques, the judge, a small group of friends, and an exchange of plain gold rings. Who knows if they would have married had the circumstances been less trying. Nonetheless, the unassuming ceremony itself illustrates just how far Jacques had traveled from her middle-class Jamaican upbringing. Before her involvement with Garvey, she would certainly have insisted on a proper wedding, so that at least all of her family could attend. Middle-class etiquette stipulated that couples announce their planned nuptials in the local newspaper before they occurred; not to do so was deemed tasteless. Within a few short years Amy Jacques had changed. Her decision to join the UNIA and her connection with Garvey were both a cause and a consequence of this change.

In Jamaica, Jacques's community had been arranged around class and color connections. Though she had been reared to be a high achiever and to fulfill her potential, it was not until after her father's death that she was able to have a professional work life and expand beyond his restrictive cocoon. New York City provided a freedom zone for Jacques, one in which she could toss aside the traditions that had kept her from fraternizing with persons not linked to elite enclaves.[67] She continued to socialize with Jamaicans in New York, but she also communicated with other West Indians, as well as African Americans. This interaction gave her exposure to different ideas that undoubtedly challenged the aristocratic values she had learned during her formative years. We can safely assume that it was this environment that stimulated Amy Jacques Garvey to rethink how her culturally constructed Jamaican identity had disconnected her from other people of African descent.

Clearly, she was not the only Caribbean migrant to become radicalized in America. As Winston James has noted, islanders entered the United States during "the midnight darkness of the moment" regarding the "question of race." "It was, therefore[,]" James argues, "not just the place that contributed to their radicalization: the exceptional times—a veritable state of emergency for black America—played their part."[68] Thus, although on the surface the UNIA—a race-first, Pan-African movement—seems to have been far removed from what Jacques was accustomed to, so was the situation of racial prejudice she found herself in. As a young woman who represented the epitome of "good Jamaican birth," she must have been shocked not only by white Americans' perception of all "Negroid" people as an undifferentiated mass—regardless of their shade of color or financial status—but also by their unwarranted hostility toward black people, which often translated into broad racial discrimination and terrorist attacks. In the first two years of her new life in the United States (1917–19), Amy Jacques was exposed to the virulent racism that accompanied the great migration of black people from the South to the North, the rise of white supremacist organizations, and the advent of race riots. Her activities and ultimate membership in the UNIA indicate that she had by then relinquished some of her culturally colored attitudes and embraced her "blackness" in a new way.

The combination of living under the racial siege of Jim Crow and the post–World War I crisis propelled a number of black radicals to the forefront of the political struggle, and unquestionably Marcus Garvey was one of the most exceptional of these figures. For his part, Garvey had reshaped his organization to embrace the tenets of African American life at the turn of the century: racial solidarity, moral uplift, and self-reliance. By the time Jacques encountered the movement, she was ready to be persuaded by it. Garvey convinced her of the "worthiness of his program, and stressed the fact that the skin-color class system of Jamaica did not exist in America, as all strata of the race were treated as one—the slogan being, 'any nigger is a nigger.'" Garvey stressed that "it was necessary for the educated and better able to join with the masses in a strong uplift-and-onward movement."[69]

Amy Jacques had to be in another context, the United States, to be "convinced" that she was a part of a black community. Joy James has shown how lynchings "transfigured" and "politicized" W. E. B. Du Bois; in a similar vein, Jim Crow America transformed Amy Jacques.[70] Her metamorphosis illuminates how Garvey's program successfully worked to unite African people from the continent and the diaspora. He collapsed class, color, religious, and geographic distinctions and then encouraged black people to view themselves as part of a Pan-African family, united for the common good and against their European oppressors. By 1922 Jacques's youthful narcissistic thinking was a mere memory; already a confident person, she had become emboldened enough to answer the call to become socially responsible to her race.[71] She was no longer a "brown" Jamaican but a black woman committed to the UNIA agenda and willing to sacrifice herself for its success.

The early years of the Amy Jacques–Marcus Garvey burgeoning courtship and subsequent marriage paralleled the zenith of the Universal Negro Improvement Association (UNIA). Black people had begun to gravitate to the organization in 1916, and by 1923 it claimed a membership of six million, with at least nine hundred branches—five hundred throughout the United States alone, and the rest in Canada, Central and South America, the Caribbean, Great Britain, and Africa. Garvey himself, of course, was a prominent reason for the organization's growth. A member of the Harlem chapter, Audley (Queen Mother) Moore, remembered that "when Marcus Garvey came on the scene, then of course a deep consciousness was awakened in me. . . . [H]e raised in me a certain knowledge of me belonging to people all over the world, the African people, and he gave me pride, and he gave me a great knowledge of the history of the wealth of Africa." Garvey's presence explains why the Harlem branch—the organization's headquarters—had the largest estimated membership, at thirty-five thousand.[1] No other Pan-African or black nationalist organization could document comparable statistics. Obviously, the black masses worldwide had responded to the UNIA's platform: to generate global economic connections between Africans living in the Caribbean, North America, and Africa via its passenger and shipping fleet (the Black Star Line); to redeem Africa from European colonists; and ultimately to link a diasporic identity with a legal African nationality.

By 1923 the UNIA itself resembled a nation. Garveyites elected ambassadors, sponsored expeditions to Liberia, sent commissioners to the League of Nations, and endorsed political candidates. Elaborate pageantry also gave the appearance of nationhood. Members sang a national hymn and wore flamboyant uniforms, and their red, black, and green flag—the ultimate emblem of an independent nation—garnished their meeting halls. All of the symbols of nationhood were evident, despite the fact that they had no territory to call their own.

As the organization grew, so did the public role of Amy Jacques Garvey. One month after her marriage in 1922, the annual UNIA August convention (marking the date of slave emancipation in the British colonies) took place in Harlem. Unlike Amy Ashwood, who had had a visible role at the previous conventions, often reciting the poetry of Paul Laurence Dunbar, Jacques Garvey was still working behind the scenes, never once sharing the limelight with her husband. Yet the issues raised at this meeting provide a sense of the concerns that were escalating when Jacques became Garvey's wife.

Marcus Garvey's agenda dominated the 1922 convention. Highly concerned about dissension within the ranks, he was determined to stifle all opinions that disagreed with his own. He condemned members who fraternized with his enemies, among them W. E. B. Du Bois, A. Philip Randolph, Chandler Owen, and William Pickens. These men had been unable, and in some cases unwilling, to organize the masses, and they refused to give Garvey credit for his intellectual prowess and his herculean effort to create a program that captured the imagination of black people. They considered him to be a charlatan and a demagogue, preying "upon the ignorant, unsuspecting poor West Indian working men and women," taking their hard-earned monies for his egregious capitalist schemes. Garvey responded to these accusations both before and during the convention by challenging these noted leaders of the National Association for the Advancement of Colored People (NAACP) to make their own records public and account for the money they had spent over the previous ten years. Feeling the need to eliminate those members who were fraternizing with NAACP luminaries, Garvey argued that the UNIA would have to "clean" itself from within in order to fight those from "without." Thus, his primary agenda was to restructure the UNIA so he could personally appoint members of the Executive Cabinet, instead of their being nominated by the membership, to ensure their loyalty to him.[2]

Garvey managed to convince the general body to amend the UNIA constitution for this purpose, but on 31 August his dominance was unexpectedly challenged by another group: the lady delegates "by some clever maneuvering were able to monopolize" this session. This move surprised the men, because "Woman's Day at Liberty Hall" had already been observed ten days earlier. At this event, Henrietta Vinton Davis had led an open forum on a "New Social Policy for the Negro," and at least eighteen other women participated. They articulated the need for a policy to ensure that children were reared to be honest and that there was no double standard of morality. Good manners and decent morals were essential to respectability, and, as Evelyn Brooks Higginbotham has noted, during this period black Baptist women "perceived respectability to be the first step in their communication with white America."[3] For their part, UNIA women considered respectability to be a key step toward establishing a sovereign black nation.

Female delegates further wanted to establish a place where men and women could learn their "social duties and obligations" to one another. This environment would guarantee that the "men of the race would stick to them" and not seek relationships with white women.[4] On the surface this discussion might be seen as a reactionary stance to protect the "market" of black men by keeping competitors out, but a closer analysis discloses that these women denounced interracial relationships not just because Garvey was opposed to miscegenation, but because they, too, were aware of the deadly consequences that sometimes arose from black men keeping company with white women. For example, Ida B. Wells-Barnett, leader of the antilynching campaign, documented that some white women willingly engaged in intimate relationships with black men and then claimed they had been raped once their secret affair was featured on the gossip grapevine. The fact that these white women protected themselves at the expense of a black man's life had devastating consequences for the black community. UNIA women believed that "Negro men must be taught to feel that their women are good enough for them and then the women must be taught likewise as to the men." By "sticking" together they protected themselves against life-threatening situations and were better able to "uplift" the "men and women of the rising generation."[5]

These limited comments by the delegates regarding white women foreshadowed future black nationalist rhetoric. A decade later, for instance, Elijah Muhammad, leader of the Nation of Islam, a separatist black nationalist organization, built on this thinking in a somewhat convoluted way. Muhammad charged that white women were white men's "bait" to entice black men away from their family obligations.[6]

With the exception of openly criticizing black men who were attracted to white women, "Woman's Day at Liberty Hall"—in addition to hosting an industrial exhibition showcasing arts and crafts and a fashion revue—was in keeping with the gender-specific roles performed by most women in political and fraternal organizations during the 1920s. But on 31 August

1922 women pushed beyond the parameters of what constituted appropriate female activism.

The UNIA's constitution was very different from that of most black organizations in that women were well integrated into the movement's structure.[7] Amy Ashwood must be credited with helping to develop a system in which women could enjoy equal participation. Each local division elected a male and female president and vice president. The constitution did not guarantee equal participation, however, as a majority of women delegates at the 31 August meeting pointed out. They elected Mrs. Victoria W. Turner of St. Louis as their spokesperson, and she submitted a five-point resolution to be adopted by the organization. These delegates demanded that women be placed in "important" positions within "the organization to help refine and mold public sentiment." They wanted absolute control over the UNIA auxiliaries, the Black Cross Nurses (women who performed duties similar to Red Cross nurses), and Motor Corps (car fleets), as well as more recognition on committees. Overall, they insisted on empowerment "so that the Negro women all over the world can function without restriction from men."[8]

Garvey had constructed the roles of men and women in the UNIA to meet his expectations for nationhood. Barbara Bair persuasively argues that these culturally constructed roles were not "separate and equal," as Ashwood had envisioned, but "separate and hierarchal."[9] Men and women were advised to wield proper influence and authority over separate spheres: public and familiar. Women were charged to make the home a haven, nurture children, and support their husbands; men, in turn, were to be providers and protectors. Garveyites believed that when men and women fulfilled these designated gender-specific roles, they replicated the lifestyle of other "successful" and powerful people the world over.

A society organized according to the principles of patriarchy was the trademark of most nationalist movements. For example, George Mosse's study on nationalism in modern Europe points out that nationalists assigned everyone their place in the social order, and "any confusion between these categories threatened chaos and loss of control." European nationalists identified women as passive guardians of the traditional order, whereas men were to dominate the public realm. In sum, "the family was supposed to mirror state and society"; by emphasizing a hierarchical structure "through the rule of the father as patriarch, the family educated its members to respect authority."[10] (Importantly, Garveyites perceived that community was thwarted by the reality of their working-class status. Even though many women wanted the choice—and choice was the key—not to work outside the home, economic hardships did not make this national structure feasible.)

Some women delegates flatly rejected being confined to the domestic sphere and struggled to enhance their womanhood and ultimately their nation by augmenting their duties in the Pan-African struggle. They were not satisfied by performing charitable duties and reinforcing male leadership; they wanted to be eligible for election to a variety of executive positions to which they felt "entitled," despite Garvey's claim that women should not be considered for "diplomatic missions."[11]

Garvey's initial response to the women's resolution was that he did not see any reason for change, "as the women already had the power they were asking for under the constitution. . . . The U.N.I.A. was one organization that recognized women." Henrietta Vinton Davis was on the Executive Council, he pointed out, and "if there was any difference made in the local divisions, it was not the fault of the policy of the UNIA, but it was the fault of individuals."[12] On all other issues raised at the meeting, Garvey's statements proved definitive, thereby ending further discussion. The women delegates, however, were passionate enough about their position to override class, geography, and other distinctions among themselves and unite against Garvey in a way that UNIA men were unable to replicate. In the end, their resolutions were modified and adopted by the convention.

The women had thus forced Garvey to concede on some level, which is surprising since, as Carol Boyce Davies correctly argues, Pan-Africanism "operates from a singularly monolithic construction of an African theoretical homeland which asks for the submergence or silencing of gender." As E. Frances White has shown, as late as 1970 Pan-African nation building had not moved beyond this formulation, and "complementary" still "did not mean equal." Men and women continued "to have separate tasks and unequal power."[13]

The UNIA women must be commended for struggling against the totalizing nature of nationalist discourse. Assertively, they helped to redefine the appropriate roles for women in the association. Although Garvey did not oppose the idea of female leadership, he was somewhat contemptuous of these delegates' desire to expand their functions as Pan-Africanists. In this confrontation, Amy Jacques Garvey must have been faced with the choice of supporting her husband, lining up with the UNIA women, or situating herself between the two forces. The record does not tell us what position she chose to take, as there are no statements by the delegates or the FBI indicating opinions by or about Jacques Garvey at the convention. Nevertheless, this persistent tension related to the making of gendered nationalist subjects would eventually compel her to take a surprising public stance.

The Garveys' personal life may have been a topic for gossip, but UNIA members did not dare to make it a part of the convention record, and Marcus Garvey clearly felt no need to explain his marital decision to the membership. For her part, Jacques Garvey kept a low profile at the convention, but the period after that proved a turning point for her UNIA activism.

To begin with, she increased her already hectic, if veiled, workload by collecting her husband's speeches and articles, the majority of which had been printed in the *Negro World*, "as a personal record." She then decided to publish them to "give the public an opportunity of studying and forming an opinion of him; not from inflated and misleading newspapers and magazine articles, but from expressions of thoughts enunciated by him in defense of his oppressed and struggling race; so that by *his own words* [italics added] he may be judged." These "gems of expressions," essays, and speeches, published in 1923 under the title *The Philosophy and Opinions of Marcus Garvey* were exclusively *his* words, but Jacques Garvey's intellect shaped how the overall scope of Garveyism would be presented to the world.[14]

Although the majority of her revisions were simply abridgments, or a combining of documents for clarity and continuity, she did locate herself in the editing process: "I have produced what I consider two of the best speeches of my husband."[15] A line-by-line comparison of five speeches reprinted in *Philosophy and Opinions*, for instance, indicates that Jacques Garvey revised some of the longer texts by deleting sentences in which he thanked delegates as well as lines that were obviously repetitious. On several occasions, she went so far as to remove entire sections from the original speech. Some of these excised portions revealed the more rebellious side of Garvey. They included, but were not limited to, statements about the use of the latest artillery, explosives, and war strategy; calls for retribution; and claims that if he had been born a slave, he "would have made some trouble and made things hot for somebody during those days."[16]

The fact that Jacques Garvey assembled this text when her husband was attempting to gather support for a mail fraud indictment helps to explain why she removed some of his more inflammatory statements. Not surprisingly, Garvey's most radical speeches are not featured in the collection. Robert Hill argues that, unfortunately, this volume "has institutionalized a distorted picture of the militant stage of the UNIA and its mass following."[17] Nevertheless, Garvey approved of this depiction of himself and the movement. The book, published in February 1923, was Jacques Garvey's first major editorial work. Though this propaganda package may have been indirectly addressed to Garvey's contemporaries, it eventually became one of the first primary collections on Garveyism.

Garvey was arrested for mail fraud after the 1922 convention. He had sold stock for five dollars a share, through the mail, for the Black Star Steamship Line Company (BSL). To keep the steamship fleet in the hands of the masses, no shareholder could buy more than two hundred dollars worth of stock. Black people throughout the diaspora had seized the opportunity to become stockholders, and African Americans led the way. During World War I many Americans had accumulated a substantial amount of wealth by purchasing stocks and bonds, and some Garveyites invested in the fleet in hopes of receiving lucrative returns. Even though a variety of institutions and business enterprises were selling stock to African Americans, including other steamship corporations, millions elected to support the BSL.[18]

Stock proceeds filled the organization's coffers, and by May 1920 Garvey had bought three shabby ships costing the UNIA more than $200,000. The purchase of these tattered vessels underscored his lack of business acumen; nonetheless, he used his tremendous organizing skills to establish an impressive cohort of UNIA leaders who were willing to aggressively recruit others while selling stock. But because the UNIA was first and foremost a racial movement, at times Garvey's eagerness to expand its membership undercut BSL profits. For example, on one occasion fruit shipments spoiled due to delays caused by additional dockage at Caribbean ports while he spread the UNIA message.[19]

Even the established African American elite, many of whom were critical of Garvey's leadership, had to concede that the BSL was a monumental achievement. W. E. B. Du Bois, an ardent opponent, acknowledged that Garvey had proved that "American Negroes can be accumulating and ministering their own capital, organize industry, join the black centers of the South Atlantic by commercial enterprise and in this way ultimately redeem Africa as a fit and free home for black men."[20]

At the same time, some leaders expressed concern about the UNIA's growing commercial focus. Cyril Briggs was forced to admit that capitalist ventures were necessary, but he warned, "No business enterprise is good enough to base the liberation movement and the morale of the Negro masses upon the success or failure of that enterprise." Not disputing the necessity of businesses, he felt that it was a mistake to link "them up directly with the liberation movement and thereby stake the entire movement upon the changes of success or failure and at the same time invite white aggression to what may be correctly considered a vulnerable spot in our armor." Briggs concluded that the sooner the Garvey section of the liberation movement recognized this, the better. Despite the success of the sale of BSL stock, the overall UNIA finances were in a shambles, due to poor business management. Judith Stein has shown that stock proceeds were siphoned off to subsidize the debt accrued from other UNIA holdings. When accusations surfaced regarding Garvey's lack of business savvy, UNIA dissidents and several BSL officers filed complaints with the New York district attorney's office alleging that Garvey had misappropriated funds. Among the claims against him were that "Garvey lost a stock book in Virginia, issued shares without paying the federal revenue tax, failed to keep records of expenditures, and used some of the proceeds to pay off the debt against the UNIA restaurant."[21]

Even under these difficult circumstances, Garvey still exhibited the confidence of a successful leader, and his unwavering attacks against his most zealous critics helped to legitimize him in the eyes of the black world. At a Liberty Hall meeting on 11 July 1920, he had gloated: "I do not care what the preacher in his criticism may say. I do not care what the politician in his criticism may say. I do not care what the journalist in his criticism may say. There is one conviction I have and that is that the Negro in this age is entitled to as much liberty as any other race on the face of the globe." "We are a new people," Garvey argued, "born out of a new day and a new circumstance."[22]

Garvey also did not let desperate financial concerns stymie the UNIA's Pan-African plan, and by 1921 the organization had sent an entourage to Liberia to survey land and negotiate with the government for a UNIA settlement. Garvey's stalwart attitude and resiliency continued to lend credence to the vitality of the UNIA, but Liberian officials would not legally commit to supporting the movement, and no doubt the U.S. Justice Department investigation had hampered his cause. J. Edgar Hoover was on Garvey's tail, identifying him as a "notorious negro agitator" and demanding that his investigators engage in "early action upon the prosecution which is now pending, in order that he [Garvey] may be once and for all put where he can peruse his past activities behind the four walls in the Atlanta clime."[23] (Atlanta, Georgia, was the location of the first federal penitentiary, and a mail fraud conviction would guarantee Garvey's residence there.)

At his trial, which began on 18 May 1923, Garvey was the first defendant called. The *Kansas City Call* reported that he quickly "dispensed with the services of his attorneys, and took his defense upon himself." According to journalist J. A. Rogers, the trial quickly "deteriorated into low comedy." Although FBI agents said that Garvey was in the "habit of counting money" from stock sales in his room with Amy Jacques Garvey after meetings, she was not implicated in the conspiracy; therefore, he was determined to have her testify on his behalf.[24] Judge Julian Mack quickly interrupted Garvey's efforts by demanding to know if Jacques Garvey was his legal wife. Dismissing the question, Garvey replied, "I am calling her as a witness." But when the court pressed for a more explicit answer, he said, "She is my legal wife at present." Judge Mack ruled that her status made her incompetent to testify. "Then I call Amy Jacques," retorted Garvey. He further asserted that if she could not testify, "his plans would be completely upset," as he would have to locate witnesses outside the state of New York. Although the court reiterated its first ruling, District Attorney Mattuck apparently did not view Jacques as Marcus's trump card and withdrew his objection to her testimony.[25]

Stylishly dressed and wearing a "large picture hat," Jacques Garvey was described by reporters as having a "slender and girlish" stature and appearing to be "much younger than Garvey." On the stand for two days, she described her role as secretary at the headquarters, where she kept all UNIA and BSL reports separate. She also sold stock, was in charge of the money collected for the organization, and made it abundantly clear that from 1920 onward she took charge of opening all the office mail, assisted by other women. Garvey, she said, "opened no mail." This was a pivotal point, and several times during direct examination she "appeared extremely nervous." On one occasion when she had difficulty answering questions without relating tangential conversations, Judge Mack spoke sharply to her. Becoming emotional, Jacques Garvey "broke down and began to weep." But Garvey interposed, saying to her, "Take your time, do not let anyone frighten or terrorize you."[26]

At the conclusion of the twenty-seven-day trial, Judge Mack instructed the jurors that they "must determine whether Garvey undertook the organization of the Black Star Line as an honorable enterprise or simply to advance his personal ambitions. The defendant had a right to buy ships and pay salaries, but not to make false financial statements." As the jury deliberated, it was reported that Garvey's codefendants (O. M. Thompson, George Tobias, and Elie Garcia) left the courtroom, but Garvey stayed and "his wife remained with him."[27] Ten hours later Garvey's three codefendants were exonerated, but he was found guilty of one count of sending false promotional materials through the mail. He was sentenced to a maximum of five years in federal prison and ordered to pay a one-thousand-dollar fine, in addition to court costs.

Garvey's initial appeal for bail was rejected, and he was immediately dispatched to Tombs Penitentiary in New York City, at which point the press quickly focused their attention on his wife. The *Pittsburgh American* reported on 20 July 1923 that "the conviction appears to be growing, that Mrs. Garvey is an able, strong-minded woman equipped in every way to do good work for the nationalist movement, by sweeping the dust of misunderstanding from the minds of some, by strengthening the bonds of unity between the members of the UNIA, by making new friends for the cause and converting some of its enemies." The *Hotel Tatler* concurred in mid-August: Mrs. Garvey has "proven [her] mettle under fire." Because of her "modest and unassuming" manner, she was not the "type from which heroines are molded, but the elevation of her brow and the toss of her head when opposed, reveals her fearless and independent spirit." No longer confined to the office, Jacques Garvey had revealed to "the world for the first time" her "intrinsic worth" to the cause of liberation.[28]

During this tumultuous time, Garvey continued to demand even more from his wife, and she attempted to fulfill all of his requests, even when it could cause her physical harm.[29] Jacques Garvey recalled that she brought a gun to the office to protect herself after a UNIA clerk had "threatened to throw" her "down the stairs" because she had reported to the BSL directors that he had lost "signed-up certificates." She later identified the clerk as a "plant" to get information against Garvey for the mail fraud trial. It is interesting that Jacques Garvey chose to arm herself with a gun, even though Garvey refused to carry one himself, stating, "No gun for me; if I am to be killed, then maybe it is my destiny."[30] Although Jacques Garvey had made sacrifices to meet her UNIA obligations, she was unwilling to be a martyr for the movement. (Other black women leaders apparently felt the same way. For example, Ida B. Wells-Barnett also carried a gun. Such self-protection exemplified another way to transgress ideas of "feminine gentility and masculine courage.") Clearly, this was a trying time for Amy

Jacques Garvey; in 1964 she recalled how "fear and sorrow now became her constant companions."[31]

Despite the physical dangers and emotional pressures of this period, Jacques Garvey stepped forward to become an ambassador for her husband and the UNIA. She said, "I only live to perpetuate the ideas of my husband just as thousands of other Negroes, imbued with his spirit, have vowed to do." She directed all of her energies toward securing Garvey's release from prison. She must have been shocked to learn that he had "only left her $50 to face the world." Although soon after they were married, Garvey had "borrowed $400 of [her] early savings, to meet an emergency of the organization," she assumed that this need for money was an exception.[32] But Garvey's lack of business acumen had encroached on their personal household, and his wife soon found herself without personal funds and with the need to raise money for his bail. It had to be unnerving for her to acknowledge that their future was uncertain and financially insecure. It took a herculean effort on her part, along with other leaders, to convince the court to grant bail and then raise the fifteen thousand dollars it required. After Jacques Garvey furnished the money—in U.S. Liberty Bonds—to the clerk of the New York court, Garvey was released on 10 September 1923. Three days later he was welcomed home at a mass meeting in Liberty Hall.[33]

At this festive occasion Garvey publicly thanked his wife, noting that she was "obedient" and "loyal" and had "carried out the instructions" he gave her. Even when others who had pledged to support him had "got weak-kneed" and "attempted to deter that poor, little woman, to strike fear and terror into her heart and told her she was doing the wrong things," she persevered. Garveyite George Alexander McGuire agreed with that assessment, hailing Jacques Garvey as a "little Joan of Arc." According to McGuire, "Never did woman for man make similar sacrifice, exhausting her mental and physical powers by day, and resisting the embrace of Morpheus by night in her untiring efforts which have brought forth the first fruits of success [Garvey's release]."[34]

Ironically, at the same time that he was praising her efforts on his behalf, Garvey was also using his wife as an excuse to justify his leaving jail. He said that if it were not for "the pale face of my wife and the suffering depicted in her countenance every morning as she came to see me I would have been as happy there [in jail] sending out the messages of inspiration and hope to 400,000,000 black souls as speaking from the platform of Liberty Hall." He was not "afraid of jail" and was as "ready to go back as he was ready to go in the first instance. The jail had no terrors for me." Only "God can strike terror and fear in the hearts of twentieth century black men." Garvey's speech, in part, represented a certain performance that was mandatory to maintain his masculinity. All UNIA men asserted their manhood by not appearing weak and effeminate. According to George Mosse, "the specter of unmanly men had accompanied modern masculinity from its birth" at the end of the eighteenth century.[35] Real men were tough, and jail served as another test to prove manhood.

Michael Kimmel cogently argues that "men define their masculinity, not as much in relation to women, but in relation to one another." Because of this, historically American men have behaved in macho ways so others will not view them as "less than manly, as weak, timid, frightened."[36] Garvey may not have thought that it was emasculating to have his wife protect and defend him while he was incarcerated, but he wanted to ensure that the membership understood that neither masculine anxiety nor insecurity pushed him to leave prison (a highly problematic homosocial institution). Rather, he left because of his inability to meet the ultimate obligation of a UNIA husband: protection of his wife.

In jail, Garvey's asthmatic condition had flared up, and on his release his physician recommended a warmer climate. Though he had to stay in the United States while his case was on appeal, he was not restricted to New York, enabling he and his wife to plan a working vacation through thirteen states, including the warm West Coast. Jacques Garvey recalled that "he took me along, as the people in the Western states were anxious to see and hear me."[37] By October 1923, five months after the trial began, the Garveys and their secretary Enid Lamos were on tour.

Jacques Garvey chronicled their trip in a series of six weekly articles published in the *Negro World*. Her goal was to describe the places they visited to show how "necessary it was to have united action to help overcome such conditions."[38] Her mission was to expose the injustices of Jim Crow America and offer the UNIA as an alternative. Jacques Garvey gave her impressions of each state by highlighting the geographic landscape, economic opportunities, and housing conditions. Though her prose was not elegant, there was a vivacity in her articles that gave them a moving quality. Like other political journalists writing during the Harlem Renaissance, Jacques Garvey used her words as a means to inspire a "collective black consciousness." Ultimately, she hoped to organize this energy into a mass awakening of black people who would recognize the importance of the UNIA's ideology and program. For instance, she described how black folks with "a little money" had migrated to southern California from the South and Midwest. Employment was plentiful in Los Angeles, "of course keeping within the limit prescribed for him by the white man who is ever watchful, ever on guard, saying, 'Nigger, thus far shalt thou rise and no farther.'" Jacques Garvey summed up the situation by saying, "Friends, members of my race, I would not advise you to try to break down those barriers." It was more practical to "turn our eyes in the other direction and look towards Mother Africa, where we will be able to rise to the heights of true manhood and womanhood and live in happiness and prosperity with our brothers and sisters over there."[39] Robert Chrisman reminds us that the *Negro World* was the "ideological arm of the UNIA," and Jacques Garvey's observations influenced and shaped the thinking of her readership by articulating what many of them had "dimly felt, sensed or observed in privacy, declaring that collective consciousness in clear, cold, black type."[40]

In all six articles, Jacques Garvey's Jim Crow discussions center primarily on the activities of the Ku Klux Klan. She reports that in Indiana the Klan's "voters are said to number between 300,000 to 400,000 in the entire state. It is said that the organization defeated several candidates in the 1922 election." Jacques Garvey did not exaggerate the political power of the Klan; scholars have estimated that in the 1920s Klan membership numbered between three and five million, with Indiana the hotbed of its political activity. Kathleen Blee's seminal work on the Klan documents that in 1924, Indiana "Klan-backed candidates won the governorship, many mayoral contests including those in Indianapolis, Evansville, and Kokomo, and numerous local offices of sheriffs, district attorneys, and others."[41] The strong presence of the Klan in every election in Indiana during the 1920s may have jolted Jacques Garvey's readership into seriously thinking about the UNIA as a rational political alternative.

Jacques Garvey also wrote about the "Southern sport among the white gentry"—lynching black men—and mob violence against black neighborhoods. Following the lead of her peer Ida B. Wells-Barnett, she understood that white people justified violence in the name of protecting their communities from "black rapists and murderers." She warned that "half of the stories of murder and rape are untrue, but propaganda distorts truth and even swallows it up when convenient." As Marcus Garvey was called one of the greatest propagandists of the period, his wife was well acquainted with its use as a political tool. But she reasoned that her husband's use of propaganda was different from white supremacist dogma because "we are not preaching a propaganda of hate against anyone," and it helped "his efforts to educate black men to see the necessity for African Nationalism, and to get white men to appreciate the righteousness of his Cause."[42]

Her single-minded focus on the Klan impelled her to pose the question, "You may ask why do I pay so much attention to the Klan? I am interested in their activities, because I agree with Mr. Garvey when he says that this organization is the hidden spirit of America." She believed that black people needed to know everything about the Klan to protect their families and communities. Nevertheless, she concluded, "Let us not knock our heads to smithereens against this high thick wall of white supremacy . . . but let us turn our eyes in the other direction and look toward Mother Africa."[43]

Jacques Garvey's description of Jim Crow America was so vivid that her writing served as a conduit to the original moment.[44] Although her articles do not represent investigative reporting like those of Wells-Barnett or Mary Church Terrell, she never let an opportunity pass to expose the underbelly of race relations in the United States and offer an analysis of segregation. Even when Jacques Garvey found herself enjoying a working vacation, she would quickly contextualize her emotions to move her feelings beyond self-gratification. For instance, she was fond of Los Angeles and its surrounding communities, writing that it "would be a real Eden to Negroes if it were not for that viper, race prejudice, with its fangs of hate ever ready to strike and kill the rising ambition and hopes of Negroes."[45]

A personal side was also revealed through her Jim Crow stories. Glenda Gilmore argues that "white supremacy entailed more than violence and the denial of economic opportunities and political rights. It forced African Americans to endure an excruciating assault on their hopes and dreams."[46] In the 1920s the majority of black adults experienced, on one level or another, humiliating pain associated with the maintenance of Jim Crow. The Garveys were no exception to this reality, as Jacques Garvey related. In St. Louis, for instance, she had become very thirsty, so they stopped at a drugstore for a soda. The clerk refused them service, stating, "Sorry, but we don't serve colored people here"—a familiar phrase to many African Americans (though most had probably never heard it begin with the word "sorry"). Jacques Garvey was "stunned, and repeated the words audibly." She "really was too upset from the incident in the day to take an active part in the meeting, but my husband, after drinking about five glasses of ice water, was evidently cooled off and spoke for over an hour." Jacques

Garvey was still "depressed" in the afternoon, so her husband took her for a leisurely drive.[47]

It is difficult to understand why Jacques Garvey seemed so surprised by this episode. After all, she had lived in New York since 1917 and had traveled to other states as Garvey's private secretary. It is hard to imagine that she had been so completely shielded from racial etiquette and legal restrictions that she was unfamiliar with the basic tenets of Jim Crow. On its face her reaction seems overly naive, but perhaps it is a mistake to think that one can become immune to Jim Crow's humiliation. No matter how often people are told they are unwelcome, it is always a distressing experience.

On the other hand, because the Garveys were treated like royalty by the UNIA membership, they seldom had to interact with white America on the same level as the majority of black people. A week before the occurrence in St. Louis, Jacques Garvey had written that a white railroad stationmaster had mistaken the Garveys for "Africans" because they were "well-clad, independent-looking people traveling first class." If they had been "traveling with bundles and had the air of 'scared to death' folks running from the South, we would have been called 'Niggers.' "[48] Jacques Garvey apparently believed that she and her husband had an aura about them that yielded respect. Maybe the Jim Crow incident shocked her because she had internalized the respect and deference granted her by Garveyites and others, and this moment was a frightening reminder that she was still black in America.

In addition to her written dispatches, Jacques Garvey was asked to speak at each location on their tour. Her verbal discourse mirrored the late-nineteenth-century "woman-tempered rhetoric," also described as "speechlets"—spontaneous talks ranging from five to fifteen minutes. According to Carol Mattingly, speechlets ensured that women did not speak too long; thus, they were able to "assure audiences that their public stance did not masculinize them." Indeed, Jacques Garvey would often simply add "my thanks to those of my husband's." By the end of the month-long schedule, however, she was struggling to confine her talks within a "feminine" time frame. She wrote, "Yours truly was called upon to speak and being fully wound up could not stop under half an hour. However, I was rewarded with a large bouquet of flowers."[49] The "however" clarified her perception that the audience did not view her lengthy talk as an indiscretion but instead appreciated her enthusiasm.

Jacques Garvey called her six articles "Impressions," but they actually constituted a refined discourse on the politics of race in the United States. Michel Foucault tells us that discourses are not passive utterances, but writing that moves beyond the places that produce texts and the people who read them. More specifically, though, Jacques Garvey's discourse not only reflected her knowledge about the United States, but also became her intellectual property, which she would draw on in the near future.

The articles were a smashing success among her readership. Garvey, in fact, used material from some of her articles in his speeches, and when they returned to New York, many wanted to hear her speak at the first mass meeting of the UNIA. Jacques Garvey remembered how "the audience clapped and called out, We want Mrs. Garvey." She rose, and when "their cheering had died down, I had caught their infectious spirit, and responded with a speech, that came to its climax in a call to rededicate their lives for service to all." Marcus Garvey acknowledged the energy, and "before he spoke he said smilingly, Now I have a rival, but I am glad she is my wife."[50]

Jacques Garvey's intense efforts on behalf of her husband and the UNIA took their toll on her physical health, and by August 1924 she was quite ill. At the annual convention Garvey explained the hardships that they had experienced. "It is no wonder that I have now a sick and half-dying wife because of the suffering that we have had to undergo." Jacques Garvey's poor health may have been a sign that she had never fully recuperated from her earlier bouts with malaria. She never disclosed a diagnosis or any treatment of her illness and only referred to it incidentally, such as she had lacked "an appetite" for months.[51]

Other writers of the time noted Jacques Garvey's small stature and how she often looked "frail." When discussing her dedication to Garvey, George McGuire wrote that in spite of her "slender build, and apparently frail constitution," she "surmounted all barriers at the risk of a general breakdown." Martha Verbrugge's study on nineteenth-century women and personal health helps us to understand why Jacques Garvey's small body was linked to her poor health: "the occurrence of illness supported the belief that women were physically weak; conversely, assumptions about female frailty made sickness a more likely event."[52] The result of this widespread belief, which carried over into the twentieth century, was that overwork and stress about her husband's pending mail fraud appeal seemed incidental to the fact that she was a petite woman who could be presumed to be inevitably sick. This idea further erroneously implied that rest and relaxation could not make her well.

We may never know the cause of Jacques Garvey's illness, but if the advertisements for products to rejuvenate the body are any indication, she was definitely not alone. The *Negro World, New York Age*, and *Chicago Defender* carried numerous advertisements for tonics, pills, vitamins, and potions, exhorting: "DO YOU SUFFER FROM: TB, Constipation, Catarrh, Bronchitis, Asthma, Weak Lungs, Weakness, Run Down, Night Sweats, Hemorrhages, Loss of Weight or Strength, Nervous Dyspepsia, Loss of Appetite, Malnutrition, Neuralgia, Rheumatism, Chronic Constipation, Bad Blood Diseases, Painful Conditions of the Kidneys, Bladder or Pelvic Organs? If you do write at once to Dr. Ivy's Free Booklet of Advice and Information."[53] Many ads specifically targeted women. The Pelvo Medical Company, for example, advertised in the *New York Age* on 25 March 1921: "WEAK WOMEN ATTENTION: If you suffer from female troubles such as ovarian pains, pains in the lower part of your stomach, bearing down pains, headache, backache, painful or irregular periods. If you have that tired, worn out, nervous feeling so common to women—Feel well and strong again." Chronic sickness was either a part of black life or entrepreneurs tapped into, and magnified, common bodily aliments. Historically, poor people in the United States have had the least access to traditional health care, and the post–World War I environment did not alter this reality, especially for African Americans. Lack of money meant that the vast majority of black people never saw a physician until their illness was chronic and often irreversible. The UNIA addressed this concern through preventive health advice. Editors of the *Negro World* ran an occasional column, entitled "Health Talks," that featured advice on how to keep one's body well.

How to remain physically and mentally fit was on the minds of many black people—especially women, since they were often the ones who nursed their families. Jacques Garvey made it her business to take care of her husband. On their working vacation, when he had an attack of asthma because of their damp room, she made sure that in their next hotel "the room was warm before taking it." She was Garvey's caregiver, but there were times when he was very attentive to her needs, and he sensed when she needed to relax. He took her on "delightful drives" through the cities they visited when she was "upset," and she cherished these times.[54] Jacques Garvey enjoyed being a passenger and sight-seer, and during these private hours their lives resembled those of other newlyweds. But these amusements and nourishing moments were too few, and it appears that she often suffered alone.

Although illness can foster dependency, it can also be a way through which people assert themselves, express frustration, and exert control over their lives, as it was for Jacques Garvey.[55] Her political life had taxed her physical well-being, and the fact that she and her new husband had a working vacation instead of a traditional wedding trip further demonstrates their hectic lifestyle. Ironically, when she was sick she had more influence over her time and an excuse not to meet all of Garvey's and the UNIA's demands. No doubt what she really needed was an extended rest, and this she was unable to get.

When the U.S. Circuit Court rejected Garvey's appeal on 2 February 1925, his wife once again had to summon the strength to deal with the inevitable. On 23 March the Supreme Court of New York refused to review the case, and a bench warrant was issued for Garvey's arrest. The couple was returning from a speaking tour in Detroit when he was apprehended by marshals at the 125th Street train station in Harlem. He was taken to the Tombs in New York to await a train that would take him to the Atlanta federal penitentiary.

Assuming control of the situation, Jacques Garvey immediately contacted their lawyer and UNIA officers. "That night at Liberty Hall I had difficulty in preventing some of the members from demonstrating on the streets. I calmed them with assurance—which I doubted—that justice eventually would prevail," she wrote.[56] Understanding the importance of remaining rational, especially when others were operating on an emotional level, Jacques Garvey thought that a public street demonstration would do more harm than good. In the end she was able to convince Garveyites not to engage in protest. Her leadership was not paternal and dictatorial but maternal and optimistic. Again, she combined socially constructed feminine qualities (consoler and comforter) to navigate a public (i.e., male) space.

This was not the first time that Amy Jacques Garvey had navigated a public space with feminine characteristics. As a spokesperson for the UNIA, she had brought hope to discouraged black people before. One of her most memorable experiences had been in Baton Rouge, Louisiana, where "the people were tense and nervous; there had been a lynching there the previous night, the horrors of which were related to [her] in detail." They advised her "not to speak and take the next train out of town, as they did not want anything to happen" to her. Jacques Garvey appreciated their concern but said that she "could not run out on them like that; they needed comfort and cheer. So [they] agreed to have an early service."

After the singing of hymns and prayers, she "preached the sermon." Her text was taken from Isaiah 40, Verses 1–6, which begins "Comfort ye, comfort ye my people." From the moans from the "Amen Corner" and expressions such as, "Tell it, sister, tell it! Hallelujah!," she felt that her talk was a success. The method she employed that night—transforming a tense moment into a setting of exhilaration—became part of her typical lecture style.[57]

Across the country, while Garvey was in prison, Jacques Garvey "preached the sermon" at a time when the majority of pulpits represented the epitome of male hegemony. Evelyn Brooks Higginbotham's seminal study on the women's movement in the Black Baptist Church notes that even "the feminist theology of the black Baptist church never altered the hierarchical structure of the church by revolutionizing power relations between the sexes."[58] In denying women the right to preach and teach in a formal setting, the Black Baptist Church was similar to most institutionalized religions of the day. Jacques Garvey was not a missionary, let alone a minister, but she aggressively took the initiative to preach. One can easily imagine her drawing from Isaiah 40:5 and repeating that "all the glory of the Lord shall be revealed" if one followed the UNIA's path. Strikingly, she selected biblical verses that could be "feminized"; that is, it was the duty of all UNIA women to bring comfort to their families, and Jacques Garvey easily moved this vernacular from the intimacy of the home to a public space. Although not a controversial declaration, her public message helped to expand what was considered "appropriate" activism for a woman.

With Garvey's incarceration, Jacques Garvey ably moved from the background to the foreground and set the tone for the UNIA during this crisis. In her husband's absence she saw herself as the organization's leader and displayed a confident persona to inspire others to have faith in her ability and judgment. She personified the stoic wife that Garvey had come to rely on and represented herself as the voice of reason to the membership.

Although her public sermons and talks raised awareness of the unjust nature of Garvey's case, legally her hands were tied and she was unable to prevent his transfer from New York to the Georgia federal penitentiary. Fear that he would have to serve the maximum sentence of five years made Jacques Garvey even more determined to be with him on the ride to Atlanta. UNIA members purchased her ticket, gave her extra money for a "drawing-room compartment in the pullman," and made sure that she was on the right train. On board, the conductor instructed her to move to another car, but she would not "budge," and in Washington she secured a private room in the Pullman. Apparently the guards were lenient and allowed Garvey to share this compartment with his wife until they arrived in Atlanta. It was in the Pullman compartment that Garvey dictated to her his instructions for UNIA officers and his "messages" for the *Negro World.*[59]

In Atlanta, Jacques Garvey was told that she could not see her husband for two weeks, so she returned to Manhattan and went directly to the Chelsea Bank to close out his personal account to pay their past due household bill. But to her astonishment, the bank manager "brought back [only] eight dollars, and a slip from the ledger clerk verifying the balance. I had to summon all of my courage to face this situation," she wrote.[60]

It is unclear why Jacques Garvey continued to have confidence in Garvey when it came to their finances. Perhaps their lifestyle gave her the impression that they had money. In any event, not only was she concerned about her personal welfare, but also she now carried the burden of once again raising funds for his legal defense. If this pressure were not enough, a few days later she was summoned to the district attorney's office to pay the $1,000 court costs and fine levied against Garvey. She brought BSL stock certificates, which were checked by the clerk. Jacques Garvey describes how "the hurt in my eyes was so eloquent, that he quickly dismissed me, saying, 'You may go.'"[61] It is interesting that in this encounter she did not feel the need to be stoic as she always had for the UNIA membership. But did Jacques Garvey really feel so downtrodden that day, or did she purposely look pitiful to stall officers of the court? Either way, an aspect of her burden had been lifted for the time being, and she could concentrate on Garvey's release from Atlanta.

Jacques Garvey's next task was to raise money to continue Garvey's legal defense. This time, though, she had to make sure that the funds would not be subject to confiscation by the district attorney's office. To this end, "I had to hide some of it in a bank in a nearby state, and a small amount in another bank in the old section of New York." To ensure that she was not followed, she traveled a variety of routes to these banks, and "sometimes the cold numbed my feet and hands, but concealed on my person was that precious money." She was also very concerned about Garvey, whom she visited every three weeks. He asked for money and "special gifts" that she could have sent directly from large department stores like "Macy's or Gimbels." She did her best to fulfill all of his requests and keep him in a good mood. In turn, he planned her speaking/fund-raising itinerary from his jail cell to maintain a constant flow of money for his legal defense fund.[62]

With Garvey jailed, the federal government began to pay closer attention to Jacques Garvey's role in maintaining the UNIA movement. New York assistant attorney Edward S. Silver advised that Marcus Garvey was "at present instrumental in the furtherance of the scheme for which he was convicted and sentenced," and that "Mrs. Garvey received her instructions from him and as a result she was using the mails to defraud the Negro people throughout the United States." This matter appeared to be "properly one coming under the jurisdiction of the Postal authorities."[63] A copy of this report was forwarded to the postmaster general and the warden in Atlanta. These communications and enclosures were "referred for consideration with other papers bearing on the matter."[64]

Acutely aware that "receiving instructions" from Garvey was not enough to implicate Jacques Garvey, the U.S. government began to try to link her exchanges with him to appeals for funds to buy a school in Virginia that was "worth a quarter of a million dollars, when in fact there was not as much as $1,000 invested in it."[65] The UNIA officers in New York had placed a down payment on the school and sought membership support to complete the purchase. But this in itself was not a crime, and once Garvey learned of the government's attempt to bring his wife into the matter, he was outraged. In a lengthy letter to Warden Snooks, he declared that his "wife made no such appeal, and [he] challenge[d] any one to honestly present such communication sent to [his] wife by way of instructions and any such appeals for funds for any school as alleged." Garvey repeated several times in the letter that Jacques Garvey had "made no appeal with intent to defraud anyone and I *dare* anyone to so charge her." He concluded that his wife was not a UNIA officer and had no connection with the school.[66] In the end, the government withdrew from this line of attack.

Well aware that the federal government was watching her every move, Jacques Garvey must have been caught off guard when she received an affirmative response to her nationalization petition, filed five years earlier. Apparently the complicated bureaucracy of federal agencies had worked to her advantage. The Department of Labor did not have a clue about her current circumstances, and the fact that she had indicated on her application for naturalization that her husband resided with her, as opposed to an

Atlanta jail cell, shows that they made no connection between the couple. It is ironic that on 6 July 1926, when she signed an oath of allegiance to the United States, government officials were attempting to implicate her in a school fraud.[67]

As the federal government was revamping its efforts to stifle the UNIA movement completely, the Garveys undertook another project to garner sympathy and support for the cause. After three months in jail, Marcus Garvey believed that another edited volume of *Philosophy and Opinions* would go a long way toward showing him in a proper light. Jacques Garvey recalls that he "asked me to get together enough of his speeches, writings, and extracts of the trial, and edit them for a book of about 400 pages; he wanted this done in a hurry."[68] Like the first volume, the second was largely a compilation of material previously published in the *Negro World*. No doubt, Jacques Garvey's advocate role clouded her ability to function as an objective editor. For his part, Garvey remained firmly committed to his platform, so he saw no need to revise his ideas or prose. Hence the reprints in the second volume are mostly identical to the originals.

The second volume of *Philosophy and Opinions*, however, does provide a few examples of Jacques Garvey falling back to a more conservative position, reminiscent of some of the editorial deletions she made in the first volume. For instance, in Garvey's last speech before his incarceration, he said, "They brought 40,000,000 black men from Africa who never disturbed the peace of the world and black men shall put up a fight that shall write a page upon the history of human affairs."[69] But in the second volume reprint, Jacques Garvey inserted the word "constitutional" before the word "fight." Her change implies that "black men" were not going to be volatile, but civil and legal. Thus, it became a civil rights argument versus the possibility of a bloody battle. In the same speech she also substituted the word "glaring" for "bloody."

Moreover, Jacques Garvey prefaced one of Garvey's most famous essays, "An Appeal to the Souls of White America," with the biblical verse "Blessed are the peacemakers; for they shall be called the children of God. Matt v.9." This verse reaffirmed that Garvey's essay was indeed a humble appeal rather than one inviting disharmony and destruction. These examples of editorial tampering in the second volume are the exceptions, however. Overall, Jacques Garvey opted for subtle changes, pruning audience responses (applause and laughter) along with subheadings. She resolved inconsistencies in dates and numbers, corrected spelling and grammatical errors, and fine-tuned Garvey's style.[70]

Time may have been a factor in her decision not to make substantial changes in the original, but we must also consider the possibility that she was becoming even more committed to controversial—and, at times, radical—political ideas. In the second volume, the thrust of Garvey's voice is never compromised. This second text was three times longer than the first and far more difficult to assemble. Jacques Garvey thought that she had managed the impossible when she was able to rush him the first copy of *The Philosophy and Opinions of Marcus Garvey, Volume II* (1925). Garvey, however, callously said, "Now I want you to send free copies to Senators, Congressmen and prominent men who might be interested in my case, as I want to make another application for a pardon." After completing this task, she was once again suffering from ill health. One of her eyes had become badly strained, she weighed only ninety-eight pounds, and her blood pressure was low.[71]

Over these early years, Jacques Garvey had become an increasingly public figure and one well versed in UNIA operations, though all of her work continued to be undertaken to "perpetuate the ideas of [her] husband." In her public speaking on his behalf and in her editing of his writings, we see a woman both emerging in her own right and dedicating herself to Pan-African ideas. Unquestionably, though, as Honor Ford Smith of the Jamaican feminist theater group Sistren points out, Jacques Garvey "typified the ideal image" of the woman in the UNIA as it developed in the United States. Even though "her literary and intellectual skills account for much of the documentation of the movement, she did not question her role as wife, . . . combining these duties with her responsibilities as a tireless supporter of Garvey."[72]

The challenge for Jacques Garvey at this point was to determine how she could keep her husband at the center of her world while maintaining her health and a sense of self. As the next chapter explores, by creating a woman's page in the *Negro World* she was able to keep Garvey's agenda in the forefront and still express her own budding ideas. These editorials also proved therapeutic because they allowed her to release stressful emotions, particularly anger and frustration, toward people whom she believed had caused her grief and anguish. Indeed, Jacques Garvey's writings on the woman's page mark a transition from perpetuating Garvey's ideas to developing her own independent intellectual perspective.

In her dual political commitment to a Pan-African agenda and to feminist ideas, and to her personal commitment to meeting her husband's needs as well as those for her own development and expression, Amy Jacques Garvey faced numerous challenges. Her solution to these apparently contradictory commitments was to adopt an approach that I call "community feminism." Her nearly two hundred editorials for the *Negro World*—most of which were written during Garvey's imprisonment—provide a window for examining this concept more fully.

In essence, community feminists are women who may or may not live in a coverture relationship; either way, their activism is focused on assisting *both* the men and the women in their lives—whether husbands or sisters, fathers or mothers, sons or daughters—along with initiating and participating in activities to "uplift" their communities. Despite this "helpmate" focus, community feminists are undeniably *feminists* in that their activism discerns the configuration of oppressive power relations, shatters masculinist claims of women as intellectually inferior, and seeks to empower women by expanding their roles and options. Best understood through poststructuralist ideas of relativism and difference, community feminism counters a macropolitical model that implies that there is something inherently "pure" or "essential" to feminist theory. By decentering feminist epistemologies, the multiple identities of black women, along with communitarian ideas (the rejection of self-interest and the autonomous individual in recognition of the self as collective, interdependent, and relational), take center stage.[1] Of crucial relevance to this theory is the interplay between helpmate and leadership roles, both of which come up repeatedly in Jacques Garvey's writings.

As the helpmate of one of the most talked about political activists in the black diaspora in general and Harlem in particular, Jacques Garvey "endeavor[ed] to be conversant with subjects that would help in his career."[2] She did this by reading a diverse mix of newspapers and magazines daily, arming herself with local, regional, and international information. In many ways, Jacques Garvey's intellectual development gave rise to her expanding position within the black liberation movement. It is hard to keep a thoughtful person, and more poignantly an organic intellectual, silent and hemmed in the corner, and Jacques Garvey was no exception.

Growing confident in her opinion on just about everything tangentially related to black people, she positioned herself to become a more visible leader in the Universal Negro Improvement Association (UNIA) by directly associating herself with the organization's most influential propaganda tool, its newspaper, *Negro World*. She took this stand when Marcus Garvey was unable to wield direct power over the organization from his Atlanta prison cell. Believing that she had a specific duty to address the concerns of women in the movement, she consolidated all of her newspaper clippings and magazines that were laced with her counterarguments scrolled in the margins, and fused them into editorial commentary. Overall, this material became the fodder for her motivational, thoughtful, and, at times, scathing analyses.

Between February 1924 and June 1927 Jacques Garvey served as an associate editor of the *Negro World* and prepared the woman's page, "Our Women and What They Think," which she had introduced. T. Thomas Fortune, editor of the newspaper during the woman's page run, was genuinely impressed with Jacques Garvey's editorial "knack," which "just seem[ed] to come natural to her." She had to "be born with genius to do it."[3] Her "genius," however, does not brilliantly shine through each weekly edition. In fact, at a glance the woman's page appears to be a hodgepodge of international sentiments regarding women. A comprehensive evaluation, though, reveals an eclectic pattern that hammered home the need for women to work as political agents as well as to perform as helpmates, acknowledging the difficulties related to this nurturing role. Although one might debate the various strategies or most appropriate means of achieving the goal, the goal was still the same—empowerment through self-determination and nationhood in Africa.

The appearance of the woman's page coincided with the most turbulent period of the UNIA. African American leaders had condescendingly denounced Garveyites as the "humblest" and "primitive minded Negroes," and the press generally referred to Black Star Steamship Line Company (BSL) ships as "floating coffins." Marcus Garvey's 1925 meeting with the grand wizard of the Ku Klux Klan had further tarnished his reputation among African Americans, along with his indictment on mail fraud charges in 1923, and his subsequent conviction and inprisonment in Atlanta in 1925.

Recognizing that the *Negro World* and its printing plant constituted the UNIA's strongest and most viable enterprise, Jacques Garvey labored, under these trying circumstances, to produce inspiring essays to galvanize the black masses to support the movement to which her husband had given his "whole existence." Margaret Ward has observed that the high points of women's participation in nationalist movements have been "also moments of exceptional political crisis, when women were either drawn into the movement because of temporary (enforced) absence of men, or they were encouraged to participate because a strong, unified front was desperately needed."[4] Jacques Garvey's broadened leadership role in the UNIA followed this trend.

For some Garveyites, however, even a crisis did not justify allowing a woman at the helm. Soon after Garvey's arrest in 1923, Jacques Garvey was forced to publicly defend her expanded role in the UNIA. Several men detailed their—and perhaps others'—dissatisfaction with her function in a commentary potently entitled "Look Out for Mud." This snipe, dated 14 July 1923, stated that Marcus Garvey "had designated three men among the chosen officers of the association to be responsible heads during his absence. Mrs. Garvey is not part of this committee. Mrs. Garvey is not an officer of the association. Mrs. Garvey doesn't actively or passively control the organization." They concluded, "It is beneath the dignity of common decency to attempt to drag the name of an innocent and helpless woman into an arena where she cannot properly defend herself."[5] In a not-too-roundabout way, these men were in effect charging that Jacques Garvey was in fact functioning as an elected official, but they cloaked their concern in language that appeared to be defending her character as a woman. In raising objections to her role, these men, who espoused self-determination and self-reliance for the "Nation" but expected the opposite in gender relations, obviously believed that politics was men's territory and were actually defending the cornerstone of their status in the organization.

In a "Letter to the Editor," Jacques Garvey replied: "[Y]ou have characterized me as helpless. . . . I am innocent of the honor of having the UNIA turned over to me by my husband, but I am not innocent of the depths to which colored men can stoop to further their petty schemes even at the expense of a downtrodden race such as ours." She concluded that "with my unusual general knowledge and experience for a young woman, may I not ask if the word 'helpless' is not misapplied?" Her statement not only publicly questioned the attitude and behavior of male leaders but focused on her confidence in her own skills and intelligence to lead the organization. By placing the onus back on them, she conveyed her sentiments in a way that forced them to rethink their accusations of her stepping beyond her "place" as a woman.[6] More importantly, while Jacques Garvey accepted her marital responsibilities to Marcus Garvey, she refused to allow other men to occupy a position of authority over her. Her community feminism empowered her to establish personal parameters regarding her public and private roles, and only her husband had the right to question her decisions.

Three years later, in 1926, George Weston accused her of instigating conflict between American and West Indian members of the UNIA. Weston, president of the New York division, alleged that she had pitted him against William Sherrill, an African American who was acting president-general, in order to personally assume control of the UNIA. Jacques Garvey batted away this accusation in a letter to the editor of the *Negro World*: "I am compelled to contra[dict] the untrue statements . . . to wit Garvey seeks to dethrone William Sherrill . . . and place in power his second wife Mrs. Amy Jacques Garvey. . . . I am not an officer of the Universal Negro Improvement Association nor am I desirous of being an officer. At no time has Marcus Garvey suggested nor intimated that he was desirous of having me act for him during his imprisonment." By this time, the pressure against her had mounted to the boiling point. One "needs the patience of a Job to deal with our people in any mass movement," she declared.[7] Even though Jacques Garvey was clearly a driving force, she made sure everyone understood who was in charge of the organization by stating, "If he wanted to place me at the head of affairs, he would have made known his desires to the people and they would have acted on same."[8]

In regard to Sherrill and Weston, she wrote, "Both of these men have conducted these affairs without even informing Garvey of their activities nor paying the slightest attention to his instruction." She summed up her position in this way: "If Mrs. Garvey rules, it will be as if Garvey himself ruled, but when Sherrill rules he exhorts the people to build up apartment houses in America and solve the problem, and Africa can be redeemed later."[9]

On several occasions, Marcus Garvey jumped into this mean-spirited fray in letters to the *Negro World* in support of his wife. Once he stated, "This is to certify that my wife, Mrs. Amy Jacques Garvey[,] has during the period of my incarceration, remained loyal and devoted to me in all her duties and obligations as a true and loving wife." She had "ceaselessly worked, with tremendous opposition, to protect and defend me during this my time of trial and suffering in the interest of a cause I almost neglected her to service." Finally, he felt "great sorrow" that his "present situation, rendered [him] unable to give her the protection necessary and to show my appreciation of her unselfish love to me and to the cause I love."[10]

Throughout her husband's imprisonment, Jacques Garvey fearlessly defended herself, both vocally and in print, against the opposition, whom she characterized as "spineless and cowardly . . . colleagues, who will shrink with fear and hesitate to move forward."[11] No doubt her stinging disapproval of Weston and Sherrill, two influential UNIA officers, further alienated her from their constituency. In addition, the fact that in her editorials she continually unleashed her frustration on male leaders whom, in general, she regarded as "indolent associates" who were willing to "bask in the Glory" and "trade on" the name and achievements of Garvey, helped to generate the reputation that she was difficult to work with.[12]

When not in a defensive mode, Jacques Garvey's writings encompassed a wide variety of topics; as a group they provide rich documentation of her philosophical worldview, her private affairs, and her sincere desire to include black women in the redemptive struggle. "The exigencies of this present age require that women take their place beside their men," she wrote. She had created the woman's page of the *Negro World* so that women could contribute to the "race first" movement "whether in the form of news articles, poems or otherwise."[13]

During this period most women's sections in newspapers merely highlighted the fine points of etiquette, fashion, and food recipes. In the *Chicago Defender*'s occasional column, "Woman," introduced in 1910, discussions ranged from the proper ways to mourn a dead husband to the ornamentation of silk stockings. One article called on club women in the North to assist our "hard working ministers in the education of the newly emigrated public from the South, into our way of living: teach them, first, to remember that they have left the South and they must wear their Sunday clothes during the week." The writer concluded, "If our club women don't get busy along this line, we may be disgraced by some unthinking individual from down home." Another article, by an irate "club woman," noted that "many of our women have become an eyesore on the street cars, in the street; in the public places and theaters, because they do not act or dress right. . . . [T]heir heads are covered with rags and shawls. . . . [O]ut in the stockyards they go into the pay office with their hands full of vitals, making loud noises, and cutting up in general." The *New York Age*'s column "Of Interest to Women," which appeared by 1917, also gave recipes, helpful hints on food preparation, and shortcuts for household chores, as well as emphasized rules on women's "appropriate" behavior and appearance.[14]

Jacques Garvey balked at the frivolity of these columns, maintaining that "fashions and [housewives'] topics only" were poor "reflections on the intelligence of our women." Believing that "men have a higher appreciation of us when they read our ambitions and achievements, and more help would be given us," she opted, instead, to create an open forum in which women could share their ideas and opinions on serious matters. "In this way we will be able to command a respectful hearing before the world, and prove that Negro women are great thinkers as well as doers." She invited the views of ladies young and old, "bobbed and unbobbed." Her appeal to "all Negro women of all climes" recognized that class barriers stood in the way of a united race movement; thus, she instructed the unfortunate women who "cannot express [them]selves on paper [to] get some one who is better equipped to clothe [their] sentiments in proper language and send them into our office." "It is common knowledge," she wrote, "that some of the most beautiful sentiments and lofty ideas emanate from the brains of women who have [had] very little education."[15] By celebrating the genius of poor black women, Jacques Garvey turned Du Bois's popular mantra of the "talented few" directly on its elitist head. It was her "aim to encourage Negro women to express their views on subjects of interest to their communities and particularly affecting our struggling race."[16]

Jacques Garvey led the way by printing editorials that situated feminist proclivities within black nationalism; her commentary thus represents a struggle on behalf of women in the context of masculinist discourse. Her feminism, however, was entrenched in her confidence that an internalized Pan-African agenda (itself based on the romantic imagining of a modern black nation) would minimize divisive differences among black people, since "the nation is always conceived as a deep, horizontal comradeship."[17]

Her political position was grounded in an array of international examples. She paralleled the UNIA's call for an "Africa for the Africans at home and abroad" with discussions of the struggles of China and India to be free from "European Powers," and she applauded the Moors' willingness to engage in warfare to keep the French and Belgians out of North Africa. Their combined actions, she argued, weakened "our common oppressor and strengthened the prestige of one of the members of the family of darker peoples of the world in the field of achievement and world power."[18]

Jacques Garvey was not alone among women in her attempts to fuel a discussion that connected the political aspirations, racial histories and cultures, and potential for collective "world power" among non-European people. A few members of the National Association of Colored Women, led by Margaret Murray Washington, were also spreading information on "peoples of color the world over" to secure cooperation and appreciation of the "darker races of the world." In 1920 a new organization—the International Council of Women of the Darker Races (ICWDR)—was formed. The ICWDR was short lived but during its heyday, 1924, 150 American and 50 foreign women of color constituted "Committees of Seven" to study the conditions and promote race literature in schools in order to stimulate "a greater degree of race pride for their achievements."[19] Both the UNIA and cultural nationalists placed the study of race history high on their agendas, and Jacques Garvey may well have applauded the efforts of the ICWDR—though they would have never extended membership to her. Although the council had similar intellectual goals, the unquestionably elite pedigree of ICWDR placed women like Jacques Garvey (those without college degrees) on the outskirts. In contrast, the UNIA and its woman's page in the *Negro World* provided an avenue for all black women, regardless of class and caste, to participate as intellectuals in the Pan-African struggle.

Convinced that the most efficient way black people could free themselves from the clutches of colonialism and rise to their highest potential was to acquire the "knowledge that has made other races great," Jacques Garvey asserted that intelligence, particularly as it related to the modern sciences and capitalism, was a globally respected virtue that was rewarded with material wealth and power. To be sure, some leaders used information deviously; it took shrewd minds to rob, steal, and cheat entire nations out of their natural resources, labor power, and possessions. Nevertheless, she warned her readers about the far-reaching hazards of ignorance: "When the mind is enslaved, physical slavery, in one shape or another, soon follows."[20]

An independent black nation could spring forth if black people used their skills and resources to develop their own territory as opposed to acculturating into the American mainstream. Acculturation, to Jacques Garvey, was akin to "parrot-like" behavior, and this is why she told her readership that "the educated man is not necessarily a thinker." Any schooled person, she wrote, could "quote from the writings and theories of great men." The "really educated" person is one "who thinks for himself and is able to discover new truths."[21]

Tapping into the most uncontested political strategy for empowerment, Jacques Garvey's writings on the imperative of education echoed themes that had been popular among African Americans since the Reconstruction era. In his discussion of the rise of universal education among ex-slave communities in the United States, James Anderson notes that as a group they believed that "political and economic independence or self-determination" could not be achieved "without first becoming organized, and organization was impossible without well-trained intellectuals—teachers, ministers, politicians, managers, administrators, and businessmen."[22]

Jacques Garvey surely would have agreed with this pronouncement. In recalling the activities of women after Emancipation, she noted how a mother would wash, iron, and perform odd jobs "so as to support her children through school, giving to them what she never had—an education." The vexed history of women's education and the even more controversial conversations on the "appropriate" public roles for women pushed Jacques Garvey to argue further that black women could superbly perform in any fashion if given the training and opportunity. She stated, "Look at her today, educated, independent and well equipped along all lines to compete with her men and in many instances outclass them."[23]

As a connoisseur of international news, Jacques Garvey regularly compared the "New Negro Woman" to that of other women in the world. She commented that women of the East (India, Egypt, Turkey) were being educated and no longer considered themselves "slaves to their husbands" but rather "intelligent, independent human beings [able] to assert and maintain their rights in co-partnership with their men." In this discussion and others, Jacques Garvey connected the worldwide "awakening of women" to their academic achievements, which "enhance[d] the prestige of their own nations and race." Not only was education pivotal to the redemption of Africa ("Africa does not want illiterate people now," it needs "job makers not job-hunters. The fellow who is looking for a job had better stay right here and keep looking"), but it would also lead to women's own personal freedom from marital bondage and the clutches of colonists.[24]

At the turn of the century, Booker T. Washington and W. E. B. Du Bois had set the parameters for a debate on formal education in African American life: despite the lack of clear boundaries between a classical liberal arts education and industrial training, an artificial distinction was created between the two. Disregarding this argument, Jacques Garvey focused exclusively on the educational needs of women, putting forth the fundamental premise that "women have been endowed with the same mental faculties as men." Careful to keep her equality rhetoric within the prescribed gender conventions, she added that although it was "common knowledge that women are not as physically strong as men," the Creator—"God Almighty"—gave women other natural gifts to "repay" them for their "physical weakness." These attributes included "graciousness and keenness of mind" and the ability to "control and order things systematically and economically."[25]

The educational concepts that Jacques Garvey promulgated in the 1920s are reminiscent of those of 1890s female reformers. In 1892 Anna Cooper, a well-respected, formally educated, middle-class club woman, whose text, *A Voice from the South*, is commemorated by literary scholars as the "unparalleled articulation" of black feminist thought, declared, "As you know that she is physically the weaker of the two, don't stand from under and leave her to buffet the waves alone." Girls needed encouragement and scholarships though "not the boys less, but the girls more."[26]

In addition, Jacques Garvey's writings reflect the prevailing attitude of racial uplift and Christian ideologies that saturated postsecondary educational institutions of the time. For example, T. J. Morgan, secretary for the American Baptist Home Mission Society (1892–1902), believed that black women's schooling "ought to be as thorough and as rigorous as men's."[27] A higher education, Morgan argued, expanded the opportunities for black women to earn a living outside of domestic service. Jacques Garvey, however, chose not to engage this point of view despite the glut of underpaid working-class Garveyite women. Instead, she focused on the missionary spirit that reinforced moral training and the need to work and sacrifice for the race.

It is also revealing to contrast Jacques Garvey's political perspective—given her strong command of international history and current affairs—with Anna Cooper's. Unlike Jacques Garvey, who saw the "race-first" movement as a path to unity and mutual respect, Cooper proclaimed that "one race predominance means death," and that a diversity of people was necessary to give "birth to reciprocity and liberty." Moreover, Cooper took the passive position that "God and time" would work out the race problem, whereas Jacques Garvey was adamant that black people could not afford to wait for divine intervention, especially since they had the power to control their own destiny. Cooper, in conjunction with other black women intellectuals who championed integration, would undoubtedly have critically analyzed the UNIA as just another "new and improved method of getting the answer [to the race problem] and clearing the slate: amalgamation, deportation, colonization and all the other ations that were ever devised or dreamt of."[28] Though Cooper did not oppose the idea of individuals leaving the United States if they so desired, she dismissed it as a political solution.

Like the efforts of other black intellectuals of comparable stature—such as Mary Church Terrell, Frances Harper, Lugenia Burns Hope, and, of course, Jacques Garvey—Cooper's struggle to uplift her race (primarily through formal education and Victorian morals) was laced with contradictions. Kevin Gaines calls attention to how Cooper used uplift ideology to uncover the "moral bankruptcy of white supremacy" while seeking the support of white reformers and capitalist elites.[29] As a Pan-Africanist, Jacques Garvey could go only part of the way with her distinguished contemporaries. She respected and agreed with their moral ideas, but it was inconceivable to her that the New Negro Woman, by being well-mannered and unnervingly accommodating, could sway white America into sharing its resources. She considered any covenant with whites impossible because racism was too entrenched in U.S. society, and colonizers were selfish imperialists who would never share power with people whom they considered inferior.

In addition to focusing on the need for education, Jacques Garvey's editorials highlighted the interplay between the familial and public lives of women. She instructed black women to be competent mothers and to affirm men in the movement for self-determination. At the same time, she went beyond a relational view of self by anchoring her discourse within the refashioning of gender roles so that women could do their part as political leaders in building the black nation. Although emphasizing their maternal role, Jacques Garvey differed from most of her peers in that she believed that their nurturing traits allowed women to run not only their homes and communities efficiently, but also their respective countries.

Dedicated to the idea that women could reorder the gender practices of their communities in feminist directions, in the editorial "Women's Function in Life" Jacques Garvey addressed "whether woman's place is in the home, in business, in politics or in industry." She understood that countries were different and women's status varied; however, "present day events convince us that women, lovely women if you please, are making their presence felt in every walk of life." The woman "of today has a place in nearly all phases of man's life"; moreover, "where such a place is not yet properly established her voice is heard in that regard."[30]

To ensure that her readership recognized that her position differed from her husband's traditional view of patriarchy, Jacques Garvey restated in numerous editorials that women must not be denied roles as intellectuals and political architects. Under the title "No Sex in Brains and Ability," she wrote that "some men declare that women should remain in the homes and leave professions and legislation to men, but this is an antiquated belief, and has been exploded by woman's competency in these new fields and further by the fact that their homes have not suffered by a division of their time and interest."[31]

She continued to bolster her opinion by answering the question, "Will the Entrance of Women in Politics Affect Homelife?," with the claim that men tend not to realize the value of women in the home until they decide to enter electoral politics or political movements; then they bemoan, "Our homes will be broken up, our children will be rejected." Despite the highly charged disapproval of some men, Jacques Garvey declared that family life had not been neglected by women's entry into politics but had in fact benefited from it because legislative policies affected the home, communities, and nation. The only pertinent question to be addressed was how much time a woman should spend in her home and how much she should devote to politics. Without hesitation Jacques Garvey wrote: "This is a matter for the individual and women are rational and reasonable enough to give as much time in the home as the exigencies of the hour demand. Woman's inherent self-sacrifice and love will influence her decision in this direction."[32]

Jacques Garvey wanted her readership to understand how the familiar and public spheres were complementary. Thus, in her editorials she also explored the private lives of women as helpmates and the important ramifications that their home life had for nation building. A helpmate role did not debilitate women, she professed, but instead gave them authority to wield influence over men. In the editorial "Woman as Man's Helper," she stated that if it were not for women, "men would plunge more deeply in the mire of mistakes than they do. What great man has ever done any profitable thing without the help of some good woman?" She offered this question to generate dialogue among her readership about the empowering nature of a woman's relationship to a man, which, by the way, put men at ease with women's expanding roles. She concluded, "However great a thing may be, or whatever other men are consulted, even if it is clandestinely done, bank on it, there is a woman in the case before all consultations come to a close."[33] Even though a woman might not occupy the limelight or a position of visible influence, she emphatically shaped the outcome of important decisions. Jacques Garvey reiterated this idea in the editorial "The Joy of Living": "A woman may be born into this world for the purpose of mothering and training the President of a nation; another may be born to be the wife of a great statesman, whose single word could decide the destinies of millions of people."[34] To speak of women being "born" was simply another way for Jacques Garvey to create a narrative around presumed intrinsic qualities in women. The idea that specific traits (good judgment, mother wit) were ingrained in the female mind and could be used for covert and overt purposes served as a means to celebrate the infinite possibilities of women.

Although Jacques Garvey encouraged black women to be guided by an African consciousness and to let their voices be heard in political and civic affairs, by no means did she want them to be "liberated" from all gender-specific roles. She believed, like Marcus Garvey, that these were innate and beneficial to both women and men, hence to the community. Women were particularly suited to be nurturers, Jacques Garvey said, despite the fact that this role set a restrictive standard for appropriate behavior. Her discussion of a black woman's relational self, however, did call into question the contemporary perception that helpmates consistently occupied a second-class status.

The social construction of the term "helpmate" has been inaccurately reduced, largely by radical feminists, to imply passivity. Jean Bethke Elshtain argues insistently that too often feminists, radicals, and reformers analyze traditional community and family as "reactionary by definition" and "repressive by nature." By doing so, they obfuscate rather than illuminate how women actually grapple with and refashion family and community in ways that are beneficial to them. For example, at the turn of the century, Deborah Gray White observes, black club women fiercely debated woman's place in the uplift movement; many concluded that "a woman exercised her greatest influence on behalf of the race in her role as wife, mother, and teacher." For them, "this did not imply notions of woman's inferiority to man" because, as club woman Alice White points out, "woman is man's equal intellectually." Moreover, most black women in the 1920s did not passively surrender to the will or whims of black men. The contested history of black female and male ideological and relational differences, which have extended across class and geographic lines, is proof that they were active and assertive in varying ways.[35]

Jacques Garvey's feminism must be understood within this cultural paradigm. Certainly, cultural essentialism is haunting, and a totalizing vision of black people is also problematic; nonetheless, for Garveyites, submissive and docile behavior was the antithesis not only to a progressive black identity (based on phenotype and a cultural commitment to the black world) but also to nationhood building, which required purposeful agency—a combination of leaders and supporters—from all of its members. As a community feminist, Jacques Garvey assisted black women in reconciling these two (helpmate and leader) different paths by exposing the underlying unity of the different approaches.

One reason that Amy Jacques Garvey was able to expend so much energy in the Pan-African struggle during the 1920s was that she was not yet a mother to her own children, although she may have seen herself as a mother to the race. Her writings on motherhood most closely resemble those of the black club women of the period. Together their words articulate the need for properly reared children. Jacques Garvey observed that "ill-bred children are a menace to any country because they develop into individuals who take on vices that often wreck their homes and endanger the safety of their communities." She viewed the proper guidance of children as important not just for race betterment, as black club women preached, but to bring character, dignity, and skills to the future nation in Africa.[36]

It was the importance of this responsibility to bear and raise children that inspired Jacques Garvey to place a section on the woman's page directly under the advice of the Universal Black Cross Nurses. The Black Cross Nurses demanded a sound health program especially for children. They were committed to reaching a standard of knowledge where they would not accept "disease as something inevitable, something inconvenient but necessary, a visitation from the Supreme Being but instead focus their efforts to transgress nature's laws."[37] The nurses answered questions relating to the care and feeding of infants and children. Good health and the formal education of mothers and children were necessary to prepare the "Negro of Tomorrow."

It was primarily the mother who shaped the minds of her children, and—not surprisingly—Jacques Garvey maintained that the most efficient, organized, and prepared woman to handle this monumental task was an educated one. In writing about the educated mother, she insisted that women should "be given every opportunity to develop intellectually so that their off-spring may inherit such a quality." Nevertheless, educational opportunities for most black women were few and far between. Jacques Garvey responded to this reality with suggestions on how women could create avenues to learn, gather information, and share it with their children. For example, she was an avid reader and instructed women to cultivate a "taste for serious reading." Do not throw away newspapers but "put a wrapper on it and mail it" to others, she advised. Books should be sent as gifts, and mothers should tell children stories from their reading material. Reading should become a family event. Jacques Garvey knew from her own childhood experience that this was possible. Her father had stimulated her intellect, and she believed that parents, particularly mothers, had the same obligation to their children. In one editorial she observed, "Meek docile women usually rear puny, effeminate men, and ignorance certainly begets ignorance."[38] As a community feminist, she advocated educating mothers not for self and personal privilege but for community advancement.

The importance of motherhood elicited the most wholehearted agreement from Jacques Garvey's readers, who submitted numerous articles exalting women's maternal role. One writer stated that a mother was to be "particularly careful of her own habits and temperaments and customs. She has to practice self control, read good books and entertain only clean and wholesome thoughts and habits that she might bequeath to her child."[39] Many statements on the woman's page proclaimed that a black woman had to sacrifice "pleasure" (movies, dances, and card games) in an attempt to formally educate her child while maintaining her virtue. Because many women throughout the world structured their lives around concerns for their children, it is no wonder that they internalized this role as a privilege. To alter one's life totally for another is indeed the ultimate sacrifice. At the same time, though, this mother-as-nurturer role placed women who had no interest in having children outside the race's womanhood. Paramount to nation building, one scholar points out, was the "possession and control of [the woman's] womb."[40]

As an intellectual committed to the exchange of ideas, Jacques Garvey disseminated the thoughts of her peers by reprinting on the woman's page stories and clippings from local newspapers and magazines on activities and issues that related to women.[41] She also repeatedly asked for submissions from her readership. Her strategy to allow debate on the woman's page was a conscious effort to foster agitation, though she never shifted from her own position that women had the right to act as political beings. She hoped that controversy would encourage women to analytically develop their own viewpoints and inspire others to take notice of and respect the ideas of Garveyites. Given that Jacques Garvey regarded the sharing of ideas—theorizing—as a form of activism, she repeatedly emphasized that contributions to the Pan-African struggle could come from the stroke of a pen or a typewriter.

Her readership responded with a range of contributions, confirming that black women's thought was not monolithic. Some agreed with Jacques Garvey that black women should stand beside black men but not be afraid to challenge them in the struggle for liberation. Other women only partially concurred with her position. They felt that their role was to be exclusively in the home and their function was solely to raise their children to be conscious citizens and support their husbands as they engaged the struggle for black liberation.

Jacques Garvey's advocacy of a range of public and political roles for UNIA women received wide support. In fact, numerous black women candidly pushed for female leadership. One article submitted to the woman's page argued: "There are many people who think that a woman's place is only in the home—to raise children, cook, wash, and attend to the domestic affairs of the house. The idea, however, does not hold true with the New Negro Woman." Black women needed to learn the essential leadership skills to uplift their race; "here are a few of the important places which the New Negro Woman desires to take in the rebirth of Africa at home and abroad: 'To work on par with men in the offices as well as on the platform' and 'To practice actual economy and thrift.'" As black nationalists, women were also "to teach practical and constructive race doctrine to the children" as well as "to teach the young the moral dangers of social disease and to love their race first." Lastly, the "New Negro Woman" had "to demand absolute respect from men of all races."[42]

These five points echoed Jacques Garvey's concept for empowerment. Black women had to make use of the skills practiced in the home (economy and thrift), cultivate their relationships with their children, and not only seek protection from men but also demand respect from all races in order to have a fluid, dialectical relationship between traditional roles and a willful feminist identity.

To Jacques Garvey's question, "Will the Entrance of Women in Politics Affect Homelife?," several comments appeared. E. Elliott Rawlins, M.D., wrote that politics would become purified by women's participation. He stressed that politics intersected with domestic life in many ways—school conditions, property and personal taxes, rent laws, health laws, morality, and crime. He suggested that the solutions to these concerns and others could be settled through politics. In sum, Rawlins agreed with Jacques Garvey that women did not automatically neglect home duties when they became political actors because their activities merely supplemented their domestic interests.[43]

Saydee E. Parham, a law student, reinforced Jacques Garvey's position by suggesting that a woman's entry into the political world would enable her to formulate and carry out laws to improve the living conditions in her community. Parham concluded: "Having better economic and better educational conditions, her children are raised in the midst of healthy surroundings, giving them high aspirations."[44]

In opposing this argument, Reverend G. E. Carter offered three ways in which women's entry into politics would negatively affect the home:

(1) Politics requires study and whole-hearted interest and the home must have the same. Both cannot have this at the same time and the home suffers.

(2) Motherhood is a natural requisite of a true woman, children need

the attention of women 18 hours a day. Politics requires at least 8 hours of any woman's time to be prepared for the task. Ten hours is not enough for the child[;] thus the home suffers through neglect of children.

(3) The love for adventure, the idealism of politics and desire to reform the evils of society will fascinate some women so much that this love will supersede the love for home and children; therefore, the race reproduction will be greatly jeopardized.[45]

Finally, Marion L. Wallace believed that the home should come before political work if the woman was a mother. She argued that when it came to holding "big political positions," a woman had to contend with the obligations of child rearing and homemaking, and she would be "better off making splendid women and men out of her children." On the other hand, if the woman had "unusual attributes" and no home worries, or if "her husband is dead and she has to raise children, the remunerations she raises from a good political position would enable her to raise her children properly." Wallace concluded that men were stronger physically, but the affairs of school, community work, and social uplift should be left entirely in the hands of "sympathetic" women.[46]

In terms of domestic responsibilities, women in the UNIA went beyond perceiving the home as a place of sanctuary. One woman wrote that "no one but a woman can make a home, and the home is the backbone of the nation. Men need it, children need it, and the woman herself needs it." This writer claimed that it was through the home that the black woman was able to fulfill her "greatest privilege, her most sacred duty and her most solemn obligation." Her "most sacred duty" was to support her husband in all facets of his life: "She is man's solace and when he needs comfort and sympathy, he needs it mighty quickly."[47]

Other comments reiterated this idea that black women must be self-sacrificing and undemanding while their husbands led the race toward self-determination. One writer stated that if a black woman "rejected her home that she was not only violating her marital vows but also her destiny." It was only through the home that a black woman was able to fulfill her "calling." Another woman contended, in her article "Girls Should Be Taught to Keep House Properly," that many divorces were the fault of inefficient housewives: "I know from experience that there is nothing a man hates more than laziness in a home. We of the UNIA want energetic useful young wives who will work for the home and for the race."[48]

Jacques Garvey agreed that laziness was akin to docility and passivity and had no place in the struggle for liberation, but she would add that divorces were not just about inefficient housewives but incompetent husbands who failed as financial providers. Such statements confirm that neither UNIA members nor Jacques Garvey herself challenged the prevailing ideology that women should be self-sacrificing wives. In essence, the task of building a black nation relied on masculine redemption, and the Garveys constructed and positioned, to borrow from Paulette Pierce and Brackette Williams, "the manliness of male-the-provider against the femininity of female-the-nurturer."[49]

When it came to black womanhood, a myriad of articles described what made a "good woman" for the black race. To begin, a good woman always had a husband or was a widow; she was never a single woman. This general opinion reinforced the idea that decent black women existed only in relation to another human being. As one writer put it, a "good woman is one who takes interest in the home, who acts as helper and companion to both husband and children. Modest, well bred, encouraging and a loveable disposition." Black women differed from the numerous white women who echoed comparable sentiments by adding that they "must do [their] best in all things and [be] satisfied with the lesser things in life, knowing [they] cannot at the present have the greatest things. Though [they] would love to have as much as other women."[50] For a UNIA woman, self-sacrifice was not immediately rewarded with material wealth, as they presumed it to be for white women. Many black women justified their lack of tangible, extravagant goods by explaining that black men were "broken down by the awful and implacable approach of doom and abiding with unshrinkable firmness the bitter blast of adversity."[51]

These comments indicate that many black women were only in partial agreement with Jacques Garvey's feminist ideas. For them, the transition from a helpmate into a leadership role was undesirable. Though an influential UNIA leader, Jacques Garvey was able to drive only a slight crack into the prevailing "patriarchal sensibilities" that race leaders should be race men. Her case was further hampered by the fact that, as Hazel V. Carby observes, leading race men, such as Du Bois, failed to "imagine a community in which positive intellectual and social transformation could be evoked" through black women.[52] Thus, Jacques Garvey's audacious call to black women to move ahead of haphazard male leadership (especially since her husband could be a prime target) challenged the idea that thinking, influential women were the usurpers of masculine agency.

Eventually, her critique of myopic gender politics became part of the militant, vanguard discourse that present-day women celebrate as a component of black feminism.

Jacques Garvey had opinions about all areas of Pan-African thought and the redemption of Africa. Therefore, although most of her editorials addressed the role of women, she knew she also had to deal directly with men. Motivating black men could be a difficult task, she believed, because they lacked faith in themselves and their potential. They had lost the "incentive to achieve big things, and produced an over burdened woman-hood," and the race was that "much poorer because of their slothful-ness."[53] Although Jacques Garvey was sympathetic to their plight, she gave them little room to excuse or justify counterproductive behavior and lack of action. Indeed, at times her chastisement of black men was harsh and aggressive.

Never short on demonstrative terms to describe black men, many of Jacques Garvey's editorials refer to them as "selfish," "unappreciative," "lazy," "parasites," and "petty." Deborah Gray White calls attention to the fact that club women, though they challenged patriarchy, never mounted "a malevolent attack against black men." Jacques Garvey, on the other hand, pitched an assault from every possible angle, ranging from black men's inability to provide for and protect black women to their lack of appreciation for their mothers and wives. Simultaneously, she consoled black women who suffered because of "the lethargy of [black] men, who are content to be servants, dependents all their lives, and lack the pluck to go out and create positions for themselves."[54] One interpretation of this vehemence is that Jacques Garvey's ultimate goal was to motivate black women to stay on course in the redemption of Africa, and she felt that black men were failing to honor their women in this task. In the editorial "Listen Women," she hoped to inspire women by counseling them not to let the "apathy of your men discourage you, as black women bore the rigors of slavery so will you bear the hardship preparatory to nationhood."[55]

As Jacques Garvey unleashed her volley against black men, she often fell into the trap of comparing them to white men. Though she identified white men as oppressors, she too often wanted black men to emulate their behavior because she believed it would be advantageous for the race. In one editorial she stated, "White men are the greatest pioneers of the age. They will brave hell itself to satisfy their women; this desire to please them is actuated by their love and respect for them." If black men "would place the right value on their women, they, too, would feel that there is nothing on God's green earth too good to give them." To understand this attitude, we need to remember that the UNIA was a procapitalist, masculinist movement, and Jacques Garvey wanted black women to reap the same material benefits as white women. She projected this position with statements like "White men, on the other hand, idolize their women and for them they will dare anything in order to merit their looks of admiration" and "They have braved the tropical jungles, slain black men, in order to get gold and diamonds with which to adorn their women; they have ventured forth into the Arctic regions so that she may have beautiful furs to keep her warm; they have exterminated the red Indians in North America, and built up a great republic, so that their women may live in comfort and luxury."[56]

This editorial suggests that she joined other black women—more precisely, 1920s classic blues singers—who connected grand attire with power. Hazel Carby has contended that the physical presence of these performers was a "crucial aspect of their power." One way that they reclaimed their "female sexuality from being an objectification of male desire to a representation of female desire" was to wear glittered dresses, furs, and diamonds.[57]

Jacques Garvey was not known for draping herself daily with jewelry and expensive clothes. Nonetheless, she believed that the devaluation of black womanhood was a global issue that called for redress. So she wrote that black women were entitled to everything the world had to offer, including what adorned the bodies of elite white women and, in some instances, successful women blues singers. Her raw description of the alleged motivation of white men seeking wealth undoubtedly captured the imagination of her readers and encouraged them to think about why they were impoverished in the midst of abundance.

Jacques Garvey's opinions of black men in many ways expose the contradictions of the UNIA generally. Though she criticized white men for being "racially selfish," she wanted black men to have that same zeal in pursuing the redemption of Africa. She was adamant that men, just like women, had to perform certain gender-specific roles. "Black men, you are failing on your jobs! Measure height of achievement and breadth of usefulness with others, and be honest enough to admit your laziness." The world expected men "to play a man's part and is fed up on your whining and 'can't-be-done' moans. Be real men, honest, sincere, determined and straight a way the race will be lifted up in the estimation of others who respect those who respect themselves."[58]

Although Jacques Garvey's vehement stance was not completely out of step with the attitudes of other UNIA women, it does blame black men (including Marcus Garvey)—not racism and colonialism—and appears somewhat inconsistent. It is puzzling, for example, that she calls on black women to support the same men whom she frequently describes as unworthy and inept. In addition, she continually urges black men to read the woman's page and respect the ideas it puts forward when no man would want to be bombarded by such scathing, generalized attacks.

Jacques Garvey's resentment of the UNIA's male leadership, which she felt did not appreciate her diligent work on behalf of the organization, undoubtedly carried over into her writings and can be better understood through the work of Anne Witte Garland. Garland documents how anger can be a principal motivator underlying activists' thinking and behavior. After interviewing a number of contemporary activists, she concluded that "anger is often at the center of their transformations from private actors in restricted universes to encompassing all the important issues of the day."[59] Jacques Garvey created a space to release her indignation through her editorials. Although her attacks could be venomous, she never doubted that she deserved a place in the UNIA movement as a leader and a challenger of chauvinistic men.

No doubt Jacques Garvey was ambivalent about patriarchal traditions. She rebuffed notions that women should be confined to the domestic sphere, but based her idea of male roles exclusively on patriarchal standards. Men should be the breadwinners so that women would have the *choice* not to work outside the home. Further, "white women have greater opportunities to display their ability because of the standing of their men." She declared that "black women [would] come out of Miss Ann's kitchen, leave her washtub and preside over their own homes" if their men would "bring home the bacon." Understanding the economic state of the black diaspora and Africa was not enough to squash her repulsion toward the black man who "is always out of a job because he is too lazy to go out and make a job for himself; he prefers to hang around the white man's factory doors begging for a job, and oftimes gets what he deserves— a kick."[60]

Only a few black club women who were in the militant vanguard wrote comparable essays. Fannie Barrie Williams, one of the most brilliant and vocal club women, was extremely critical of black men who failed to defend black women against degrading slurs and sexual exploitation. She challenged them with the question, "Is the Colored man brave enough to stand out and say to all the world, 'Thus far and no further in your attempt to insult and degrade our women?'" In short, the New Negro Woman was revolutionizing the old type of male leadership. "We are women of the newer type, striving to make our race sublime—conscious that the time is ripe, to put our men on the firing line."[61] On another occasion, Fannie Williams urged her sisters not to mimic black male leadership, "whose innumerable conventions, councils, and conferences during the last twenty-five years have all begun with talk and ended with talk." In 1922 Mrs. Robert Patterson, socialist candidate for the Pennsylvania General Assembly in Philadelphia, joined the attack, stating that "we need women who are not content to trail along in [the] foolish political paths of Negro men."[62]

Although their rhetoric rarely matched the intensity of Jacques Garvey, other Garveyite women submitted articles criticizing masculine dominance. These women, along with other progressive African American women, challenged black men to step up their activism or be prepared to be put down and led by those who were better equipped—and no one was more prepared for leadership than Jacques Garvey herself.

Throughout her editorials, Jacques Garvey identifies "innate" qualities in black women that enable them to fulfill a host of duties. Not surprisingly, perhaps, she herself possessed the majority of these traits. She consciously personified the type of black woman that the UNIA needed—intelligent, industrious, willing to sacrifice self to better her home, community, and nation.

Jacques Garvey also generalized from her own experience in identifying her expectations for others. Unwavering as a helpmate to her husband, she expected all women to occupy this role even if it caused them discomfort. She suffered as the wife of the movement's leader, so she expected others to bear similar crosses. For instance, producing the woman's page "certainly [was] a hardship"; she had "to put in eighteen hours of work daily and sometimes [got] only three hours of sleep." Lack of rest magnified her physical ailments, and she often complained of "eye trouble" and was "handicapped by prolonged illness." Eventually she had an unspecified minor operation. Jacques Garvey knew that it was difficult to grieve in silence, and she urged women to "find an outlet for one's woes";

however, "strive always to show a calm exterior, thereby you will command their [black men's] respect and gain their sympathy."[63]

This advice may sound a bit manipulative and counterproductive. One would think that she shuddered at the thought that someone wasted energy on pity. Based on her record, she should have preferred that vigor be placed into productive action for nationhood. Her statement may be out of character, but it reveals an emotional side that she made every effort to keep private. Jacques Garvey was a sensitive human being despite the no-nonsense image she projected to the world.

Occasionally Jacques Garvey's personal decisions did taint her theory. Too often she labored on behalf of Marcus Garvey until her physical health was compromised. Similar to other committed activists, she consciously and unconsciously became a sacrificial lamb for his needs and the UNIA's goal. Jacques Garvey's acts of self-subordination unfolded in many forms, but overall they signaled the multiple practices of feminism in the 1920s. These circumstances require that we create concepts to grapple with seemingly problematic forms of feminism that are endemic to a historical moment. The concept of community feminism (which at times resembles a tug-of-war between feminism and nationalism) gives us a channel through which we can observe the larger implications of both Jacques Garvey's personal choices and her political activism.

By placing the UNIA's nationalist ideas within a feminist paradigm, Jacques Garvey was able to keep her husband at the center of her world without shifting her intellectual self completely to the periphery. The difficulty, as Carol Boyce Davies points out, is that "Afrocentric feminism sounds like a contradiction in terms, for if it is Afro-centered then the feminine/feminism is already an appendage, an excess, easily expelled or contained within."[64] In editorials, however, Jacques Garvey expressed her feminism as a cornerstone of the UNIA's platform. It was obvious to her that skilled, smart women were not only an asset to themselves but to their families, communities, and the UNIA as well.

Although Garveyites imagined a gendered community inherently grounded in a system of differences, Jacques Garvey contested the socially constructed categories and roles that limited the personal and intellectual development of women, and her feminism became a linchpin to unite all black women to reach their full potential for the black nation. Overall, her writings exemplify how one woman maneuvered between what most view as intrinsically oppositional forces—nationalism (a doctrine that first and foremost advocated popular freedom and sovereignty to determine one's destiny) and feminism (a doctrine of equal rights for women that challenged women's oppression and subordination)—and brought them together in one theoretical construct dedicated to establishing an independent nation in Africa.

One of the most salient features of Jacques Garvey's editorials was her stout assertion that women must claim their equality to men even though she herself lived in a male-dominated marriage. That apparent contradiction assumes that she simultaneously rejected and accepted codes of patriarchy. In the Garvey household, as in most homes of the 1920s, the parameters for the wife, helpmate, mother, and daughter were based on patriarchal principles.[65] Though a universal idea, patriarchy was diverse in its specific structures and effects. For example, capitalist patriarchy was so pervasive in the United States that in some cities married women were barred from working in certain professions, such as teaching, because it was believed that their husbands should maintain their status by being the primary breadwinner.[66] Social norms dictated that women, especially middle-class women, function as self-sacrificing nurturers who deferred to their husband's and father's wishes, making their family obligations the priority in their lives.

Moreover, race women believed that they had an additional moral obligation to be efficient housewives because their domestic responsibilities to their husbands and children were paramount for racial progress. According to Stephanie Shaw, even elite black women were not excused from performing household duties, and they devoted as much energy to their communities as to their families. In an Afrocentric community, to borrow from Elsa Barkley Brown, "community is family."[67] Thus, Jacques Garvey's domestic behavior should not be seen as merely a reflection of her inability to challenge patriarchy wholeheartedly or to take a critical stand against her husband for the sake of their marriage, but more as an expression of her talent to maneuver between her family and the larger world. In doing so, she, along with other race women, mastered community feminism.

The notion that women ought to be leaders as well as helpmates was central to "talented-tenth" uplift rhetoric. Certainly, Jacques Garvey was not the only black woman who had a strong gender lens that focused on declaring that women had the right to multiple identities and the wherewithal to successfully engage on contested terrain: the vast majority of African American women lived lives that reflected this reality. But elite African American integrationists of the period believed that it was the duty of women to engage in a specific brand of community leadership, such as the social work detailed in Jacqueline Rouse's biography, *Lugenia Burns Hope: Black Southern Reformer* (1989). The majority of activists were reluctant to admit that women could move beyond domestically situated activism.

Jacques Garvey's position also becomes exceptional when contextualized within nationalist political rhetoric (including Marcus Garvey's), which stipulated that racial progress was inextricably tied to men and women "functioning" within gendered spaces to guarantee masculine control. And though male dominance (at the heart of masculine political thought) could not simply be reduced to role playing, it was often performed; Jacques Garvey's writings questioned what was presumed by many UNIA followers to be indispensable to nationhood—masculine dominance. Cynthia Enloe, who has explored women's relationships to nationalist movements internationally, posits that nationalism, "more than many ideologies, has a vision that includes women, for no nation can survive without culture being transmitted and children being born and nurtured." Nevertheless, even though women, too, have suffered abuses, "they have been treated more as symbols than as active participants by Nationalist movements organized to end colonialism and racism." Enloe goes on to observe that women are frequently urged to fulfill the roles of "ego-stroking girlfriend, stoic wife or nurturing mother." These traditional identities are nonthreatening to male nationalists; therefore, women who refuse to be maternally confined have an "uneasy" relationship with men.[68] Other scholars have also critiqued the way nationalism invariably entails the subordination of women largely due to the symbolic creation of "nation" as a patriarchal construct.[69]

Yet Garveyites conceived of Africa as a motherland, and, like many anticolonial struggles, the Garvey movement was an oppositional discourse to that of Western colonists, the progenitors of patriarchal nationalism. Keeping this complexity in mind, Jacques Garvey gave the straightforward message that women should be powerful in their own right and progressive actors in the making of a public world—a place that, ironically, honored masculine forms of chauvinism. Thus, in many ways, her editorials and activism pushed for what Partha Chatterjee calls a "new patriarchy." Jacques Garvey wanted women to be "active agents in the nationalist project—complicit in the framing of its hegemonic strategies as much as [she was] resistant to them because of [women's] subordination under the new forms of patriarchy."[70] This explains why many of her editorials cried out "God, Give Us Men!" but detailed the potential of women and opposed ideas that pigeonholed them domestically.

Despite her efforts to balance feminism and nationalism—with the textual link of the principle of self-determination—Jacques Garvey's espousal of a liberation narrative that granted women equal status was too often constrained by a rigidly bound nationalistic expression. That is, her unflinching commitment, both emotionally and ideologically, to the idea that the only solution to the problems of oppressed people of color was the divine right to control their homeland's resources took precedence, regardless of whether men or women assumed the lead in pursuing that goal.

The excruciating pace involved in producing the woman's page and leading the defense committee to pardon Marcus Garvey eventually took its toll on her physical and emotional health. The woman's page of *Negro World* ended abruptly on 30 April 1927; Jacques Garvey remained an associate editor for two additional months and only a contributing editor thereafter. She elected to put all of her energy into securing Garvey's release. Finally, her efforts (and those of countless other Garveyites) paid off when President Calvin Coolidge commuted his prison sentence on 18 November 1927. By this time the U.S. government had sensed the depth of his followers' loyalty, and officials were feeling the pressure by others who believed that Garvey's punishment was unjust. On 26 November he was discharged from the Atlanta prison into the custody of the U.S. Immigration Commission. Garvey's attorney, Arim Kohn, Jacques Garvey, and other UNIA officials tried unsuccessfully to get a stay of execution on the deportation order. Six days later Garvey gave his farewell address, as a choir sang the Ethiopian national anthem, from the deck of the SS *Saramacca* in New Orleans. Marcus Garvey's tenure in the United States marked the peak of the UNIA in terms of organized membership, economic resources, and political and radical militancy.

As her husband sailed to Jamaica, Jacques Garvey stayed in New York to raise money to pay off his legal expenses and to "finalize all other matters preparatory to joining him in Jamaica." On 10 December he received a hero's welcome in his homeland. He immediately wrote Jacques Garvey that he had purchased a home for them and to bring everything from New York: "Say darling I do not want you to leave even a piece of paper behind for I want all my books."[71]

The packing and shipping of their belongings, including a large collection of breakable antiques, proved to be a difficult assignment. After two estimates, Jacques Garvey "realized the immensity and costliness of the task." Apparently she informed him that packing "everything" was a formidable chore. Garvey responded, "I notice you are repeating the same news that you are packing. . . . I am surprised that you should be telling me about the quantity of things, I know all about it so when I tell you to ship everything I fully knew what I was about." He further warned her that "I am waiting in Kingston only for you but I can wait no longer than the 13th of January for I sail the 14th on my tour of Central America etc."[72]

Frustrated and beleaguered, Jacques Garvey wrote that Garvey "had no thought" of the particulars required to send items by freighter, but what was most disappointing to her was that he had not mentioned their "promised vacation together alone." She reasoned, "If the last three strenuous years did not warrant it, then what more would?" A vacation would rejuvenate their relationship, but Garvey's main concern remained the UNIA. They had been married under trying circumstances, and it seemed as if they always faced a crisis. In her view, Garvey's dismissal of a holiday confirmed that their marriage would continue to take a backseat to the movement.[73]

Amy Jacques Garvey arrived in Kingston on 26 December 1927, after she had dotted all the i's and crossed all the t's on their New York homestead. It had been almost ten years since she had lived in Jamaica. Her family and close friends knew about her marriage to Garvey and her transformation into a passionate Pan-Africanist activist. Some would quickly embrace her, but many of her former peers might have felt the need to distance themselves until they had time to observe her behavior and evaluate how different she really had become. Jacques Garvey had to have mixed feelings about how she and Garvey would relate to one another as husband and wife residing in the same household. Though both of them were committed to maintaining the UNIA, there were no guarantees of their personal future together.

Jamaica in 1928 still largely reflected the society that Amy and Marcus had left in 1917 and 1916, respectively. The island had remained largely rural, and even the most vocal naysayer could not deny the botanical beauty of some areas. Most significantly, though, the British colonial state had succeeded in maintaining a racial hierarchy. Of its million citizens, black people remained numerically the majority, but they were politically and economically dominated by "intermediary" ethnic groups—coloreds, Chinese, Lebanese, and Jews. White residents had declined from 3 percent to 1 percent, but they continued to function as colonial gatekeepers, which translated into a manipulative control of corporate capital. As was the case in other English-speaking Caribbean territories (Grenada, Trinidad, Dominica, and Barbados), racial discrimination and cutthroat capitalism prevented the vast majority of blacks from owning the economic means of production, clinching their aggregate status as a group whose labor power was exploited well beyond human decency. In addition, poor black people still lacked access to postsecondary schooling; this magnified the probability that they would have to work for low wages as adults, primarily producing export crops such as bananas, coffee, citrus, pimentos, and sugar.[1]

These conditions spurred the Garveys to take a greater interest in Pan-Caribbean issues on their return to Jamaica. While maintaining their dedication to Pan-African liberation, they quickly tailored the platform of the Universal Negro Improvement Association (UNIA) to deal directly with Jamaican workers' concerns as well. With a small entourage, they toured the island to build up local UNIA membership, making sure to reach the rural districts despite the unpaved roads. Garvey gave talks emphasizing the need to establish a university that would be available to all who desired a higher education. He also echoed the sentiments of farmers and peasants who wanted to acquire their own cultivatable land to produce crops. Harking back to their days in the United States, the couple encouraged the building of a national steamship line to assist independent farmers in transporting their goods to the world. Their prolabor position called for a "minimum wage, an eight-hour working day, housing and medical attention on the estates, prohibition of child labor, assurance against accident or failing health," and the right of workers in trades to organize into unions. These efforts doubled the number of registered UNIA members in Kingston.[2]

As revolutionary nationalists, the Garveys adamantly talked about racial solidarity as a means to counter colonialism and solve the "Negro problem." In her characteristically blunt tone, Amy Jacques Garvey said, "If the Negro does not organize and keep organized and place himself on a good sound economic foundation he will starve to death and be eliminated altogether."[3] But like racial uplift ideology in the United States, which too often reflected conservative middle-class aspirations and was plagued by color contradictions, their rhetoric was also designed to appeal to the problematic agenda of the Jamaican business elites, many of whom were "brown" or colored and unashamedly expressed contempt for black workers. When Marcus Garvey had first organized the UNIA in Jamaica, he had wanted elite support. On his return, he continued to have an ambivalent relationship with this group—which became even more precarious with his increasing fame—complicated by the fact that his in-laws were proud to be "brown" and privileged. His wife, however, had learned to embrace a "black" identity in the United States. Jacques Garvey's new political stance placed her at the vortex of race, class, and color tensions in Jamaica, demonstrating how a black identity can sometimes be an unstable racial category.

On some level it had to be unsettling for Jacques Garvey to be sympathetic to the needs of the black masses while her family continued to bask in their distinct "brownness." Her position might remind some of the "tragic mulatta" popularized in late-nineteenth- and early-twentieth-century American literature. In fiction, the debate around this character ranges from seeing her as a figure designed to enlist the sympathies of whites to a more subversive character who deconstructs the categories of race and problematizes the relationship between black and white people.[4] The heart of the tragedy lies in the mulatta's desire for the privileges associated with whiteness. Jacques Garvey, unlike her chameleonlike fictional counterpart, maintained a consistent ideological position on race. Her commitment to black liberation and self-determination turned her away from a "brown" identity and its attendant advantages. At the same time, though, her commitment to capitalist notions of success, which were similar to her husband's, also prevented her from completely rejecting bourgeois ideas. She and Garvey were thus lodged in a cauldron of competing beliefs that spawned a dubious relationship with workers and capitalists alike.

With Garvey once again in the limelight of the liberation movement, Jacques Garvey retreated to the domestic front to instill order in their new home, called "Somali Court," on Lady Musgrave Road. It was located in an exclusive section of St. Andrew, near the governor's mansion, an area largely inhabited by upper-class whites. Garvey was proud that he was able to buy such a prestigious property, not only because it symbolized a bourgeois lifestyle but also because he had always believed that all black people deserved to live well, even if it meant that the majority of his neighbors were white. In a letter to his wife while she was still in New York (affectionately calling her "Mopsie"), he described the "three bedrooms, drawing and dining rooms, bath and other rooms, piazzas, outroom bldg. pantry, garage[;] [it's] with a flower garden and one acre of garden and trees, we can get more land adjoining later." To make sure that she would approve of the home, Garvey had enlisted the opinion of his mother-in-law, who was "pleased with it."[5]

Having been raised in an affluent Kingston neighborhood and having lived in the United States in a Harlem apartment—albeit modest—that was filled with costly antiques, Jacques Garvey was accustomed to some degree of opulence. Perhaps this is why she later characterized the same property as "a three bedroom, one bathroom house, with the necessary outbuildings," but "there was no tilework and the finish was poor." The details about the inferior construction would have made clear to her audience that, in her mind, they were not living in the lap of luxury, even though the majority of Jamaicans would have disagreed and the American press reported, "Garvey's Black House was [filled with] liveried servants."[6]

Once their furniture arrived from New York, Garvey "arranged it just where he wanted it. I [Jacques Garvey] was allowed to sort and classify the books."[7] Jacques Garvey's phrasing to describe this simple domestic event gives us another glimpse into their home life. Both she and Garvey valued books, and perhaps under these circumstances it was a privilege to arrange them. Further, in addition to indicating her love of knowledge, her comments might also have signaled to other men that they should take part in making their home a haven. Notwithstanding these possible interpretations, the fact that Garvey "allowed" her to perform the task of alphabetizing books is evidence that he tried to control the entire organization of their household, an impression that runs counter to the UNIA's notion that the home should be in the hands of women—another small example of the discrepancy that sometimes appeared between the man and his ideas.

On completing his speaking tour in Jamaica, Garvey wanted to visit Central America, but his request for a passport was denied. Rupert Lewis has shown that a major tactic of colonial authorities was "to pin him down to Jamaica" so they could "watch" him and prevent his "personal contact" with the main UNIA branches.[8] After some discussion, the Garveys agreed that since authorities had not restricted his freedom in the West, Europe would be the best place to jump-start the fragmented movement and enlist sympathy for their cause.

In April 1928 the Garveys left Jamaica—with Hazel Escridge, a personal secretary from New York—for a stay in West Kensington, England. It was here that Jacques Garvey noticed her husband's tendency not to reflect on the immediate past. She recalled him saying, "I never look back; there is no time for that; besides it would make me cautious. How could I dare for the future, when the past is written with so many warnings?" At the time, journalist J. A. Rogers noted that despite Garvey's three years in jail, he looked "younger" and seemed "as undiscouraged as ever."[9] Garvey's ability to move beyond the negative indicated his resiliency, but Jacques Garvey did not always appreciate that remarkable quality. She was still disappointed that he had not kept his promise to take a private vacation, and her frustration with him continued to mount. In hindsight, she interpreted Garvey's political attitude as "impersonal," saying, "Those who get hurt in the tense moments of the adventure are only regarded as necessary props to the build-up of the hero."[10]

As soon as a UNIA office was set up in West Kensington, Garvey began contacting dockworkers, whose potential courier status made them fundamental to the spread of Garveyism, as well as African students, the majority of whom were male and from wealthy families.[11] Despite these efforts, the turnout at the first major meeting was disappointing. The amused press reported that there were "9800 Empty Seats," adding, "Each member of the audience had a choice of fifty seats." Taken aback by the inertia of the black masses there, the Garveys soon reasoned that they had to revamp their strategy, since "seamen would lose their jobs and students would be flunked in their examinations" if they were "keeping bad company." The flamboyant displays of pomp and chivalry that had characterized the UNIA in New York thus disappeared. Jacques Garvey observed that Garvey had to opt for "greater silent, penetrating forces" if the UNIA was to be effective. Other activists concurred. In fact, Ladipo Solanke, a leading Nigerian student spokesman at University College, London, suggested to Garvey that he go to Africa on Garvey's behalf "in a secret mission to organize in every country."[12]

Another important change to accommodate the London conditions had to do with the UNIA's relationship with whites, particularly white women. In Jamaica white people were few in number, and in the United States members reluctantly interacted with them. The prevailing sentiment was that there was no reason to trust those who had colonized and oppressed and had no respect for anything African. In London, though, Garvey employed a white stenographer and formed an auxiliary for the English wives of African male members. (However, these women were not allowed to become registered members or participate in "internal discussions.")[13]

The support of white women in the cause of racial uplift was not novel; every major black organization promoting integration in the United States touted its white members. But black nationalists held the opinion that racial uplift was about reducing dependency on whites; self-sufficiency produced self-respect and the power to determine one's destiny. Many Garveyites around the world would have debated the inclusion of whites in their movement had it become a part of the international discourse. The UNIA female vanguard of 1922, in particular, would have objected, since the presence of white wives was a slap in the face to their efforts to secure black families. Other Garveyites, however, might have agreed with Jacques Garvey, who apparently did not have a problem with the members of this auxiliary, whom she described as "sincere in their work to enhance the standing of the men whom they had chosen to marry."[14]

No one could question that the Garveys were black nationalists of the highest order. Their speeches and writings were filled with references to political power based on racial unity. In the end, Garvey's decision to enlist the support of white women and Jacques Garvey's belief that it did not contradict their philosophy substantiate that they were more problack than antiwhite. Charles Hamilton has pointed out that Pan-Africanism has both short-term and long-term dimensions. To achieve the long-term goal of a united African continent, "reformist" objectives are often adopted. The Garveys viewed their decision to organize these white women as a short-term strategy to unify a "scattered Ethiopia."[15]

In late July 1928 the Garveys, with secretary Escridge in tow, began their tour of Europe. Though they always tried to travel first class and lodge in the best hotels, their trip was not a conventional upper-class journey abroad, but one to investigate firsthand the politics and policies of European countries as they related to people of African descent. The tour also served as a recruitment strategy to bring together the greatest array of black people for the August 1929 UNIA convention.

Their sojourn began in France, about which both Amy and Marcus had strong opinions prior to their arrival. Several years earlier Jacques Garvey had argued that it was reasonable to expect France not "to give up her possessions in West Africa, when her factories are waiting for the raw products to keep her people employed and to furnish them commodities at minimum prices." But she was appalled by the large number of Africans used by the French in Morocco during the Arab war. "That is the horror," she said, "the tragedy of it—brothers in race and blood thrown against each other to keep all servitude to the white European!"[16]

Carrying this ideological baggage with her, Jacques Garvey and her husband were escorted in Paris by members of the Comité de Défense de la Race Nègre and updated on racial activities in the colonies. From these conversations, Garvey concluded that the French administrators had adopted the "usual method of exploiting the Native African." During a speech attended by at least six hundred people at the Club de Faubourg, Garvey contended that members of the African diaspora had a "legal right to many portions of the African continent and that his race did not intend to forfeit this right."[17]

On the subject of black people living in France, he had declared that there was "absolutely no difference between the white Frenchman, the white American and the white Englishman on the question of race." The French simply interact in another way because "she had not a Negro domestic problem." These conditions led Garvey to echo many of his contemporaries: "Comparatively speaking, the black man ought to be more sympathetic and friendly toward France than any other major nations, like England and America, because he is better treated." (The fact that African American and West African soldiers had fought for France in World War I had made the French a bit more tolerant of members of these groups, as opposed to North Africans—particularly Algerians—toward whom they remained arrestingly hostile.) Tyler Stovall has documented that in the twenties the French were by no means color-blind, but next to other Europeans and white Americans they were more accommodating and openly condemned racial discrimination; thus, a trickle of the African diaspora had chosen to settle in France. Because racism there was not as violative as that of the United States and Britain, Garvey believed that the French internal policy of "courteous treatment for all" was detrimental in the long run, because it prevented Africans in France from developing a critical race consciousness.[18]

The Garveys enjoyed visiting all of the tourist sites. Jacques Garvey recalled an episode involving a Frenchman who joined them one evening for dinner. "With his broken English and my schoolgirl French we seemed to have carried on the conversation as a team." Before they left, the Frenchman asked Garvey if he could arrange to have another meeting with "Mademoiselle." Garvey responded curtly, "She is my wife." The Frenchman was "embarrassed" and believed that Garvey had not considered the question in the spirit in which it was given. Apparently Garvey was jealous that another man was attracted to his wife and, moreover, that she enjoyed his company. Later Garvey asked her, "Why don't you put on some weight? You are so frail." On some level, he believed that she was enticing the Frenchman not only with her intellect but also with her body. She responded, "But how could I?" Their pace had been hectic and constant since leaving the United States, and there was no end in sight.[19]

Garvey's protective nature did not stop his wife from socializing and engaging intellectually with other men in Paris. As a journalist, she took an interest in the serials produced there, especially *La Race Nègre*, the monthly periodical of the League for the Defense of the Negro Race, founded in 1927 by Lamine Senghor and Tiemolo Garan Kouyate. Kouyate, a Sudanese instructor with communist leanings, was the league's general secretary and wrote the most erudite essays. He and Jacques Garvey continued to correspond after she left Paris, primarily exchanging *La Race Nègre* for the *Negro World*.[20]

From Paris the Garveys traveled to Berlin. Like any tourist, Jacques Garvey walked up and down the streets to get an up-close-and-personal view of people's lives. She was immediately taken with Germany's remarkable recovery from World War I; only a smattering of French colonial troops (from North Africa, Madagascar, and Senegal) still occupied the Rhineland territories. Although aware that Germans "were the people who made up the colonial powers, who had joined others in partitioning Africa to buttress their economy," she and her husband still agreed that it would be wise for the African diaspora to seek an alliance with them. As Garvey put it, "There is no fooling around Germany with the Germans. Every man is serious; he has a purpose, and apparently he is living for it." Furthermore, German discipline produced a kind of "character" that acted as a "safeguard against abuses" from other people.[21]

Jacques Garvey was so impressed with Germany that she was inspired to write an article for the *Negro World* based on her observations of its imperial development. Building on Garvey's views about the importance of "discipline," she added that the "compulsory military training" for all young men and the "special care" given to girls' "physical development" was excellent. Unlike the Belgians and French, who were "frail-looking," the Germans had "splendid physiques," which made for a "sturdy population, ready at any moment to demonstrate fitness to rule." Germany was "strenuously preparing" itself to get what it wanted: its commercial planes were up-to-date; it had expanded trade in the East; it had a sizable police force, a thriving local industry, and a higher birthrate than other European countries, because "every encouragement is given to women to become mothers." Jacques Garvey warned black people not to let themselves be used "as tools" to "stop the brutal Hun from overrunning Europe." Germans had "been trained to want to achieve what seems impossible to others," and Africans should have that same nationalist zeal. In fact, her husband wanted to create an empire comparable to Berlin in Africa.[22]

Jacques Garvey had keyed in on a fundamental obsession of the German state in 1928—the culture of the body. Since World War I, German leaders had become preoccupied with the "purification" of the body. They wanted to distinguish themselves from their enemy, the "feminine" intellectual or cerebral French, and convey to the world that they were hardworking, productive, and physically and morally fit. Germany wanted to be to viewed as the first modern nation, an image predicated on a healthy, "performance-oriented" nationalist community.[23]

Jacques Garvey's article could have easily been written by a publicist for the German state. However, the shift from a focus on the development of a "healthy" citizenry to the "purification" of society based on principles of "race" would not become obvious until 1933, under Adolf Hitler's Third Reich. Nevertheless, Marcus Garvey's initial endorsement of postwar Germany, Hitler, and fascism generally have become the cross on which his intellectual crucifixion has taken place. Garvey's dictatorial leadership style and his obsession with having disciplined followers—men and women who were willing to place themselves on the firing line and end racial oppression through violence—are hallmarks of fanaticism. Furthermore, the UNIA's racialized fraternity and bourgeoisie morality not only existed alongside, but also could have been a slip away from the racial purity extremism of a fascist nation-state. Tony Martin succinctly points out the similarities between the doctrines of Garveyism, Mussolini's fascism, and Hitler's Nazism: "In their fierce nationalism, in their doctrines of racial purity, in their uniformed indoctrinated youth groups, in their conversion of the crowd into disciplined uniformed units, with some qualifications in their anticommunism, in the impassioned oratory of their leaders, in their pageantry, the atmosphere of excitement surrounding their movements . . . bore certain resemblances."[24]

Garvey himself celebrated these comparisons. When J. A. Rogers wrote in 1927 that "Mussolini and Fascism is like Garvey and Garveyism," not only did the *Negro World* publish his article but also Garvey later boasted to Rogers that he had not quite hit the nail on the head. Reportedly he said, "We were the first fascists. We had disciplined men, women and children in the training for the liberation of Africa. The black masses saw that in this extreme nationalism lay their hope and readily supported it." He bragged that "Mussolini copied fascism from me but the Negro reactionaries sabotaged it."[25]

At the same time that Garvey praised fascism, Jacques Garvey was more critical of it as a form of government. "Fascism as Mussolini of Italy exemplifies it, is absolute dictatorship, the mind, body and soul of Italy being in the hands of one man," she wrote. Though his "policy" had "pulled Italy out of the financial mire," many Italians charged, "Our mouths are muzzled, we dare not act as free men, or express our opinions in the press on the public platforms; our country is being run by a despot against the wishes of the masses." Understanding that fascism suppressed the politics of the subaltern, Jacques Garvey explained how her vision was different from Garvey's in that she dreamed of a government that "will be a democracy in the truest sense of the word, for the benefit of all classes, where money and color will not be the standard by which one will be measured, but by his service to humanity."[26] For Jacques Garvey, then, black nationalism was not demagogic or loaded with reactionary baggage and certainly not a stepping stone to a fascist government.

In all fairness to Marcus Garvey, he took a scathing view of German nationalism when it made a quantum leap to Nazism and of Mussolini when he invaded Ethiopia in the fall of 1935, destroying one of the three independent African nations. He published a number of articles condemning these atrocities and pleading that the League of Nations stop their imperialism. Informing black people that the fascist intention to establish a supreme race spelled extermination for Africa, he emphasized that black people "are in sympathy with Jews because they are an oppressed minority," and he attacked Mussolini for committing war crimes against "innocent women and children of the civil population of Ethiopia."[27]

But during their German tour in 1928, both Amy and Marcus admired what they saw. Perhaps if they had conversed with the communists living there, they would have had a clue that the brewing fascism could only mean ruin to Africa. No doubt they would have reconsidered their desire for an alliance had they been aware that German political parties had submitted a parliamentary petition to withdraw all "colored troops," who were "wild people" and a "dreadful danger" to whites.[28] Most likely the Garveys did not study the living conditions of Africans and their approximately five hundred African German children, whom authorities regarded as a menace, because their numbers were so small and the population was transitory. Nonetheless, it is difficult to understand why they were not more judgmental considering that Germany also had pillaged a little corner of Africa. The Garveys' approval can best be explained by recognizing that their critical eye was trained on the Euro-American elites who had benefited most from the Atlantic slave trade and who continued to prosper from colonialism. The Treaty of Versailles had deprived Germany of its colonies in 1919, and, compared to France, Britain, and the United States, its exploitation of Africa was relatively minor. Furthermore, an interesting commentary printed on the *Negro World* woman's page in 1925 drives home the message that Euro-Americans were the main oppressors of black people and polluted the world with racism. The writer announced that a female member of the British Parliament, speaking about "Black Troops on the Rhine," said, "we women of England have no love for the women of Germany, but we shall boycott French goods unless France puts an end to the despoil[ation] of German women and girls by their black troops."[29] It was not a German representative calling for intervention, but a British woman who had spread venom against black men.

Other black intellectuals concurred with the Garveys' analysis of who were the most harmful whites to the black world. As early as 1884, Frederick Douglass had written to friends that "the leprous distillment of American prejudice" had crossed the Atlantic to Paris. And in 1923 Claude McKay wrote that in his travels abroad, "everywhere I [have] been treated much better and with altogether more consideration than in America and

England." Dr. Raphael Armattoe of Togoland underscored this perception when he explained that "at one time all Africans born in the French Empire were citizens. It was only when the Anglo-Saxons brought their influence to bear on the French that the position changed and fewer Africans were regarded as citizens."[30] The Garveys' notions of who qualified as "oppressors" similarly rested on a construction of whiteness based on the Anglo-Saxon/Anglo-American model.

On a personal note, the Garveys' legal national status as British subjects had not conferred on them a citizenship with adequate rights and protections even though "it was the black subjects in the British possessions that were feeding the English people," Jacques Garvey announced at a Liberty Hall meeting. Puzzled by these conditions, she later wrote that "the fact that Negroes from any part of the British common-wealth of Nations, being born under the British Union Jack, should have been rated as 'aliens' in England" clinched their persecution as a people. "When Uncle Sam lynches her black boys with her uniform on their back, and John Bull calls her ex-soldiers aliens," then it was "high time for some dull, apathetic Negroes to think in terms of nationhood."[31]

From Berlin, the Garveys returned to London. On 2 September 1928, the opening day of a series of speeches presenting the case of African peoples to the English for their "consideration and adjustment," both spoke at the Century Theater in the Westbourne Grove area of West London. Jacques Garvey, who preceded her husband, was just "given fifteen minutes" to articulate a ringing message from "Negro women to the white women of London." She began by noting that it was "difficult to deliver" such an important speech within a "short space of time." Though Jacques Garvey had kept her early talks within the prescribed "feminine" time frame, she now became publicly critical of this gendered discrepancy that apparently had no national boundary. Nevertheless, in her limited time on stage, she raised many issues, moving back and forth between complimenting white women and chastising them for their unwillingness to learn more about black women the "world over."[32]

Jacques Garvey's comments were a reflection of her ambivalence toward white women generally. On the one hand, she recognized that they were discriminated against as women in a male-dominated society: "Know this, that we suffer even as you do, because the color of our skins does not make us different in our physical bodies, does not make us different in our ambitions, and in our aspirations and in our hopes. No. We hope for as much as you have hoped and longed for." At the same time, their whiteness empowered them to insult black women with the Jim Crow statement, "I am sorry; we do not serve black people in here." As an Anglican, she lambasted this behavior as unchristian and, in yet another turn, appealed to them as women, who have a "finer conscience, or perhaps more conscience, in them than men have." "Think twice" and "remind your men" that "we are all human beings, and as children of God, we deserve equal treatment, equal fairness, equal justice in common with all humanity." Jacques Garvey's appeal on religious grounds, the allegedly highest and most moral authority, was a popular propaganda tool of countless activists, regardless of their political leanings. The English were "surprised" by her "force and conviction," but Garveyites were not. By now they were hailing her as "the greatest Negro woman of our race," who was unshakable in her commitment to present the cause of the black woman internationally to the European world.[33]

Following his wife to the podium, Garvey further elaborated on her appeal to the English people's sense of humanity and love of God. A longer time slot, however, gave him the opportunity to discuss many ideas, including how "God intended" that Africans and Europeans have different political and social outlooks; "that is why geographically he suited you for Europe and suited me for Africa." He also attacked colonialism and U.S. imperialism.[34]

After the speech, Garvey and secretary Escridge left for Geneva to present to the League of Nations on 11 September a petition on the need to consider the question of Negro liberation and anticolonial measures. This was the second petition forwarded to the league on behalf of the UNIA. The first, which had been brought to the attention of the U.S. State Department in September 1922, included the statement that the petitioners, representing 400 million Negro people, "desire to bring before you the fact that our race is now seeking racial political liberty; that we desire to found a Government of our own, and that we shall be given the opportunity to exercise that liberty that is common to all free men of all races and nations." A "non-action" endorsement from the American consul followed, but State Department documents warned that "quite a large number of American negroes" are "part of this agitation."[35]

It is alleged that 20 million copies of the second petition circulated among Europeans, and Garvey was assured that their concerns would be fully discussed at the League of Nations assembly session in 1929. Jacques Garvey did not participate in what her husband would later cite as his most "successful accomplishment" in Europe, because "he had not suffi-cient money to take [her]" to Geneva.[36]

At the end of October, the couple left England for a North American tour beginning in Quebec. Garvey had scheduled a meeting with UNIA division presidents in Toronto on 2 November to discuss the agenda for the Sixth International Convention of African Peoples of the World, to be held there the following August. His deportation from the United States prevented his return, so Jacques Garvey made that leg of the journey without him. On 23 October, accompanied by secretary Escridge, she embarked on a speaking and fund-raising trek for the UNIA.

On this trip, just as she had throughout Europe, Jacques Garvey demonstrated how a community feminist functioned. She was able to move easily from the role of wife in Paris, to that of independent thinker and leader of women in London, to that of Garvey's deputy in the United States. Her ability to alternate between helpmate and leadership roles was the epitome of a community feminist. Both she and Garvey understood the necessity of political flexibility; in fact, their helpmate/leader functions were now reversed, since Garvey had the task of creating her U.S. itinerary from Canada, as he had similarly done from prison. They communicated by letter and telegram, often addressing each other by their affectionate nicknames of "Mopsie" and "Popsie" despite the tension that existed between them. Clearly, they worked particularly well together when Jacques Garvey had more occasion to act independently.

In the United States, she was able to draw hundreds to hear her speak, and the *Negro World* advertised her "monster mass meeting[s]" by displaying an elegant seated portrait of her, modestly attired in a sleeveless dress, hair pulled up, a single strand of white pearls around her neck. But the pace was grueling; her schedule "allowed no rest, except on midnight trains." When she arrived in New York on 28 October 1928, Madame DeMena—assistant international organizer and another powerful woman of the UNIA—joined Jacques Garvey and her secretary, serving as a traveling companion for the remainder of the trip.[37] Although Jacques Garvey did not comment on their relationship, DeMena's inclusion on the trip suggests that at the very least they had the benefit of a mutual respect. And when Escridge left to vacation with relatives in Buffalo, DeMena's presence saved Jacques Garvey from the impropriety of a woman traveling cross-country alone.

At the Commonwealth Casino on the evening of 30 October, Jacques

Garvey enjoyed an "uproarious welcome." UNIA members offered "affection" to the "talented wife" of Garvey. The *Negro World* reported that she gave a "splendid address," describing her travels throughout Europe as well as "the activities of herself and husband." In conclusion, she "urged the membership" to undertake more "strenuous endeavor[s]."[38]

The next day she went to Philadelphia and received a "tumultuous ovation" at the Mt. Zion African Methodist Episcopal Church. Garveyites were there to "honor the bravest little woman [they] know and to drink, as they delight to do, from the fountain of Garveyism." A delegation from the Democratic Headquarters Citizens' Organization, on behalf of presidential candidate Al Smith, and a representative from the Democratic Women of Philadelphia, of which Mrs. Franklin D. Roosevelt was chairwoman, presented Jacques Garvey with a bouquet of flowers in "appreciation for her leadership among Negro women." Jacques Garvey was pleased by this unexpected display of "inter-racial good will." She received twenty-five dollars from the local division and a gold key inscribed with her initials from the city. At this event, Jacques Garvey, described as "graceful as a queen and as charming as a rose," stuck to her script, detailing the Garveys' recent activities and discussing how they had struggled to educate Europeans on the aims of the UNIA. She ended by "inspiring members to nobler heights."[39]

Amy Jacques Garvey never seemed to disappoint her audiences. Though sleepless nights and fatigue were her constant companions, she became energized by the presence of fellow Garveyites. Her U.S. tour confirmed that they appreciated all of her personal efforts for the movement. Perhaps they had sensed her frustrations and feelings of isolation, which were layered into her editorials on the woman's page. Whatever the reason, at this point in her life she needed recognition, and on every public occasion members took the opportunity to let her know that she was not alone. They affirmed her by giving her gifts and expressing their love and respect.

Everywhere Jacques Garvey went, she appealed for UNIA funds, and people gave generously. She kept her husband informed of her fundraising, and on two occasions he wired her for money. His monetary requests had become frequent, and Jacques Garvey seemed a bit perturbed. Clearly, she had not relinquished her patriarchal ideas that husbands were to perform as primary breadwinners, and to her his requests were direct signs of domestic failure. Despite her frustration, she sent him a total of eight hundred dollars via Western Union, "practically every cent

I had raised at paid meetings, after paying all expenses, and giving the branches a percentage."[40]

While his wife was still in the United States, Marcus Garvey, who was viewed as a menace by Canadian immigration officials, was apprehended and charged with illegal entry. Both his peers and contemporary scholars reasoned that his detainment was a response by Canadian officials to American diplomats' fear that he could influence the upcoming presidential election. He had published several scathing articles on Republican presidential candidate Herbert Hoover, whom he linked with Harvey Firestone, the culprit who had forced thousands of Liberians to work as slaves on rubber plantations.[41] Garvey had made impassioned pleas to American voters not to vote for Hoover—"A vote for Hoover is a vote for slavery." In addition, he urged African Americans to cast their ballot for the more progressive presidential candidate, Al Smith, the Democratic Catholic governor of New York. Though Canadian immigration officials detained him for only one day, they limited his stay to one additional week; thus he had to leave by 7 November.[42]

After notifying his wife of these unforeseen circumstances, Garvey arranged for them to meet in Bermuda. Jacques Garvey, however, was confused about the schedule, and she wrote back inquiring whether she should return to Toronto after Detroit or go directly to Bermuda. "If you care I will speak Brooklyn seventh, Newark eighth you wire & make arrangem[en]ts & inform me." Garvey quickly responded to "Mopsie," detailing her arrangements to sail first from New York, then from Bermuda on 10 November. From Bermuda to Jamaica, "we will have first class passage." Garvey's last sentence was undoubtedly intended to smooth over his wife's anticipated displeasure with the second-class tickets he had purchased for her and Escridge. (Once on board, however, Escridge had enough money to upgrade their tickets to the first-class accommodations that they were accustomed to.)[43]

They traveled according to plan, but when the Canadian SS *Forrester* docked in Bermuda, British officials would not let Garvey on the pier, so that evening Jacques Garvey spoke on his behalf. She was hailed as an "inspiration"; "cleaving to the side of our Leader, she has braved all and dared all." Her "fortitude, determination, and sagacity stand out as monuments." Unlike her other speeches, which concentrated on her European travels, this one cleared up points of confusion about the UNIA. First, since many people continued to misinterpret its platform, she said, "You must not think that we intend to dump the entire Negro population of

Bermuda in Africa." For one thing, some people were not worthy of being sent—for example, those who lacked technical skills or a progressive Pan-African consciousness; "the weeding-out process," she believed, would prevent this from happening. The UNIA simply wanted to be able to send a Bermuda representative to the League of Nations or to "any other place where one is needed."[44] Although lightly stated, Jacques Garvey had highlighted a fundamental organizing principle of Pan-Africanism: that black people the world over needed the power to voice their complaints before an influential decision-making body, and this could only occur with political backing.

Further, she clarified, black nationalists were not antiwhite; in fact, "our people must work side by side with the exponents of western civilization, absorb the best of it and return with it to our brothers and sisters on the Continent."[45] Over the years, the Garveys had conveyed how the United States and the West Indies had been "splendid training grounds" in terms of Western education. Though formal schooling had always been a key strategy of uplift ideology, for Jacques Garvey it was not meant to acculturate the lowly black masses to become philosophers who, in the words of one contemporary observer, "intellectualize black people to death." Africa, she had written earlier, "needs black men and women who have mastered the sciences, literature and the art of modern government in this Western Hemisphere to go over and teach their brethren."[46] Jacques Garvey's statements are reminiscent of other anticolonial nationalists who divided the world into two domains—the material and the spiritual. The material was the "outside"—the economy, science, and technology—a domain where the West excelled; thus, its accomplishments had to be carefully interrogated and replicated. By comparison, the spiritual domain marked the "inner" and "essential," represented by religion and family, stamps of cultural identity. Thus, a core feature of anticolonial nationalism in Africa and Asia, as Partha Chatterjee points out, was to imitate Western material skills; the greater one's success, the greater the imperative to preserve the uniqueness of one's spiritual culture.[47] Anticolonial nationalists like Jacques Garvey set out to launch a modern national culture that was nevertheless not Western.

In Bermuda, Jacques Garvey also tackled accusations that Garveyites were not law-abiding citizens. "We of the U.N.I.A. believe in constituted authority, and advocate respect for and a proper observance of the laws of any country in which we find ourselves." To hammer home the reasonableness of Garveyites, she asked aggressively, "Who is Red? We are not

Reds! Nor are we Socialist! We are a people banded together whose principles are self-love, and amity with all peoples." It is ironic that Jacques Garvey would make such a distinction, since three years earlier she had given an equally sharp response to "whether a connection existed between [the] African repatriation movement and communism." In May 1925 she said, "The time has come when everyone who fights for some measure of reform or justice is labeled 'communists' as though the term meant something incorrigibly bad or vicious."[48] It is unclear what accounted for her philosophical change that apparently accepted, at least to some degree, the popular Western conception that positioned communism and socialism as principal threats to world peace. The fact that Marcus Garvey's personal enemies in the United States fell into these camps may have magnified her antileftist tilt. A closer reading, however, reveals her annoyance that white authorities found it so difficult to believe that black people could select their own leader and organize independently from other groups.

After a brief stop in the Bahamas on 22 November 1928, the Garveys arrived in the Kingston harbor and disembarked to a 1:00 A.M. heroes' welcome. Overall, Jacques Garvey viewed their journey as a success, and she complimented her husband on his "splendid work in organizing and financing the underground movement to all parts of Africa."[49] One has to wonder why they did not include a brief tour of West Africa on their journey. After all, Garvey had political connections and UNIA branches in West and South Africa, as well as supporters in Kenya and the Congo. Neither had yet visited the continent that had provided the ammunition for their discourse. To touch African soil and share firsthand impressions would have gone a long way with fellow Garveyites. Money may have been an issue, but they were able to scrounge up funds to go everywhere else. It is more probable that the restrictions on Garvey's passport and the difficulty in locating a country to sponsor their visas prevented them from visiting West Africa. Moreover, the Garveys undoubtedly had a plan that could only be executed one step at a time, and on this trip they concentrated on laying the foundation to unite the African diaspora.

Back home in Jamaica, the Garveys' financial status was still far from certain. By 1929 the *Negro World* was reduced to selling advertisements for skin "whiteners" to generate income. Garvey admitted that since 1922 he had "never yet received a full check for salary" from the UNIA.[50] He was a politician without a secure political post. To address these two concerns—financial and political stability—at once, he decided to begin publishing the *Blackman*, a daily paper to compete with the conservative *Daily Gleaner. Blackman* would generate a local income, along with giving him an instrument to voice his political concerns and agenda. To his wife's dismay, Garvey cashed in his life insurance policy to obtain funds for a printing press and office space in Kingston. In his typically grand style, he bought not a small office but Edelweiss Park, which included a large outdoor amphitheater that eventually became a "centre of the social and pleasure life of the Corporate Area." Garvey was a master of propaganda but still a novice when it came to money management, so Jacques Garvey pleaded with him to let her "put aside a portion of the money, but he refused."[51] By March 1929 the first issue of *Blackman* was hot off the press. Garvey, of course, was the editor, and though the newspaper did not have a woman's page, Jacques Garvey continued to publish her trademark feminist editorials.[52]

From the first time that Garvey had been imprisoned in the United States until now, Jacques Garvey had been preoccupied with money difficulties. It is likely that Garvey's perpetual mismanagement of funds had made her even more conscious of the times that money had slipped out of her hands and into his. This problem intensified in Jamaica, where poverty was abundant and where they no longer had immediate access to the most solvent UNIA branches. These circumstances helped to shift the focus of Jacques Garvey's editorials. Many of them were reprints from the *Negro World*, under the same title but with a slightly abridged text, yet her monetary concentration is more pronounced because she published fewer articles in *Blackman*.[53] Feminist issues persisted, but overall her *Blackman* editorials were more concerned with poverty and empowerment. Other themes consistent with this topic included the virtues of intellectual development, self-sacrifice, and endurance to overcome obstacles. These qualities would bring, Jacques Garvey believed, financial rewards and political sovereignty.

"Poverty is Slavery," she wrote, because it is an ill whose "cure is not within easy reach of its victims." In asking "why is the Negro race the poorest of all races, yet Africa is the richest continent in the world?," she joined other writers who critiqued colonialism. It began with the forced removal of Africans during the horrific transatlantic and East African slave trades; the 1884 Berlin conference, where Europeans carved up the continent for economic gain, sealed the fate of African people and their natural resources. Although her analysis is not as sophisticated as that of her contemporary, R. Palme Dutt, who addressed how the traditional methods and tactics of bourgeois domination (violence, lawlessness, and corruption) were used against colonial subjects to build the "democratic foundations" of Western imperialism, she did respond to a pivotal question, noting, "All Negroes have not learned the value of Africa, and not knowing they have not made united efforts to hold and protect same." This essay dealt not only with the larger Pan-African question but also with local financial issues. Jacques Garvey told her readers that to be "truly independent one must have money invested." But to ensure that all understood that the ultimate goal was beyond material possessions, she concluded by saying, "A sound brain is better than a bank account, if the owner knows how to use it."[54]

Jacques Garvey consistently reiterated the importance of acquiring knowledge, and not simply for monetary rewards. In "Some Fallacies about Children," she exhorted, "Never let children get ahead of you mentally." Though Jamaica was poor and could offer a secondary education to only a few, there were ways to get around these limitations. For instance, she noted, "In this world of progress grown-up folk can go to night school, get good books and magazines from free libraries and pay only a few pennies for newspapers." This is how Jacques Garvey herself kept abreast of what happened off the island, so others could do the same. She felt that children should not have to remark, "Mother is so dumb, she doesn't know whether the world is moving or standing still."[55]

Postulating that a formula of self-help plus intellectual development equaled empowerment, Jacques Garvey turned to the popular philosophies that had taken root in the African American community and recharged them in Jamaica. Admittedly, working-class African Americans had felt removed from these discussions, and Jamaican peasants had comparable reasons to feel alienated—both struggled to meet daily living expenses and were not privileged with leisure time to contemplate what was going on outside their immediate communities. Moreover, capitalism and colonialism ensured that there would always be a surplus workforce no matter how hard one labored. It was easier for someone who had access to a middle-class income, as well as assets, to work exclusively as an intellectual, and the Garveys fell into this category. They were not required to work as wage laborers and had the resources to travel abroad. Nevertheless, their elite external lifestyle did not quash their rebellious spirit. In fact, Jacques Garvey's travels had made her more attuned to issues of poverty and fair distribution of wealth—questions that had become essential to her thinking and writing.

In a further step to deal concretely with poverty and disfranchisement, the Garveys organized a Jamaican-based party—the People's Political Party (PPP). The PPP was formally launched at the Sixth UNIA Convention, held in Kingston in August 1929, with 15,000 delegates attending.[56] The pageantry that had become legendary in the United States, as well as the chaos and internal bickering, marked the occasion. Before the convention, George O. Marke, the former supreme deputy potentate of the UNIA, had sued the organization for back payment of salary totaling $35,000, and Garvey had contested his claim in court, arguing that he had "never earned one penny of it hardly." Marke was not the only disgruntled leader; even Henrietta Vinton Davis, a longtime supporter of the UNIA and the Garveys' former housemate, had requested $12,000 in back salary. In the end, Garvey chastised the New York contingent as "wicked men, vicious men, crafty men, greedy men, men without honor, men without character, men without any respect at all for their race."[57] It was this entourage that had mishandled the UNIA's finances during his incarceration, Garvey claimed, resulting in the bankruptcy of the organization.

During the convention Garvey decided to safeguard the remaining UNIA assets by reorganizing under a new name "UNIA, August 1929, the World." The new and improved UNIA, based at Edelweiss Park, consolidated Garvey's power and further split the movement into American and West Indian factions, despite the fact that Kingston had been selected as the site for the convention "to bring the American Negroes into closer contact with the Negroes of the West Indies for trade and commercial and industrial relationship."[58]

After the convention, the Garveys shifted their activities from the UNIA and to the PPP. On 9 September 1929, in Cross Roads, Jamaica, Garvey pronounced himself chairman of the PPP—a political organization "sponsoring the election of fourteen men to the Legislative Council of Jamaica." Garvey, who had already included himself in this group, said, "There are fourteen things that I hope to do in the Legislative Council after my election."[59] This manifesto made Jamaican history by establishing a modern political party, though loosely organized, whose platform defended the interests of the masses.[60] Unlike the earlier objectives of the UNIA, the PPP did not mention women's issues; instead, it focused on labor protection, a minimum wage, land reform, fair distribution of wealth to improve urban areas, a Jamaican university, legal aid, and a national park. Progressive critics, particularly members of the Communist Party, were not convinced that the PPP was sincerely behind the Jamaican workers because of its continued close alliances with local businessmen. Conservative critics, such as the Jamaican Supreme Court, believed that the PPP's tenth plank, which called for a law to impeach and imprison judges who illicitly made arrangements with lawyers and deprived clients of their court rights, was an attack against them and therefore illegal. Legal retribution against Garvey by the court was swift. He was charged with "contempt" (a "first class misdemeanor"), and sentenced on 26 September to three months' incarceration at Spanish Town prison, twelve miles from Kingston, and fined one hundred pounds ($400).[61]

Jacques Garvey once again attempted to make her husband's jail confinement tolerable. This task was magnified when they learned that he suffered from diabetes. She "arranged with the proprietress of a lodging house nearby [the prison] to look after Garvey's laundry, and send in all of his meals." On one of her regular visits, which were cumbersome due to the unpaved roads, he informed her that the creditors of the Edelweiss Park property had threatened foreclosure if they did not receive payment. According to Jacques Garvey, he told her: "I am powerless to help, being here; you are the only person who can save the situation, by mortgaging the home and giving a bill of sale on the furniture." She felt she had little choice in the matter and "acceded to his wish."[62]

Once released from prison, on 19 December, Garvey began campaigning for office. This proved difficult, since poverty made the vast majority of his supporters ineligible to vote (a citizen had to either pay a tax or earn £1 per week or £25 a year to vote). Only 7.75 percent of the Jamaican population was registered for the election. Soon the Garveys were convinced that those Jamaicans who could vote were "intimidated" and felt that retribution would be taken against them by the government if they cast their ballot for Marcus Garvey. These conditions forced the Garveys to conclude that his chances of being elected were nil, and that they should put their efforts into helping other candidates on the PPP ticket. On election day, political apathy resulted in only a 2.74 percent showing.[63] To some, Garvey appeared "to be losing such influence as he possessed."[64] The Garveys' disappointment, however, was eased by the election of three PPP candidates: Dr. Felix Gordon Veitch, from Hanover Parish; R. Ehrenstein, of St. Thomas; and Philip Lightbody, a journalist whose nationalist views most closely resembled those of Garveyites. Most exciting, though, was their personal news: after seven years of marriage, Jacques Garvey was pregnant.

For years Amy Jacques Garvey had written about the value of motherhood, but after more than seven years of marriage she still had not had a child herself. Though she makes no mention of this in her correspondence or memoir, gossip and rumors regarding her "womb" must have hovered over her. No doubt today's observers would have questioned her husband's medical history, perhaps hypothesizing that his multiple ailments could have rendered him impotent, but in that era childbearing and rearing were viewed as exclusively a woman's responsibility. In fact, once she did become a mother, Jacques Garvey performed the role as seriously and singlemindedly as any other woman of the period. Despite her early feminist call to women—and mothers in particular—to perform public leadership roles, with the birth of her own children she withdrew from politics. Motherhood absorbed most of her time and energy; even her husband's needs and concerns were pushed to the background. As wifehood gave way to motherhood, Jacques Garvey moved away from the specific political/personal balance of her community feminism. Transformed by issues directly related to providing the essentials for their children, she ultimately removed herself from active participation in the Pan-African struggle.

In the 1920s, many American women, especially activists, intentionally delayed motherhood in order to complete their education, travel, or fulfill other personal desires.[1] But there is no evidence that this was the case for Jacques Garvey. She knew that Marcus Garvey wanted children; in fact, this was her explanation for why he decided to marry her instead of the older Henrietta Vinton Davis. Her delay in getting pregnant probably had more to do with the poor health and physical weakness she had complained of during her sojourn in the United States, as well as Garvey's frequent absences and the stress associated with serving as a leader of the

Universal Negro Improvement Association (UNIA) during his repeated periods of incarceration.

When Jacques Garvey returned home to Jamaica at the age of thirty-three, many people may have believed that she was unable to have a baby, since most Jamaican women had their first child in their late teens or early twenties.[2] Once she and Marcus Garvey had a lengthy period of time together uninterrupted by separations, she did finally become pregnant. Jacques Garvey was thirty-five years old when Marcus Garvey Jr. was born on 17 September 1930. Like most Caribbean women, she gave birth at home, assisted by a trained nurse. Her mother and sister Ida were nearby. Garvey was at his office when the baby was delivered and was notified of the happy news by telephone. Jacques Garvey remembered that later he hurried home to "see what the baby looked like, beamed all over his face, and returned to the office, like most proud fathers, to say, 'I have a son.'" No doubt Garvey was elated—he was a first-time father at forty-three, an age when most Jamaican men were already grandfathers. He also must have been relieved that his wife was doing well after the birth, since she had had a difficult pregnancy. Indeed, in her first trimester her physician had ordered her to bed for six weeks. Everyone around her was made aware of her delicate state and tried to shield her from stress and anxiety. On one occasion, a wooden statue of an "African woman holding a light" was removed from the Garveys' open veranda by vandals, and when the pieces were found, they were not "brought home on account of my condition."[3]

Although Garvey apparently had done his best not to worry his wife during her pregnancy, the couple was clearly having financial problems. At one point, when he needed money to pay pressing UNIA bills, he went to her with an "acceptance" to sign in order to obtain funds presumably from her personal savings account. In the past Jacques Garvey had always given in to her husband's monetary demands, but this time she stood her ground. The house and furniture were already mortgaged, and she had recently "backed other notes for him. I was in no condition to be further harassed." In response to her refusal, which must have shocked him, Garvey immediately packed his suitcase and left the house. He returned later that evening and pleaded with her once again on behalf of the organization. Jacques Garvey was "lying down, too worn out and disgusted for words; I shook my head in refusal." Two days later "I felt as if I was losing the baby." She summoned the physician and her mother, but not Garvey, who had taken up residence at a nearby house shared by his widowed sister, Indiana, and two UNIA secretaries.[4]

During this crisis Mrs. Jacques stayed with her daughter and offered support. When Garvey returned later that week, his mother-in-law "did not scold him, only asked what had happened." He poured out his "financial woes" to her, Jacques Garvey claims, and then confessed that he could not "take it" when his wife "turned him down," because "she is all I have to depend on." Mrs. Jacques was well aware of Garvey's financial troubles, since her daughter was constantly withdrawing funds from her savings account and other assets willed to her by her father. In addition, that week she had witnessed her daughter sending the "gardener and maid" to Garvey "for their pay." They had returned to inform her that Garvey had said that "he had no money" and that they would stay on an additional week out of respect for Jacques Garvey and in hope that their salaries would materialize. Mrs. Jacques's comments to Garvey are not recorded, but she must have used her "soft" nature to convince him to do the right thing, because that night he went back to his wife and they "never discussed the incident" again.[5]

Jacques Garvey narrates this story as if death were figuratively knocking at her door, and that was the only reason she did not try to reconcile these money matters at the time. She and Garvey had both sacrificed their personal lives for the UNIA, but she was adamant about not putting their baby at risk. To be sure, Garvey also wanted a healthy child, but he was not prepared for her change of heart. From this period Jacques Garvey began pushing her husband away from the center of her world and replacing him with their child. She would still be a helpmate to Garvey, but now regarded motherhood as her ultimate duty.

The birth of Marcus Garvey Jr. coincided with the beginning of the Great Depression. By 1930 the domino effect of the 1929 stock market crash in the United States had created a slump in the world economy. Practically every country was affected by this phenomenon, though its duration and severity differed significantly from region to region. In Britain, as W. R. Garside has shown, Parliament passed the Colonial Development Act of 1929 to keep its colonies from diversifying their economies, thus making them dependent on imports, which would in turn, it was hoped, stimulate employment and income in the British market. But as the depression intensified, the 1929 act proved a dismal failure for Jamaica. Shifts in the terms of trade, combined with natural disasters, resulted in a reduction of one of the island's most profitable commodities, fruit. Devastating hurricanes in 1934 and 1935 further curtailed fruit production, and the American fruit market collapsed in 1935. Lower dividends followed, and any hope of financial independence for small producers disappeared.[6]

Moreover, the population was increasing as Jamaican nationals began to return home from Central America because of the depression. The failure of the economy to cope with this growth laid the foundation for acute unemployment. Countless Jamaicans—landless and unemployed—moved throughout the city, scrambling for provisions and settling into the "pens" of Kingston, properties on the outskirts of town.[7]

The lack of an increase in home food production magnified the effects of the depression. In 1930 the rising demand for goods pushed Jamaica to spend as much as 9 percent of its national income on imported food. Patterns of consumer expenditures in 1930 show that about 49.4 percent of a household's income was spent on food alone.[8] Jamaica's economy was deteriorating rapidly, but the Garveys were determined that their son would not suffer for want of any material needs. Indeed, from the moment of Junior's birth, it appeared that his mother's middle-class roots were reasserting themselves: an announcement appeared in the newspaper, and a formal christening ceremony took place at St. Luke's Anglican Church (even though Garvey was a Roman Catholic). In Jamaica, Anglican services were noted for being "unemotional and decorous"; whites were generally associated with this orthodox church, which had a "high snob value for the social climber." The Garveys selected "professionals" as godparents: Mr. J. Hume Steward, a merchant of Spanish Town; Dr. Samuels, a dentist in Kingston; and Mrs. Stewart of Half-Way Tree. Although it was Amy Jacques Garvey who possessed the middle-class pedigree, Marcus Garvey seemed equally committed to these decisions. It was he who submitted the birth announcement and arranged for the elaborate christening.[9]

To be fair, these activities were probably more a reflection of the jubilation of new parenthood than an excess of middle-class decorum. Still, there were other indications that Garvey was increasingly adopting a self-aggrandizing attitude, which affected both his personal and business affairs. For example, after the People's Political Party (PPP) elections and the implementation by the U.S. House of Representatives in 1930 of the "quota system" restricting immigration from the West Indies, Garvey intensified his efforts to develop black entrepreneurship in Jamaica.[10] Although this was a step forward in the national democratic revolution and a justifiable tactic to empower people of African descent, who had been discriminated against by banks and other credit agencies, it also relied on the conservative idea that opportunities and increased wages would trickle down to the masses from their employers.

Garvey instructed workers to study their employer's interests and "give him an honest day's work so his business [can] succeed," contending that this would create "the opportunity for increased remuneration." In theory, it made sense to argue that when "he [the laborer] gets his pay . . . he is an independent man"; but the reality was quite different.[11] Even the most "philanthropic and paternalistic" capitalist, R. L. M. Kirkwood, managing director of the West Indies Sugar Company (WISCO), in testifying in 1938 before the Jamaican government commission, admitted that although his company planned to "invest ten thousand pounds per year in Jamaica over a period of years" and provide family dwellings for its workers, there would not be "any significant wage increases." Kirkwood added that due to the island's "disorganized" labor force, it was impossible to "determine a fair wage level." He concluded that "those companies which could afford to pay their labour more than the standard rates should devote their attention to housing, medical facilities, recreation grounds and clubs, rather than to embark upon a process of competitive wage increase." Thomas Holt accurately observes that WISCO "deliberately created a situation of chronic underemployment at low wages, ostensibly for a larger social good."[12] Garvey's labor rhetoric failed to acknowledge these real-world conditions. Though he continued to be a champion of the masses and was well aware of the hardships that most workers endured, at times his speeches and writings undermined their interests.

Marcus Garvey still believed that workers had legitimate grievances, but in his opinion they were unable to articulate them in a way that would impress government officials. Unlike the common folk, he was able to "speak for himself before anyone, and he was assuming the responsibility to interpret the sorrows and suffering of his people, not only to the local government, but to the imperial government." Garvey claimed that he was the explicator of the people and understood the power inherent in that role. Literary scholar and novelist Ngugi Thiong'o has suggested that intellectuals who serve as interpreters sometimes see themselves as "scouts and guides" in their own linguistic space. Unfortunately, too often these thinkers fall into the trap of locating power solely in those who can articulate it, failing to see its source in the people themselves. In Jamaica it was becoming more evident that Garvey saw himself as the "cultured representative" of the masses, even though he had criticized this attitude among African American leaders in the preceding decade.[13]

While her husband was addressing labor issues in an abstract and public vein, Amy Jacques Garvey was becoming concretely aware of poverty and the difficulties of making ends meet at home. This began to change her ideas about what constituted waste and excess. On one occasion in 1931, she suggested to Garvey that he spend less on his personal secretaries. Both secretaries were paid U.S. salaries and had access to a car (a major luxury, since most people on the island traveled by foot, donkey, or mule, or hitched a ride on the back of a truck). In addition, Garvey gave them presents, took them on costly outings, and after a year of employment paid for their vacations in the United States. All of this occurred when "we at home are suffering great deprivations, and he was being pressed to meet organization bills." In response to her complaints, Jacques Garvey recalled that he "calmly and deliberately" told her that because he received most of his financial support from the United States, the African American secretaries had to be accommodated, "I thought you realized this long ago," he reportedly told her.[14]

On the surface, Jacques Garvey knew that her husband felt the need to keep the secretaries materially happy so they would remain "loyal" to him. But perhaps since she had also been his personal secretary and had ended up as his wife, she was a bit jealous of all the time that he spent with these women. Given, too, that money was short and she and her son were doing without, it is understandable why she wanted him to change his spending habits.[15]

Essentially, she was responding to what appeared to be elaborate expenditures when they had their baby's future to secure. Her father had labored and invested the family wealth to ensure his family's lifestyle, and she expected Garvey to do the same for their child, especially since Garveyites were adamant that men needed to function as heads of households and take full responsibility for their financial success. Other Jamaican women born at the turn of the century held similar views, believing that it was the "task" of men to "donate money" to sustain the family.[16] Throughout her memoir, *Garvey and Garveyism* (1963), Jacques Garvey claims that her husband continually drained both their household funds and her inheritance to meet UNIA debts. But with the birth of Junior her attitude about Garvey's haphazard money management changed: she went from simply voicing her complaints to refusing his requests and openly criticizing his pecuniary mishaps. The overall tenor of her memoir reveals that although saying no to her husband could be painful, because she had always done everything in her power to help him achieve the goals of the UNIA, it was also necessary. Now she and her child were struggling financially, and she was forced to heed the advice she had given her readership over the years on how to stretch a dollar. No longer could she merely offer suggestions on "making do" as an outside observer; now she herself had to make do.

Of course, class struggles are relative. When journalist Harold Stannard described the housing conditions of agricultural workers of the West Indies in 1938, he stated: "The first time I saw one of these hovels I could hardly believe that it was intended for human occupation. Stands of dried bamboo are woven round a framework of stakes and 'the room' thus formed is covered with palm thatch. There is no furniture except sacking on the earth and some sort of table to hold the oil-stove." Conditions in Kingston were even worse: "shacks were put together anyhow out of the sides of packing cases and sheets of corrugated iron." Thus, a poor Jamaican woman who "made do" by supplementing her family income with her "own account" work—domestic service, dressmaking, hairdressing, and selling the surplus food staples of small farmers—would accurately have viewed Jacques Garvey's complaints as petty. After all, the Garveys lived in a modern home in a prestigious neighborhood, they had a maid and a gardener, a car (American Garveyites had sent them a Buick in 1929, and when the engine gave out, they sent a Hudson), and a telephone in their home.[17] But all that glitters is not prosperity, and maintaining a middle-class exterior, in any culture, is difficult without a steady monthly income.

Jacques Garvey found motherhood extremely time-consuming. Although she had extended family support, particularly from her mother and sister, she could no longer give Garvey and the UNIA the kind of energy she had provided before. Her helpmate role was now primarily to care for her son, and she was annoyed when Garvey's decisions impeded her ability to meet her maternal obligations. For example, at one point she wanted to purchase a Jersey cow with some of the money they had been given when Junior was born. As a nursing mother, she most likely intended to wean him after nine months and therefore was eager to have a ready source of cow's milk.[18] In recalling the incident, she describes the irritation she felt at having to sell a calf "and all my ducks and fowls to pay for the cow," because Garvey was "unable to return the amount" he had borrowed from Junior's funds.[19] The fact that Garvey had to borrow his son's money indicates that Jacques Garvey controlled these funds, and

Garvey could not simply help himself. Despite the fact that Garveyites argued that financial matters were the responsibility of fathers, Jacques Garvey apparently considered the management of the household finances to be intrinsic to her maternal duties.

Since motherhood for Jacques Garvey was a full-time undertaking, it is understandable that there is no evidence that she contributed essays to the *Blackman* after Junior's birth in 1930.[20] In early February 1931 Garvey suspended publication because of debts related to the printing press, but, as always, he persevered and in July 1932 began an evening newspaper, the *New Jamaican*, published in St. Andrews. Jacques Garvey apparently never wrote for this organ, either.[21] Interestingly, critics perceived the *New Jamaican* as confirmation that Garvey was "racially dead," that he was now a man who had "completely dropped the great cause and is only interested in making a living for himself and his family." Jacques Garvey, on the other hand, had to view this publication as direct evidence that he continued to put the movement before his family. At this point Garvey was in poor health, and others pleaded with him to retire and "start life on your own. For your family's sake, give it up." His wife claimed that he could not stop; if he tried to, the suffering of his people would "haunt" him.[22]

In the writings and recollections of Jacques Garvey, there are many indications that she and her husband had always experienced some degree of marital strain. Garvey's editorial in the *New Jamaican* of 1 September 1932, entitled "The Question of Love," suggests that these tensions were pervasive. He begins the piece by asserting that "love is really a personal matter." For instance, "One man will love a woman because of her beautiful hair." From this point on, the essay hints strongly at autobiography. "A man marries a woman in the first instance of loving her, for her hair." As the marriage develops, he may begin to realize her "shortcomings physically and otherwise, not consistent with the love that the person had in the first instance, because of the beautiful head of hair." Garvey describes how a philosopher sympathetically reasons with his spouse about her "repulsiveness or bad disposition" as a means to reform her. If the spouse accepts these suggestions, "the lover will find himself not only loving the hair of a person, but loving the person completely." But when the woman "refuses to conform . . . then you have a variance that cannot be interpreted as love." He concludes that "a little sympathy and a little willingness to adapt oneself . . . would insure as genuine a love as man could want."

Here Garvey is attempting to discuss "love" from a nonpersonal stand-point, as a "philosopher," but the fact that he uses "hair" as an example of attraction is significant, because in Jacques Garvey's memoir she talks about how her hair "thrilled" her husband. Her hair was ultimately a metaphor for her "brown" beauty. Though beauty was only one aspect of Jacques Garvey's identity, it was initially an important one for Garvey.[23] While we need to be careful about over interpreting a single editorial, it is fascinating to explore what appears to be Garvey's revealing indictment of his marriage.

In this essay Garvey stresses the importance of "adapting oneself" to avoid "domestic confusion and upheavals." In his view, marital "gain" is related to compatibility and complementarity, and he offers a model to resolve marital difficulties based on bargaining. Although Jacques Garvey might well have agreed with this statement in principle, in practice both were unwilling to give up their dominating traits to accommodate the other. Jacques Garvey was not going to turn back the clock and sacri-fice herself for her husband when she had a child to provide for. As the "philosopher," Garvey did not see himself as the one who needed to conform; therefore, their marital problems were destined to remain unresolved.

No doubt Jacques Garvey exhibited kindness, warmth, and compas-sion, but these qualities were not central to her temperament. Because of her commitment to the Pan-African struggle and later to her mothering duties, she had little time to coddle and console others; thus, she could be both brash and aloof. On the surface, her impetuous personality seems to have conflicted with the helpmate role that she wrote about and charged other women to commit themselves to. Nevertheless, the fact that she was not always cheerful does not mean that she was unhelpful. In addition, as she matured with motherhood, her ideas of what constituted a helpmate probably also changed. By the early 1930s she was apparently quite vocal with Garvey about her money-related concerns, and she refused to always back down and accommodate her husband's wishes, as she had done early in their marriage. Raising a child in an economically depressed world had made Jacques Garvey even more conscious of working-class struggles. In many ways, this moment provided a bridge to move her from her earlier UNIA political and intellectual activities, in which she demonstrated her skills as a community feminist, to an astute political awareness of ex-ploited workers and actions on their behalf.

As in most marriages, the Garveys' financial problems exacerbated their marital strains. At one point, Jacques Garvey was summoned by a bailiff for "over a year's taxes due on the home," and she went to court and arranged for payment. As their money troubles continued to worsen, debt forced Garvey to suspend publication of the *New Jamaica*. Nevertheless, despite these pressures, the couple continued to live as husband and wife, and on 16 August 1933 Jacques Garvey gave birth to their second son at their Somali Court home. He was christened Julius Winston Garvey at St. Luke's Anglican Church. One might have expected the couple to name their second child after an African leader or a noted African of the diaspora, not after Julius Caesar and Winston Churchill; the Garveys, however, identified these names with the power and strength of these leaders.[24] Obviously, they held high aspirations for the child, who physically resembled Garvey at birth.

With the birth of Julius, the joys of motherhood became twofold for Jacques Garvey. But raising her children in Jamaica also reawakened her to unresolved issues of her "colored" past. One day, while out walking with the three-month-old Julius, she bumped into a former schoolmate, who greeted her with, "I haven't seen you in ages. What are you doing with this little black baby?"[25] Jacques Garvey later recalled this incident as if it had affected her a great deal. Her former peer's question no doubt called up a whole network of "colored" ideas. First of all, her schoolmate never entertained the thought that the baby might be Jacques Garvey's child, because middle-class "brown" Jamaicans customarily married a person of comparable hue. The former schoolmate knew her family, as well as the importance of fulfilling "colored" expectations. Confronted with the fact that she had steered away from the practice of marrying "light," Jacques Garvey also had to have been reminded of the belief system that she herself had once subscribed to. If she had stayed in Jamaica, she would never have associated, let alone married, a man like Marcus Garvey, who was poor and black and had no legitimate ties to her family's lifestyle, no matter how hard he courted elite support. Years later her sister, Mrs. Ida Repole, asserted that if their father had lived, Jacques Garvey would not have married Garvey, implying that his paternal authority would have prevented such a major break from tradition.[26]

In recalling the incident, Jacques Garvey does not share how she responded to her schoolmate's query. One would hope that she repeated her belief that "Black is beautiful" and that everyone in the African diaspora should value their African heritage. But regardless of what she said, she had to have felt a twinge of pain, not only for herself but also for her child. Her marriage to Marcus Garvey had shattered any hope of rekindling certain relationships, and this fact was complicated by her present anger with her husband. Although her duties to the UNIA, and later her children, were time-consuming, they also gave her an excuse not to wholeheartedly confront the ideology of her past, which was plagued with contradictions.

Jacques Garvey had largely shielded herself from the gossip and disapproval that surrounded her choice of a husband. But would she be able to do the same for her children, whom she loved so dearly? What would their future hold if they were snubbed by their own people? Though there was no legal color bar in Jamaica, it was in fact "difficult for a really dark man or woman to get any of the better and more responsible jobs."[27] In hindsight, Jacques Garvey analyzed the encounter with her former schoolmate as an informed black nationalist intellectual would, explaining that the "concept of skin-color distinction, and the idea of raising one's color by marriage dies hard with our people."[28] But we cannot really know the full impact of this incident at the time.

As the mother of an infant and a toddler, Jacques Garvey was indeed domestically occupied. Homebound but not unhappy, she now found satisfaction chiefly in nurturing her children, which was quite different from nurturing her husband or the Pan-African nation. In the preceding years, she had been in a position to influence her husband's political decisions by offering him her opinions and analysis of events. For this role she had been rewarded by the UNIA membership and hailed as the "Joan of Arc" of helpmates. Nevertheless, her status had not automatically translated into real power in the movement; indeed, it seems that she constantly struggled against feeling powerless within the realm of patriarchal power. With her children, on the other hand, she experienced a sense of real and absolute power. "Pregnancy, birth, and breast-feeding are such powerful bodily experiences and the emotional attachment to the infant so intense," Evelyn Nakano Glenn has observed, "that it is difficult for women who have gone through these experiences and emotions to think that they do not constitute unique female experiences."[29] These experiences were so profound for Jacques Garvey that she was willing to sacrifice personal desires to fulfill maternal responsibilities. Essentially, motherhood empowered her to take positions against her husband to protect their financial welfare. As her marital relationship became more precarious, her mother-child relationship became a rock of stability.

In her earlier writings, Jacques Garvey had not conflated "woman" with "mother," but as a mother of small children, it appears that she was too busy not to differentiate between the two. The records do not reveal her romanticizing motherhood during these years as a "labor or love," but she was apparently so taken with child rearing that she was no longer a tireless UNIA worker. She did not lend herself to the editorial/publication staff of either the *New Jamaican* or Garvey's new publication, the *Black Man: A Monthly Magazine of Negro Thought and Opinion*, which first appeared in December 1933.[30] As an intellectual, her words had always been her primary means of production, but now she concentrated her efforts on raising the next generation.

Ironically, Jacques Garvey's absence from the political scene coincided with a peak of political activity for many Jamaican UNIA women, who were also affiliated with female-centered organizations. More than any other black nationalist group in the early twentieth century, the UNIA had emphasized female participation. Women were always central to the organization's management and annually elected to leadership positions. In the 1930s some of these women applied skills learned in the UNIA to Jamaican women's organizations. Indeed, in one of the few works that deals exclusively with early political organizing among Jamaican women, Joan French and Honor Ford-Smith's *Women, Work, and Organization in Jamaica, 1900–1944* shows that "the UNIA was the training ground for many of the middle and working class women leaders of the thirties."[31] Liberal Jamaican feminists such as Amy Bailey, Una Marson, Satire Earle, Adina Spencer, and Jacques Garvey's U.S. traveling companion, Madame DeMena, were all committed Garveyites. They were also active in the Women's Social Service Club (WSSC), formed in 1918, and were outspoken critics of female unemployment.[32]

The social work of middle-class women in Jamaica was consistent with the ideology of "housewifisation." This term, coined by Marie Mies in 1981, is used to account for "the concentration of women in sectors where the tasks and duties performed are extensions of housework, or defined as in keeping with the natural labour of women." Basically, this ideology supports the notion that the biological ability of women to have babies should be extended so they can become the "social nurture[r] of mankind." Thus, if a middle-class woman wanted to work outside the home, she should apply herself to "good works on a voluntary basis." Eventually the WSSC became the most prominent Jamaican women's organization of the early twentieth century. This club and others like it allowed women to organize in "women's arms" and later to resist the colonial definition of the ideal woman, one who believed it was in her best interest to maintain male privileges.[33]

As a community feminist, Jacques Garvey had pressed black women to serve their communities as both helpmates and leaders, and these activists were doing just that. Nonetheless, Jacques Garvey herself was not involved in any of these groups. It is perhaps unfortunate that she did not participate in this movement, which provided opportunities for women to expand their horizons and their relationships with other women. Not only might this have been a potential source of female friendship, but also it would have provided her with the company of women who did not allow men to mediate their lives—experiences that Jacques Garvey might well have benefited from.

Meanwhile, as Jamaican women were consolidating their activism in their own organizations, the UNIA was struggling to remain solvent. In addition, in the United States the UNIA now had to compete with thriving rival movements, such as Father Divine and the Communist Party in Harlem. To deal with this pending crisis, and because in Jamaica he felt isolated from world affairs, Marcus Garvey decided once again to relocate to London.[34]

When her husband departed Jamaica for London in March 1935, Jacques Garvey was left with sole responsibility for their children and inadequate financial resources for their care. Moreover, by this time Garvey was bankrupt. The Edelweiss Park property had been foreclosed, and Garvey had sold the household furniture to generate funds.[35] What remained was "a bedroom suite, the books and two large pictures and vases." Jacques Garvey reports that Garvey instructed her to "rent out the home, get two rooms somewhere, as my mother's home was being remodel[ed], and in time he would send for us."[36] Black nationalism unapologetically argued for a patriarchal family structure, and Garvey had spoken out against "female-headed" households, but now he was leaving his wife to care for their sons alone. Whatever else it may say about the state of their marriage, the fact that Garvey could leave without his children exemplified his freedom from daily child care responsibilities and Jacques Garvey's role as the primary caregiver.

When Marcus Garvey moved to London without his family, Jacques Garvey became the head of the household in Jamaica. Garvey had always been the patriarch, making the final decision on most family matters, but with the birth of their children, Jacques Garvey began increasingly to challenge him on issues. Hence, their home eventually became a repository for more tension than ease and more distance than familial warmth. When Garvey left the island in 1935, both of them must have exhaled with relief to be free of the pressure of living under the same roof.

After thirteen years of marriage, the Garveys had separated by choice. Even though the preceding years had been made difficult by Garvey's pecuniary mishaps, life without her husband was arduous for Jacques Garvey. She was free of a day-to-day marital accountability, but her parental obligations had increased. For all intents and purposes, she now was a single mother—one of a host of Jamaican women who raised their children without any daily interaction or assistance from the father. Edna Brodber has documented that the absence of a man from a woman's life was a "social fact" in Jamaica. This social fact was also indicative of an economic one: the vast majority of these women were poor, their husbands often working in a different parish or off the island in order to provide their families some financial support. Of course, in the years during and immediately following the Great Depression, poverty was not limited to female-headed households. By 1935, 25 to 33 percent of urban wageworkers were unemployed, and the average weekly salary of the bulk of employed laborers had fallen to new lows.[1] Nevertheless, financial problems were particularly severe for mothers trying to raise children on their own.

Jacques Garvey's middle-class inheritance was not enough to cushion her nuclear family against financial bankruptcy, and creditors continued to stalk her. Bills went unpaid, and on one occasion she was summoned to court because of a physician's debt incurred during and after her first pregnancy. She arranged to pay monthly installments "out of the small irregular amounts [Garvey] sent us." In addition to the gradual dissolution of her personal inheritance, the financial resources gleaned from the Universal Negro Improvement Association (UNIA) were atrophying along with the organization's membership. At one point Jacques Garvey admitted that she "missed the thoughtfulness and unsolicited services of Garveyites in America." Over the years they had sent cars, gifts, and money to Jamaica, but the depression prevented even the most loyal members from giving as they had in the past. Though many of these Garveyites were born in the West Indies, Jacques Garvey attributed their generosity to living in America. She believed that the American atmosphere had "mellowed" Jamaicans with the "spirit" to give and do for others, "unlike most Jamaicans at home, who had nothing to give but their services, and even this they withheld."[2]

Jacques Garvey was more critical of Jamaican Garveyites in part because she had direct contact with them now, and it seemed to her that they had forgotten what the UNIA had done for them in the past. This feeling is illustrated by her recollection of an incident that involved a Jamaican physician who had worked at the UNIA headquarters in New York City while he was a medical student at Howard University. Years later, in Jamaica, when she took Julius to this doctor, he merely gave her son a "once-over" look and proclaimed him a healthy child. On leaving the office, they passed the dispenser's window, where the receptionist asked for payment of the fee. "I told her that the doctor had not prescribed any medicine, so I did not think he would charge me." In Jacques Garvey's mind, this doctor should not collect money from her not only because he had not provided any real service, but also because her husband had assisted him during his time of need. If Jacques Garvey had had the money to pay the doctor, she might not have been so put off by his fee, but she was financially strapped and had to "borrow a shilling" from a friend for "tram car fares" after paying the amount due. She was soured by this experience, believing that only a money-hungry human being would not honor a past act of kindness. She also had to wonder whether the doctor would have charged Garvey for the same nominal service. Unfortunately, she chose to regard this physician's behavior as representative of all Jamaicans, whom she callously stereotyped as people who "go to bed with the 'gimmies' and wake up with the 'wants.' "[3]

Times had changed, and Jacques Garvey had not yet adjusted to the fact that she no longer commanded the kind of deference that had once been showered on her by fellow Garveyites. To add insult to injury, she lacked adequate financial resources to fill this void with material comfort. Like most female heads of households, Jacques Garvey found herself the lord—or in this case the lady—over a few pence, and she complained about her money problems to anyone who would listen. In this respect, her attitude differed from that of other middle-class people during the depression. Most were too proud to let others know their plight and ashamed that they could not provide for themselves. Letters written by middle-class Americans to President and Mrs. Roosevelt, for example, indicate that they were embarrassed by their misfortune and that what they wanted was not charity but a loan. These letters largely emphasize that the authors had "never as yet begged."[4]

Middle-class Western culture of this time, regardless of precise geographic location, was deeply infused with a work ethic. The idea, most notably promoted by Booker T. Washington, that hard work and self-help were the rudiments of success resounded. In the 1920s Jacques Garvey herself had been critical of black men who were waiting for a handout, declaring that they deserved a swift "kick" for not creating a job for themselves.[5] When it came to her own needs and expectations during the depression years, however, she refused to be silenced by a false sense of pride. To some, she must have sounded like a broken record; nonetheless, she would not pretend that her family was doing well and evidently saw her own complaints not as a form of begging but as an expression of legitimate entitlement.

Garvey, on the other hand, wanted to keep their personal affairs confidential and was critical of his wife for discussing them with others. He wrote to her that he "would appreciate if you keep our business to ourselves instead of talking to or writing to people who only care about their own affairs." Was Garvey embarrassed, as were so many others who labored to maintain a middle-class lifestyle, that he was not able to adequately support his family? In the same letter he also stated, "What I can do I do when I can and other people have nothing to do with it, for it is not their business and they do not care."[6] Garvey did periodically send money home, and he sent suits to his sons; thus, he had not completely abandoned his familial responsibilities. But his efforts were not enough to satisfy his wife. Jacques Garvey could not finagle or postpone feeding, housing, or clothing their children, who were at the rambunctious and needy ages of five and three. She bewailed to Garvey the need to provide clothes and other basic provisions. Indeed, recent research suggests that female household heads in Jamaica continue to allocate a larger share of their budget to children's goods than to other necessities.[7]

The 1930s were difficult worldwide because of the Great Depression, but Jacques Garvey tended to characterize her family's suffering as if it were far more horrendous than others'. It may help to put her reactions in perspective if we consider the findings of researchers that economic strain can produce what has been called the stress-distress paradigm: a slew of emotional reactions, especially mental depression among women and hostility among men.[8] The Garveys shared a fiery spirit that often surfaced as animosity but also prevented them from becoming deeply depressed. Obviously, they knew that the black masses were chronically poorer than they were, but they elected not to adopt the coping strategy that encourages people to appreciate what they have because times could be worse. Their expectations were high. In a political context, this had the advantage of encouraging them to dream of a Pan-African world, one that would bring substantial prosperity to all Africans at home and abroad. In a personal context, the Garveys believed that they deserved the best and complained when anything fell short of their desires.

In many ways, the Garveys turned complaining into an art form. Both of them were elaborate, excessive, and biting in their criticism of others (and, at times, of one another). At one point Jacques Garvey even admitted that she was "full of arguments and contradictions."[9] Their attitudes and charges against others sometimes made them difficult to be around; by the same token, however, it was their verbal and written forcefulness that made them such powerful and persuasive figures.

Writing and talking were the cords that bound the Garveys to life, and during their separation they maintained an open dialogue. They even showed signs of affection for each other, continuing to use their nicknames of Mopsie and Popsie even in their most embittered exchanges. Garvey always made it a point to send greetings to Jacques Garvey's sister, mother, and aunts, and he was careful to mention that he appreciated all of the sweet treats that his wife sent him.

Garvey's letters from this period indicate that his political and personal life was difficult in London. He described a UNIA office that was fraught with tension, and he wrote of his inability to hire capable clerks and trust-worthy housekeepers. One maid, he claimed, had "searched the home and my pockets and drawers from end to end. She and the people around knew more of my business than I knew myself, and nobody would tell me what was going on." He was also upset by the alleged behavior of Eric Walrond, an acclaimed Guyanese journalist and novelist, who, Garvey believed, had been "making love to all of them [the female staff] at one and the same time."[10]

Garvey's London residence and the UNIA office were in a shambles, and Jacques Garvey must have read between the lines of his letters the implica-tion that many of his worries would be alleviated if she would come and take care of the household and UNIA business. But Garvey still did not arrange for his family to join him. Jacques Garvey understood that he was not receiving enough money to support a household in addition to the work of the UNIA and the publication of the *Black Man* magazine, "so our going was deferred for these priorities."[11]

For two years Garvey labored to regain his leadership among the black masses and to keep his Pan-African ideas alive, while his wife struggled to make ends meet with their children in Jamaica. Though she was not desperate enough to become a wage laborer, Jacques Garvey most likely supplemented her household allowance with support from her family and the minimal aid from UNIA members in Jamaica.

At last, in May 1937, Garvey arranged for his family to join him. He wrote his wife with instructions to collect the tickets and prepare to sail on 8 June. As always, he had a list of tasks for her to complete prior to the trip. He wanted her to bring "as many of the two Vols of *Philosophy and Opinions* as possible and about 500 of the Hymnals." It is unclear if Jacques Garvey requested an additional ticket for a maid, or if Garvey made that decision to ensure that his wife would travel with ease. In any case, Jacques Garvey, her maid, and the two boys departed Jamaica as scheduled, arriving at Avonmouth on 21 June 1937.[12]

When Garvey met his family at the dock, his wife found that "in appearance he had not changed much, though his hair was thinning out in the front." What was obvious to all present was his delight in seeing his children. Jacques Garvey noticed that her husband was particularly taken with Julius's physical appearance; his youngest son still looked and now walked like him. Garvey believed that he "must have been just like him as a boy." After riding a "boat train" to London, they arrived at their home at 2 Beaumont Crescent in West Kensington.[13]

It was an unexpected blessing that Garvey could afford to lease only part of the house, for the cramped quarters inevitably helped to bring the family closer together. In the weeks that followed, the father tried to make up for lost time with his sons. He enjoyed taking them out, especially to the cinema. Quickly the boys became something of a novelty, Jacques Garvey recalled, because "colored children were rarely seen in England at this time." Garvey was "intrigued by English remarks such as these: Aren't they lovely? . . . [S]uch big black eyes! What beautiful white teeth! They speak English, too. Can I touch him for luck?" Apparently he was so exhilarated to be with them that he found himself "intrigued," as opposed to upset, that his children had a carnivalesque appeal for his white English neighbors.[14]

That fall, the children settled into school and Garvey prepared for UNIA regional conferences. The family reunion had lasted less than two months when, on 12 August, Garvey set sail with his secretary, Daisy Whyte, for organizational meetings in Canada, the British West Indies, and Central America. He left written instructions for Jacques Garvey, who was placed in charge of the London headquarters. This was the first sign since the birth of their children that she was wholeheartedly active in the organization.[15]

To manage UNIA business again must have been like riding a bicycle for Jacques Garvey. She was able to mount the seat and peddle away, bringing order to the chaos that had threatened to engulf the office. She rode alone for three months, and when Garvey returned on 20 November, he pronounced his trip a success; there is no evidence that he was disappointed with his wife's performance, either.[16]

In February 1938 the Garveys found a house that they could afford to rent on Targarth Road, near the UNIA office. Since the house had not been occupied for some time and was in bad shape, Garvey convinced the owner that some rent was better than none at all. The structure was exceptionally damp due to the long vacancy, but it was large and allowed them to live once again in spacious comfort. Garvey took control of setting up this household, as he had done in Jamaica, by placing furniture where he saw fit and assigning particular rooms to his family and staff. He put Jacques Garvey and the children in a rear room on the top floor; his secretary had the large front room and the maid the smaller one. Garvey lodged on the second floor, in a set of rooms that included his bedroom, the bathroom, and a library. The first floor contained two sitting rooms and the basement, the kitchen and dining room. Jacques Garvey was not pleased with these arrangements and asked Garvey to transfer herself and the boys to the back sitting room on the first floor, but, she claims, he replied, "No up there the children are out of the way, and not distracting to me." As someone who prided herself on knowing her husband better than he knew himself, she suggested that his caustic response was similar to what his own father would have said. Garvey wanted to be different from his father, but she observed that "although a man may strive to be what he wants to be, he is made up of what has been, the genesis of which gives him impulses to do and become what he does not wish to be; therefore he usually denies the labels his actions merit."[17]

It is unclear why, in this analysis, Jacques Garvey did not plainly call her husband impatient or selfish, especially since she had said as much on other occasions. One can speculate that her dissection of this conversation demonstrates that she was grappling for a more meaningful and compassionate explanation for his behavior since his comments related to their children. Though Jacques Garvey never implicated herself as the catalyst for his foul moods, as an intellectual she needed to ground his personality in some verifiable source. Overall, her analysis teeter-tottered between reactionary and historical truths. It was reactionary because she sought to find direct evidence, linked to his past, to explain his insensitive behavior. And though Garvey's disposition may have been characteristic of his father, it also could have been spurred by the desperation and the pressure he felt to pump air back into his suffocated movement.

Once again, tensions in the Garvey household were compounded by problems in the UNIA: living conditions for black people throughout the world were worsening, the annual convention attendance over the last four years had been poor, and UNIA membership had dropped to an all-time low because of the popularity of rival organizations such as New York UNIA Inc. (formed after the 1929 UNIA convention), Father Divine, and the Peace Mission movement. The Pan-African movement had brought the Garveys many joys and disappointments over the years, and their marriage had reflected this ebb and flow. When Jacques Garvey first pledged UNIA membership in 1919, she was just as committed as Garvey, and when she made her marriage vows to him in 1922, she was equally vested in their union. Although their differences were often personal and not political, UNIA business did sometimes trigger a showdown. But it took a medical crisis—Junior contracting rheumatic fever—to reveal the true extent of their marital discord.

Poor health had loomed over the Garvey household for years. Chronic fatigue and weight loss had dogged Jacques Garvey, and bronchitis related to acute asthma, along with diabetes, afflicted Garvey. In London, a favorite game of Junior and Julius was "machine gun bombardment," which required Junior to kneel on one knee on the uncarpeted floor, behind an armchair, in order to aim his toy weapon. This game eventually had crippling consequences for him. "That knee became drawn and painful," Jacques Garvey remembered, and "the fever lasted three weeks." Completely attentive to the needs of her sick child, Jacques Garvey relinquished her UNIA duties to nurse him. She had to keep pressure, including blankets, away from his leg; maintain a fire in his room; and climb up and down two flights of stairs to get food and hot water from the kitchen. Her attention to Junior also kept Julius in the house, and he soon developed bronchitis from lack of fresh air. Jacques Garvey later said the situation brought her to the "breaking point," and Garvey was little help because he did not "know how to attend to them" and it pained him to see them sick and suffering. Though there was a live-in maid and Garvey's secretary in the home, Jacques Garvey still believed that it was her role to care for her boys, and she did everything in her power to make them well.[18]

Julius's illness ran its course, but Junior remained sick. Garvey began climbing to the top floor daily to visit with his son. Junior said that the pain was "like lightning striking through it, and my heart trembles." Garvey told him to be brave; he did not want him to "become a weakling. When the asthma bothers me, I try to throw it off, knowing full well that when the body becomes weak the forces of man, and even nature, seek to brush you aside." Garvey was a firm believer in the power of positive thinking. Only a month earlier, during a speech at St. Kitts, he had declared that "there is nothing outside of you as strong as what is inside of you. That power inside you is stronger."[19] No doubt Junior tried to follow his father's suggestion, but by the end of the fourth week the doctor informed the Garveys that he needed to be seen by a bone specialist and to be hospitalized. For three months Junior stayed in the orthopedic ward of the Princess Beatrice Hospital. His parents visited him often, and Garvey pampered him with chocolates and made sure that he did not get behind in his schoolwork by bringing him volumes of Arthur Mee's *Children's Encyclopedia.*

Junior was finally released in July, just as his father was preparing for his annual visit to Canada, where the Eighth Annual UNIA Convention would take place in August. The morning before his departure, he gave his wife "four pages of typewritten instructions, and told [her she] was again in charge of the office." Because Garvey pushed everyone around him to work hard, his loyal secretary, Daisy Whyte, was too physically exhausted to travel with him, so he arranged to have a secretary sent from New York to meet him in Canada. Jacques Garvey and Whyte held down the fort at home, a task made more difficult by the fact that Garvey had left them only ten dollars a week for staff salaries and household money. Jacques Garvey "earned the compliment for my sex, from one of the English typists in the office, when she said, '[I]t takes a woman to do it.'"[20] As she had during Garvey's imprisonment, Jacques Garvey faithfully completed the tasks he had assigned to her. Although her helpmate/leadership role (a glimmer of her earlier community feminism) was now visible only to the typists, Jacques Garvey clearly remembered the Englishwoman's comment with pride, hearing it not only as a personal compliment, but as one for her sex as well.

As the UNIA August convention was drawing to a close, Junior's leg, which had become slightly drawn after the plaster had been replaced with a hip-length wool sock, grew worse. A specialist sought his mother's consent to have his leg straightened out for replastering, a procedure that would entail anesthetizing him with ether. The doctor also felt that what Junior really needed was heat, so after the replastering he recommended that he be sent to an orthopedic hospital in the south of England that specialized in ultra violet-ray treatment. After another consultation, it was suggested that Jacques Garvey take Junior back to the West Indies for sunshine instead. Jacques Garvey reported that one of the female doctors who also knew Garvey asked her, "Where was the objector?" When she told her that he was in Canada, the doctor said, "You must decide. This child is intelligent and must not be allowed to grow up as a cripple."[21] Relocation for health reasons was something that Jacques Garvey was certainly familiar with, having, in 1917, fled the warm tropical air of Jamaica for a cooler climate. Now her son required the opposite move.

She elected to resolve this difficult question without any input from her husband, making the immediate decision to take their child back to Jamaica. Here again is evidence that Jacques Garvey had assumed full control of her children's development, even if it meant leaving Garvey completely outside the decision-making realm.

Years later, in recalling this critical decision, Jacques Garvey rationalized that she had had to rely on her own good judgment in Garvey's absence. He had always expected her to do this; that was why he had placed her in charge in the first place. Once she made the decision to go, she "sold a diamond ring, booked our passages and cabled an S.O.S. to my aunt for the balance." (The fact that she had a diamond ring to sell indicates that though she lacked cash in Jamaica, she still had personal property in the form of jewelry and land.) In her memoir, Jacques Garvey describes hasty preparations for her departure. She told "no one of my plans until the night before sailing."[22] It is likely that she kept her voyage secret since she knew that Garvey would not approve and may have thought that he would try to stop her.

Jacques Garvey presents her decision to leave London as if she had no other choice, as if Junior's health mandated it. But perhaps her concern for Junior had deflected attention from what she had wanted to do for some time. The two years she had spent away from Garvey had been difficult, but the great distance between them may have made it easier for her to gloss over his imperfections, as well as her own. Time and distance can transform memories into romantic testaments on caring and the desirability of a person in one's daily life. In London she had once again seen Garvey up close and personal, and seemingly his flaws again grated on her; thus, she may have been seizing the opportunity to be released from his smothering clutches. By now, the demands of wifehood had completely given way to those of motherhood, but she still may have felt the need to steal herself and children away from London because she feared that her husband would object.

Jacques Garvey was not the only one concerned about Garvey's reaction. When she told Daisy Whyte of her decision, the secretary apparently became "upset and said, How am I going to tell Mr. Garvey?" To handle this phase of her plan Jacques Garvey wrote two letters to her husband, "one containing a statement on the office transactions, and the other marked personal explaining the urgency of Junior's case, and that we would stay at my mother's home."[23] She entrusted these letters to Whyte and instructed her to give them to Garvey when he returned.

In early September 1938 Jacques Garvey and her two sons set sail from the Royal Albert Docks, bound for Jamaica via Amsterdam. The calm ocean gave them the opportunity to "rest and revive" their "spent bodies."[24] This relaxed state yielded a peace that must have eased Jacques Garvey's mind and affirmed to her that she had done the right thing. At the same time, she must have been somewhat apprehensive about what her surroundings would look like when they docked in the Kingston harbor. From April to June the island had been in a state of rebellion.

That year, 1938, marked the centenary of West Indian emancipation, but the mass of Jamaicans had not experienced the political and material promises of freedom. Thomas Holt has shown that by the late 1930s, "access to small plots of land no longer meant freedom—for the peasant fruit growers who supplied United Fruit nor for the migrant workers cutting cane for WISCO—West Indies Sugar Company." There had been a general shift in industry toward a more cutthroat capitalism. This reshaping had strained the network of personal relationships between employer and employee. No longer were laborers allowed to graze their animals or chop wood on the estates they worked. Though the roughest phase of the Great Depression in Jamaica occurred between 1931 and 1933, working conditions in 1938 were still poor. A survey of all estate properties revealed that there were "2,513 barracks accommodating a maximum of 22,620 persons in 8,596 rooms, fewer than half of which were judged to be in acceptable condition." Of these 2,513 barracks, 258 of them had no latrines and 567 others were unsanitary. Only approximately "1 out of every 8 barracks was supplied with water, either piped or drawn from the wells; 38 percent made no provision at all, and about half received water from rivers and ponds." The sugar properties were deemed to be the worst.[25]

Not surprisingly, WISCO was the first target of the protestors at the Frome Sugar Estate in the parish of Westmoreland. On 29 April a misunderstanding over the payment of wages led to a riot. A strike followed, with workers demanding that their pay be raised to a minimum of four shillings a day (80 cents). More than a hundred armed police incited the workers to defend themselves, and four people were killed, fourteen wounded, and eighty-five arrested. After this, sporadic strikes by dockworkers and banana loaders on the waterfront in Kingston and St. Ann's Bay eventually ignited a march through Kingston that closed down public services, factories, and ship transport. Jamaican workers held protest meetings all over the island, and by 2 June workers were in rebellion in almost every parish.[26] Amazingly it was reported that only 12 people were killed, "32 wounded by gunshot and 139 injured. Of the 745 persons prosecuted, 265 were found not guilty where 40 were convicted and given a variety of punishments."[27]

To regain control, the British and local elites sent British troops to reinforce the police and then appointed a Royal Commission to investigate the social and economic conditions in the Caribbean colonies. In the end, a concession was offered: the local political leadership would be assigned a greater role in the island's government. It had been more than seventy years since Jamaica had had a system of self-government, and the people responded with the call to create a political party dedicated to the workers of Jamaica. On 18 September, just days before Jacques Garvey's arrival, the People's National Party (PNP), led by Rhodes scholar and lawyer Norman Manley, was inaugurated.

The first modern political party on the island had been Garvey's People's Political Party (PPP), which had at its base a racial appeal. But with the rebellion and the expansion of labor unions, class issues had begun to surpass those of race and color. Jacques Garvey accurately observed that it was not a "race riot or a color riot; these desperate men and women felt that they must now, with their own hands, destroy anything and everything, that represented the class barrier, which had kept them away from good food and decent homes and, in short, a happy life."[28] This class struggle marked the beginning of the liberation movement of the workers on the island, and Jacques Garvey's return coincided with this new period in the history of modern Jamaica.

When the ship docked in Kingston, a large crowd was assembled on the pier. "The angry neglected masses were on the march," Jacques Garvey later wrote. Rumors had floated that Marcus Garvey was coming home, so a crowd of workers had gathered, many of whom had been loading a banana boat nearby. Jacques Garvey evidently was caught off guard by the reporters' questions—"Do you intend to take any part in politics in Jamaica? Will you pave the way for Garvey to come later on?"[29] She does not say how she responded to these queries, and Jamaican newspapers do not record her arrival, but no doubt she privately acknowledged what many other Jamaicans felt—that though Marcus Garvey was not physically present, his ideas pervaded the island; in many ways, he had served as a catalyst for all the changes that were now taking place.

The next day Jacques Garvey took Junior to a specialist at the Public General Hospital in Kingston. He stayed there a few days to have his leg replastered and then returned every two weeks for the next two years as an outpatient. This time around, hospital bills were not an issue; because of her "financial condition, I was not billed." Once again Jacques Garvey was struggling economically, and it did not help that she had arrived "just in time to lose [their] home by private sale, as the rental could not pay the mortgage, taxes, water, insurance and repairs for damage by termites, which are prevalent in the tropics."[30] At the end of this financial fiasco, which was compounded by a lien on two linotype machines purchased for the printing plant, Jacques Garvey received only two hundred dollars for the sale of their home. She and her sons moved into her mother's house, as initially planned, and she wrote Garvey two letters explaining the state of their affairs.

When Garvey learned of the loss of his home, his mind may well have echoed his own words: "Own your own house and land; then you will be a respectable citizen. . . . [D]on't let it get away from you." But whatever he thought, Jacques Garvey received no reply from him personally; his secretary informed her only that he was "angry because [she] had taken the children back to Jamaica."[31] Jacques Garvey had anticipated his disapproval, but not his pain at having the children taken from him. He was apparently so upset that he flatly refused to correspond with her but kept in constant contact with his sons. In two separate letters dated 8 December 1938, Garvey told Junior and Julius that he was "surprised to have not found you [children] at home when I returned from Canada, but I know as children, you have nothing to do with what happened. I am hoping, however, that you are well." Garvey also made it clear that he would "not be returning to Jamaica."[32] Nevertheless, his correspondence to his sons resonated with genuine concern and affection for them. In one letter he told Julius to have his grandmother write on his behalf and he would send him whatever he needed. Garvey enclosed one pound ($4.00) for a Christmas gift and wrote that clothes and books would be forthcoming.

When Daisy Whyte went to Jamaica on vacation in January, Garvey made good on his promise to his children. He had her bring them a package containing two suits for each child, books, and two letters, each with one pound enclosed. Jacques Garvey was offended by the amount and told Whyte to "tell him that when he is able to make it up to the past four months of support, he should mail it." Finding herself in the middle of a marital war zone, Whyte stressed to Jacques Garvey that her husband missed and worried about the boys and that he was depositing five shillings ($1.00) a week in a savings account for them. She concluded her plea on his behalf by stating that he felt "that with your family connections they were alright."[33]

Garvey was correct to assume that Jacques Garvey's family would assist her. Several years later, in a letter to UNIA secretary general Ethel Collins, Jacques Garvey wrote, "If I did not have family who were comfortably well-off, I would be in a worse plight." But her reply to Whyte that day in January 1939 was that Garvey "should have known that the attitudes of relatives and some friends would be, put colloquially, if you make your bed hard, you must lay down in it." Since Jacques Garvey had chosen to marry Garvey, a poor black man, then she had to take full responsibility for the outcome. Also, she did not want to have to depend on others when she had a husband. Garvey had submerged "the roles of husband and father" and sacrificed "his family on the altar of African redemption."[34]

The boys thanked their father for his gifts in letters dated 11 January 1939. Junior informed him that his mother pushed him in a wheelchair and that he felt better. He also asked him, "Why don't you send money for us for food and school and movies. Grannie feeds us and we live in her house, but we need lots of things." Julius echoed these sentiments, adding that "I thought you forgot all about us, as you never send us any money."[35] Since the boys were only nine and six years old, it is likely that their mother coached them to say this. Garvey seems to have reached a similar conclusion. After receiving several letters along these lines, he finally wrote Junior that "I am not prepared to [blame?] you [for] all it contains. I am always thoughtful of you and Chubbie [Julius], and I know the unreasonable statements are not yours." Garvey always replied to both sons that he was glad to hear from them and that they must stick to their studies; on one occasion, he told Junior that he was "glad to know you have taken your condition like a man." (Garveyite "men" had always symbolized ultramasculinity. They were charged to be imposing, strong, and brave warriors.) Garvey never inquired after their mother but wrote instead to "tell Grannie to look after you."[36]

Garvey sent brief letters to his sons every week, enclosing pocket change and money for school fees.[37] But this was not enough to maintain them in the fashion that Jacques Garvey deemed fit. Because Junior was sick and "needed constant care," she "could not take a full time job." It was during this period that she "took charge of [her] share of [what remained of her] father's estate and started to develop it to be revenue bearing."[38] In other words, she took advantage of an elite option and became a landlady, renting her property to generate a steady income. Jacques Garvey was developing a new attitude about her role in financially supporting her family. She had been raised in a household whose well-being was served by the father, and she had initially expected her husband—and all other black men—to do the same for their own families. In the 1920s she had been critical of black men who failed on the job, keeping black women in "Miss Ann's kitchen." But changed circumstances had forced her to rethink the role of breadwinner.

Jacques Garvey was taking on the role of breadwinner at a time when it was still uncommon for a middle-class woman to do so. During the 1938 rebellion women did not demand equal pay but only an increase in wages. This position was "a reflection of the male breadwinner ideology which was imposed on the working class."[39] Meanwhile, middle-class women continued to be consumed by and to defend an ideology that kept them relegated to the home. Even women like Amy Bailey and Una Marson steered clear of the riots and supported the men of their class in the hope of winning concessions for them. Overall, Jamaican women, regardless of class, wanted to be financially solvent, but they were not advancing themselves to become financially independent from men; therefore, Jacques Garvey's attitude can fairly be seen as a precursor to that of the later liberated woman.

With Jacques Garvey's return to Jamaica, the Garveys' marital ties completely unraveled. It was not easy for Jacques Garvey to be head of the household, especially since this time around her husband had not sanctioned it. Essentially, she had traded away a potentially higher household income and greater social acceptability with her husband for the ability to make the family's decisions and control its resources. Garvey's unwillingness to communicate with her signifies the strength of his refusal to accept what she had done. Robert Hill notes that this breach "represented the end of the last major working relationship that he [Garvey] had been able to maintain from the days of the early UNIA."[40]

The couple's political working relationship was severed by their marital problems, and their marital problems made their marital vows, particularly to "love and cherish in sickness and in health," null and void. In early January 1940 Garvey suffered a stroke, which left him partially paralyzed and affected his speech. Since he refused to go to the hospital, he was nursed by an entourage consisting of Daisy Whyte, his personal secretary; a white housekeeper; and two clerks. Jacques Garvey does not indicate that she was the least inclined to visit him in London, even though she had been informed that "with care he might have two years" to live. Two months later, when Junior's leg was out of plaster and he could walk without crutches (making it possible for him to travel without much difficulty), she nevertheless opted to send Garvey a photograph of the children instead of taking them to see him. Whyte wrote her that "tears came down his cheeks" when he saw the picture, and he "insisted on keeping it under his pillow." But Garvey's response did not soften his wife. In fact, she believed that "lying paralyzed on one side and unable to get around he now felt and understood the suffering of Junior, who might

Photograph of Marcus Jacques Garvey (right) and Julius Jacques Garvey, Jamaica, 1940. Photograph by W. G. Morais. Schomburg Center for Research in Black Culture.

have been a permanent cripple." She asked, "Did the picture of his two sons arouse his paternal instincts?"[41] Unquestionably, her bitterness about his previous lack of support was so intense that even the gravity of his illness could not alleviate it. There is little doubt that Jacques Garvey no longer saw herself as his comforter or nurturing helpmate.

Garvey dictated several letters informing his children that he was sick. Writing to both boys on 1 June 1940, he stated, "I am dropping you these few lines to let you know that I am still sick and think of you." On 9 June Whyte notified Jacques Garvey by cable that "Garvey Relapsed Sinking." He had apparently suffered another stroke or possibly cardiac arrest and died the next day. A telegram to Jacques Garvey on 11 June confirmed that she was now a widow.[42]

Strikingly, Jacques Garvey's writings offer no indication of how she felt or the reaction of her children to this news. Although they were no longer close, Marcus Garvey had been part of her life for the past twenty-one years; with him she had matured politically and emotionally. During their courtship and the early years of their marriage, she had catered to his unending needs and represented herself as the epitome of a helpmate. He had helped her realize her journalistic skills, and with his aid she had grown confident as an intellectual. When men in the UNIA were critical of her, he had publicly defended her right to occupy a leadership position in the movement. He had also understood—at least at one point—the degree to which she had suffered. In a 1925 message addressed to black people of the world, Garvey had stated that he had given everything to them and that Jacques Garvey had "suffered and sacrificed with me for you." He concluded, "I have left her penniless and helpless to face the world, because I gave all to you, but her courage is great, and I know she will hold up for you and me."[43]

They had been a leadership team, poised to direct the Pan-African cause, and they had tried to submerge their personal problems for the benefit of the movement. With the birth of their children, however, Jacques Garvey's helpmate role had shifted from her husband to her children. Garvey had difficulty adjusting to this change, and Jacques Garvey grew impatient and then bitter with what she saw as his lack of support. An intense marital tension grew between them, and by the end of Garvey's life they were not even on speaking terms. In the beginning they had brought out the best in each other, but by the end of his life their interaction unleashed venom, not camaraderie.

Ironically, Garvey's death revitalized Jacques Garvey's dedication to his ideas and her commitment to spread the UNIA's agenda. Letters from UNIA leaders assured her "that while we too have forgotten you in the past, there will be many [members] whom shall never forget you and his children, so continue to be brave, as you have always done, and for which we have always admired you." At the UNIA convention in New York City in August

1940, she gave evidence of having begun this next phase of her life, sending the following message to be read to the participants: "Through a cruel chain of circumstances I greet you as a widow, a mother of two fatherless sons, as a bereaved member of the Negro race, who has lost the active leadership of Marcus Garvey."[44]

The 1940s set the tone for the direction and intensity of Amy Jacques Garvey's renewed public commitment to the philosophy of Garveyism. By the time of her husband's death, the Universal Negro Improvement Association (UNIA) had gone through a stream of national officers, experienced countless financial setbacks, and divided along U.S. versus Caribbean lines. Jacques Garvey had witnessed the decline and divide of the UNIA, and she had watched her husband labor to keep his ideas in the forefront of the Pan-African struggle. Few leaders in the history of Pan-Africanism had been as dedicated as Marcus Garvey, but despite all of his efforts, a dwindling membership now made the future of the organization appear bleak. After his death, Jacques Garvey had to decide whether to abandon a sinking UNIA or try to help resuscitate it. This was one of many decisions that she would have to make as she grieved (in her own way) the loss of her husband.

Jacques Garvey's sorrow was undoubtedly tempered by the years they had spent living apart. Significantly, she wrote that his death left her a "bereaved member of the Negro race," not a bereaved widow, suggesting that she was no more personally affected by it than any other black person. She believed that all conscious people of African descent mourned the loss of Marcus Garvey, and she never suggested that her private pain was more intense than others who respected and loved him.[1]

In his will Garvey had requested that his body be embalmed and sent to Jamaica. (The preferred method among many people of African descent is to have the deceased buried "back home"; cremation is often rejected because of a belief in the sanctity of the body and spirit.) Case studies indicate that widows feel a sense of obligation to carry out their spouses' last wishes, especially when connected to the disposal of the body, and Jacques Garvey was no exception. Wartime hostilities, however, prevented the timely removal of Garvey's body from London, so she had no choice but to have his remains placed in a vault until the end of the war.[2]

"In the universal language of mourning," Hosea Perry writes, "the external expression is the funeral ceremony." If Jacques Garvey had attended the elaborate memorial service held for Garvey at St. Marks Methodist Episcopal Church, Harlem, on 21 July 1940, she would have experienced a real sense of his demise. The rite began with a short but colorful parade from the Garvey Club headquarters on 133d Street to the church. Under the direction of UNIA general secretary Ethel M. Collins and high chancellor Thomas W. Harvey, the program included presentations by two bishops, four priests, one judge, three attorneys, eight local UNIA presidents of Greater New York branches, students of an African philosophy club, civil leaders, and local talent. Funerals allow for closure; without them, family members can remain in a state of anxiety or limbo. Although it was unknown how long it would be before Garvey's body could be shipped home, Jacques Garvey was committed to the idea that her husband would have a public burial and that Jamaica would "be the final resting place of his body."[3]

In addition accepting the fact that Garvey would not have a timely formal funeral, Jacques Garvey had to contend with UNIA matters in the aftermath of his passing. On 28 June, just eighteen days after his death, she received a letter from Ethel M. Collins stating, "The headquarters could easily be shifted back to Jamaica where you are, along with Miss Whyte when she can get to you, and myself and Mr. Harvey could continue here [in the United States] as National Representatives and report to you." This proposal does not appear to have been echoed by anyone else in the UNIA leadership. In fact, UNIA commissioners later voiced their feeling "that it would be very cruel to place this burden" on Jacques Garvey's "shoulder," given the "death of Garvey" and her "added responsibility of taking care of the children." Just as they had in the 1920s, UNIA male leaders were still in the business of preventing legitimate power from slipping into Jacques Garvey's hands under the guise of "protecting" her. Whatever her reaction to their opinions, she elected not to take Collins up on her suggestion, thereby taking the decisive step not to become engrossed in UNIA affairs. Jacques Garvey believed that the United States was the best place for the headquarters because Garveyites there had always been the most numerous and had better access to resources. She therefore wrote letters notifying the various UNIA divisions that UNIA headquarters had been transferred from London to the United States.[4]

On 18 August 1940 UNIA delegates from the United States, the West Indies, and Canada converged on New York for an emergency meeting to discuss the future of their organization. Though she did not attend, Jacques Garvey dispatched a five-page letter outlining matters that would ultimately monopolize her attention for decades to come. Her foremost concern was that her children be able to continue their formal education, so she challenged UNIA members to support them financially in their studies. She also admonished members that "whatever you may do in your deliberations, always remember this;—You can't leave Garvey out of the U.N.I.A." Perhaps she feared that as the movement surged forward, her husband's contributions and thereby her own might vanish from the collective memory. She urged the membership not to try to fill Garvey's position "because it is not empty." Garvey gave his program to the UNIA forever, she wrote, and members need only carry out the organization's platform, which was "in a nutshell Africa for the Africans, those at home and those abroad."[5]

Moving to another political level, Jacques Garvey observed that the UNIA was now in its second stage of "quiet, penetrating work," a stage that would require a change in leadership style. She did not favor the appointment or election of another imposing, powerful, figure; nor did she propose an alternative vision, such as a collective council. Instead, she simply explained why a change needed to occur. The first stage of the movement had required Garvey to awaken "the sleeping Negro" and arouse "in him a consciousness of his potentialities as a MAN." Indeed, ideas of manhood had long been a feature of the movement. In a speech in June 1922, Garvey had stated, "Now, understand the Universal Negro Improvement Association represents a manhood program, a program of unity and love, a program of charity but we say charity begins at home."[6] Jacques Garvey now took up this mantra, but for her, manhood also served as a means to allow women to be women.

She had always argued that the socially constructed masculine attributes of breadwinner and protector of women freed women from carrying the burdens alone, thereby giving them more time to develop other pursuits as well as their "feminine" nature.

But in 1940 Jacques Garvey thought that a new approach was called for. There was "no necessity now for shouting," she argued. "The Negro is awake; he is shaking himself, and looking around. Teach him now quietly." It would be self-defeating to "let the other fellow hear [giving him leverage to manipulate] how he [the black man] is to stand firm on his two feet, get his balance and use his brains as well as his brawn to make a place for himself among the nations of the world."[7]

Garveyites responded to Jacques Garvey's communiqué by voting to give her family a monthly allowance of fifty to one hundred dollars. But they rejected the idea that another president-general was unnecessary and elected James Stewart to fill the office until the next formal convention in 1942. A leader in the tradition of Marcus Garvey, Stewart was a good writer, a captivating speaker, and headstrong in his beliefs and commitment to Pan-Africanism. He relocated the UNIA headquarters to his hometown of Cleveland, Ohio, and made Jacques Garvey's former foe, William Sherrill, the head of the UNIA's National Public Relations Committee, based in Washington, D.C.[8]

A new UNIA appeared to be on the move, and though Jacques Garvey refused to be its leader, she did want to be a part of the decision-making body. Since joining the organization in 1919, she had never been elected to an office; she claimed that she was not "desirous of being an officer" but had always functioned as a member of the executive council. Stewart, however, did not recognize, let alone take advantage of, Jacques Garvey's leadership assets. Her history with Sherrill may have been part of the problem. It was public knowledge that she had once accused Sherrill of not regarding the redemption of Africa as the UNIA's top priority; instead, she had argued, he sought to solve diasporic problems by building up "apartment houses" in America.[9] This disagreement reflected the factionalism in the movement, that of taking local versus international approaches to black problems.

Undoubtedly personal antagonisms were also at work here. Over the years, Jacques Garvey had developed a reputation for being opinionated, controlling, and uncompromising—qualities that her husband had also possessed. The Garveys' commitment to Pan-Africanism yielded, at times, similar attitudes, but though Garvey's disposition was viewed as a masculine double-edged sword (when handled with finesse, these attributes would grant him what he wanted for the movement or keep presumed enemies out of his camp), this same weapon in Jacques Garvey's hands was interpreted as nothing short of a dagger, a tool for stabbing all who got in her way. Garvey was celebrated as a man who refused to humble himself in the face of adversity, whereas Jacques Garvey was criticized as a woman with a volatile temperament who could not be subdued. Stewart's response was to keep her in the dark and to rarely solicit her ideas. Exasperated by his behavior, she later wrote, "For years I have never heard one word from that man [Stewart]."[10]

At the 1942 UNIA annual convention, Stewart was reelected president-general. Among the only surviving correspondence between him and Jacques Garvey is a letter regarding payment on Garvey's burial vault. In June 1942 Stewart had informed her that he had in his "possession funds for the renewal of the rental of the vault for the body of your late husband our Beloved leader."[11] Jacques Garvey, pleased that the organization was honoring this financial responsibility, replied with the name and address of the cemetery in London. But this spark of confidence in the UNIA was short-lived. Delegates at the August convention passed a motion that allowed Stewart to place in escrow the money collected from the divisions for the Garvey children until they reached the age of twenty-one.

After the convention, several officers informed Jacques Garvey that Stewart had used improper balloting for the election and had inappropriately spent the money collected from UNIA divisions for the vault. N. H. Grissom, commissioner of the Wisconsin Division, echoed these accusations in a letter to Jacques Garvey saying, "He [Stewart] was dead wrong in his actions, he utterly failed to come up to his own agreement with the contributions, he told each division, he would refund their donations toward this vault."[12]

Jacques Garvey became increasingly disgusted with Stewart, whom she labeled a "discredited, dishonest man"; in 1945 she wrote that it was remarkable to her "that people in the UNIA would allow themselves to be fooled by him, after he collected over $600 to pay for the Chief's vault, in 1942, and did not pay a cent of it." Her contempt was shared by Ethel Collins, who also expressed frustration with other UNIA officers. Collins wrote to Jacques Garvey that "in my speaking at all times, I speak for the support of the organization, and not individuals, and so I am misunderstood."[13] Misunderstandings, misinformation, and radically diverse opinions on how to achieve the Pan-African goal kept the UNIA swimming in a sea of dominating personalities.

With an ego of her own, Jacques Garvey complained as she distanced herself from the UNIA parent body; still, she remained closely affiliated with the original Garvey Club members in New York. Her political commitment made it nearly impossible for her to sever her ties to the UNIA altogether, despite her disrespect for Stewart and his entourage. Stewart angered Jacques Garvey so much that she eventually refused even to refer to the organization he led as the UNIA. Writing to B. Gibbons, president of the New York Garvey Club, she stated, "My reason for using A.C.L. [African Communities League] alone, was because of Stewart, I did not want him to say that I influenced divisions to forsake him, so I ignored him, and let him fade out."[14]

As she grew tired of her antagonistic relationships with the male leadership, Jacques Garvey began to consider her prospects for affiliating with the UNIA and ultimately the Pan-African cause in a different way. Philosophically, she began to view the UNIA as a collection of sects, making it an inadequate political vehicle; but its business antics and nepotism did not seem unusual, and she felt there was little guarantee that she would find a better organizational home elsewhere. Finally, she decided to strike out on her own. To ensure that she would not be stifled by others, she created "Garvey's African Communities League" with the objective of bringing "cultural and ethical development to people of African Descent" and named herself "Successor and Director of All Allied Garvey Associations and Societies."[15] Under this banner she was able to function independently even though the group she envisioned never fully materialized.

Although Jacques Garvey had made it clear that she did not want to lead the UNIA, by 1944 she was identifying herself as Marcus Garvey's natural "successor." A spiritual connection with her late husband had redefined her attachment to him and his ideas and had in turn engendered her political rebirth. Four years after Garvey's death, she now felt the need to "relay what M. G., our Chief, has thro words, and spiritual contact, told me to do and say."[16] J. Bowlby's scholarship on the processes of mourning points out that the last phase of "healthy mourning" results in the achievement of a different relationship with the "lost loved one, in which, through identification, the griever continues to carry out the goals and ideas attributed to the lost loved one." Jacques Garvey felt that she had a continuing relationship with her dead husband, and she was committed to fulfilling the goals that he "channeled" to her. Intimacy with Garvey's spirit increased his emotional importance in her life. She would explain his intervention with phrases like "the chief is worrying me to have it done" or "he appeared to me in a dream recently, and urged me to go forward."[17]

For Jacques Garvey, moving forward meant integrating "Garveyism into the folds of organizations, groups, etc." In 1944 she wrote, "My work of the last six months is to get Leaders of thought and action through all the different agencies of expression that modern man uses, to understand Garveyism—which as you know is Nationalism, by stages of course, for all people of African blood." The work of Marcus Garvey had "outgrown the limited capacity of one Organization"; thus, she was no longer concerned about membership affiliation or making every person of African descent an active member of the UNIA. To drive home her point, Jacques Garvey informed Wyalt Dougherty, representative of the Union of People of African Descent, based in Washington, D.C., that her "policy since the death of [my] husband, is that groups can travel along different roads, and work according to their own fashion, and liking, as long as there is an awareness and appreciation of each other's work—but all having the same goal and strengthened and inspired thereby."[18]

Retreating from confrontational dialogue, Jacques Garvey wrote countless letters to Garvey's friends and foes to meet her new objective. No longer exclusively rooted in the UNIA, she became more effective as a team player—a move that signaled the beginning of her transformation into an organizational woman for the Pan-African movement.

It may seem somewhat ironic to call Jacques Garvey an organizational woman at this time, given that she had never been so far removed from the inner workings of the UNIA and that her own organization, Garvey's African Communities League, was supported primarily by a few members from the Garvey Club in New York. But by calling her a team player, I mean to underscore the fact that she was most effective when not consumed by defending her right to be a political player; thus, her decision not to "bottle up Garveyism in one or two organizations" also freed her to view former competitors as comrades in the Pan-African struggle.[19]

The execution of Jacques Garvey's new agenda required forming a coalition from the different Pan-African groups. As she explained to A. Philip Randolph, president of the Brotherhood of Sleeping Car Porters, "when there is no unity . . . we both lose precious time ridiculing each other, we become loud-mouthed trying to convince each other that 'I should not be dictated to.'" Emphasizing how enemies of the Pan-African cause relished their disharmony, she stated that they "chuckle" and say "they will never unite, so I will get them one by one." By "unity" Jacques Garvey did not mean "conformity of effort." In fact, she rather welcomed "diversity of effort, as we respectively cover much more ground, in our different journey to the focal point."[20]

Once she had committed herself to the goal of unifying a dispersed and divergent movement, Jacques Garvey began to assay the political terrain. She concluded that the Atlantic Charter, the joint declaration of peace issued by President Franklin D. Roosevelt and Prime Minister Winston Churchill on 14 August 1941, required an intellectual critique. The charter was a military alliance, an expression of Anglo-American solidarity against the domination by conquest "upon which the Hitlerite government of Germany and other governments associated therewith [i.e., Japan]" had embarked. To secure a better future for the world, the charter stipulated that nations would not seek territories nor make territorial changes without the freely expressed wishes of the inhabitants concerned, the right to self-determination and self-government, collaboration among nations for social and economic security, and freedom from fear that follows the defeated enemy and the disarmament of the aggressors' nations. Issued as a press release, the Atlantic Charter provided no specific plan of how to translate this lofty rhetoric into political reality. Roosevelt later conceded that the charter was essentially a "beautiful idea"; the British needed hope because they were losing the war, and the charter "gave it to them."[21]

On 1 January 1942 representatives of twenty-six nations, led by the United States, Great Britain, the Soviet Union, and China, endorsed this important document. They signed a Declaration by United Nations that became the first landmark document in the evolution of the "United Nations" (a term coined by Roosevelt). Diplomatic relations took a decisive turn as countries began positioning themselves to align with the United Nations in order to receive protection and postwar consideration, particularly material assistance from the United States and Great Britain. Even James Ford, national committee member of the Communist Party, agreed that "a world-shaking realignment of forces is taking place." This "unity of forces on a world scale to wipe fascism from the face of the earth" could serve as a means to "develop a path for freedom and democracy for peoples throughout the world," he predicted.[22]

The intellectual and political significance of the Atlantic Charter, as well as its propaganda value, was driven home to Jacques Garvey by Eleanor Roosevelt, who arrived in Jamaica on 9 March 1944 for a two-day visit as part of a three-week goodwill tour of the U.S. bases in the Caribbean and Latin America. In a letter to Adam Clayton Powell Jr., Jacques Garvey described Mrs. Roosevelt's press conference, in which Jacques Garvey gave her "impression" of the charter as a "fine Declaration of faith, whose importance can be real" when the points are implemented and "applied to all the peoples of the world." While praising its possibilities,

Jacques Garvey was careful to note that the charter primarily concerned the "oppressed nations of Europe."[23]

Comments by both Roosevelt and Churchill confirmed Jacques Garvey's assessment of the charter as Eurocentric. Roosevelt had indicated that his "sole purpose" in drafting it was to "save French Africa" from "laws passed in France under German pressure." Defeating the Germans in North Africa was clearly his goal, even though the French resisted the Allied invasion. To placate the French, Roosevelt gave a radio message assuring them that the United States had "no desire to take over any of her territory and that, at the end of the war, whatever we were obliged to invade, we would return to them."[24]

Churchill, on the other hand, saw the Africa invasion as just the beginning; he told Roosevelt: "If all goes well . . . we might control the whole North African shore . . . thus saving some of the masses of shipping now rounding the Cape. This is our first great prize." Never did either Churchill or Roosevelt want to free Africans from colonizers, despite the charter's declaration to "see sovereign rights and self government restored to those who have been forcibly deprived of them." In fact, Churchill made it abundantly clear that the charter should not be applied everywhere. For example, he stated that "[i]n the Middle East the Arabs might claim by majority they could expel the Jews from Palestine, or at any time forbid all further immigration. I am strongly wedded to the Zionist policy, of which I was one of the authors."[25]

The Atlantic Charter's major racist shortcoming became the catalyst for Jacques Garvey's first project to popularize "materially" the work of Pan-African organizations. Determined to move beyond symbolic gestures, she conceptualized a "collective" writing of memorandums to inform the United Nations of Pan-Africanist demands.[26] She introduced her idea through a personal letter-writing campaign to leaders in the fight against racial injustice.

One man whom Jacques Garvey targeted was Adam Clayton Powell Jr. As one of the editors of Harlem's *People's Voice*, Powell had held a mass "symposium for the one billion people of the darker races" in the newspaper's 28 March 1942 edition. Identifying himself as a speaker "on behalf of free Negroes of the Western Hemisphere," he also pushed for a free Africa, India, and China. Both a preacher and a politician, Powell had a diverse base of supporters, whom he represented through the Abyssinian Baptist Church in Harlem and the People's Committee, a militant protest organization in Harlem aimed at economic empowerment and political equality with the slogan "One People, One Fight, One Victory."[27] An ambitious community leader, Powell was "perceived as one who would stand up to the authorities and not equivocate"; he was the kind of man whom Jacques Garvey would want on her team. Powell was busy solidifying support for his bid for Congress when he received her letter, but he took the time to reply that he wanted to support her efforts "to bring to pass the complete freedom of Africa and Africans." He assured her that he "shall with a few friends try to put forward a program which will meet with your approval."[28]

Jacques Garvey notified a host of other activists to give them detailed instructions on what their individual memorandums to the United Nation should include. For instance, she told Powell to "have a committee draw up a Memorandum proposing an African Freedom Charter, applicable to Africans in Africa, abroad, and all peoples of African descent (whether 100% or 1%)." (Acknowledging mixed-race peoples but unwilling to split hairs, Jacques Garvey continued to repeat the North American "one drop" rule of African identification; for her, however, it was a means of inclusion, not exclusion.) The memorandums would be the first step in writing a new charter that would "restore to them [African people] their manhood rights, by declaring for them the following Six Freedoms—Economically, Socially, Educationally, Politically, Spiritually and Morally." These freedoms were the only way that African people could completely determine their own destiny.[29]

Powell's memorandum, Jacques Garvey suggested, should start with a preamble that referred to past and present contributions of Africans to civilization. Another paragraph should detail the Six Freedoms, and the closing one should show "the natural consequences of the continued denial of manhood rights, because of color, to peoples enlightened by the pressing needs of war, and ironically by pressing needs of peace too." Jacques Garvey indicated the "lines on which the Memorandum should be drawn" and "what international action we want taken." When she commissioned Nnamdi Azikiwe, director of the *West African Pilot*, a black nationalist newspaper published in Lagos, Nigeria, to write *The West African Press Delegation Memorandum*, she asked that he emphasize self-government in Gambia, Sierra Leone, the Gold Coast, and North and South Nigeria, as well as survey the import and export situation with suggestions for government improvement.[30]

Each contact was charged to write a memorandum "in their own wording." This approach, Jacques Garvey hoped, would make "the representation more universal, and not stereotyped." She assured her contacts that "our international plan will not interfere with local efforts to relieve local conditions; but rather strengthen all local efforts."[31]

As a burgeoning organizational woman, Jacques Garvey became more conscious of collective input and approval; thus, she told her contacts to make sure that they "put the resolution to the meeting [of their constituency], and have it seconded and carried." It was only then that the memorandum could be forwarded to President Roosevelt, Prime Minister Churchill, Premier Stalin of Russia, and General Chiang Kaishek of China. Correct in her assessment of who constituted the United Nations heavyweights, Jacques Garvey argued that these men were "the Architects of our Fate in a world, under demolition and reconstruction." More radical activists like Claudia Jones, representative of the Young Communist League, however, refused to accept this premise; she stated, "While pretending to be fighting for the rights of small nations for democracy, the British ruler denies to its colonies the most elementary democratic rights."[32] It is hard to imagine that Jacques Garvey would take issue with Jones's statement, but seemingly she was so exhilarated by the possibilities of the period that she believed that it was important to appeal to powerful men like Churchill.

Self-government was an explosive topic among Pan-Africanists. Keith Byerman has shown that one of the common assumptions that frequently shaped this discourse was that "Africans were incapable of achieving the standards of modern civilization on their own." Reform of colonial practices and immigration to the continent were solutions that Garvey had pushed and that Jacques Garvey was trying to move beyond—although not as forthrightly as Claudia Jones, who questioned whether it was better for African people to support British imperialism in the conflict when compared to their status under German rule. Jones believed that this argument was "dangerous because it is a vicious acceptance of the status of Negroes as inferiors, who must be ruled, regardless." Jacques Garvey took the most popular, intermediate stance in this debate. Although she did not want to simply substitute "masters" of African peoples, she did feel that the process to end colonialism should not be abrupt and the West African memorandum should reflect this. In the end, the completed document requested "self-government within the British Commonwealth, by stages of course, being ten years of Representative government, and five years of Responsible government, internally independent and then dominion status."[33]

When Dr. Harold Moody, a Jamaican physician and chairman of the London Missionary Society, became aware of the multiple memorandums, he asked Jacques Garvey for a single, summary document that could be presented at a July 1944 conference on Africa. Impressed by Moody's determination to "do something which would be of positive and permanent value to Africa," she mentioned his plan to W. E. B. Du Bois, stating, "He warrants your encouragement and suggestions." When Du Bois pledged his support, Jacques Garvey became even more excited about the vast possibilities of the conference.[34]

In response to Moody's request, Jacques Garvey labored to complete a comprehensive document as if Marcus Garvey himself had ordered it. "The Chief's Spirit drives me on," she said. "I must obey it, it directs me in all I write, say or do." Though she lacked the funds to pay a research assistant and her fingers were sore because she could not afford a typist, she pressed on. She did most of the work "in bed, propped up, and finally [I] had to summon God's aid to strengthen me, as I had to do all the typing myself." Four months later, she informed New York Garvey Club president Gibbons that she had "just completed the Memorandum Correlative of Africa, the West Indies and the Americas" for the July meeting. Proud of her accomplishment, she declared that "it is the only work of its kind done by a member of my race, and I have done same under great handicaps."[35]

Addressing the *Memorandum Correlative of Africa, the West Indies, and the Americas* to the United Nations representatives, she wrote that African peoples should be able to "share, as Partners, in this post-war Democracy, [as] our centuries of blood, sweat, and tears, [have] contribut[ed] to humanity's comfort and happiness." An analysis of the loopholes in the Atlantic Charter and an appeal for an international African Freedom Charter and Council represent the heart and soul of the memorandum:

As millions of men of African blood, cheerfully give their lives in the globular war, in answer to the call of the United Nations, to help save the world for Democracy, in like manner, we call on the United Nations—for the sake of Democracy to save Africans from the hands of saboteurs of justice by declaring for an African Freedom Charter which will give Africa and all peoples of African descent, everywhere, their share of Democracy—in principle and in fact—and free all of them from their present disabilities—economically, socially, educationally, politically, spiritually, and morally.[36]

Jacques Garvey described this text as a "sacred document" that elevated Pan-African discourse to new heights. Since she freely admitted that she was unable to keep up with the activities of African Americans due to the "dearth of American reading matter" in Jamaica, she was no doubt unaware of Roi Ottley's *New World a-Coming* (1943) and W. E. B. Du Bois's *Color and Democracy* (1945) (even though she was corresponding with Du Bois), books that also analyzed the Pan-African world.[37] Her sixty-six-page document is a somewhat miniature version of these works, as well as of a host of others that appeared during World War II. It also stands as a testament to the fact that she was intellectually grounded in a set of concepts that resonated in the diasporic intellectual community of the time while simultaneously raising the debate to another level.

Like Ottley, Jacques Garvey offered a study of black nationalism and the contributions of Africans to world development, celebrating what Ottley described as the "Negro's aggressive attitude" that took center stage during the war. "Negroes want tangible assurances that the loud talk of democracy is in fact meant to include them," he wrote. Jacques Garvey would add that "this is why the Africans at home, like his kin abroad, fight and die willingly. They feel that their human and material sacrifices, are the means of laying the foundation of a better world, in which, in their respective habitats, they will be able to live as free men—unhampered and unexploited." And, like Du Bois, Jacques Garvey offered a scientific glance at the real-world contributions (size, location, terrain, population ratio, crops produced, and colonial imperialism) of Africa and the West Indies largely based on statistics compiled from the *World Almanac*. Du Bois had asserted that "COLONIES AND THE COLONIAL SYSTEM MAKE THE COLONIAL PEOPLES IN A SENSE THE SLUMS OF THE WORLD, DISFRANCHISED AND HELD IN POVERTY AND DISEASE." Jacques Garvey expounded on this idea by noting that Africans in the New World "work and suffer, under similar disabilities as are imposed on Africans in Africa. Briefly it is this. . . . No black man, carrying either a British or American passport, is given the recognition, and accorded the same privileges, as a white man with similar passport."[38]

Jacques Garvey not only echoed but also moved beyond the works of Ottley and Du Bois by omitting any personal material in the summarized *Memorandum Correlative*. When she had written her "Impression" series for the *Negro World* in the 1920s, her firsthand observations had been the basis for a portrait of Jim Crow America; during her European tour, she also wrote of her own experiences. By removing herself from this document, she ensured that her analysis of the facts would not be muddled by personal stories that could easily be disputed or singled out as an aberration. Her decision to exclude her personal reflections was not an indication that she no longer viewed herself as an authority on the Pan-African world but represented an attempt to make the *Memorandum* an authoritative document rather than a commonplace memoir.

Most significant, though, was Jacques Garvey's reluctance to use the word "Negro" in the document. In a letter to Du Bois she explained that he "*must avoid* any reference to the word Negro. Regardless what white Scientists say, in order to have the hearty cooperation of all, and we will, we must not use the word. To the mind of the African it is synonymous with slavery, serfdom, it is just as if it were spelt with two g's." Continuing, she argued that "White America has abused the word 'Negro,' its reference means a low person to be kicked about. No, don't use it. Except where an Organization bears the name. That is why M. G. later organized the A[f]rican Communities' League." Correct in her assertion that whites tended to associate negative images with "Negroes," Jacques Garvey's analysis was later rearticulated by Black Power advocates, such as Stokely Carmichael and Charles Hamilton, in the 1960s. Du Bois, however, never responded to her suggestion and in later writings continued to use the word "Negro," balanced with the word "black." Essentially, Du Bois's position was that "if men despise Negroes, they will not despise them less if Negroes are called 'colored' or 'Afro-Americans.' "[39]

In her sensitivity to the ways in which language can shape and stifle political options, Jacques Garvey was far ahead of her peers. For her it was not just a matter of what others thought of her race, but of what people of African descent thought of themselves. Only in recent years have scholars investigated how "the control of language and the terms we adopt take on enormous political significance," influencing the way we think about our political situation. "Indeed, language can be viewed as essentially political," Ruth Grant and Marion Orr have shown, since "language necessarily reflects, reinforces and reproduces the power relations within every society."[40]

"Africa for the Africans, at home and abroad" had been Marcus Garvey's motto, and he had been extremely conscientious about language and identity. He capitalized and used the word "Negro" at a time when most of the African diaspora still preferred the term "colored." During the two world wars "Negro" had gained predominance in America, but Jacques Garvey now rejected it, preferring instead "Africans or people of African decent [*sic*]." Her shift from race to "ethnicity" and "culture" as the defining characteristic of the group evoked not only similarities that moved beyond the "cuss of color," but also the importance of homeland for a homeless diaspora.[41]

The idea of connectedness, as opposed to that of displacement, rooted Jacques Garvey's identity concerns in an imagined "African" community. As Paul Gilroy convincingly argues, "The need to locate cultural or ethnic roots and then to use the idea of being in touch with them as a means to refigure the cartography of dispersal and exile is perhaps best understood as a simple and direct response to the varieties of racism which have denied the historical character of black experience and the integrity of black culture."[42] Unity was her call, and emphasizing one Africa was a means to combat the borders and fragmentation that had weakened the Pan-African world.

The last section of the *Memorandum Correlative* provided an overview of race issues in the United States, describing Jim Crow and its armed forces. The document concluded with the Greater Liberian Bill (also known as Bilbo's Bill), a "Freedom for All" appeal to the United Nations, and Marcus Garvey's hymn. In essence, the *Memorandum Correlative* explained the aims of "African-Nationalism,—just what each territory wants, its potentialities, and the ambitions of our people to have political freedom and economic independence."[43] This document, among its other reasons for being of historical interest, is compelling evidence that Jacques Garvey deserves a place among the intellectual leaders of the movement to empower Africa and Africans.

Once her comprehensive memorandum was drafted, Jacques Garvey enlisted the New York Garvey Club to print it. "As you know I cannot print it here [in Jamaica], not even a simple letter," she wrote to club president Gibbons. She was "powerless at this end to do anything financially, I have made my full contributions, by doing all the work, in a sick state of body, and grieved state of mind."[44] Making it clear to others that she had done her part was not just about tooting her own horn, but about her conviction that everyone should participate on some level. The club was her only organizational base, and she believed that together they could complete this difficult task if they followed her instructions. Her plain but meticulous directive left no room for error and was reminiscent of the orders that she had received from her husband over the years. "When you get the Memorandum from me, you must not show it around," Jacques Garvey explained. "Keep it safely, until the printer gets it." Always willing to share ideas, she did not fear that others might lay claim to the fruits of her scholarship, but she did not want the document to get bogged down while a variety of organizations decided whether to approve it. If it were subjected to that sort of review, she predicted, the memorandum "would have been going around and creating controversy until the next war comes and would not be ratified." "Not one word is to be changed"; she wanted to do "all the proof reading, when you send me a proof, and it must be registered." She also wished to print the document in the form of a "booklet, 6 by 9 inches, sewn in the center with cloth cover." "A whole Race's welfare is depending on the speed with which you can have same printed," she emphasized. And in case that was not enough to galvanize the club members, she added a warning meant to strike a chord of fear: "Don't fail, or God will fail you."[45] No longer having the wrath of Marcus Garvey on her side, Jacques Garvey reminded her compatriots that they must answer to a higher power if her expectations were not met.

Such dramatic language is featured throughout Jacques Garvey's writings, and it undoubtedly added a sense of urgency to her correspondence. Confidentially, though, she told Nnamdi Azikiwe that she "never for a moment believed that our Memorandum of Demands, because of its rectitude, would bring moral adjustments." Nevertheless, it was essential that "we present our demands and suggest means of rectification, when world readjustments were under consideration." Otherwise, "our omission would be used as a plausible excuse, for unfair adjustments against us, on their plea of ignorance of our desires and ambitions, therefore innocence of guilt on their part."[46]

Once they received it, the Garvey Club members critiqued the *Memorandum Correlative* and particularly questioned the inclusion of Mississippi senator Theodore G. Bilbo's Greater Liberian Bill, introduced in 1938 and 1939 to assist African Americans with volunteer repatriations to West Africa. Marcus Garvey had enthusiastically supported the bill, for which UNIA members had collected over 50,000 signatures.[47] Since Garvey's death, Jacques Garvey had written three letters to Bilbo regarding his bill, because she believed that it would be important for years to come. She wanted to include a copy of it in the *Memorandum* so readers would have a chance to "make suggestions to the Bill, before it is re-introduced" in Congress. Bilbo indicated that the war had hampered efforts to pass the bill, which "asked for million of dollars," but he promised to continue working for its passage. Changing times, however, had caused fellow

Garveyites, some of whom had initially supported the bill, to have a change of heart. James A. Blades, on behalf of the Garvey Club, wrote to Jacques Garvey that "the name Bilbo stands out in the minds of American blacks with the worse elements of Southern thought and action." Therefore, "To ask the race in the United States to accept anything coming from Bilbo as having any possible good, is sheer madness. . . . As a good Christian, would you accept a plan from the devil as to how you may get to heaven?" How could the Garvey Club "sponsor a program, which in the American black man's mind will come straight from the master of Hades himself?"[48]

This was not the first time that Jacques Garvey had bumped heads with Garveyites over the charge that she was colluding with racists. For example, at one point she had corresponded with Ernest Cox, a representative of the White American Society, an organization that condemned miscegenation and advocated the colonization of African Americans and the superiority of the white race. Cox and Marcus Garvey had had extensive contact, and occasionally Cox addressed UNIA meetings during which Garvey told members to read his works, *White America* (1923) and *Let My People Go* (1925). For Jacques Garvey, maintaining a relationship with Cox was a purely political matter. She reasoned that "Mr. Cox is a white man, and an exponent of 'White America,' but his ideal of race purity appeals to us, as we also do not want to use miscegenation to solve our Race problem in the U.S.A." She saw nothing wrong with seeking his assistance in obtaining support for the Greater Liberian Bill. But when N. H. Grissom, commissioner of the Wisconsin UNIA Division, learned of Jacques Garvey's discussions with Cox, he told her that the UNIA belongs to "Negroes in the world, not whites and as long as you shall solicit white support—you are deadly wrong and I am opposed to any effort on your part in this direction."[49]

Initially, Jacques Garvey responded to this criticism by stating that whites who agreed with the Pan-African agenda should be used for political leverage and their access to resources. Garvey had always lined up with whites who supported his agenda, and Jacques Garvey had supported the activities of white English women who were married to Africans in London. Unlike Garvey, though, she had learned to back away from an unpopular decision. When she received a letter from Gibbons "regarding the rabid, rude attitude of the Senator [Bilbo]" and containing his suggestion "that we exclude same from the pamphlet," she "gladly acted on" his request.[50] Adjusting the *Memorandum Correlative* to exclude the bill was another example of Jacques Garvey's political rebirth and newfound ability to function as a true organizational woman who was willing to listen to and incorporate the opinions of others.

After the removal of the bill from the *Memorandum* had been agreed upon, the Garvey Club members began production. Out of frustration with the situation, Gibbons informed Jacques Garvey that "we didn't want to burden you with matters we felt we must put through. The total cost of printing the Memos and 3000 pamphlets is $515 approximately. . . . [W]e have paid on account $205.00 which leaves a balance of $310." In addition, "production [by] the printer cannot be guaranteed, due to the war." It was important to Gibbons that Jacques Garvey understand that the club members were not complaining about their assignment but "simply feel that you should know." This report of a financial shortfall must have reminded Jacques Garvey of the many conversations she had had with her husband regarding financing publications. Experience had made her sensitive to these difficulties, especially since she was the one who usually handled the logistics. She responded to Gibbons that "re cost of printing, I see where you have done your very best, under the circumstances." She told him to use good judgment in deciding whether to sell the pamphlets at $1.00 or $0.75, "seeing that we have to give away so many to High Officials of governments etc."[51]

The individual memorandums were part of "our world-wide representations" to world leaders questioning the "depth and breadth of the Atlantic Charter" and fostering a "something must be done attitude in our favor." With the *Memorandum Correlative* finally approved, Jacques Garvey continued to enlist others in her sustained effort to introduce international reforms. She was especially determined to engage the assistance of W. E. B. Du Bois, crediting his "calm, calculating judgement . . . and knowledge of international affairs." Though Du Bois's leadership had been somewhat eclipsed by younger African Americans like A. Philip Randolph and Adam Clayton Powell Jr., Jacques Garvey still viewed him as an ardent race man. Nevertheless, her willingness to reach out to Du Bois meant overlooking his past criticism of Marcus Garvey. An outspoken enemy of Garvey's, Du Bois in 1924 had written that Garvey was either "a lunatic or a traitor" and without doubt "the most dangerous enemy of the Negro race in America and in the world." During the mail fraud trial, Du Bois had observed that Garvey had convicted himself with "his swaggering monkey-shines in the court room."[52]

But much had happened to Du Bois in the intervening years. He had been forced into retirement from his teaching position at Atlanta University in 1944, and he was on the verge of returning to the National Association for the Advancement of Colored People (NAACP) that spring as director of special research, a title that loosely translated into minister of foreign affairs. This was a perfect post for Du Bois, who had by then traveled to most European countries, Asia, Africa, and the West Indies. He wrote that "contacts with foreign peoples and foreign problems and the combination of these problems with the race problem here [in the United States] was forced into one line of thought by the Second World War." These conditions, Gerald Horne has shown, helped strengthen Du Bois's conviction to "meld the NAACP with the Pan-African movement" and ultimately "devote the rest of his life" to "the liberation of Africa and world peace."[53]

By 1944 the differences that Du Bois had had with Garvey were water under the bridge, and he was more than willing to "cooperate" with Garvey's widow "in any possible way."[54] For her part, Jacques Garvey had told Du Bois that "personal feelings must be forgotten in the Unity of effort that is being forged for Africa." As activists on the same political stage, they were both stimulated by the exigencies of World War II and ever more committed to international questions of diasporic racism and colonial exploitation of Africa. Recognizing the demands placed on Du Bois, who was now seventy-five years old and highly selective about his political undertakings, Jacques Garvey returned to a theme from her earlier community feminism. She wrote Du Bois that she wished that she knew his wife personally, because she "would try to get her busy, making you see what a fine opportunity presents itself" for "*international Service*," by writing a memorandum. Always believing that wives had an inordinate amount of influence over their husbands, Jacques Garvey was unaware that Du Bois had initially been attracted and "held" to his wife, Nina Gomer, because of her "rare beauty and excellent household training." Mrs. Du Bois appreciated his work, but he thought that she was too "busy to share [in it] because of cooking, marketing, sweeping and cleaning and the endless demands of children." When his wife suffered a cerebral hemorrhage in 1945, Du Bois wrote a family friend that he believed it had been brought on because she "worked so hard cleaning and washing."[55]

No stranger to household obligations herself, Jacques Garvey told Du Bois that she was able to "combine housework, the support of my boys, and my work for my Race." Since the early days of the Garvey movement, she had juggled multiple responsibilities and she inaccurately assumed, perhaps, that this was the lifestyle of other women married to prominent leaders. All wives of race men were drawn into the movement, Jacques Garvey believed; thus, she just could not imagine that Du Bois had an apolitical wife. Nevertheless, she also knew the costs wives and families sometimes had to pay: "I know that Mdme DuBois, has many a time been sacrificed on the altar of *Service to Race*."[56] Whatever the reasons—her inability to fully recover from the death of their firstborn was undoubtedly a major factor—Mrs. Du Bois was not a part of the helpmate tradition that Jacques Garvey had advocated over the years. It was not until after the death of his wife in 1950 and his marriage to writer, artist, and longtime friend, Shirley Graham, that Du Bois would find a political partner.

Du Bois's attention to Jacques Garvey's *Memorandum* request was sidetracked by his need to prepare for the first session of the United Nations Conference, scheduled to be held in San Francisco in May–June 1945. Black desegregationalists and Pan-Africanists alike believed that a collective black agenda could galvanize anticolonial forces at the meeting, whose overall purpose was to build an international organization to maintain peace and security worldwide. At Du Bois's suggestion, the NAACP had sent telegrams to an array of African American organizations (labor and community groups and clubs) soliciting their views on what should be included in their platform. Armed with a cadre of ideas, the African Americans attending the conference had high hopes for the session. Jacques Garvey was also excited and had predicted to Adam Clayton Powell Jr. that "the United States of America, the greatest Democracy in the world, and as such, still keeps up a yearly record of lynchings of her dark skinned citizens, will not blush to give us" a vote for decolonization. Unfortunately, their hopes were quickly replaced with frustration. The delegation was led by President Harry S. Truman and the inexperienced secretary of state Edward R. Stettinius Jr. NAACP leader Walter White was stunned when Stettinius announced that the American delegation had "decided neither to introduce nor support a human rights declaration as an integral part of the charter which the nations had gathered to draft." The secretary's lack of "bold moral leadership," White points out, caused the United States to lose political influence.[57]

Though disappointed in the stands taken by the U.S. delegates, Jacques Garvey was impressed by the progressive positions on racism and colonialism embraced by representatives from Russia and China. Earlier she had anticipated that "China being a Colored Race, just emerging from racial abasement will cast her vote for us" and that Russia's "sixteen States, made up of one hundred and seventy two different races, cultures, and creeds, [and now being] autonomous Republics, free to develop, along their own culture and racial lines—will certainly give us number two vote." Rupert Lewis points out that although Jacques Garvey's "formulation" was inaccurate, she recognized "the fundamental fact that natural and racial oppression had been uprooted in the USSR. She did not fall into the narrow anti-communist outlook of so many Nationalists who claim to be Garveyites."[58]

The African American "consultants"—including W. E. B. Du Bois and Mary McLeod Bethune, in addition to delegates from Haiti, Liberia, and Ethiopia—did their best to pressure the body to address political repression in Nigeria, Sierra Leone, South Africa, and the Rhodesias but were unsuccessful.[59] In the end, all were disappointed by the failure of the conference to place all colonial possessions under United Nations trusteeship, which would have guaranteed a path to independence.[60] Yet anticolonial lobbying at this meeting did permit another benefit: intimate and personal interactions among the various delegates. Jacques Garvey missed out on this because she was absent—Jamaica did not send a delegation to the meeting. At times like this—and especially during pivotal negotiations—living on the island exacerbated her feelings of isolation. This is why she put so much effort into stimulating a discourse—and a forum for it—that she could participate in from her home. Though her locale often positioned her outside important Pan-African conversations, her cosmopolitan thinking and dedication to the cause of black empowerment made her just as astute as other anticolonial stalwarts.

By July 1945 the *Memorandum Correlative* had been printed, and the next order of business was to make it available to the public. While Marcus Garvey was in prison, he had instructed his wife to send copies of *Philosophy and Opinions* and his pardon materials to ambassadors, consuls, and a host of American leaders. Having witnessed the power of mass distribution, she wanted nothing less for the *Memorandum*. As an organizational woman with only one solid base of support—the Garvey Club of New York—Jacques Garvey once again aggressively pushed for its assistance. She encouraged club secretary Alice Allman to "co-operate with others in selling the Memorandum books, which were piled up at the back of the office, so that the persons who loaned the moneys can get some back. I think they could be sold at street meetings and at halls and churches." Allman responded that the club had sent several hundred copies to UNIA divisions but had "not received any word on how the sales are going as yet, when we do we will be glad to tell you." Evidence that the *Memorandum Correlative* was falling into the hands of intended parties finally appeared when Jacques Garvey received a note from Ambassador Guillermo Belt of Cuba indicating that he had obtained her document by mail and looked "forward with great interest to reading the Memorandum."[61]

The *Memorandum* was just the beginning of Jacques Garvey's renewed dedication to the Pan-African cause. Ironically, the death of her husband had reinvigorated her political commitment, and as she grew more confident in her leadership abilities and conversant as an intellectual on Pan-African affairs, she began once again to write essays and editorials, as she had done for the *Negro World* some twenty years earlier. This intellectual work in turn strengthened her analysis of Pan-Africanism as an ideology and sharpened her understanding of how to put it into practice. Therefore, when the Fifth Pan-African Congress opened in Manchester, England, in October 1945, she was well suited to serve as its convenor.

Amy Jacques Garvey's political rebirth depended on her ability to destabilize and navigate established chauvinistic politics. The depth of her commitment and her sustained political efforts are revealed by her role in organizing the Fifth Pan-African Congress, held in Manchester, England, in October 1945. The four previous congresses (1919, 1921, 1923, 1927) all had been structured around the struggle against imperialistic political, economic, and territorial domination. Initially, the congresses were a by-product of a movement begun by Trinidadian lawyer Henry Sylvester Williams in 1900 and revived by W. E. B. Du Bois. Over the years the congresses had been hampered by minimal African and working-class participation, but the 1945 meeting was attended by several young African leaders (Kwame Nkrumah, Nnamdi Azikiwe, and Jomo Kenyatta) as well as working-class delegates, many of whom had attended the World Trade Union Conference in France just days before. The result was the most powerful gathering of Africans and peoples of African descent ever assembled, all working together to defeat imperialism.

W. E. B. Du Bois, by this time affectionately known as the "father of Pan-Africanism," had proposed this fifth meeting. After she had asked him to write a "one-man Memorandum," Du Bois had requested that Jacques Garvey serve as co-convener. For most of her political life, Jacques Garvey had struggled to have her ideas taken seriously by her peers. Often she found herself at the center of activities but, ironically, at the same time on the margins of the decision-making body. Du Bois's proposal, and even more significantly the fact that he wanted her "reaction and suggestions" to an enclosed draft letter to call the congress after the war, signaled that she was finally being included among the vanguard.[1]

Excited about the prospective meeting, Jacques Garvey believed that Du Bois's "esteem [for] and confidence" in her would "be helpful to those whom we serve, and in turn our collaboration will encourage others to submerge personalities and close ranks for the common weal."[2] Her close working relationship with Du Bois at this time demonstrates just how far both of them had come from their bitter disputes of the 1920s. For example, during the Second Pan-African Congress (1921), which paralleled the heyday of the Universal Negro Improvement Association (UNIA), Du Bois was annoyed when the press confused the congress with the UNIA, which he superciliously characterized as a "people's movement rather than a movement of intellectuals." The Garveys' determination to bring together Africans the world over was laudable, but the UNIA's weakness, Du Bois wrote, "lay in its demagogic leadership, its intemperate propaganda, and the natural fear which it threw into the colonial powers."[3]

Although time had transformed Du Bois and Jacques Garvey's hostile relationship, Du Bois was still squeamish about instilling revolutionary "fear" in colonists. The goal of the Fifth Congress, he wrote, "shall be for consultation and information," to set "before the world the needs of African Negroes and of their descendants overseas." He made it clear that "no political changes in relation between colonies and mother countries will necessarily be contemplated except in cases where it is evident that no freedom of development is possible under present circumstances." However, George Padmore, chairman of the International African Service Bureau, who was joint secretary (with Du Bois) of the congress and its planning mastermind, spoke with a different voice. He informed Du Bois that the Provisional Committee in London had "every reason to believe that there will be unanimous agreement upon the fundamental aims and objects" of the congress. These were, simply stated, that "political consciousness naturally assumes the form of National liberation, self-determination, self-government—call it what you may. They [Africans] want to be able to rule their own countries."[4]

On this point Jacques Garvey's thinking was closer to Padmore's; she was also ambivalent about Du Bois's "thin" intentions, believing that the "broadest objective should be stated and nothing more." Her two lengthy letters, written two days apart, further critiqued Du Bois's draft letter. As the only proposed female co-convener, she joined an impressive entourage: Du Bois; Dr. Harold Moody, president of the League of Colored People and former president of the London Missionary Society; Paul Robeson, chairman of the Council of African Affairs; and Max Yergan, executive director of the Council of African Affairs. In spite of their elevated political status, Jacques Garvey did not doubt her own opinions and expressed them without hesitation. To her, it was regrettable that the congress "could not be held before the war is over, so that United Africa would speak as never before." She was concerned that after World War II, "the Nations of the world would be in a state of complacency and do not care how we burn, as long as they are no longer being bombed and blasted."[5]

Jacques Garvey also proposed that the congress organize a permanent body called a Pan-African Union "to watch over the interest of our people the world over." In addition to eschewing the term "Negro," she suggested that the group avoid the word "native" when referring to Africans or West Indians, which was also "offensive." She wrote, "Africans argue, and rightly so, that one does not refer to the natives of England, or the natives of France, why then are they called natives, with the inference of contempt for their condition of handicap and suppression[?]" Carefully naming and accurately locating peoples (in Central and South America, the West Indies, America, London, and Africa) was an obsession with Jacques Garvey, because "the slightest word can be misinterpreted, purposely of course, to upset a magnificent effort for the future of our Race." She learned this lesson from her "dealings with men of big affairs in Europe."[6]

Further, it was of "vital importance, from all angles," that a "born African" be named one of the conveners of the congress. She identified Nnamdi Azikiwe, a Nigerian, who was the editor-and-chief of four newspapers and chairman of the West African Press Delegation. Her suggestion was well reasoned, for Azikiwe "adore[d] Garveyism." Indeed, he had argued that the Garvey philosophy, "with its elements of race pride, race consciousness, nationalism and its correlant of economic stability, appeals to the modern political enthusiast, who keeps his head clear and steers away from chauvinism or enthocentricism; for it will aid in ameliorating various political, economic, social, and other problems which affect this modern age." Determined to revolutionize African journalism, Azikiwe in 1937 had founded the *West African Pilot*, a newspaper he used to guide public opinion on the Nigerian independence movement. I. F. Nicolson points out that "Zik's own nationalism had in it ideological elements of something wider than nationalism-pan-Africanism, international socialism, and the old West African Nationalism of the Lagos intelligentsia of the twenties." Educated at Lincoln and Howard Universities, Azikiwe was a formidable athlete, poet, and businessman, as well as journalist. In the eyes of Jacques Garvey, there was no African more stellar—it did not hurt his case that he had completed her memorandum request. Despite these attributes, he had a "variable character, with great charm on occasions, but on others difficult and unpredictable." Aware of Azikiwe's finicky personality, Jacques Garvey warned Du Bois, "If you me[e]t him, perhaps you may not like him personally, but we have long ceased to allow personalities to hamper unity of efforts, in this great and wide-spread work."[7]

Somewhat embarrassed by the length of her letters to Du Bois, Jacques Garvey wrote: "Try not to be bored. . . . I want you to thoroughly understand my thinking regarding our people, so that in your plans will be implemented my thoughts, that are worth-while, even if hazily expressed by letter." Correspondence thus served its purpose, but Jacques Garvey also believed that it was no substitute for a "heart to heart," face-to-face talk. To further ensure that Du Bois had a thorough grasp of her ideas, she told him to read a "letter over twice, so that you can catch the unexpressed references." Jacques Garvey used repetition and long explanations to validate her points so that Du Bois would not dismiss her intellectual contribution. This was a real possibility not only because her comments critiqued his letter, but also because during the 1940s, race men seldom worked on a par with race women, and W. E. B. Du Bois was no exception. For instance, at the first session of the United Nations, he had referred to the remarks by his co-consultant, Mary McLeod Bethune (president of the National Council of Black Women and former appointee to President Roosevelt's cabinet) as a harmless "nuisance."[8]

For virtually all of her political life, Amy Jacques Garvey had had firsthand experience with chauvinistic men. Perhaps this is why she concluded her last missive to Du Bois with the statement: "Now dear Professor, perhaps you may misunderstand the tone of my letters, as I have been so accustomed to talk with M. G. and take part in Conferences with men, as 'man to man' that I don't think or act, as if I 'were just a woman.'" Such phrasing suggests that Jacques Garvey's sense of herself positioned her outside those constraints based on an assumed fundamental "natural" dichotomy between men and women. The "natural attitude," Mary Hawkesworth has shown, "implicates gender in the ideology of procreation." This, however, was not a problem for Jacques Garvey, who believed that the body and sexuality were biological features (male and female hormones, reproductive organs). This "natural" view also meant that there were culturally specific characteristics associated with masculinity and femininity. In her 1920s editorials, Jacques Garvey had charged black men to be "real" men—breadwinners with strong backbones—socially constructed masculine attributes. Joan Scott argues that the "idea of masculinity rests on the necessary repression of feminine aspects—of the subject potential for bisexuality—and introduces conflict into the opposition of masculine and feminine."[9] At the same time, Jacques Garvey advocated more flexible feminine attributes that allowed women to function as both helpmates and leaders. But recognizing that her thinking on this point differed from other radicals, she felt the need to clarify what might appear to Du Bois as an "unnatural" feminine position.

Jacques Garvey appropriated a masculine identity to ensure common understanding between herself and Du Bois. For some reason she did not want to alienate him in the way she had done when she clashed with male UNIA leaders. Perhaps she had more respect for him because of his unquestionable commitment to "uplift" the race, as well as the deference afforded him by other leaders whom she respected. Her aggressive and forthcoming "tone" had previously been interpreted as bossy and uncompromising; to a chauvinistic mind, her voice was a "nuisance" at best and "unfeminine" at worst. By explaining her confidence and intellectual demeanor as being outside the scope of "just" an average woman, Jacques Garvey failed to critique the false notion that the political/public domain was best suited for men. At the same time, though, her explanation undercuts the claim that masculine and feminine "traits" are fixed, in that locating herself outside of "woman" ruptured gendered classifications. To be sure, Jacques Garvey was not making a universal claim, but her self-perception fundamentally undermined essentialist viewpoints of "woman," which were grounded in archaic ideas of femininity.

Du Bois did not respond to her letters, and there is no surviving record of the final letter of invitation; thus it is unclear if he implemented any of her suggestions in response to his draft of the letter convening the Fifth Pan-African Congress. A year passed before she resumed correspondence regarding the meeting. By July 1945 she had received a letter from George Padmore on behalf of the Provisional Committee in London officially inviting the UNIA to participate. Already ahead of the game, Jacques Garvey had enlisted the services of New York Garvey Club president B. Gibbons to arrange a meeting to choose a delegate and collect funds for travel expenses to London. She urged Gibbons to select a person who was "educated, honest and courageous." Measuring up in "statesmanship" was the only way to "make our contribution." Four Jamaicans met these qualifications, and L. A. Thoywell-Henry (who was also active in the People's National Party) was the number one delegate. Jacques Garvey did her best to facilitate his travel plans, as well as arranging a rushed meeting for him to address in New York. As delegates from Garvey's African Communities League, Jacques Garvey named V. G. Hamilton and K. Boxer; from the UNIA she tapped Alma La Badie.[10]

As the only scheduled female co-convener, Jacques Garvey took on the issue of female participation at the congress. She had asked Padmore to have invitations sent to Una Marson, who "could represent West Indian Women," and Ivy Tracy Timothy, who was born "of an English mother and West Indian father, and has suffered from the inequalities meted out to English-born Colored people."[11] In many ways Marson and Timothy were personifications of Jacques Garvey herself. Marson was a middle-class social reformer, poet, and journalist who came to prominence during the 1938 Jamaica rebellion. Her reports on the conditions faced by middle- and working-class women, published in the *Jamaican Standard* in 1938, gave insight into the need for social services. Despite her efforts, Marson's critique was not taken seriously by many middle-class male activists who viewed women like Marson as a "thorn in the[ir] flesh." They wished to protect the "helpless" working-class woman and assert their own ego against the presumed emasculating structure of the dominant culture. Rarely were women included in Jamaica's leadership since these men believed that women were best suited to deal exclusively with "apolitical, social concerns." Marson, nonetheless, persevered and, like Jacques Garvey, she was uncomfortable with—and often rejected—those dominant cultural definitions of black women's work that stifled their agency to develop as political leaders. Yet Marson and Jacques Garvey were never fully able to transcend middle-class values, and their outlook during this period too often failed to address wholeheartedly the needs of poor women, though they attempted to represent such experiences in their writings. Timothy, on the other hand, was a mulatta who had "suffered" as a mixed-race person. Jacques Garvey now identified herself as "one hundred per cent African," but she was indeed "brown" in Jamaica and still sensitive to culturally loaded issues surrounding mixed racial identities.[12]

Seeking to ensure that the congress had the best Pan-African minds available, Jacques Garvey also contacted W. A. Domingo, another enemy of her husband. Domingo had been the first editor of the *Negro World* but eventually became a member of the Socialist Party and an outspoken critic of Marcus Garvey. "From a purely impersonal attitude or opinion," Jacques Garvey was able to contact Domingo, since she herself preached and practiced UNITY. His "knowledge of world affairs as it affects our people," his "ability as a journalist," and his "contacts in America and West Africa—well fits [him to be] a Representative of our Race, and the Nationalist Movement."[13]

Later she explained to George Padmore that she had mailed suggestions to Du Bois some time ago but had not heard from him. Insisting, once again, that Azikiwe should be a co-convener, she enclosed a copy to Padmore of the document that echoed her *Memorandum Correlative* concerns to the congress. Anticipating comments concerning the level of her participation at the meeting, she included a brief section entitled, "Why Should Mrs. Garvey Sponsor Such a Resolution?" Her answer was simple and direct: her husband's role as founder of the UNIA/ACL and in dignifying Africans and people of African descent justified her presence and, she hoped, would silence all critics.[14]

When the Fifth Pan-African Congress finally opened in the Chorlton Town Hall, Manchester, England, on 15 October 1945, Mrs. A. Garvey was present, but unbeknownst to many, it was Amy Ashwood Garvey who took her seat, not Amy Jacques Garvey. Jacques Garvey was unable to attend because she "did not have a cent to go." Once again, she had missed a crucial opportunity for interpersonal dialogue with leading Pan-African intellectuals. To her displeasure, Ashwood was present at the invitation of W. E. B. Du Bois. In the years after Ashwood's contested divorce—beginning as early as 1924—she occasionally wrote to Du Bois, and in January 1945 he had resumed their correspondence.[15]

Ashwood and Jacques Garvey were both steadfast Pan-Africanists, and though aware of the tension between them, Du Bois apparently had dismissed Jacques Garvey's comments in April 1944 that she "was surprised to hear that M. G.'s Ex-wife 'Amy Ashwood' is in America, from 1920 she has lost no time in vilifying him, and ridiculing his movement, now blossoms *forth as his widow*, and *the Brains* of the *Garvey movement*. Professor don't we realize that the dead has no power!!" Twenty days later, she added, "please refer to me as *A. Jacques Garvey*, and omit the Christian name of 'Amy,' as M. G.'s Ex-wife, is in America, impersonating 'the widow,' and she has a bad rep, for rackets and schemes, I would never like to be further mistaken for her. . . . [S]he purposely misleads the public so as to exploit them with her schemes and rackets."[16]

Although they were dissimilar in appearance, mistaken identity followed both women; their shared first name and surname generated much confusion. Moreover, Ashwood perpetuated this misunderstanding by calling herself Garvey's widow. Even those Garveyites who were not around during the divorce fiasco were confused, for "Miss Amy Ashwood's allies were telling people about her two sons in Jamaica," even though the first Mrs. Garvey had never had children. Wanting to reassure Jacques Garvey, Gibbons wrote "we ourselves know better" but to put the confusion to rest, he asked her to send him a "picture taken with yourself, Winston and Marcus together, so that queries may be satisfied."[17]

Jacques Garvey admitted to all who would listen that she was "very sensitive on this matter," as Ashwood "caused my family much pain." Her pain escalated to hostility when she received a clipping from the *Amsterdam News* picturing Ashwood with the caption "Garvey's Widow." Livid, Jacques Garvey sought to quickly clarify the situation by writing the editor. C. B. Powell responded that he would give her statement "publicity as soon as possible."[18] Though Jacques Garvey believed that the damage was already done, she further attempted to stop the recycling of the photograph by writing New York's *People's Voice* and Chicago's *Defender* that Ashwood was not Garvey's widow.

Ashwood was in a sense a widow of Garvey, but it is unusual for an ex-spouse to take on this identification. It is unclear what she hoped to gain. Perhaps the notoriety and the spoils that sometimes followed were enough for her to continue this charade. Jacques Garvey was told, for example, that in Monrovia, Liberia, Ashwood "posed" as her and "apparently accepted money from the British Government [and] leased several houses to sublet for (9) years." Tony Martin points out that the Garvey name guaranteed her attention, adulation, and even celebrity status.[19]

Maintaining distance from Ashwood was the easiest way for Jacques Garvey not to confront their unacknowledged connectedness, for her anger closed off any possibility that she would deal directly with their problematic relationship. Audre Lorde, who has thought seriously about tensions between black women, surmises that they often fall into the trap of thinking, "I must attack you first before our enemies confuse us with each other." Lorde maintains that "black women should try to see each other more clearly, as opposed to stewing in a passion of aversion." On the surface, Jacques Garvey claimed that she was motivated by self-protection; her beleaguered body and wounded soul struggled against the fiend, Ashwood. But no matter how hard she tried to justify her harshness and cruelty toward the woman, Jacques Garvey recognized that her anger contradicted the core of her call for UNITY. Jacques Garvey cautioned Azikiwe "to look out for her [Ashwood]" not because of a "personal axe, if she was honest to Race and Homeland, we would only be glad to use her, despite what she had done in the past, but she is slippery and most immoral. I have risen above personal feelings in all of my efforts for Africa."[20]

This assessment of Ashwood—and of Jacques Garvey's feelings toward her—were not altogether true. Ashwood was a bit unconventional: her schemes to earn a livelihood were erratic, and her adventurous spirit kept her on the move; throughout her adult life she never stayed in one country more than four years.[21] But she was just as dedicated as Jacques Garvey when it came to advancing the political interests of African peoples and standing up for women's issues. At the last session of the Fifth Pan-American Congress, for example, Ashwood gave a moving speech exposing the sexist agenda of the meeting. "Very much has been written and spoken of the Negro, but for some reason very little has been said about the black woman." The black woman "has been shunted into the social background to be a childbearer. This has been principally her lot." Most concerned with the fact that Jamaican women's wages were much lower than men's, she felt that black men were "largely responsible, as they do little to help the women to get improved wages."[22]

In theory, Jacques Garvey would not have taken issue with Ashwood's comments, but her anger made it difficult for her to acknowledge Ashwood's positive and timely contribution. Similar political agendas do not automatically generate sincere, open communication; moreover, in the case of Ashwood and Jacques Garvey, their tension was stoked by their loss of the male companion Marcus Garvey. Both women had complained about his moody temperament and other character flaws, but, as Audre Lorde points out, "we have also been taught that a man acquired was the sole measure of success, and yet they almost never stay."[23] Garvey's death was not enough to achieve closure on their mutual hostility; it just evolved into another level of rage.

The Fifth Pan-African Congress went down in history as the most important point in the Pan-African movement's turning from a "passive to an active stage." Indeed, the Congress Resolutions were sophisticated intellectual indictments of political, economic, and social imperialism. "The complete and absolute independence of the peoples of West Africa is the only solution to the existing problems," proclaimed the ninety delegates. Each geographic region had specific resolutions, although West Africa was the most powerful bloc present. Since U.S. representation was minimal, the New York Garvey Club organized a special session. Fraternal greetings were offered by A. Philip Randolph; Jones Quarterly, secretary of the African Student Association of America and Canada; and Lester Taylor, secretary of the International Convention of African Peoples of the World. Finally, a special supplementary resolution was presented by delegates of the Garvey Club. Padmore assured Jacques Garvey that he read her "comprehensive memorandum" for African redemption. A condensed version of her enclosure to Padmore, which addressed the need to create a Federation of the British West Indies and to remove barriers and restrictions—especially connected with transportation and "entering our Motherland"—was entered into the final proceedings.[24]

After the congress, Jacques Garvey continued to correspond with leading Pan-African intellectuals like Padmore and Azikiwe, whom she encouraged to work together and arrange an African Goodwill Mission, a tour of speakers throughout the continent. Sticking to her agenda to fold Garveyism into existing organizations, she cautioned them not to change "the methods of various societies and organizations of our people abroad, but that their efforts should be channeled toward support of the Nationalist Movement."[25] Jacques Garvey's urging of these leaders to respect different organizations' autonomy was an ongoing example of her organizing spirit. Yet however invigorated by the blossoming of Pan-African leaders, she undoubtedly suffered a great deal for having missed the congress, especially since the reason was lack of money. She had been able to maintain a middle-class Jamaican lifestyle (a gardener and maid one day a week) via her inherited rental property, but it was not enough to permit travel off the island. Growing ever more accustomed to disappointment, Jacques Garvey was constantly readjusting to the idea that although she was "bottled-up" in Jamaica,[26] Garveyism need not be. She reasoned that she could best disseminate her redemptive African philosophy through journalistic work, which had always been her chief mode of production. Acutely aware of her restricted circumstances, she once again funneled energy into writing.

I n the years following the Fifth Pan-African Congress, Amy Jacques Garvey's determination to create an intellectual interest in Africa persisted, as she once again began to produce essays and editorial commentary. Her writing thus became her avenue of participation in the stimulating Pan-African dialogue that blossomed during and after World War II. Not only was she able to generate internationally focused discourse that circulated well beyond Jamaica, but also her work as editorial consultant for *The African: Journal of African Affairs* was another way to disseminate Garveyisque ideas. Further, as an activist invested in the efficacy of an educated constituency, she revived her husband's African Study Circle. These specific activities advanced her general purpose: that a well-informed citizenry of Africa and of the African diaspora should and would recognize their connection to one another and be willing to struggle for a common liberation.

By 1944 the *The African*, printed in New York, and the *West African Pilot*, a daily newspaper published in Nigeria, had become the main vehicles for Jacques Garvey's discourse. The wartime atmosphere gave her writing a new sense of urgency, and her release from the restrictive clutches of male leaders of the Universal Negro Improvement Association (UNIA) freed her to direct her more caustic rhetoric away from them and to the real enemies of the "Darker Races" of the world. In one essay, for example, she wrote that the nation that "boasts of being 'most civilized' " because of its ability to "manufacture automobiles, warships, bombers and jet propelled planes" is "usually hypocritical in actions, vague in manifestations, and contradictory in principles."[1]

Overall, the bulk of her political essays articulated the possibilities of the coming era and the necessity for New World diasporians to actively participate in the decolonization of Africa. The Garveys' treatises on anticolonial measures had been extensive. As Rupert Lewis points out,

Marcus Garvey was an anticolonial champion long before it was in vogue to explore race consciousness and advocate decolonization. More specifically, Jacques Garvey's 1920s essays had detailed the horrendous status of women under colonial rule in Africa, China, and India. Notably, however, in the 1940s gender-specific discussions in Jacques Garvey's writings were minimal. In fact, the twofold (helpmate/leadership) concept of community feminism faded from Jacques Garvey's political vocabulary. Instead, she mainly advocated refocusing the battle against Germany and Japan to include postwar decolonization for Africa. As she put it, "approximately 300,000,000 peoples of African blood (100% and 1% inclusive)" were giving "their best services" and the "wealth and resources of their lands to [the war] effort." Indeed, between 1936 and 1938 annual imports of strategic material from Africa to the United States grew about 2.3-fold, and between 1938 and 1942 Britain increased imports of chromium ore from Africa from 172,000 to 328,000 tons, and steel from 300,000 to 530,000 tons.[2]

In the war against fascism Africans undoubtedly had made huge sacrifices of material and human resources, but colonists did not perceive their contributions as down payments toward independence. As progressive forces around the world contemplated how Africans would benefit from the battle, their inquiries, Jacques Garvey contended, were "side-tracked, with assertions, which amount to this, 'Boys, if you don't help us, put out this forest fire, we will all be burnt alive.' So on the job." As she located herself firmly in a battle against men "drunk with material power" and "bereft of spiritual grace," her typewriter became her weapon of choice and her ideas the arsenal.[3]

By words and implication, Jacques Garvey interpreted the real postwar agenda of Western Europe to be nothing short of figuratively swallowing up Africa. Imperialist aggression would, moreover, hinder the progress of New World diasporians because "citizenship of a minority member in any country does not guarantee full rights, unless that person belongs to a strong nation, whose heavy arm the government of the would-be mobsters fear or from whom they want to court favor." Africans abroad were in a precarious position, she warned, and lack of protection could make them victims akin to the Jews in Germany. Would the "six million Jews" massacred "by civilized, Christian Europeans" have been "decimated with impunity, if after 1914–1918, they had fitted themselves for the years ahead by uniting under their own vine and fig tree?" The Jews after World War I, she argued, "ignored Palestinian Nationalism and remained European minorities, mere toys at the mercy of temperamental majorities—played with, then tossed aside, dismembered, dying in human dump heaps." The Jews had "proven to their own sorrow and loss" to all who were doubtful how "futile it is for any people to weaken their national existence by being absorbed in alien countries." "Overseas Africans" needed to acknowledge a kinship to the African continent and "service her in her rehabilitation" so that they could "benefit from Africa's national prestige and protection wherever you choose to live."[4] Jacques Garvey was careful not to bluntly blame the Jewish victims of the Holocaust. The tragic plight of some five hundred Jewish refugees was brought home to her in 1941, when the British government granted them sanctuary in Jamaica. But her analysis of their diasporic community complicated the indictment of Adolf Hitler commonly pronounced by her contemporaries.

Prolific commentary about Hitler by black writers around the world had accelerated when he refused to shake the hands of black Olympians during the 1936 games. Most noticeable was his unflinching dismissal of African American Jesse Owens, who had broken several track-and-field world records. Hitler's public display of racial contempt convinced many black people that they could expect nothing from the Nazis except possible enslavement. In fact, Hitler never downplayed his desire to exploit Africa's resources once he had access to the continent; as early as 1938, rumors circulated that British prime minister Neville Chamberlain was considering that the best way to satisfy Hitler's aspirations was to give him an African territory. Thousands of East Africans from Tanganyika marched through the streets protesting these reported plans.[5]

Despite the evidence of Hitler's racism, in the United States "Aryan" propaganda had tried to rouse African Americans against the Jews. Here, a transformed Hitler was depicted as struggling to free black people from Semitic economic exploitation. "Capitalizing on the dissatisfaction of disfranchised and underpaid American Negroes," Mercer Cook wrote, "the Fascists have attempted to convince them that they could be no worse off under a nazi government." Although no respectable black leader accepted this disinformation, it did complicate the thinking of some. In 1939, for example, Cook, W. E. B. Du Bois, Countee Cullen, and other African Americans sponsored a campaign to assist Senegalese and French West Indian soldiers. But one black columnist denounced this move to support the "French" and accused African Americans of having sold out as a result of Parisian openness to black culture. The writer asked: "What had France done that made her more noble than Germany?" Why should aid be given to Senegalese soldiers who were helping a white nation to exploit other Africans? Was the campaign to save France inspired by "the fact that some of [them] may have flirted with a blonde or two in a Paris café?"[6]

Communist Ben Davis was most forceful in campaigning across the country against the "imperialist [Allied] war." He told black people not to become "cannon fodder" to "smash Hitlerism," when "Hitlerism is enforced against [them] at home." Those who were skeptical of Allied antifascism charged that the world of black Britons was no better; William Harrison, secretary for the International African Service Bureau, wrote that black people in England were "subjected to an indignity which no black visitor to Nazi Germany has ever received."[7] Racial prejudice thus became an Achilles' heel in U.S. and British foreign policy, weakening the crusade against fascism.

Because Africans at home and abroad had never been treated well by Europeans, unrelenting prejudice had made "the Negro even more Negrocentric than segregation and exploitation have forced him to be."[8] But Negrocentric or black nationalist zeal did not necessarily evolve into the Pan-African, anticolonialist thinking that Jacques Garvey envisioned. The effort of African peoples' to participate fully in World War II illustrates this point. African Americans organized to wear military uniforms as well as to work in defense industries, for they reasoned that their participation in these war efforts would win them rights as full-fledged citizens. Executive Order 8802, which prohibited racial discrimination in U.S. defense industries, was a major victory for them. In London, progressive activists who were otherwise opposed to African and Caribbean troops' "doing the white man's work" nevertheless demanded that the armed services drop the color bar. Their Negro Welfare Association succeeded in placing black officer candidates in the Air Ministry, two of whom were children of Dr. Harold Moody, the Jamaican activist who had requested Jacques Garvey to write the *Memorandum Correlative.*[9]

A similar lack of concern for African independence was evident on the Continent. Both France and Britain conscripted hundreds of thousands of Africans. As one Kenyan explained, "we had been told that unless we joined up and helped the Government, Kenya would be occupied by Germans and Italians." So, "to keep out these 'monsters,' and also to escape the boredom and difficulty of being unemployed in Nairobi," he enlisted. Rita Headrick has demonstrated that the "universal desires" of African enlistees were better food, more money, and a vocational education.[10] The French sweetened their package by promising voting rights to all Africans who signed on. Africans were far from waving an imperial flag nor were they cooperating in their own oppression, but building a Pan-African nation was incidental to their more profound needs: trade skills and the rights associated with full-fledged citizenship.

Jacques Garvey was not critical of people of African descent struggling for their human rights via their full participation in the war effort. She had also encouraged black Jamaicans to fight for empowerment on their island. But "no matter what progress our people make as a minority group anywhere, or even as a majority in small islands," she wrote, "as long as Africa, our ancestral home with its teeming millions of our people are exploited and kept in ignorance, just so long will their condition reflect discreditably on the progressives of our race."[11] Jacques Garvey thus contended that no real achievement could occur until the most downtrodden members of the race (i.e., those who lived in Africa) were empowered on their own terms. An imagined Africa had to be at the center of diasporic thinking to recover all that was noble in African culture, as well as to protect what Africans had achieved abroad. In 1948 diasporic Jews fervently supported—politically, financially, and emotionally—the new State of Israel and Jacques Garvey expected nothing less from the African diaspora.

The fundamental reason why New World diasporians had not galvanized support for Africa, she reasoned, was because "cunning oppressors" had "fooled and befuddled" them into believing that they were not "units of a mighty whole whose center is Africa." The Caribbean area is called the "West Indians," but "are they Indians? No, their forebears were brought from West Africa, so, truthfully speaking they are West Africans, not Indians." Central and South America's African children "are absorbed in the Spanish and Portuguese population" and taught to "turn their backs on Africa." Latin American culture is a compilation of "African-Spanish-Portuguese," and when one considers what "North Africa has contributed to Spain and Portugal in the past, then Central and South American culture is basically African," Jacques Garvey argued. And in the United States, 14 million "sons and daughters of Africa are called 'Negroes'" by whites. The word *Negro* has been so "debased that new words such as 'niggard' have been coined from it to mean a low, mean person." It was no wonder, she proclaimed, that a white settler in South Africa had the nerve to "suggest that legislation should be passed there to call Africans 'Negroes' and that the white settlers alone should enjoy the honorable name of Africans."[12]

Jacques Garvey's analysis is clearly a questionable assessment of racial identities, as well as a distorted analysis of history in order to portray the all-absorbing power of imperialism. A prominent East Indian community did indeed reside throughout the Caribbean, and it is ahistorical to argue that the North African influence in Latin American culture was enough to describe Latin America as "basically African." Jacques Garvey was in the habit of molding her arguments to suit her purpose, even if that meant oversimplifying her case so as to reveal her prejudices. But her decision to transfigure and homogenize multiethnic/racial peoples into an African body demonstrated her fervent political determination to mobilize a scattered race.

The "ties of blood that bind us transcend all national boundaries," she wrote. Moreover, differences in dialects and languages were "being overcome as all of us are learning the language of freedom," which resulted from an emancipated mind.[13] Marcus Garvey had been fond of pointing out that there was a thin line between "mental slaves" and "chattel slaves," and his widow, guided by his inspirational spirit, continued this conversation by terming liberating linguistic distinctions "the language of freedom." She held that an individual of the dominant race maintained "his vaulted position of superiority" by keeping other human beings ignorant or "hypnotized victims," who "act against their own interest." In contrast, Garvey had "taught his race to think for itself, to work for itself and to love itself"; he had freed their minds and given them a goal: economic and political liberation. Jacques Garvey hoped to see that work continued.[14]

In 1945, before the war ended, she saw promising signs that Garvey's and her goals were being taken up in the Nigerian workers' strike. One month before Japan surrendered, 200,000 Nigerian workers activated one of the few weapons available to colonial subjects, a large-scale strike. After the British government refused to grant a 50 percent wage increase, which would have paid them fifty cents per day, the workers closed down all transportation and governmental services. A. O. Imoude, president of the Railway Workers Union, and Nnamdi Azikiwe, Jacques Garvey's intellectual comrade, were the commanding figures to rise from this struggle. People of African descent worldwide took up the charge to support the demonstrators and fight for a free press in Africa. Jacques Garvey viewed this strike as an example of African unity against the British Empire and as a crucial step toward the liquidation of imperialism throughout the Continent. She was proud of Azikiwe and told him to begin a lecture tour, for "everyone wanted to see the leader of the Nigerian strike."

Three years later, another leadership notch was added to Azikiwe's belt, when he opened the African Continental Bank, after it had "dawned on [him] that political freedom was not enough; economic freedom must be won also."[15] For Jacques Garvey, this marked the beginning of the post–World War II Pan-African liberation movement. Azikiwe's revolutionary leadership and the collective activism of the black masses gave her hope for a united, free Africa in her lifetime.

Though in theory Jacques Garvey was sympathetic to all Pan-African and Pan-Asian liberation movements, when she observed Chinese agents in Jamaica "collecting funds from the Chinese people, for the Nationalist Party in China," she privately shared her concern with Azikiwe: "in the name of God, why must our substance be wasted. Black Chinese, Brown Chinese all supporting China." The agents' motivation to involve their people was honorable, yet, in her eyes, the brown and black Chinese, who had equal percentages of African and Chinese blood, proudly called themselves "overseas Chinese" and had dismissed their African heritage.[16]

These observations were the catalyst for her 1945 article, "China Milks Africa in the Caribbean," published in Azikiwe's *West African Pilot*, which was by then netting the largest newspaper sales in West Africa. In this essay, Jacques Garvey linked the financial success of "7,000 Chinese" living in Jamaica to the exploitation of islanders. She explained how people of African descent were often forced to swap their produce for essentials at grocery stores at "give-away prices," enabling the Chinese to become "a produce dealer at a handsome profit." Black Jamaicans were manipulated to "underwrite" financial contributions to China. She cautioned: "Peoples of African descent, these islands are yours, because you and your fathers have toiled and bled for them. Take hold of your economic controls." Otherwise, she admonished, the Caribbean might become the "colonies of China."[17]

Although the Chinese were a minority population and had first immigrated to Jamaica in 1853 as indentured servants, by the 1940s they were mostly prosperous entrepreneurs. Their patriotic activities were much appreciated by the Chinese government, and to Jacques Garvey they modeled the possibilities for nationalist allegiance. They demonstrated to scattered Ethiopia how to "contribute of your means and ability to the rehabilitation of the land of your forebears, the continent of Africa." Yet Jacques Garvey also claimed that Chinese in the Caribbean exhibited colonizers' oppressive tendencies. What she saw as the presumed eagerness of the Chinese to exploit black Jamaicans was due to myths of black inferiority, which translated into a lack of respect for them. This is why successful Chinese traders "who owe all to these islands . . . give all to China."[18]

In her concern about relations between the Chinese and the black diaspora, Jacques Garvey was not alone. In 1948 Layle Silbert explored mainland Chinese racial prejudice toward black people. For example, postwar visitors to Shanghai were greeted by "grinning blackface" advertisements of "Darky" toothpaste on billboards along the main streets. Enterprising Chinese businessmen unapologetically explained that white teeth against dark skin showed the effectiveness of "Darky" toothpaste. "But as the Chinese customers brightened their teeth they darken[ed] their minds with the repeated association of Negroes to an odious word" and with a picture based on "a false cult of inferiority."[19] Silbert's discussion on the spread of bigotry against blacks in China during the 1940s attributed the phenomenon to the same forces as did the Garveys' comparable study of the late 1920s—Anglo-American foreign influence. Signs of racism had appeared in large cities where Western powers had staked out concessions during the world wars. And as the American government poured money into Nationalist China, exporting popular cultural media (books, movies, and magazines) bearing implicit assumptions of black inferiority, the seeds of race hatred toward blacks germinated. The African diaspora, thousands of miles away, in Europe and the Americas had no means to correct these false images.

Tensions surrounding Chinese identity in the Caribbean persisted, so much so that in 1959, when the first "Miss Jamaica" of color, Sheila Chong, was crowned, a petition surfaced asserting that a Jamaican woman had never been crowned "Miss China," so a Chinese woman had no claim to be "Miss Jamaica." These questions regarding Caribbean identity—whether aesthetic, political, or economical—were really about representation and the lack thereof. As late as 1960, Jacques Garvey still had an ambivalent relationship to this group, reportedly saying that black men and women should "acquire the economic stability that [their] 90% of the population should have in relation to the 30,000 Chinese here."[20] Although she never turned her eyes away from Africa, she affirmed that wherever black people lived—especially in the Caribbean, where they were the majority—they had to stand up for their entitlements.

Based on her timely articles on diasporic issues—as well as her journalistic experience and editorial work—Jacques Garvey was consulted by several magazine editors for various purposes. She worked most closely with the staff of *The African*, soon becoming one of its contributing editors.[21] By 1947 she was an associate editor, with David A. Talbot and George S. Schuyler, a conservative writer and former foe of Marcus Garvey. Because *The African* suffered from lack of financial support, Jacques Garvey was initially consulted on how to increase its revenue. She promptly stated that although she appreciated her complimentary copy of the periodical, the staff could not afford to send many free copies "as the Magazine must be made to carry itself." In the same letter, though, she provided a list of people who did deserve unsolicited copies, including Nnamdi Azikiwe; George Padmore; Sylvia Pankhurst, editor of the *Ethiopian News and New Times*; D. G. Tackie, editor of the *Gold Coast Independent*; C. V. Jarrett, editor of the *African Standard* in Freetown, Sierra Leone; Mons Lescott, president of Haiti; and secretariats in Washington, D.C., that were affiliated with the Central and South American republics.

After recommending a list of "honest" people who could serve as "agents" (distributors) and the names of other editors who could be consulted, she provided two contacts at Jamaican bookstores who wanted to order the magazine. Jacques Garvey's list served the magazine well, as agents reported back to her on their progress. Eventually, she collected the monies that Caribbean magazine agents received from sales. She kept meticulous records on these funds, which she dispatched in lump sums to *The African* office.[22]

As another way to generate revenue, Jacques Garvey suggested that *The African* sell postcards of the Garvey family. Five hundred postcards were printed at a cost of $10.71, paid for by the editor, "as a token of our appreciation for your [Jacques Garvey's] kind assistance to the magazine—for Editorial services and otherwise."[23] The postcards were so popular that a second batch of one thousand was printed, and Jacques Garvey received a percentage of all the sales.

When *The African* was reorganized under the editorship of Ridley A. Lewis, he informed Jacques Garvey that "we have reached a large number of persons in the higher intellectual bracket but in my opinion we have missed the great middle class to whom the magazine is really aimed." It is unclear if the "higher intellectual bracket" meant the elite, or if Lewis viewed the middle class as a mediocre-thinking lot, but who could finance the journal. Either way, Jacques Garvey was concerned by this statement, responding that she hoped he would "not lower *the Africans* intellectual standard" by changing the format to accommodate the middle class.[24] Most magazines seeking middle-class readers, such as the *West Indian*

Bulletin or *Ebony*, highlighted local social events and individualistic messages regarding wealth and prestige. As a political journalist, Jacques Garvey had always ridiculed this type of reporting, and since she sought to inspire the impoverished masses, she resisted any apparent equation of class with intelligence.

These initial exchanges between *The African* editors and Jacques Garvey opened a floodgate of her demands for improvements. In an authoritarian tone, she advised the editorial board to "put two staples to hold the magazine, one is not enough. Try to get issues out regularly, as finances permit. And do not lessen the high tone and cultural outlook of the magazine." In terms of content, she proposed her new mandate: that there be "*three main features of news*, apart from the feature articles etc." She identified specific revisions, including the need to change "West Indian Topics" to "Caribbean News." Concerned that news about Africa was sadly lacking in other periodicals, she challenged the editors to outshine them in this area. This could be done with a news feature called "The African Horizon," for which every effort must be made to get news from all parts of Africa. A feature on "The American Front" was also needed because when "the war is over, Aframericans will be still fighting" for their rights. She specifically identified the Caribbean islands, Africa, and the United States because this is where "our people are in large numbers."[25]

Jacques Garvey was metamorphosing from an isolated political woman into an organizational player. This was not an easy feat, because she was strongly attached to her own ideas. In this case, not all of her suggestions were taken up: *The African* continued to refer to the Caribbean area as the West Indies, and did not introduce news features on Africa and the United States. However, the magazine did adopt her suggestion to start a column for "pen-pals." Here she was on firm ground, since it had become abundantly clear at the Fifth Pan-African Congress that most Africans, at home and abroad, knew little about the rest of the African world. Acutely aware of this, and of the fact that many Africans lived in relatively remote areas where reading materials were not easily accessible, Jacques Garvey advocated an African pen-pal column to address this problem. This section would help Africans to get information and make contacts with "more progressive elements of our people." Conversely, knowledge of Africans and their lives would encourage black people in the New World to strive to uplift their race. Such "exchange of views, information and ideas is one of the best means of creating fellowship and love between

Africans at home and abroad."[26] The editorial staff was sold on this idea, and the pen-pals section became a regular feature of *The African*.

In addition to her magazine work, Jacques Garvey's other main project during the postwar years was reviving the African Study Circle, initially founded by her husband. Pointing out that contact with others broadens the outlook and increases the intellect, Jacques Garvey proposed that the Study Circle was another way to move beyond the colonial propaganda that kept peoples of African descent divided and ignorant of each others' accomplishments. As she put it, "Knowledge dispels the Ignorant fumes that becloud Reason." The immediate purpose of the Study Circle was to develop interest in African history and to counter the "misinformation, much distorted information in respect to the historical background of black people of the world."[27]

This agenda of Jacques Garvey's—uncovering "one's true self" and "pinpointing . . . one's centre"—has subsequently become a central organizing principle in contemporary Afrocentric scholarship.[28] Critics of this discourse point out that slavery and colonialism—phenomenal periods of victimization and exploitation—are in some part erased from a neatly packaged, ancient heroic African narrative. Jacques Garvey's reconstruction of the African landscape, however, included texts on slavery and colonialism, because she did not interpret these tragic moments as negative reflections on the identity of peoples of African descent, but as expressions and outgrowths of an unjust capitalist, political, and racial power. By studying the history of both Africans and New World diasporians, she wanted to show a common racial origin and history that would inspire common understanding and mutual progress.

Although Jacques Garvey indicates that the long-term goal of the Study Circle was to promote participants' pride in the achievements of their race and to expand their honorable legacy, she was also clearly motivated by heuristic ideas. High levels of illiteracy engulfed the black world, and helping others to learn would give rise to literate communities. As an intellectual who never underestimated the potency of dialogue as well as the transforming power of literature, Jacques Garvey continued her tradition of educating the mind and soul for action.

Her first step in this effort was to write a circular letter for the Study Circle; she then expended considerable energy trying to get it printed. Yet her very commitment to the "principles and ideas that Marcus Garvey enunciated, fought, struggled and died for" had produced restrictions against her that were so tight, she was not even permitted to print the circular letter in Jamaica. She explained this with, "war, of course is an excuse for every handicap." As usual, she turned to the New York Garvey Club for assistance, as there was "no other group that [she could] depend on like [them]." Explicitly detailing how she wanted the four typed pages prepared, she asked that five thousand copies be printed and sent to her as follows: "see that in each package, you put all the pages to make up a letter, whether it is numbered 1,2,3 and 4 pages, all must be in the one package," and then "mail two of the packages every week to ensure delivery." The Garvey Club was to keep two hundred letters and wait for further instructions on how to have them "distributed among member's relatives in other cities, or the Caribbean."[29]

Once the letters were printed, Jacques Garvey apparently contacted UNIA divisions directly, but there is no surviving correspondence seeking input or approval from any member at the national headquarters. She instructed individual chapters to organize their members "to educate our people about their history, and teach them to take the right pride in their race."[30]

In her attempt to realize her vision of a Study Circle, Jacques Garvey was building on an established history of literary societies. Internationally, groups were formed and collaborative efforts were devised, beginning in the nineteenth century, to concentrate individual interests in common purposes of study. On the whole, these activities were educational, providing a forum for intimate intellectual dialogue and literary investigation, as well as possible channels for publication. Political and social concerns sometimes crept into these conversations, moving the participants to address these issues.[31] The Study Circle should be placed within this philological tradition. Its format was both formal (Jacques Garvey advised participants to elect a chairman, secretary, and treasurer) and intimate (meetings took place in private homes, churches, or clubs). She envisioned that small units of black people worldwide would gather to study books by and about black people. Dramatizations, plays, and other means of expression would also be used to "develop social interest in things African."[32] Essentially, Jacques Garvey's Study Circle combined creative performance and critical debate in the pursuit of knowledge.

Although her 1940s articles had become less gender-oriented than her earlier writings and community feminism as a mobilizing concept had vanished, this would seem to be largely because she no longer had Marcus Garvey to produce an analysis of the overall Pan-African program. Thus she herself took charge, which left her little room to do anything else. When it came to the Study Circle, however, she once again overtly targeted women. She told B. Gibbons to "get an intelligent group of women to start Circles in their homes, so that during the winter seasons, [they] could do real study work and cultural work."[33]

Bringing together like-minded women for literary fellowship was not a new phenomenon. In fact, Jacques Garvey's suggestion to organize genderized units was fully in step with the history of Western literary societies. Since men and women were presumed to be different, masculine and feminine literature maintained their differences. Western white women were located in a domesticated arena, where "academic" education—studies in the classics, history, mathematics, and the physical sciences—was "most visibly absent." Genderized literature of the late nineteenth and early twentieth centuries had helped to maintain socially constructed roles, and separating men and women into the public and private spheres, respectively, was the subtext of related discourse.[34] But on the cusp of the 1940s, women were reading more diverse forms of literature, and Jacques Garvey wanted to capitalize on this trend by providing controversial, stimulating studies to ignite them into action for racial upliftment. Further, during this personally and politically transformative moment, the Study Circle showed how community feminist ideas remained fundamental to Jacques Garvey's way of thinking (even though they were no longer overtly promoted in her writing, she remained convinced that literate women developed literate families for a progressive black nation).

Cross-culturally, literate women should come together in circles as "sisters" to talk over texts for self-improvement and community uplift. Anne Knupfer's analysis of African American women's literary clubs at the turn of the century holds true for the 1940s in that, in addition to literature, most "clubs included the study of philanthropy, home, education, art and music." Jacques Garvey recognized that such clubs' leisure reading and other activities were forms of "classical" high culture. Knupfer's discussions clarify how, given the racialized history of the United States and the Caribbean, it is not surprising that "classical"—as opposed to "folk"—studies were color and class-coded. Privileged women participated in these clubs and generally excluded others, largely based on color, class, or other subjective "deficiencies."[35] Jacques Garvey attempted to break such boundaries between women by creating reading groups in which all women could participate. In doing so, she attacked the notion that reading was a leisurely activity of the well-to-do, usually elite whites. She also challenged the foundational structure that kept literature and a certain form of language—which Carolyn Cooper terms a "primal facilitator" in the "process of self-definition and articulation—away from the masses."[36]

To guarantee that participants read the proper texts, Jacques Garvey told them to contact responsible authorities on African history through the Garvey Club of New York or Dr. L. D. Reddick, curator of the Schomburg Collection of the New York Public Library. She also provided a book list including but not limited to Selwyn Jones, *South of the Congo* (1943); Negley Farson, *Behind God's Back* (1941); J. A. Rogers, *Sex and Race: Negro-Caucasion Mixing in All Ages and All Lands* (1941, 1967) and *One Hundred Amazing Facts about the Negro* (1957); Melville Herskowitz, *The Myth of the Negro Past* (1941); W. E. B. Du Bois, *Black Folk: Then and Now* (1939); Donald Pierson, *Negroes in Brazil: A Study of Race Contact a Bahia* (1942); Xavier Herbert, *Capricornia: A Novel* (1943); Paul Laurence Dunbar, *The Complete Poems* (1913); Denis Saurat, *Watch Over Africa* (1941); and Nnamdi Azikiwe, *Renascent Africa* (1968).[37] In compiling this list, Jacques Garvey pulled together cutting-edge scholarship by black and white writers, documenting a range of experiences—European, African, and African diaspora—and past achievements.

Most of the texts she selected have become literary classics, but some presented grossly inaccurate information and were saturated with racist language. For example, Pierson's *Negroes in Brazil* argued that humane and intimate relations were the general rule during slavery and that barbaric and extreme cruelty were relatively rare. Negley Farson, based on his travels throughout Africa, opined in *Behind God's Back* that Africans had the "best chance of progress" under the English and unabashedly remarked that the laws of the Belgian Congo were "too lenient to be regarded as real punishment by the native," because "the native needs a good beating."[38] The fact that Jacques Garvey recommended these texts and others that include bigoted and false conclusions suggests that she wanted to instigate lively debates about not only African splendor, but also slavery, colonialism, and future possibilities for the race, as opposed to having participants memorize a static narrative of ancient African advancements and achievements. In other words, she had by no means slipped into a revisionist mode, wherein readers obsessed with origin and myth may disregard any narrative presumed to represent an antithesis to the "glory" of African civilization.[39]

Since many books from her reading list were published on the eve of and during World War II, they also helped to deepen Study Circle participants' understanding of why the world was falling apart. For instance, J. A. Rogers's work determined that the drive to create a "pure" and "superior" race with the "right to enslave and use the rest of humanity" was created from "scraps of false philosophies of past centuries; a quotation from this or that prejudiced traveller; lines from this and that semi-ignorant divine of colonial days," passages from the Bible or from some "badly mixed-up ethnologist, all jumbled together with catch-phrases from greedy plantation owners, slave-dealer and other traffickers in human flesh." This combination had brought to life a "monster . . . to ravage and slaughter: His name: Adolf Hitler. His purpose: World Domination." To replace the conglomerate of myths about African people with verifiable facts about their contributions to humankind became one intellectual purpose of Study Circle groups. Jacques Garvey encouraged them to publish small pamphlets on the "Black man's contributions in all parts of the world" to help deflect criticism about their potential for self-government.[40] Overall, her reading guide included sophisticated and meticulous—while at times, racist—scholarship in her effort to draw together a disparate population. Her idea was that the unification of African peoples for the decolonization of Africa was the ultimate way to bring the order of self-rule out of the chaos of World War II.

Establishing reading circles was an ingenious way to cultivate literate communities. But it was also a daunting task to implement on an international scale, because wherever black people lived, formal, organized schools were few in number. In Africa, colonial education had mostly generated "native elites" through selective recruitment of students. French West Africans were usually admitted to the best schools after they had signed a pledge to serve for several years in the colonial administration—where they would be given separate jobs and unequal pay. Peggy Sabatier documents that in 1940, only about 0.5 percent of the children of the general Francophone West African population were enrolled in primary school, and 0.01 percent of the total population had attended secondary schools.[41]

Africans often attempted to satisfy their desire for education and information through newspapers. The unparalleled growth of African-controlled newspapers in Kenya between 1945 and 1952 partly fulfilled this need for political news and reading material from an African source, considered "more attractive than information controlled by Europeans and government." Nnamdi Azikiwe alone owned four newspapers in West Africa. One Study Circle from Guachapali reported that its members read "both local and foreign newspapers and from correspondence," especially since it was difficult to obtain several copies of the same book after World War II.[42]

It was not long before the British colonial administration connected the spread of scholarly knowledge to decolonization movements. And because it was inconceivable to the colonial mind that Africans would struggle for self-determination on their own, the administration believed that the growth of Zikist nationalism in Nigeria and Kwame Nkrumah's appointment as general secretary of the United Gold Coast Convention in 1948 were the result of Cold War communist infiltration into Africa. Determined to resist what they perceived as the spread of communism, the British began their particular Cold War witch-hunt by suspecting the extramural lecturers and the Oxford University Delegacy of Extramural Studies to Ghana and Nigeria. Most tutors of nonvocational adult education wanted to sustain British power in West Africa, but a few agents in the delegacy refused to become another propaganda outlet for colonial aggression. Their progressive, "left-wing" politics were identified as subversive by colonial administrators determined to stop this succor to political independence. Officials would curtail the already minimal access to adult education and possibly disrupt Study Circles because they filled an educational need.

In the United States, illiteracy among African Americans was widespread, aided by the parlous state of public schooling. Similar to the whole of Africa, good schooling in the South, where the majority of African Americans still lived, remained a privilege, not a constitutional right. The teacher-to-student ratio substantiates this. In 1945 in Mississippi, for six months out of the year only three black teachers taught 190 children in all subjects in grades five through eight. In 1944–45 southern states spent about $40.00 annually per white pupil but only $10.00 to educate a black child. Underfunded districts, underpaid teachers, a shortage of classroom space, and "a kind of curricular and programmatic bankruptcy steeped in intellectual confusion about what was needed in the postwar era summed up the state of public education between 1946 and 1960." These conditions produced a southern populace with almost a million people over the age of twenty-five who had not finished a single year of school.[43]

Closer to home, Jacques Garvey's Study Circle can also be understood as a response to contemporary debates surrounding secondary education in Jamaica, where educational reform began after the 1938 labor rebellion.

In the 1940s the Kandel Commission of Enquiry into Secondary Education proposed two systems. The first maintained the elitist tradition of secondary education for a wealthy few. The second proposal was an attempt to liberalize and expand secondary education for the "lower middle and subordinated classes" by establishing a Common Entrance Examination for secondary schools. In theory, this test would "guarantee equal access for every child." Heated debates, however, stopped the implementation of the second proposal, which threatened to unlock the upper and middle classes' hegemony over secondary schooling.[44] By advocating reading groups, Jacques Garvey positioned herself politically outside the Jamaican bourgeoisie. She was acutely aware that there were few avenues for exposing working-class children to nonvocational literature, and this concern fueled her argument that forming Study Circles would be most beneficial to the young. She explained the "great amount of good that it will do to educate our people, especially the younger ones, to the truth of Race, and so enable them to be inspired to live up to the past achievements of our people, it will give them a goal, it will give them Hope, it will give them Faith in the possibilities of our Race."[45] Thus the Study Circle was not just to enrich or broaden the intellectual identity of adults, but to awaken or catalyze an informed, positive identity in children as well.

The principal forum for exposure to the Study Circle were full-page advertisements placed in *The African*. Even though Jacques Garvey was aware that the magazine needed paid endorsements, and she remained concerned that the editors did not accept "cheap advertisements" to "maintain its dignity," she nevertheless wanted free space. She justified her request by arguing that her name, as a contributor, would "cause many of our members to take this magazine." She was further convinced that the publication would thereby "have the advantage of drawing from the Circle an intelligent following that will be easier to lead, and more willing to support the magazine."[46] Jacques Garvey believed that better-prepared readers would be better positioned to appreciate the logic of Pan-Africanism and anti-imperialist struggles. These arguments, combined with the fact that she did not receive payment for her articles, swayed the editors to let her swap free advertisement for her services.

The few surviving records of the Study Circles indicate that, although they did function, some groups needed more guidance than others. This is not surprising since Jacques Garvey provided only a basic structure and reading lists, as opposed to specific logistical suggestions such as how often they should meet or how discussions should proceed. For example,

Irene Ford of Cleveland, Ohio, the home of the UNIA national headquarters, wrote, "we want to hear more a bout the Circle so we can go forward in the work of it." Ford concluded: "We get ready to get the books and litture we can get. So we can get rite down to study them. So we want to hear from you as soon as you can." But other circles did not rely on Jacques Garvey, taking it upon themselves to create and implement their own activities. For instance, Daiziel Fuller, assistant secretary of the African Study Circle, auxiliary of the Guachapali Division, reported how her group sponsored an "all isthmus competition on Negro History among the youth of our race." Enclosed with the letter was a copy of the questions that they hoped met with Jacques Garvey's approval.[47]

Jacques Garvey's vision was that as micro-units of a grand, African-centered whole, Study Circle members would share in the responsibility of creating collaborative learning communities. It was her hope that the Study Circle would thus help to generate an antiracist, anti-imperialist, African-identified constituency. Although she recognized that New World diasporians could not, as Stuart Hall puts it, "travel back through the eye of the needle," Jacques Garvey did believe that a reconnection to an imagined African community was possible, indeed, desperately needed for the decolonization movement.[48] She also wanted Africans to be exposed to, and learn from, the multiple experiences of the Pan-African world. In this sense she continued to carry out Garvey's program, which linked education and the absorption of certain developments of Western civilization to the rise of Africa, an Africa entitling all of its members across class and gender divides.

Essentially, the Study Circle was another way for Jacques Garvey to merge all of the ethnic and cultural differences of the African world—as well as seal the profound rupture that diasporian Africans had suffered—into a unified nation, ready to mount an attack on the political forces that kept them separate, divided, and weak. This dialectical flow and exchange, Paul Gilroy explains, resulted partly "from the affiliation of diaspora cultures to Africa and the traces of Africa that those diaspora cultures enclose."[49]

But pulling together this eclectic black world required more than learning the "language of freedom" at its most fundamental level. Collaboration and exchange would require key players to be multilingual, and this was the major problem with the Study Circle reading lists. All of Jacques Garvey's selected literature was in English; thus, the targeted

Africans, as well as African diasporians, were limited to those who had been colonized by British-Anglo forces. In all fairness to Jacques Garvey, she was not fluent in other languages, and she tried to remedy this linguistic problem by also identifying Puerto Rican Arthur Schomburg's massive multilingual, international history collection for the reference of Study Circle participants. But in general, all other languages were marginalized, and English was clearly dominant.

During this period of the 1940s, in addition to investing a considerable amount of time and energy in creating an intellectual Pan-African readership and community, Jacques Garvey also began to assume a more active role in Jamaican politics. As the next chapter explores, over the next several decades she became a constant presence at political meetings on the new Jamaican government. Her activism in Jamaican politics offers yet another window on her intellectual and political world.

A quintessential criticism—both current and historical—of professional public intellectuals is that they are not grounded in the specific, lived realities and communities of the people they pledge to serve. W. E. B. Du Bois, for example, was reserved in manner, which he unapologetically characterized as withdrawing "sometimes ostentatiously from the personal nexus." To put it baldly, he rarely spoke to his New York neighbors; he even admitted that his "leadership was a leadership solely of ideas." His attitude was characteristic of other black intellectuals who frequently made disparaging comparisons between themselves and the masses. Such self-imposed alienation ensured these theorists marginal status in their black communities.[1] But marginality was not (nor is) the common fate for all black thinkers. Jacques Garvey's political activity—both in her local neighborhood and in the larger Jamaican community—demonstrates that her Pan-African vision was not besmirched by such arrogance and elitism. Moreover, the main obstacle to her involvement in both Jamaican politics and in the Pan-African struggles (with the efforts of other black nationalists, Pan-Africanists, and leftists) was finally the onslaught of a larger international event, the Cold War.

After her husband's death in 1940, Jacques Garvey and her children settled into her mother's charming bungalow on the outskirts of Kingston, on the same land where she and her siblings had been born and raised. Although many years had passed since she and her father had kept stray cattle away from their property, Jamaican society in 1943 was still split along complicated racial and ethnic lines. Distinct groups continued to characterize the population: blacks (78.1 percent), "browns" (17.5 percent), East Indians (2.1 percent), whites (1.1 percent), and Chinese (1.0 percent). Generally, Jacques Garvey continued to be classified among the culturally and biologically diverse "brown" population, and she lived in a "brown" community. Finally, her family's rental property not only continued to be her chief source of income, but also led others to perceive her as comfortably middle-classed.[2] Despite this appearance, Jacques Garvey's lifestyle was not pretentious, and she was just as concerned about the rudiments of daily living as those Kingston residents who were confined within the city's pens of poverty.

Unemployment, underpayment, and lack of access to the means of production had generated striking economic differences in Jamaican society. A redistribution of wealth and institutional resources—particularly higher education—were profoundly needed to balance this divide. Moreover, at this time employers seldom displayed regard for the care of their workers. For example, both peasant farmers who worked on estates and urban workers received little or no financial compensation after an injury.

More hazardous even than the workplace were Kingston's roads. The majority had been carved out of mountainsides, and continual masonry was needed to buttress dangerous points. When it rained there were never enough workers to keep the roads safe, and avalanches were frequent. Poorly kept roads were a reflection of larger municipal problems; Kingston was then undergoing a transition from using both tramcars and motor buses to using buses exclusively. Motor buses were cheaper than trains to maintain, required no steel tracks, provided curb service, and offered easier expansion of routes.[3] But with the convenience and reliability of buses came heavier wear on the roads, especially in the suburbs, and maintenance was increasingly inadequate.

The roads leading to Jacques Garvey's property were no exception; since her children left home for school daily, and she traveled at least three times a week by bus to attend political meetings, she was especially concerned.[4] After a man was killed by a trucker rounding one of the curves, she led a campaign to have dangerous areas of the street repaired. Mounting a one-woman challenge to a system that had minimal consideration for the well-being and personal safety of black people, she wrote to the director of the Public Works Department on behalf of twenty-one residents, who also signed her complaint: "for the safety of the traveling Public, we respectfully ask that you survey the area."[5]

Although most of her writings addressed international activities, Jacques Garvey never distanced herself even from neighborhood struggles in Jamaica. But with characteristic energy, her main political efforts were expended in the broader local arena by visibly supporting the People's National Party (PNP). The PNP had been formed in 1938 after middle-class

Jamaicans—teachers, professionals, and civil servants—became politically mobilized by the successful working-class rebellion of 1938. Essentially the PNP was a nationalist vehicle to expand local political leadership with the goal of universal adult suffrage and independence from imperial policy. Norman Manley, a "light-brown" member of the Queen's Counsel and a lawyer, led this charge of the intelligentsia. By 1944 Manley had called for the state to intervene and control "public works . . . investment of money . . . and the national economy to the extent of securing work for everybody."[6] The PNP's mild form of socialism also criticized the large capitalist estates that cut off the peasant farmers' access to the means of production. Overall, the PNP argued that freedom from the Crown would stimulate economic and social reforms.

Given that the core of the PNP platform was political independence from Britain, during the November 1944 campaign Jacques Garvey "routed" for the party. This meant that she spoke to and covered two to three group meetings each night. Her observations were chronicled, but the *Daily Gleaner* refused to print them. Accustomed to its censorship, Jacques Garvey understood all too well how the paper's "policy of reasonable excuse[s] for not publishing views from [her] pen" kept the public uninformed about competing ideas.[7]

Opposing the PNP was the Jamaican Labor Party (JLP), under the dictatorship of Alexander Bustamante, Manley's cousin. The JLP had been launched in 1943 as the political arm of Bustamante's Industrial Trade Union (BITU), founded during the 1938 strike. Bustamante had positioned himself as a leader in the rebellion, since workers had responded to his charisma and populist rhetoric. He had organized the JLP to narrowly address bread-and-butter issues, offering an immediate better life to Jamaican workers and denouncing the PNP as a party diluted by middle-class intellectuals and Marxists. If that charge were not enough to taint the character of the PNP as unresponsive to the masses, "Busta" proclaimed that its objective of self-government would mean "brown man rule," an idea that was extremely unpopular among the predominately black members of the BITU.[8] With the approaching December 1944 election, the first to include universal adult suffrage (property and income qualifications had been eliminated) and a popularly elected House of Representatives inaugurating a limited form of self-government, the PNP and JLP fought a highly contested and, at times, malicious campaign.[9]

Jacques Garvey wrote, "Abuse and violence seem to be the program of Bustamante." Such criticism had to surprise many, since JLP candidates often compared Bustamante to Marcus Garvey. Bustamante's spellbinding oratory, self-confidence, and courage were in the tradition of Garvey, who was still an inspiring political figure for the black masses. In fact, attempts to "destroy" Bustamante were compared to the elitist attacks that had been leveled against Garvey. Bustamante was a warrior to many working-class people who had faith in him and celebrated his willingness to take to the streets and march. "Busta" proclaimed that he was the voice of workers, and in turn they chanted, "We will follow Bustamante until we die!"[10]

But as an independent thinker Jacques Garvey could not be drawn in by emotional rhetoric or co-opted by popular will. She looked beyond Bustamante's charm to analyze the core of the JLP platform. JLP candidates recited the desires and needs of laborers—higher wages and improved working conditions—but they opposed state intervention in the economy. Bustamante did not rally around occupational, safety, and health measures in addition to an acceptable minimum wage. The ruling elite was also attracted to Busta's conservative capitalist solutions for the fledgling economy, remedies that failed to address larger political objectives necessary for self-government. Thus the conservative *Daily Gleaner*'s bias in favor of Bustamante explains its refusal to print Jacques Garvey's criticism of him.

Ironically, as Rex Nettleford notes, PNP leader Norman Manley viewed the BITU and PNP as "two sides of the same coin." In fact, Manley admitted that it was difficult for him to accept some of Jacques Garvey's ideas.[11] Manley held democratic views, but his assumptions about self-government were largely based in the British parliamentary tradition, and Jacques Garvey questioned European paradigms as a means to achieve self-determination. Moreover, Manley precariously argued that the laboring classes measured independence by their relationship to the Crown, but as a practical intellectual, Jacques Garvey understood that workers linked their independence to the ability to directly bargain for their livelihood. This might be the reason why the Jamaican voting masses, who were politically articulate, repeatedly challenged PNP candidates to explain what socialism meant for them.[12]

Indeed, Manley had trouble connecting with black peasants, small tradesmen, and landless laborers, who perceived him as aloof. Observers point out that his difficulties were also due to the PNP's unwillingness to openly link color with poverty. Ken Post observes that the party's nationalism was based more on a concept of shared Jamaican history and culture than on racial unity; thus PNP Marxists resisted using race as a rallying mechanism.[13] Jacques Garvey contested many of Manley's positions but this one most adamantly. For years she had emphasized that racial unity was essential to confront European imperialism directly. Although African peoples were divided culturally, linguistically, and geographically, they were "united by nature." For Jacques Garvey, nationalism in Jamaica was not just a nation-state struggle, but a part of other liberation movements resounding throughout Africa and the diaspora. She always reasoned that the best way to politicize the masses for a powerful independence movement was through a call for racial unity, rather than for building electoral machines. A racialist agenda, she argued, was imperative to address color stratification and move across class differences to produce an impenetrable political bloc. But her ideas were not easily assimilated, as Carl Stone poignantly notes: party affiliation, not race or class, was the organizing mechanism for political consciousness in Jamaica during this period.[14]

These philosophical differences between Manley and thinkers like Jacques Garvey created an untidy PNP political base. It also positioned Jacques Garvey as a person loathed by some but needed within the party ranks. Since close to 80 percent of the Jamaican population was black, its vote had to be courted for the PNP's survival—and who better to do it than an intellectual who could connect with them on the basis of black identity and whose sincerity was unquestioned. This was important because a news story in the *Daily Gleaner* had charged Manley and the PNP with "insincerity to their promises to the laboring classes of Jamaica [and] insincerity in their promises of a Utopia through their method of Government."[15]

The *Daily Gleaner*'s editors and other critics of the PNP forced Jacques Garvey and other progressive PNP activists to maximize neighborhood cluster meetings to attract supporters for canvassing purposes and to ensure a large voter turnout on election day. PNP activist Daphne Campbell explained that when her group met, political matters were discussed and attempts at community advancement were made by "the training of people in different aspects." Campbell also recalled that more women were attracted to the cluster groups because "women were anxious to find a way out." Since they were at "the base of the ladder," they wanted "to find somewhere, they need[ed] to find somewhere to align themselves, to associate and find a better life, because in these groups there [were] a lot of little opportunities . . . like finding jobs and that kind of thing."[16]

Women like Jacques Garvey and Campbell were not merely rallying around a nationalist male leadership, they believed that the PNP could enhance the well-being of all Jamaicans, regardless of class and color. Specifically, Jacques Garvey argued that the PNP had "to fight ignorance, which is being used by selfish interests to destroy our future, through ignorant, or self-seeking men." She wanted to "see that vested interest[s] do not put their puppets into the New House of Representatives, nor can we allow ignoramuses under the guise of Labor, to misrepresent us there."[17] In many ways, Jacques Garvey protected the PNP from alienating the working class while she performed as a "vote-catcher," keeping the "brown" intermediate class in a dominant position.

Yet she was not a PNP puppet; she was not oblivious to her role, and she used it to show PNP leaders how racial issues were connected to the class divide. Clearly, her political agency was dialectical, as can best be understood from Aggrey Brown's analysis of the PNP and JLP. "The biggest irony," Brown notes, was that "only a handful of intellectuals question[ed] the covert and overt manipulation of the Jamaican population by the country's political *cum* labor leaders, only to have those very techniques used against them in justification of their ostracism by those leaders." In the end, Bustamante prevailed: the JLP won 41.4 percent of the votes, the PNP 23 percent. Twenty-two House of Representative seats went to the JLP and five to the PNP.[18]

In pointing out the PNP's failure to deal with the racial-class nexus, Jacques Garvey tapped into the underlying shortcoming of this middle-class movement—a deficiency that continues to resonate in the Pan-African world. As Cornel West put it, middle-class activists are generally "concerned with racism to the degree that it poses constraints on upward social mobility."[19] Thus, as the hue of the urban political tier darkened, the middle-class activist movement did not guarantee that the issues that kept the majority of black Jamaicans on the periphery would be sufficiently addressed.

Her highly charged local and international activities began to take a toll on Jacques Garvey's health. A spectrum of illnesses ravished her body in the 1940s: Teeth were extracted, her eyesight was failing, and earaches, throat troubles, rheumatism in her wrists, and full-blown influenza overwhelmed her. It seemed that she endured one crisis after another. For instance, soon after Jacques Garvey was bitten by a dog, her leg became arthritic. Her unstable financial situation required that she attend to her ailments "according to [her] means," and she often paid her medical fees in installments. Sharing her hardships with Nnamdi Azikiwe, she wrote that she was "weakened in body, but strong in mind." Over the years, Jacques Garvey's mental strength had often compensated for her physical problems, but she recognized the need for a long vacation to rest and rejuvenate her body. She hoped, once the war ended, to be permitted to spend a summer in the United States and Canada with her sons.[20]

But a vacation off the island was costly, and although her family was well-off, extra money had to be saved for her boys' schooling. Living on a tight budget was nothing new, yet Jacques Garvey admitted that her family lived "very humbly since [Garvey's] death, in my Mother's home, and I work too. But I never anticipated that I would have it so hard after his death."[21] She does not elaborate on what type of work she did, but evidently it did not greatly enhance her purse. Moreover, the monthly stipend of $50 to $100 promised her by the parent body of the Universal Negro Improvement Association (UNIA) never materialized.

After James Stewart was elected acting president-general of the UNIA in 1940, he had sent a circular letter asking that the association's divisions "by special collection and contribution, raise a substantial amount and forward [it] to the Parent Body" so that each month money could be sent to Jacques Garvey and her children. Although Stewart stated "with regret [that] . . . so few divisions . . . reported as they should in this direction," members did not believe him; neither did Jacques Garvey. She received many letters from Garveyites complaining about Stewart and the fact that they had sent money, once a week in some cases, specifically for her family. One member wrote, "I am worried—very much re[garding] the administration of the UNIA presently[,] for we have the most selfish-arrogant and highminded president the UNIA has ever had."[22] Stewart's response to criticism substantiates much of the gossip. When one member clarified that he was in fact only "Acting" president-general, Stewart responded that "subordinate officers" had made an "error" when they had ordered UNIA letterhead referring to his position as acting. "Acting," he said, implied that the position was temporary and that the permanent person would return. "I am sure that you can readily agree that the person in whose stead I am delegated to act will not return to us. Hence my authority is absolute as President." Stewart also had problems with Executive Council members. Minutes from council meetings reveal confusion, accusations, and dissension within the ranks.[23]

Committed Garveyites were worried about the welfare of Jacques Garvey and her children and held Stewart accountable for the crisis, demanding a plain explanation. In a flagrant, and slightly facetious show of concern, Stewart ran a full-page photograph of Marcus Jr. and Julius Winston in the *New Negro World*, the UNIA monthly magazine, posing the question, "Have You Forgotten Them?" This 1942 piece gave no information on the status of the boys; worse, the picture was taken when they were around the ages of five and eight when they were already nine and twelve. Stewart deliberately distanced himself from Jacques Garvey. To members who threatened to withhold support from the parent body until this matter (and others regarding UNIA finances) was resolved, he haughtily remarked, "Mrs. Garvey is not quite in the position to inform you . . . [about] irregularities." All information should be obtained from him, he insisted, as "others are apt to become confused in mind by inquiry of something for which they lack facts at their disposal."[24] It was this kind of arrogance and deceitful behavior that caused many Garveyites to reject Stewart as a leader and label him a fraud.

Loyal members who dismissed Stewart's directives communicated directly with Jacques Garvey and did everything in their power to assist her. They would send her small sums of money, and during the Christmas holiday, she could count on larger donations of twenty-five to thirty dollars from a variety of divisions. She was always extremely gracious and thankful, explaining that the money would be spent on household goods, books, and so forth. The New York Garvey Club was particularly attentive to her needs; during the summer of 1946 they raised enough money to pay for her and her sons' vacation in the United States and Canada. Her visit to New York was timed to correspond with the Eighth International Convention of African Peoples of the World, sponsored by the club.

As Jacques Garvey prepared for the trip, Jamaica was in disarray. Bustamante was on trial for manslaughter as a result of a riot waged by union members, and sanitation workers had just gone on strike, leaving garbage piled high in the city streets. It was surely a relief for Jacques Garvey and her sons to be able to leave the turmoil and arrive by plane in Miami on July 11 and in New York two days later.[25]

Jacques Garvey had already told Garvey Club members that she wanted to stay in an inexpensive place, "as I do not want a show, we need every penny to buy things we need and to get recreation we longed for." But her primary concern was her children's safety, and because of her hostile interaction with Stewart, she identified him as a source of trouble. "I trust Stewart & his gang will not try to hurt my children," she wrote. Stewart was an alleged thief and of questionable character, but to accuse him of possibly harming her children was extravagant, unless Jacques Garvey was aware of threats not evident in the historical record. As a protective mother, she tried to anticipate problems that could arise during their visit. She specifically requested that they reside in a private location so "that the public should not know where we stay, so that the boys can go back and forth to take shows, museums, Libraries etc., without dread of being hurt."[26]

It had been seventeen years since Jacques Garvey had been in the United States, but she still believed that if her work was made known, it would be "hampered by the watchful eye of imperialists' Agents." On the surface, this might explain her concern for the boys' safety; "real work is dangerous," she argued. It also suggests that she perceived herself as a rebel-rousing political agent in the United States, and with that status, she knew, harassment and stalking followed. But despite her repeated plea for anonymity, her instructions to Chairman Gibbons reveal that she expected to be noticed: "press conferences and other interviews" should be held at the Garvey Club, she reminded him.[27] Jacques Garvey wanted to be acknowledged on this trip as the widow of Marcus Garvey and a leader in her own right—but she also wanted to control and secure the setting.

When the Eighth International Convention of African Peoples of the World opened on 4 August 1946, three thousand people took their seats in the Golden Gate Ballroom on Lenox Avenue. In the tradition of the UNIA annual conventions held in the 1920s, the meeting opened with a parade through Harlem led by officials riding on horseback. The convention delegates resolved to demand that President Truman establish a federal inquiry to investigate recent lynchings in Georgia and that the findings be made public. Chairman Gibbons also called for political and economic security for all people of African descent, declaring that "swords shall be unsheathed for but one purpose—death to Africa's enemies." At another mass gathering on 25 August, Jacques Garvey was one of the principal speakers, along with Mexican consul general Enriu L. Elocondo and the Cuban consul general Reinaldo Fernandez Rebull. At this meeting, attendees discussed a resolution to support Ethiopia's claims for payment of reparations from Italy. Once again, Gibbons said that he was excited about the wholehearted willingness of representatives of the republics to go on record in favor of freedom for Africa.[28]

On at least one occasion during the month-long convention, Jacques Garvey gave an inspiring lecture that she later claimed helped "launch the African Nationalist Movement" in the United States "so as to better able carry on the African program." Entitled "Can Black People's Future Be Made Safe?" and delivered at St. Augustine's Church in the Bronx, the speech was an overwhelming success. One listener recounted how his "heart and spirit was moved as never before . . . having heard many women speak, but never and before in life like you." When he left the meeting, "a deep feeling of regret crept over [his] soul thinking . . . only if [he] would have been blessed to have . . . [touched] the hem of [her] garment." Such reactions provide some evidence that Jacques Garvey's sense of self-importance as a leader was not an illusion, even though, as Winston James has shown, "Many Caribbeans shared a marked tendency to exaggerate and gloat about what they perceived to be their contribution to the struggle." Her lecture was followed by musical numbers performed by Marcus Jr. and Julius Winston.[29]

On arriving home, Jacques Garvey gave a report to the *Daily Gleaner* on her travels, analyzing the post–World War II climate. She applauded the "advancements" made by black people living in the United States and Canada but lamented juvenile delinquency in America, which she directly linked to absentee mothers. World War II had given mothers and elder sisters, particularly white women, opportunities for gainful employment in the defense industries, and thus children were not given the attention they had previously received. This produced an increase of "rage" among youth, she argued. Community officers and law enforcement agencies also contended that working mothers were the main catalyst for child neglect and juvenile delinquency. Statistics do suggest that the war had a direct influence on juvenile behavior in every city in the nation, resulting in more arrests and cases brought to court. But Karen Anderson properly warns that juvenile misconduct also received more attention during and after World War II, which led to tighter enforcement and arrests, thereby exaggerating the public's perception of delinquency. Notably, the idea that mothers figured more prominently than fathers in the delinquency of youngsters was a popular notion, one that continued to resonate decades after the war.[30]

At this time, however, Jacques Garvey was wise enough not to place all the blame on mothers. She explained, "I think another contributory cause to this state of affairs is the dangerous lethal weapons which so many hardware stores" displayed. Furthermore, "attractive advertisements encourag[ed] [youngsters] to 'buy switch blades, [and] dagger-shaped knives." These observations reflect that Jacques Garvey had noticed how war magnified masculine socialization for aggressiveness and violence. In every U.S. city, "so-called commando gangs of boys" mimicked militaristic organizations and their accompanying violence. These gangs were firmly rooted in American society by the war's end: "even young children are forced to join" clubs or societies "at the risk of being beaten to death by other club members."[31]

The circumstances that created juvenile delinquency were not unique to the United States. In Jamaica, discrimination and mobility, especially movement from the country to the city, were also cited as important etiological factors in a 1950 study. Personal aggression, rather than property offenses, characterized the behavior of wayward youth. As unemployment rose, working-class areas featured gangs of boys who fought with knives.[32] Jacques Garvey responded to these mushrooming difficulties by keeping her own sons on a tight schedule and under close supervision. She had specific goals for them and was determined that they remain focused on school. She felt that providing the best education for her sons was her most important responsibility.

Educating children was no easy feat in Jamaica, since secondary schools were still reserved for the middle and upper classes. Curbing the growth of formal schooling had been an early strategy of the Jamaican Assembly—planters, businessmen, lawyers, and merchants—to control the labor supply. The 1943 census confirmed that primary education had diminished illiteracy considerably, with 71.2 percent of males and 75.0 percent of females between the ages of 6 and 14 attending public schools. But secondary schooling continued to be an exclusive realm, with only 7.7 percent of males and 8.3 percent of females between the ages of 15–19 attending.[33] Jacques Garvey struggled to ensure that her sons would be a part of that 7.7 percent.

With no disposable income, Jacques Garvey was always looking for ways to drum up money for her sons' books, fees, and uniforms. One of her ideas was to reprint *Philosophy and Opinions*. While in New York, she had received an estimate for printing costs from the William Frederick Press Company: $2,450 for the first 1,000 copies and $1,525 for an additional 1,000. She also needed $65 for spacing the text and illustrations per thousand, and the publisher wanted half the money on deposit. Although the Garvey Club offered to help finance the reprints, the project was just too costly, so Jacques Garvey prepared her children for scholarship exams instead. She explained that "this is the only means by which they can be educated. . . . [S]econdary education costs a lot out here. Some schools charge as high as seven pounds per quarter of three months."[34]

All of her preparations paid off, for one year after Garvey's death, Marcus Jr. won a scholarship at Calabar High School. Jacques Garvey proudly exclaimed that "he got the highest marks in the entire school in Latin and honors in Spanish." He was the youngest boy in his class and his teachers described him as "brilliant." Three years later, Jacques Garvey prepared Julius for his scholarship test for Wolmers Boys' School. In the end his young age prevented him from winning the full award, but he did receive a partial scholarship. Jacques Garvey had a more difficult time with Julius and periodically was disappointed with his academic performance. In communication with Wolmers' headmaster, Jacques Garvey shared that she "tried very hard to impress in [Julius] the serious consequence of laxity in his work." She believed that her son needed regular reminders that he had to make the most out of his Wolmers opportunity.[35]

At age fifteen, Marcus Jr. passed the Cambridge University senior examination. Although he liked to write, his mother was against this professional choice, "as that d[id] not pay" in Jamaica; she was "keen on economics, as this is really the base of all activities, industrial, commercial, and banking." As a practical intellectual, she instructed her sons that their schooling was not just about acquiring knowledge, but maintaining a class position. Occupational choice was important to her, and she conveyed that it was only obtainable if they worked hard. Unlike many parents, however, Jacques Garvey did not transfer her own unfulfilled aspirations onto her children, nor did she articulate that their employment was a means to secure her old age, a sentiment often voiced by working-class parents.[36]

She also kept her sons busy in a variety of extracurricular activities. On weekends they played football and cricket. Marcus Jr.'s foot had fully recovered, but his mother "always [had] to keep him nourished and warm at nights, yet getting fresh air." The boys also enjoyed sea bathing and sometimes a movie. In England they had acquired a "taste for good acting" and were "rather critical" of most films they saw in Jamaica. (It is somewhat remarkable that they could even recall living in London, since they were only five and eight years old at the time. Clearly, their mother was largely responsible for their remembrances; as an adult, Julius described how she read letters sent to him by his father, "some repeated so often [that Julius] began to imagine [he had] been there.") In the summer, her children required more of her attention; on one occasion she wrote that having them "home for two months vacation, [she] could not write [her] article."[37]

Mothering her sons was not the only caregiver role that Jacques Garvey performed during these years. In the last months of her aunt's life, Jacques Garvey nursed her when she became ill, "as old folks do not want to go to the Hospitals out here." Although her aunt was also supported by other siblings, sometimes familial responsibilities took their toll on Jacques Garvey and she became worn out from having to "carry the entire burden" of her family.[38]

While she negotiated the roles of dutiful mother and niece in her private life, Jacques Garvey continued her activism in Jamaican politics. Since the 1920s she had been acutely aware of the power of nationalism, but by the late 1940s she became particularly sensitive to class issues. It had become increasingly clear to her that the political framework of both the PNP and the JLP impeded the development of racial and class mobilization among the laboring masses, largely due to these parties' flirtation with conservative elites. The PNP's ineffectiveness was exacerbated by the onset of the Cold War. During this period the propaganda against Marxists increased substantially, and Norman Manley buckled under pressure from international and national communities to purge their hard-core, left-wing activists. The harassment against PNP progressives—Ken Hill, Frank Hill, Richard Hart, and Arthur Henry—climaxed with their expulsion from the party in 1952, when they were accused of disseminating communist doctrine.

The following year, the PNP refused to criticize the British invasion of Guyana, which ousted the progressive People's Political Party from power.[39] Thus, even though the PNP had acquired more mass support since the 1944 election, the shedding of its left-wing activists and socialist policies made it quite similar to the JLP. Not surprisingly, center and right-wing middle-class elements soon began to dominate the PNP, quickly eliminating the party's key economic aim of state participation in the economy. By 1954 the JLP and PNP differed on few issues—and only in degree, not substance. The modern Jamaican movement had been started by workers in 1938 but ended in the hands of upper-middle-class leaders, who by the 1950s had abandoned the workers' interests.

As Jacques Garvey became increasingly disillusioned by the PNP, she also found herself progressively cut off from the rest of the world. During World War II the black press in the United States had enjoyed unprecedented power because of its voluminous international circulation. A New York City post office examiner observed "the undue feeling of triumph the [N]egro is experiencing over the fact that he is fighting back" through black publications. Walter White, president of the National Association for the Advancement of Colored People (NAACP), explained that the war gave African Americans a sense of kinship with other colored peoples of the world and that their struggle "is part and parcel of the struggle against imperialism and exploitation in India, China, Burma, Africa, the Philippines, Malaya, the West Indies, and South America."[40] Jacques Garvey agreed with this idea and clamored for reading material in order to accurately interpret international events. But as U.S. Cold War influences reached hemispheric proportions, capitalist nations worldwide aligned against the perceived threat of communism. As a result of this ideological warfare, dissenting publications and activists considered sympathetic to communist ideas were tagged "red" and subversive.

"America [spent] billions of dollars yearly to fight communism—an ideology," Jacques Garvey observed. In fact, an inordinate amount of money was used to persecute progressive activists and their organizations. The NAACP was one of the first targets. The "aim was to destabilize the NAACP, drive friendly whites from it on the grounds that they were likely to be reds, and intimidate Blacks from joining on similar grounds." Under Walter White's leadership, the NAACP's militancy waned, and he too began to view W. E. B. Du Bois as his nemesis. Du Bois had refused to buckle under the anticommunist attack, continuing to advocate equality and socialism. Determined to extinguish all controversial flames, White ousted Du Bois from the NAACP in 1948, accusing him of "radical thought."[41]

Walter White was not the only leader who sheltered himself against anticommunist propaganda by becoming a watered-down progressive. A. Philip Randolph separated the "interest of Black labor from the radical left," since Marxists were now perceived as infiltrators. Like a number of other African American leaders, Randolph wanted political support from the Truman administration, since the president had proposed to "increase federal assurance of civil rights for the black majority"—but this assurance came "while curtailing black radical dissent."[42]

Essentially, to expand their civil rights on the domestic front, many African Americans elected to subscribe to anticommunist rhetoric. This agenda articulated by designated African American leadership, influential journalists, and intellectuals "eclipsed" the Pan-African politics that had characterized the immediate post–World War II period.[43]

Cold War victory necessitated a consensus of opinion, and so where foreign policy ideas were concerned, the U.S. Office of Censorship wanted a monolithic press. When the press underwent an overarching about-face, black journalists who had been critical of colonialism and supportive of African diasporic issues found themselves "blacklisted or dropped from leading African American papers." Medias that stimulated intellectual exchange were squashed, as radicals insulated themselves against undemocratic tactics. By 1950, Penny Von Eschen persuasively argues, "there was a fundamental transformation of anticolonial discourse and a dramatic narrowing of coverage of Africa and the Caribbean in the black American press."[44]

The United States had been an important venue for Jacques Garvey's literature. With the demise of the nation's radical black press, it became more difficult for her to keep abreast of African and anticolonial discussions. Although she continued to work as a journalist, her recorded output pales compared to her production in the 1940s. Still serving as the collector agent for *The African* and *African Opinion* magazines, she maintained her commitment to distribute these journals, but readership declined and sales dropped.[45] This caused publication to be sporadic, and in 1951 *African Opinion* was no longer distributed due to lack of capital.[46] U.S.-influenced bans against literature in Jamaica also became widespread in 1959, when Fidel Castro ousted dictator Fulgencio Batista, a former "friend" of the United States. Ninety miles north of Jamaica, Castro berated U.S. imperialism and resolved to reduce Cuba's economic and political dependence on America. Overall, the Cold War curtailed not only the leftists' political function, but that of nationalists and Pan-Africanists as well.

With few avenues—including *The Drum*, published in Johannesburg, South Africa—to circulate her articles, much of Jacques Garvey's writing simply became a defense of Marcus Garvey's character against slanderous statements and false facts, printed mainly in the *Daily Gleaner*. Still inundated with endless requests concerning Garvey and Garveyism by students, teachers, and political activists, she also spent a great deal of time replying to inquiries. The record suggests that she answered every letter with care. Establishing a ritualized response, she first wanted to know if the writer was "white or colored" and what prompted him or her to take an interest in Marcus Garvey, apart from just collecting historical information. She never explained why these questions were important, nor do the records indicate that she gave different answers depending on the race of the questioner. She seemed to be most interested in *who* the people were; to her, their race was important to their identity.[47]

Almost everyone who requested information from Jacques Garvey stated that they were writing theses, dissertations, or books. David Cronon led this pack of scholars with the publication of *Black Moses: The Story of Marcus Garvey and the Universal Negro Improvement Association* (1955). Jacques Garvey answered all of Cronon's questions, and he acknowledged that she had freely given of her time, providing factual information about her husband along with scarce copies of his publications. For her part, Jacques Garvey was impressed with Cronon's research and applauded the citations that enabled readers to follow up all of his references for a deeper understanding of Garvey and his motives. But reading the book was difficult for her, because it vividly brought to her mind "the horrors of the past years," and she found herself defending Garvey. She had received a copy of *Black Moses* while "under-going financial difficulty, and to read again the concerted efforts to destroy Garvey, while [she] suffer[ed] that stark reality of his years of giving all" was excruciating.[48]

Her praise of Cronon notwithstanding, Jacques Garvey detailed the shortcomings of his book in an extensive critique that centered on the author's characterization of the UNIA as a program of "escape, either emotional or physical." It was difficult for her to imagine how Cronon could write that the movement was an escapist program for African Americans after he had read "so much of Garvey's utterances and writings." She told him that his analysis seemed to be an "effort to appease Black American leadership." That is, by presenting the UNIA as a movement outside African American political life at the turn of the century, Cronon portrayed Marcus Garvey and his followers as somewhat reactionary, apolitical "foreigners." Garvey had "dared to come into their theater of action and steal the show," Jacques Garvey wrote, and African American leaders were jealous of his ability to lead millions when they could only sway hundreds.[49]

Jacques Garvey also wished that Cronon had consulted her on the Ashwood question. He had written that she and Amy Ashwood had been friends in Jamaica and that Ashwood had invited her to the United States. Jacques Garvey explained that she met Ashwood "for the first time in New York City," and that they never had a "past relationship." It was "very painful" to be so associated with Ashwood, because "her way of life has been entirely different to mine." This analysis was not altogether true. Having two children produced a stationary, but not static, lifestyle for Jacques Garvey, whereas Ashwood was free to live a nomadic existence. But they had both remained steadfast Pan-African intellectuals; Jacques Garvey's activism was connected to dispersing ideas of empowerment, and Ashwood tied her political work directly to financial schemes. In the end, Jacques Garvey thanked Cronon for his "work and effort to place Garvey in an historical setting of American life and development," and she sent kudos to the University of Wisconsin Press "for being broadminded enough to publish same."[50]

As Cronon's *Black Moses* rolled off the press, Jacques Garvey had only three copies of *Philosophy and Opinions* in her possession. UNIA president James Stewart had never returned the three hundred volumes he had taken in 1940, and this loss magnified her financial despair. Furthermore, she was constantly bombarded with requests for these books. Jean Blackwell, curator of the Schomburg Collection in New York City, indicated that the two volumes of *Philosophy and Opinions* in the collection's possession were "almost worn to shreds and we are anxious to obtain fresh copies."[51] Once again, Jacques Garvey investigated the possibility of publishing reprints to meet these demands.

Jacques Garvey and William Sherrill, who was back at the UNIA helm, discussed how they could get the books back in circulation. Although willing to pay interest on money loaned to her for the reprints, as well as giving the UNIA a certain number of the books to sell as reimbursement, Jacques Garvey refused to give up the copyright. The fact that the copyright was even mentioned appalled her; in disbelief she asked, how could these men "bare-facedly" try to take her copyright away? Sherrill clarified that there must have been a misunderstanding between Jacques Garvey and UNIA officers—he did not oppose her maintaining the copyright "to this[,] your brain-child." But he did regret that she "felt it necessary to speak so bitterly" about the attitudes of the present UNIA leadership. He explained that she was not the only one experiencing personal hardships; as president, he received no pay and only expenses in the field.[52]

To say that Jacques Garvey was suffering financial hardships was an understatement. By 1956 both her sons were attending universities, where it was nearly impossible to keep them, especially Julius Winston, who attended medical school in Canada: "[W]ith fees raised and instruments and books at a height I cannot stomach the petty meanness of Negro men toward us." She contended, "I cannot publicly denounce them [the UNIA leadership], but when I get a chance as this, I have to point out to them their unworthiness."[53] Thirty years earlier she had denounced many black men in her *Negro World* editorials on these same grounds, but this time around she believed that demeaning public comments were politically inappropriate, especially since her UNITY philosophy discouraged internal

Amy Jacques Garvey viewing the bust of Marcus Garvey erected in Jamaica on 4 November 1956. Photographer unknown. Schomburg Center for Research in Black Culture.

bickering. Still, Jacques Garvey's personal history reveals that when she felt attacked, she defended herself, to the surprise of many.

In the midst of this turmoil, Jacques Garvey finally saw the fruits of her labor rewarded when the Jamaican government acknowledged the heroic nature of Marcus Garvey's lifework by unveiling a bust of him in King

George VI Memorial Park. Although George Padmore commented that the ceremony revealed a "typical West Indian mentality to make a big show of erecting public statues to men," and that the money could be better spent by endowing a scholarship or building a school, Jacques Garvey was more optimistic and thankful for the organizing committee's effort to "commemorate the worth and work" of her husband.[54] As a compulsive organizer, she made herself available to the committee, but her suggestions to hire a Jamaican sculptor, as well as her concerns about who should write the program, were bureaucratically bypassed. No doubt she was perturbed by the standoffish behavior of the committee and its decision not to involve her directly. If the members were not aware of her skills in the beginning, her letters to them revealed that she was capable of sound suggestions. One has to wonder why they tactfully disallowed her participation. Perhaps they had heard that she was opinionated and difficult to work with. Did they fear that she would take over the project? Or maybe they did not see her as a "legitimate" organizer of big affairs. Whatever the reason, during most of the planning stages her voice was silenced by others in positions of power. One year later they finally invited her "to be associated with the committee," and Jacques Garvey graciously replied that she was glad to be of service. The lavish ceremony took place on 4 November 1956. Jacques Garvey sat on the platform, without her sons—who were abroad at school—but with a host of dignitaries. Evidently she was not asked to speak, but she was introduced to the audience.[55]

This event was a high point for Jacques Garvey. Only nine months later, in August 1957, her mother became ill and died.[56] Although she seldom referred to their personal relationship, Jacques Garvey's mother had been an important support system for her and her sons, especially after Garvey's death. Her loss appears to have prompted Jacques Garvey to reflect on her own life: it was at this time that she began to seriously write the first chapters of her memoir. Cronon's book had not satisfied inquiring minds about Marcus Garvey, and who was in a better position to set the record straight than his widow? Instead of rescinding her commitment to the anticolonial struggle during the repressive Cold War, as others had done, she took this opportunity to focus on it and to remember her life with Garvey, while simultaneously defending his character and motives to the world.

I n the last period of her life, Amy Jacques Garvey continued to focus on preserving and spreading the legacy of Garveyism, especially the Pan-African concept. At the same time, her increasingly leftist political perspective was revealed on her long-awaited trip to Africa, as well as in her commentary on the Jamaican political scene following independence. These efforts absorbed all of her time and energy in the 1960s and until her death in 1973.

Since the 1920s, Jacques Garvey's organizing activities had sought to further the decolonization of West African nations as people of African descent endeavored to restructure their societies. The antecedents of these largely nationalist movements were well established in the Pan-African struggle that came into its own during the early 1940s—including the Fifth Pan-African Congress and Jacques Garvey's memorandums—as well as in other power shifts around the globe: the rise of the Soviet Union, liberation struggles in Indochina, the independence of China and India, and the Asian-African Bandung Conference. Indeed, within this political milieu, "West African nationalism and various brands of Pan-Africanism," Hakim Adi poignantly argues, "could mix with everything from Fabian Socialism [to] Marxism-Leninism." The Cold War undoubtedly induced colonial officials to quicken the pace of self-government in the commonwealth as a defense against the real and imagined "threat" of communism. Thus, although the decolonization process was a hard-won fight, driven by Africans to remove imperialist footholds in Africa, it was largely channeled by British colonial administrators into establishing new forms of control, primarily through economic regulation, the "Africanization" of civil service positions, and the direct grooming—by Europeans—of future politicians.[1]

"Despite the greed of the colonialists fighting among themselves to keep Africa in perpetual suppression and oppression," Jacques Garvey said in 1960, "Africa shall be free." And when her longtime friend Nnamdi Azikiwe invited her to attend his inaugural ceremonies as the first African governor-general and commander in chief of the Federation of Nigeria, she eagerly seized the opportunity to visit—for the first time in her life— the continent that she had written about for over forty years. Marcus Garvey had always been denied entry into Africa, "so the dearest wish in his heart was not accomplished"; Jacques Garvey thus viewed this opportunity "with gratification and joy." It would have been out of character, though, for her simply to go to Africa as a tourist; she described her travels as a "West African good-will tour."[2]

With financial assistance from her adult sons, Jacques Garvey was able to make the trip, arriving at the Lagos airport on 11 November 1960 for the installation ceremony. The historic oath taking took place on 16 November, and all of the other inaugural events, including a thanksgiving service at the Cathedral Church of Christ, were a royal operation. Over 37 African heads of state, about 170 distinguished international figures from countries outside the continent of Africa, and more than 32,000 Nigerians were present.[3]

Although appointed by Queen Elizabeth II to the post, Azikiwe asserted that his governorship was "an instrument of constitutional authority," as opposed to "an instrument of absolute authority" as it had been during the colonial era. That is, as a constitutional ruler, Azikiwe avowed that he exercised power to "reflect the wishes of a democratically constituted authority." But Jacques Garvey was most impressed with his belief that "the existence of a stable and constitutional government in Nigeria [could] become a motive power for the revival of the stature of man in Africa and an impelling force for the restoration of the dignity of man in the world." This paraphrase from Azikiwe's lengthy inaugural speech, along with other extracts, Jacques Garvey explained, should be taught to school children not only in Nigeria, but also all over the Pan-African world. Children of African descent should "learn the words and be able to recite them just as American children are taught Abraham Lincoln's Gettysburg speech. This would inspire them to leadership and service."[4]

At one point during the weeklong activities—and in the company of Mr. Mildred F. Johnson, first vice president of the Afro-West Indian Affairs and founder of the Afro-West Indian Society in London, and W. B. Williams, federal member of the West Indian Parliament—Jacques Garvey delivered a public lecture in which she "preached" the "philosophy of Garveyism." She discussed the Universal Negro Improvement Association (UNIA) slogan "Africa for the Africans" (those at home and those abroad) and motto "One God, One Aim, One Destiny." Johnson followed with a talk "to promote goodwill and understanding between the West Indians and their African ancestors." Then together they left Nigeria for Ghana at the invitation of President Kwame Nkrumah. Jacques Garvey was just as elated about this last leg of her journey as she had been about visiting Nigeria, for she looked "forward to meet[ing] many of [her] relatives that [she had] not seen for two hundred years," referring to her "Ghanaian ancestors" who had been taken from West Africa as slaves and deposited in the Western Hemisphere.[5]

This yearning of Jacques Garvey's—to return "home"—has become an integral part of the Pan-African theme. A return home harks back to the first generation of Africans who were uprooted from the continent and absorbed into the transatlantic slave trade. Whether in the form of repatriation petitions or returning one's spirits in a ritual or ceremony or ashes in death, diverse records, folklore, and myth all speak to the attempt to "go home." But the Garveys' desire to foster a relationship with Africa, in conceiving of an African nationality and of Africa as a homeland, should not be understood as the popular but misapplied idea that they advocated a romantic "Back to Africa" movement.[6] This is an important distinction, because they argued that an Africa redeemed from colonial rule would give New World Africans international influence and strength to demand fair and equal treatment for themselves wherever they lived. The Garveys were fully aware that the majority of black diasporians had no desire to return to another oppressive setting and, moreover, that most of them were unequipped to build up Africa in practical ways.

By 1960, however, diasporic Africans were taking an interest in the motherland as never before, and African leaders were encouraging both short- and long-term emigration. On one occasion in Harlem, St. Clair Drake recalls Nkrumah inviting "almost ten thousand people . . . to come to Africa as teachers and technicians." This had been the Garveys' call since the 1920s—a fact that may help to explain why Jacques Garvey had no ambivalent reactions toward Africa during her stay there. This in itself was unusual, as Leslie Alexander Lacy notes: "Black bodies in exile" often developed a "refugee" mentality. More specifically, in Ghana, Lacy remembered, "the moves you make appear to reflect political acumen, but in reality they are based on acute anxiety, blind acceptance of an ideology you vaguely comprehend, a confused fusion of the political rhetoric you learned back home (which of course has nothing to do with the present political culture), and equally irrelevant, what you read in the daily newspaper." Similarly, on a visit to Ghana Richard Wright constantly experienced a sense of dislocation that prompted him to pose the question, "How much am I a part of this?"[7]

Admittedly, Jacques Garvey often wrote about Africa from the perspective of a united race, downplaying differences to emphasize a common heritage, mission, and future. An end to colonial rule constituted the core of both her and her husband's diatribe; thus, it is no surprise that Kwame Nkrumah wrote in his highly circulated autobiography, "of all the literature that I studied, the book that did more than any other to fire my enthusiasm was *Philosophy and Opinions of Marcus Garvey* published in 1923." When Nkrumah named Ghana's national shipping line the "Black Star Line Limited," the Garveyesque connection was sealed. Fundamentally, Nkrumahism, as Michael Williams points out, is an "assimilation, advancement and refinement of Garveyism."[8] In many ways Garvey was a modern mentor, in that Garveyism was a political program directed toward the redemption of Africa, although later Garveyism became in some ways a mere shadow of its former self, manipulated to meet the diverse objectives of later thinkers and activists.

Many of Jacques Garvey's colleagues brought the complementary nature of Nkrumahism and Garveyism to her attention. Jean Blackwell, curator for the Schomburg Collection in Harlem, wrote her, "It must warm your heart to have lived to see him so appreciated after all these years." Blackwell, like so many of Jacques Garvey's comrades, had failed to interpret this political surge as also being an effect of Jacques Garvey's own contribution to the Pan-African effort. Fortunately, both Azikiwe and Nkrumah were perceptive enough to acknowledge not only Jacques Garvey's historic role in the movement, but also her contemporary importance in the next phase of African liberation; hence, they took it upon themselves to invite her "home" as a guest of their respective governments. Yet Jacques Garvey saw her "return" as representing something beyond herself. In fact, she stated that "to the African I represented the spirit of Marcus Garvey—the 'Returned One.' "[9]

Even prior to landing in Accra, Jacques Garvey said that she was "glad to see the progress Ghana has made since her independence." It had only been three years since Nkrumah had been named president of the republic, but his proposal to rebuild its economy along socialist lines and to produce a self-reliant, democratic state addressing the needs of the people was in full swing. Most notable were the substantial numbers of new hospitals and schools that had been built. Since education had always been a high priority for Jacques Garvey, her itinerary included a visit to the Bureau of Ghana Languages. Housed under the Ministry of Education, the bureau had been set up by Nkrumah to "facilitate the achievement of his Pan-Africanist goals."[10] Nkrumah understood that communication was the key to building a united Africa; so the bureau was composed of schools to teach languages, particularly English and French, as well as translator skills. In addition, African languages were studied as degreed subjects. Essentially the bureau, later called the Ghana Institute of Languages, was a unique setting for higher learning, promoting the idea that "through the teaching and learning of modern languages, . . . communication competence, cultural understanding and general economic development among the comm[uni]ty of nations, particularly in Africa," would come to pass.[11]

Jacques Garvey "marvelled" at the "rapid development and progress of Ghana." She attributed it to Nkrumah's "dynamism, in both personality and in leadership," along with the fact that he "also mixed freely with the people." Jacques Garvey was not alone in her assessment of Nkrumah's personality. C. L. R. James, secretary of the West Indian Federal Labor Party, remarked that "thanks to Nkrumah's unselfconscious autobiography, the Ghana revolution shows . . . the relation between people and leader," including his "sympathy for the ordinary people, his intuitive understanding of them, his respect for them." However, one scholar points out that the many accolades for Nkrumah were in fact an indication that so many activists' "own reputation[s]" were "invested in a certain image of Nkrumah's significance as a Pan-African leader and as the living embodiment of the International African Service Bureau."[12]

In Ghana, Jacques Garvey was equally interested in the Women's Division of Nkrumah's Convention People's Party (CPP). Years before her trip, she had befriended Evelyn Amarteifio, secretary for the Federation of Women in Accra, regarding the need to expand the federation to include women in the diaspora. She charged Amarteifio to "explain to Dr. Nkrumah how important it will be as a link between all Units of the Race—in the West Indies, United States, and the Homeland, not only for women's pursuits but as a means of publicizing Africa's national activities to the Western World." This expansion would make it "possible to get financial aid for social services, as well as technicians and scientists" in Africa.[13] As an activist who always looked toward securing the future, she appealed to her natural constituency, women, to serve as leaders.

Stability and prosperity in Ghana—along with other West African states—required a thriving economy that was coordinated with regional developments. It was through the Trade Union Congress (TUC)—so integral to the CPP that one membership card was used for both organizations—that both Nkrumah and Jacques Garvey addressed workers on 29 November 1960. In a number of speeches Nkrumah clarified that "public officers and state workers" not only had to "reali[z]e their obligation to the State, but also accept fully the responsibility which they share for the task of reconstruction in which we are engaged. The nation expects from you all maximum dedication to its service." (A national minimum wage was established, but workers were expected to maintain a forty-four-hour workweek, and in 1961 all wage earners would lose 5 percent of their income to supplement the welfare programs.) Following Nkrumah's lead, Jacques Garvey urged her audience at a TUC meeting to undertake every job assignment with a "deep sense of responsibility in the interest of the country and its people." Although in awe of Nkrumah, she knew that he could not carry the burden of a free Ghana alone. Every citizen had to do his or her part to unite as "one people, one race with one destiny" to ensure its promise.[14]

No longer the young woman who avoided the limelight, Jacques Garvey was a confident activist, always willing to speak to an organized gathering. At every turn she gave her opinion on issues related to the Pan-African struggle, and on 29 November 1960, while in Ghana, she addressed the impending crisis in the Congo.

On 30 June 1960 the Belgian Congo had become independent, largely due to the stoic leadership of Patrice Lumumba. A brilliant thinker and orator, Lumumba exemplified the ideological sophistication that Africa needed. But like other Europeans, the Belgians never intended to relinquish power, and one month before independence they reinforced their military might in the Congo to ensure neocolonial domination. As prime minister, Lumumba refused to be a puppet of the new state and ordered the Belgian troops to leave the Congo, condemning their "external aggression" and "colonialist machinations." The troops refused to go, igniting a crisis that drew in the United Nations and the United States as allies with Belgium. The Belgian authorities called Lumumba an unscrupulous communist who had to be contained because he was serving Soviet interests. (He had accepted Soviet assistance, but during the height of the alleged Soviet intervention, only about 380 Soviets and Czechoslovaks were up against 14,000 United Nation troops, which essentially functioned as U.S. agents, and thousands of Belgian military officers.)[15]

People of African descent the world over were in sympathy with Lumumba and the Congolese. Nkrumah sent troops and spoke out in support of the prime minister: "no outside power—not even the United Nations—has the right to unseat [Lumumba] by military force or intrigue with other Congolese, no matter how hard they find it to work with [Lumumba]." To Africans and to the sympathetic diaspora, the future of African liberation required that the people of the Congo make their own decision through Parliament or their assembly. Nkrumah tried to support Lumumba, but behind the scenes Ghana's many white officers held different sympathies. Nkrumah's Congo policy soon became shaded by complicated Cold War politics. Jacques Garvey, however, was free from the policy-making fray, unhesitantly proclaiming it "the responsibility of Africans, not Europeans, to see that the law and order was maintained in the Congo." But the enemies of African liberation proved too strong, and Lumumba was assassinated on 17 January 1961, with the U.S. Central Intelligence Agency playing a major role in the murder.[16]

Jacques Garvey's trip to Nigeria and Ghana appears to have been a major highlight of her intellectual life. As soon as she was back in Jamaica, she began chronicling her impressions of African nationalism in a number of unpublished essays, as well as in her personal correspondence. Since she had been so closely connected to Africa for decades, she rejoiced in experiencing the "atmosphere of the Old and New Africa." Essentially, she had been renewed by her trip to the motherland. Aimé Césaire's poetic verse from his "notebook of a return to the native land" in many ways captures what she must have felt: "Suddenly now strength and life assail me like a bull and the water of life overwhelms the papilla of the morne, now all the veins and veinlets are bustling with new blood and the enormous breathing lung of cyclones and the fire hoarded in volcanoes and the gigantic seismic pulse which now beats the measure of a living body in my firm conflagration."[17]

Everywhere she went, Jacques Garvey reported, she had been "treated royally" and acknowledged as Mrs. Garvey, the wife of the man who was a "son of Africa" and who had "used every means available to enlighten world opinion of the facts and truth" about Africa that had been "suppressed by white news agencies." African leaders gave Garvey full credit "for his prophetic warnings and declarations." In fact, one prominent Nigerian told Jacques Garvey that "whatever our leaders say today, Garvey said more than forty years ago."[18]

Jacques Garvey's articles and letters from this period return in style to her 1920s "impressionistic" reporting. They capture the diversity of Africa and its peoples, yet remain committed to her unity theme. In this "New" Africa, all belonged to the "whole, yet sharing it, with the joy of knowing that they are masters of their destiny in their own country." Although she provided details on the efficiency of the railroads and buses, ten-story office buildings, and modern equipment like air conditioners and elevators, she pointed to the fact that every aspect of African life was "manned by Africans."[19] Self-reliance was imperative to a prosperous Africa and could be used to unite regional countries and, eventually, the entire continent. A reciprocal relationship between ideas and economy produced like minds similarly dedicated to the Pan-African goal. Jacques Garvey's essays considered these ideas in the context of the magnitude of change worldwide.

She also described how black diasporians' freedom and national identity were located in Africa's liberation. More specifically, she discussed the direct links between freedom struggles in Africa and the civil rights movement in the United States, making use of the example provided by the problems faced by African ambassadors to the United Nations. By 1960 the United Nations had become the chief mechanism through which racial disputes were addressed within an international format, and since it was headquartered in New York, America's Jim Crow practices had become the focus of world attention. When African diplomats were treated with the same contempt that African Americans experienced daily, it became a highly visible matter, calling into serious question the U.S. human rights record. For instance, in December 1960, when a Nigerian diplomat was refused restaurant service, the National Council of Nigeria and the Cameroons issued a statement indicting the United States: "A country devoid of respect for human dignity, a country with completely bankrupt racial policy, a country which still lives in the dark ages, had no claim to leadership of free men." Other African envoys recounted how housing discrimination affected their ability to function as statesmen. The Ghana embassy even filed a complaint with the State Department regarding racial harassment.[20] In her essays Jacques Garvey explained that American civil rights laws were altered, in part, due to the presence of African representatives at the United Nations and because embassies and consulates generated "constant embarrassment to the State Department when they were mistaken for and mistreated as American Negroes."[21] Numerous contemporary Cold War scholars also point out how African criticism of America's racial problems helped break down Jim Crow by exposing the contradictions of U.S. foreign policy compared to its domestic laws.[22]

The Garveys had always articulated how racial problems throughout the diaspora could not be resolved without engaging issues of African independence and self-determination, especially since, as Jacques Garvey put it, black people are "all one in the eyes of the white world." So "lets us [sic] clasp hands across the seas—the U.S.A., the West Indies, Central & South America, and right across to the continent of Africa. All of one blood, what happens to one Unit, affects the prestige of the others." The 1960s proved this hypothesis correct, as calls for freedom and liberation echoed simultaneously throughout Africa and the black diaspora. Nor were the Caribbean territories left out of this equation, as in 1962 both Jamaica and Trinidad and Tobago were the first British holdings to achieve political independence.[23]

Since 1944 the march toward self-government in Jamaica had been slow, with each step announced as the "final" one such that—as Gordon Lewis notes—"colonialism, for Jamaicans," ended "not in a bang but a whimper." But Jacques Garvey contended that the main reason "why the West Indies [had] not attained independence after many years of talking about it, [was] because of the false propaganda about Africa and Africans." She argued that misinformation about Africans helped to "swell" the Jamaican "ego, and make them feel that there is nothing in their ancestral continent for them to emulate, and that they are more civilized than Africans."[24] Once again, the importance of black diasporians locating their center in Africa was seen as fundamental to their progress as individual nations.

When Jamaica became independent on 6 August 1962, the two-party system of representation completely took hold of the island. The Jamaican Labor Party (JLP) and the People's National Party (PNP), which had been formed during the World War II period, were unchallengeable. With independence, the "browns" supplanted the whites in political representation. Yet the "browns" were internally divided into conservative and leftist camps, with the conservative upper-middle classes wanting to maintain a hegemonic power; under no uncertain terms did they want to revolutionize Jamaican society. Although Jamaica was desperately poor, its conservative leaders were "even more desperately determined to copy Western social and economic patterns." Jacques Garvey agreed that there could be no "progress unless the means of livelihood is guaranteed and secure," but she was critical of a Western blueprint for advancement. She encouraged Jamaicans to embrace the new "African personality"—one who "refuse[d] to be a copy plate of the European." By "unearth[ing] his ancient history, long hidden from him; he applies his traditions and customs to the demands and tempo of the times," building "character in his people [and] giving them incentives and ambitions to become full fledged men and women."[25]

Bourgeoisie interests nonetheless retained their hold, and social arrangements that kept upper-middle-class "browns" in a dominant position over the black masses continued. The adoption of Western models for redevelopment initially translated into a Jamaican economic boom based on the production of cosmetics, textiles, cement, and containers of all sorts for export markets. This period is often referred to as the "miracle years." Most factories were located in the Kingston metropolitan area, where the economy was heavily infused with foreign capital, primarily from North America. But during this time the rate of absolute poverty grew considerably; it is estimated that between 1958 and 1968 the absolute income of 30 percent of the population fell from J$32 to J$15 per capita. Unquestionably, the rich got richer and the poor got poorer at the hands of foreign investors. Seemingly, Jamaican leaders desired to "become heroes in colonial garb." For her part, Jacques Garvey remained adamantly opposed to governmental administrative "manipulation of the economic interest of the submerged black masses by an alien economic elite." By this time clearly identified with the left, she criticized the government for not dealing with workers' issues: "Those who have bread and a little butter should not get more butter, while the majority do not know where the regular daily bread is coming from."[26]

Even though Jamaican workers were plentiful, and thus to the capitalist mind, exploitable, they did not assume a passive stance and, in fact, grew increasingly rebellious under the system. In 1960 Reverend Claudius Henry, leader of a Rastafarian group, in conjunction with an armed New York–based organization, planned a coup against the Jamaican government. Although this attempt ended in dismal failure, other working-class rebellions followed.[27] (Trevor Munroe points out that in countries like Jamaica, the "relative weakness of the working class" can be attributed to "its isolation from the world revolutionary process, and predominance of non-proletarian ideologies in the national-liberation movement," as well as "its deep and many-sided ties with small land holding and petty commodity production.") The escalating violence was often centered in Kingston, where Jacques Garvey lived. Anthony Payne argues that "the violence served to arm and, above all, politicize sections of the Kingston lumpenproletariat." Jacques Garvey was extremely disturbed by the political upheaval on the island, which she blamed in part on the Jamaican government for having stifled "peaceful protest and demonstrations" through legislation that regulated meetings and marches. "It's impossible for any opponent of the two political parties—the JLP and PNP (and I am an unrelenting opponent of these two institutions and their policies) to make his voice heard in the country," she proclaimed.[28]

As the years of independence multiplied, so did Jacques Garvey's disgust with the Jamaican government. "Brown" and middle-class herself, she nevertheless felt a strong sense of solidarity with the black workers. "The blood and tears of black people have enriched Jamaica, [so] why should they be at the bottom of the economic ladder?" she asked. "The facade of political independence" produced a setting where "food, clothing and housing," the "three essentials necessary to man's existence," were all "controlled by minority groups (Chinese, Syrians and Jews)," along with "foreign cartels and companies." These conditions made her hold even more firmly to the legacy that she had helped her husband create. Although she did not insulate herself from current political happenings, she increasingly narrowed her concentration to give the public what she felt it needed to make the most of revolutionary times. Dusting off her memoir, "Garvey and Garveyism" (she had completed a first draft in 1955), Jacques Garvey was more determined than ever to have it published. Both this text and *Philosophy and Opinions*, she believed, "would inculcate a sense of pride in black awareness, dignity, love and unity[,] qualities that make for good citizens" that were essential for racial progress.[29]

In 1957 Jacques Garvey's memoir was rejected for publication. This must have surprised her, since she had reworked the earlier draft specifically to "appeal to white publishers." It is unknown exactly how Jacques Garvey revised the manuscript once she had decided to publish the book herself; by 1962 she had rewritten it a total of five times. At that point she began to solicit support from friends with access to publishers.[30] After UNIA President William Sherrill received her letter, he made an appointment to see noted Afrocentric scholar J. A. Rogers in order to obtain names of printers and "other information relative to having [her] book printed." Rogers reported, however, that he had to "find money and publish" every one of his books himself.[31] Realizing that she would have to take a similar route, Jacques Garvey felt pressed for time, especially since she continued to suffer from ill health. She believed that when she "passed on, much of the authentic story of his [Garvey's] life will be lost." Yet her narrative went beyond securing Garvey's place in history—the preservation of her own political legacy was also at stake. Fortunately, her financial appeals were soon answered when two African American Garveyites—George Willis and L. B. Fraser—consented to loan her more than half of the cost of the printing and a few hundred dollars for other expenses.[32] These funds were combined with her life savings to publish her book, which was printed in Kingston in 1963.

Overall, the appearance of *Garvey and Garveyism* went almost unnoticed.[33] Her cluttered narrative was plagued by poor organization and many undocumented quotations. Since her husband's death, she had called herself the authentic voice of Marcus Garvey, and she "could quote for hours from his speeches"; thus, she apparently felt no need to provide citations.[34] The lack of scholarly support and recognition of the book—there were no reviews of it in academic journals—did not altogether dampen her spirits. In fact, she took the few praiseworthy statements about the book and inserted them on her circular letter/mail order form.[35] This type of advertisement had been her principal form of disseminating information in the past, reminiscent of the African Study Circle's circular. Finally, she used the last of her savings to send free copies to libraries throughout the world. "This was a financial loss," Jacques Garvey wrote of her own investment, "but it paid off in terms of perpetuating the memory of Garvey and his work."[36]

Garvey and Garveyism also gave the world an extensive, introspective view of Jacques Garvey herself. Her personal life, which she had always labored to keep private, is revealed in surprising ways. The pain and frustration of living both with and without Marcus Garvey, the financial deprivation, and the ridicule and sneers that she had felt from misinformed people are woven throughout the memoir. Her sense of urgency and her belief that she had not only participated in but also helped to create significant historic moments underscore the narrative. This text confirms the degree to which Jacques Garvey had invested in securing herself a place in the black radical tradition.

After publishing the memoir, she turned her attention to retrieving her husband's body from London, where it had been held in a vault since his death in 1940. After World War II, Amy Ashwood Garvey had begun a battle with Jacques Garvey in the British courts over who was actually the "rightful kin" of Marcus Garvey and therefore entitled to his remains. When George Padmore reported in the *Chicago Defender* that the wives of Garvey were fighting over his dead body, B. Gibbons, on behalf of the New York Garvey Club, wrote Padmore a scathing letter accusing him of bringing "the attention of the world on the action introduced by Amy Ashwood into the Chancery Court relative to the question of the possession of Marcus Garvey's remains."[37] Although Ashwood Garvey had contested her divorce from Garvey in 1922, he believed that the action was legal and married Amy Jacques several months afterward. Decades later, though, Ashwood still refused to accept this judgment because she had never signed a divorce decree.

Over the years both women had appropriated Garvey, and their competing interpretations of his legacy was another site of their dispute. A 1960 article entitled "The Ghost of Marcus Garvey: Interviews with Crusader's Two Wives," which appeared in the popular African American magazine *Ebony*, reveals their differences and helps to substantiate the impression that Ashwood was just as entitled as Jacques to his legacy. The author describes Jacques as "thin and intense" and Ashwood as the "heavier" one who "wears African tribal robes," but both were "persuasive conversationalists."[38]

The two wives agreed on Garvey's main contributions to the modern world, in terms of awakening the black masses to the importance of racial unity, but in separate interviews each gave different opinions on other features of Garveyism. For example, Ashwood believed that Garvey would have "adjusted his program to changed conditions," but Jacques denied that he would have altered it, because "every plank in his platform . . . is valid." No doubt since the 1920s, both women had spent countless hours sharing their opinions about Garvey. Jacques Garvey even felt comfortable saying during the interview that "when I talk, I talk for Garvey. I feel I can interpret how he would feel if he were alive." But talking about Garvey, at least for Jacques Garvey, was not an easy experience. There were moments when reliving her years with him could be quite painful; Rupert Lewis recalled that after giving interviews, she would sometimes become physically ill from being "emotionally caught up in evoking his spirit."[39]

Once the *Ebony* article appeared, Jacques was disturbed to find that it also featured Ashwood. "You did not tell me that you intended to write a symposium," she admonished the author. Her son Julius agreed that it was "not fair to give Amy Ashwood's statement place beside [his mother's] as he ha[d] read and heard so much of her campaign to 'down Garvey' since they were divorced."[40] The inheritance and regulation of Garvey's body was indeed a literal and figurative question.

Despite Jacques Garvey's efforts, her husband's remains were not returned until the Jamaican government wanted them for ceremonies that would proclaim him the country's first national hero. Jamaican officials were unaware of the history between Jacques and Ashwood, but when they began the proceedings to recover his remains, they found themselves in an "embarrassing position" with the British government, which "demanded proof of ownership" of Garvey's body. Ashwood, who was living in Spain, returned to England and contacted her personal attorney in New York, who proved, to the satisfaction of British officials, that she and Garvey had never received a final legal decision; therefore "neither one" was divorced. Ashwood quickly signed the necessary paperwork to release his body in 1964. No doubt she was motivated by a promise (which never materialized) from Jamaican politician Leslie Alexander to "sponsor the publication of her book on the biography of Marcus Garvey and that she would be given recognition at the ceremony and a gift of $1,000 to cover her expenses in coming from Spain to sign the agreement."[41]

Meanwhile, Jacques Garvey was unaware not only that the Jamaican government was orchestrating the return of Garvey's body, but also that Leslie Alexander had begun a campaign to collect money from merchants and businessmen for that purpose. Once she learned of Alexander's actions, she told him to "stop this sort of thing, and to refund moneys subscribed, for myself and two sons do not want it said that it was through the benevolence of business men that M. G.'s body was brought back home." By this time (1964), she was so disgusted with her government's unwillingness to deal with the economic crisis of the black masses that she had a change of heart and now wanted Garvey's remains shipped to an African country where a shrine could be built. When she informed Alexander of her plans, he "got angry . . . and said that [she] was a disloyal Jamaican." After this encounter, Jacques Garvey received a message that the Jamaican minister of development and welfare wanted to see her. For the first time, in the minister's office, she was informed that "his Government had decided to bring Garvey's body here for reinterment, and that Mr. Alexander was [her] Agent."[42]

It is mind-boggling to consider that the Jamaican government would set out to remove Garvey's twenty-four-year-old remains without notifying his widow. The explanation that communications may have simply broken down between the two parties is hard to swallow. Rather, the omission seems to have been a deliberate slight of Jacques Garvey, who, although involved in Jamaican politics and absorbed in global Pan-African networks, continued to be marginalized politically on the island. In addition, she had been critical of conservative Jamaican leadership. Changing times had shifted the political tide to embrace some Pan-African ideas, but in Jamaica there was still no social or ideological space for the likes of Jacques Garvey. To some she must have appeared an oddity, possessing a black consciousness but occupying an explicitly "brown" and middle-class hegemonic position. She had no political instrument that could be used on her behalf and that would give her visibility and public recognition. Clearly, Jacques Garvey understood that she was outnumbered and overpowered. In the end she cooperated "against odds" with the government, still stipulating that "this young nation should conduct this whole procedure with dignity, sincerity and decorum."[43] To add insult to injury, Amy Ashwood had positioned herself to release Garvey's body and the Jamaican government recognized her at the London ceremonies celebrating his removal.

When his remains were finally returned to Jamaica in November 1964, Marcus Garvey was pronounced by the government to be an official national hero. As Gordon Lewis has shown, Garvey served "the need of every newly independent nation to create its own national Pantheon of father figures." But not all Jamaicans were elated about his elevated status, and some voiced their objections. Misinformation about him heated the controversy, and a substantial portion of Jamaicans were of the opinion that the core of Garvey's message, embracing an African identity, was unacceptable. Jacques Garvey sent rebuttal letters to dissenters and wrote two articles for the *Daily Gleaner* on "Garvey's Activities for Jamaicans."[44]

Her articles set the stage for the ceremonial activities surrounding the reburial of his remains. Garvey's body was first visually surveyed by his son, Dr. Julius Winston Garvey, who as the representative of his "family and with the official approval of the Ministry of Development and Welfare . . . [did] not think that it should be [an] opened [casket] to the view of the public."[45] A group of Jamaican dignitaries, led by the prime minister, took part in the Victoria Pier ceremony and the procession conveying the body to Holy Trinity Cathedral, where it stayed for five days. After a Mass was celebrated on 15 November 1964, the participants proceeded to King George VI Memorial Park for the reburial. An estimated thirty thousand people gathered at the park, and a pamphlet based on *Garvey and Garveyism* was distributed free of charge. Jacques Garvey delivered a message and her sons, Marcus Jr. and Julius, read the epistle and the gospel. The "reinterment proceedings were important," Jacques Garvey wrote, "because many of those paying homage" were "white men, brown men, and even black men in good social position, who in the 1920s and 1930s laughed at Garvey's determined task to lift the Black masses everywhere economically, socially, and politically at the stature of other races. It is a triumph for Garvey and Garveyism."[46]

The continual spread of Garveyism, evidenced through Jamaican and West African independence, gave Jacques Garvey cause to celebrate the vindication of her husband, and by 1965, the civil rights movement in the United States was added to her slate. With the advent of the Black Power movement, largely nationalistic in political orientation, African American activists had shifted the direction of their struggle. More specifically, when Willie Ricks prompted Stokely Carmichael to voice the slogan "Black Power" at the 1966 James Meredith March, it marked the public division between the professed "non-violent, direct action" protest led by Martin Luther King Jr. and a more militant stance in which activists argued that "a non-violent approach to Civil Rights is an approach Black people cannot afford and a luxury white people do not deserve." Jacques Garvey believed that this public split was positive, describing it as "the younger group of freedom fighters" separating from the "conservative interracial groups, such as the N.A.A.C.P. and the Urban League" in their demand for Black Power—"a drive to mobilize the black communities, as the only way to achieve meaningful change."[47] Jacques Garvey was so inspired by this movement that she wrote an essay to historically situate the source and course of Black Power in the United States.

The outlines of this essay germinated when a researcher asked her to respond to a series of questions about the impact of Marcus Garvey on leaders like Malcolm X and Martin Luther King Jr. Other scholars were also posing this question, having pointed out that Garvey was the modern mentor of black nationalists and that mainly his ideology had inspired West African nationalism, Pan-Africanism, and ultimately Black Power, all of which redefined political, social, and economic boundaries within societies in West Africa as well as the black diaspora. Jacques Garvey contributed to this body of thought, allowing King and Malcolm X to speak for themselves by citing their speeches commenting on Garvey's influence. Discussing Malcolm X, she had especially strong evidence on her side: both of his parents had been active members of the UNIA in Detroit, and Malcolm had said that "every time you see another nation on the African continent become independent, you know that Marcus Garvey is alive."[48]

Jacques Garvey recalled the time she had met King when he visited Jamaica in 1965. King had laid a wreath at Garvey's shrine and told a crowd of over two thousand how "Marcus Garvey was the first man of color in the history of the United States to lead and develop a mass movement. . . . You gave Marcus Garvey to the United States and he gave to the million of Negroes of the United States a sense of personhood, a sense of manhood, and a sense of somebodiness." At this event Jacques Garvey gave King a copy of *Garvey and Garveyism.* Jacques Garvey wrote of this first recipient of the Marcus Garvey Prize for Human Rights: "The Rev. King had the financial support and sympathy of influential white Americans . . . and he was doing what he was guided to do in the interest of Civil Rights for Negro Americans . . . [but] he was stopped forever, in the midst of his work by an assassin's bullet."[49]

Given that bullets kill people, Jacques Garvey argued that Black Power was an effective "weapon of defense" against injustices. Moreover, an "ideology (whether it is red/communist or black/nationalist), in the minds of people" cannot be destroyed. Throughout most of her adult life, Jacques Garvey had witnessed how ideas can empower and motivate people to struggle for change, and in this essay on Black Power she once again identified the importance of cross-fertilization of Pan-African thought. She pointed out that because African Americans were roused to struggle for liberation and took an interest in "African nationalism all over the world," they gained, as a minority in the United States, "prestige and international backing." Geographic alignments were no longer rigid borders, as Africans worldwide viewed their struggles as one. It was this black UNITY, Jacques Garvey asserted, that generated Black Power. She concluded that "Black UNITY is black power, the only power a despised, oppressed minority is capable of attaining." As an intellectual with a dynamic mind, she encouraged activists to create strategies that allowed them mobility and "flexib[ility] in expression and pronouncements so as to cope with the exigencies of the moment, keeping the goal always in mind—to change an existing system that holds them down." After this essay appeared in a two-part series in *The Star*, Jacques Garvey wanted it to reach a wider audience, so she personally published it, along with two other essays—"Marcus Garvey's Impact on Jamaica and Africa" and "The Power of the Human Spirit"—in a pamphlet entitled *Black Power in America* (1968).[50]

Jacques Garvey went on to write several essays offering her opinion on economic conditions in Jamaica, the United States, and Africa, as well as on Marcus Garvey's impact on world events.[51] But in 1970, when primary UNIA documents turned up in New York City, the frustration that she had felt over the years reached the boiling point. After struggling for decades to ensure that the Garvey legacy was understood within the larger scope of Pan-African and anticolonial history, Jacques Garvey was unprepared for what must have seemed to her crass, opportunistic appropriation of their heritage.

Boxes of UNIA documents were discovered by members of a community-based group, "The Community Thing," directed by a Mrs. Sims. Scholar Robert Hill informed Jacques Garvey that the papers were the "remaining records of the UNIA Headquarters in NY."[52] After receiving several telephone calls regarding the find, Jacques Garvey understood that Jean Huston, curator of the Schomburg Collection, had "paid a man $2,000 for a large portion of the papers, and these are now safely housed at the Library." The remainder of the documents, Jacques Garvey believed, had been turned over to famed sociologist Dr. Kenneth Clarke. Jacques Garvey immediately informed Clarke that she had "exhausted" herself "preserving and interpretating the work of Marcus Garvey." Moreover, she had "made available to Researchers, Students, and writers all the material" kept at her home and papers that she had sent to the West Indian Reference Library. "Never" had she "charged any one," and therefore she wanted "to see all the papers, documents, letters, etc." in his possession "turned over to Mrs. Jean Huston, Curator . . . so that they can be easily available to the public."[53]

In response, Clarke wrote Jacques Garvey that approximately "one-third of the total amount of these materials were in the possession of Mrs. Sims and her associate Mr. Tatum" and that "they were in complete control of the [papers]." He, Clarke, did not "have the power, nor can

I assume any right or responsibility to turn this material over to anyone." Soon Jacques Garvey received a cablegram from Mrs. Sims informing her that the culprits who initially "stole" the papers were associated with the Schomburg Library. In addition, Sims warned, the Schomburg archival facilities were deteriorating; she thus proposed to place the materials elsewhere, and Jacques Garvey agreed.[54]

Between telephone calls and letters from a variety of scholars, activists, publishers, and archivists, Jacques Garvey was overwhelmed by the fiasco.[55] Now seventy-four years old and in poor health, she was in no shape to travel to the United States to clarify matters. Perhaps this is why she ultimately decided that the materials were not a serious find. One reporter wrote that Jacques Garvey threw "cold water on the recent claim that a cache of papers belonging to her late husband represented a gold mine." It was speculated that Jacques Garvey believed that their value was exaggerated "so that people could cash in on them as Garvey Papers."[56] She also concluded that if the materials included personal correspondence, then they belonged to her, according to the terms of Garvey's will. In the end, these documents were cataloged at the Schomburg Library; they represent a major collection of UNIA business and archival documents.

This experience soured Jacques Garvey's perceptions of some scholars, who, she believed, were making a career "trading" on Garvey's name for financial reward. Eventually she accused both Robert Hill and John Henrik Clark of giving "speeches on Garvey" to increase their professional status for profit. The fact that $10,000 was eventually paid for the Garvey Papers and that scholars were earning incomes off the propagation of Garveyism must have been infuriating to Jacques Garvey. For close to fifty years, she had made herself freely available to researchers, students, and political activists, even though she continued to suffer monetary hardship during the last years of her life.[57] Since she was motivated solely by her commitment to keep the philosophy of Garveyism (and of course her own intellectual work) alive in the minds of black people, the earning power (no matter how meager) of others was, in her mind, a prostitution of Garveyism. On one occasion, she remarked that "the pickings using the name of Garvey is good these days."[58]

Openly bitter during the last years of her life, in a 1972 interview, recalling her difficulty in publishing Garvey and Garveyism, Jacques Garvey said, "I had to send my manuscript back five times and had no help, neither from my children nor from friends; they did not feel the way I felt about the movement. . . . I can truly say I had no help in all this trouble and no one to thank." Although she may not have had the support she desired, the evidence that two former Garveyites loaned her part of the money for publication counters this accusation. But again, her comments are important because they express how she at times felt about the people around her and her belief that she was in the trenches alone. That belief was substantiated by the fact that prior to the advent of noted Garvey scholars, Jacques Garvey had done much of the major work to preserve and disseminate Garveyisque ideas. She was correct in stating that "the rebirth of Garveyism in the United States and all over the world, was brought about by my intelligent and dedicated actions in bringing about or having these books published at great cost to me physically, emotionally and mentally."[59] Even though almost every prominent scholar credited her for keeping that legacy alive and for interpreting Garveyism to the world, she still felt unappreciated.[60]

Jacques Garvey's emotions were mirrored by other black female activists who gave their lives to political struggles. For example, Ida B. Wells-Barnett's autobiography offered similar melancholic sentiments regarding lack of recognition.[61] Physically and mentally worn out at the end of their lives, Jacques Garvey and Wells-Barnett both believed that others understood neither the passion of their commitment nor their sacrifices for their causes. Perhaps their unyielding dedication made them hyperjudgmental of others who appeared less committed or more motivated by greed and prestige.

The last few years of Jacques Garvey's life, however, offered notable redeeming moments. In 1971 she won the Musgrave Gold Medal, which honors "distinguished eminence." Established by the Board of Governors of the Institute of Jamaica in commemoration of Sir Anthony Musgrave, the medal acknowledges leaders in promoting literature, science, or art of the West Indies, especially Jamaica. Jacques Garvey was selected "in recognition of her dedicated and distinguished contributions to the peoples of African descent and particularly for her erudite dissertations on the philosophy of Garveyism, which have earned her a lasting place in the field of historical writings." In 1972 the first hall at the Jamaican College of Arts, Science, and Technology (CAST) to be named after a woman was named after her. At the ceremony, Jacques Garvey placed the sign bearing her name on the wall. It was reported that she addressed the gathering "on the role of women in Jamaican society and encouraged the residents of the Hall to win the respect of their male counterparts."[62] She had worked toward this goal on various levels since joining the UNIA in 1919; fifty-two years later, she still believed it was an important undertaking for women.

Her last award came directly from the Jamaican government, which voted in 1973 to give Widows of National Heroes a $6,800 annual tax-free pension. Cabinet members believed that she was entitled to the funds not only as Marcus Garvey's widow, but also in view of her "own distinguished contribution to the progressive movements of black people of the world, along with [her] work in advancing black consciousness and awareness." Although grateful for their "assessment of [her] worth to [her] race and [the Jamaican] nation," it was impossible for Jacques Garvey to compromise her principles by accepting the pension. At age seventy-eight, she still lived on a tight budget, a limit she attributed to the Jamaican government's unwillingness to regulate the economy. No amount of "money" was "adequate compensation" for the personal sacrifices and the "harassment" she had suffered from the "governmental administrators whose lust for political power and personal aggrandisment" transfigured her into "an implacable enemy" because she opposed their manipulation of the economy.[63] Jacques Garvey understood why the black masses lived on the economic edge and felt that this issue merited publicity, so she took the opportunity to critique economic policy. In an extended essay, she asserted that "the priorities for financial help should go to those who have no proper shelter . . . lack of opportunities to earn daily bread and the necessities of life."[64]

In touch with a world where progressive Africans were rejecting "all the things originating from metropolitan powers, including capitalism as an appropriate economic form," Jacques Garvey was influenced by this thinking, especially since over the years she had witnessed the "high price paid" to develop African capitalism by exploiting the working black masses. Her essay advocates that the government should function as a "wholesaler" to end monopolization and to ensure the fair distribution of resources. Overall, her criticism reflects her "effort to have a Better Jamaica from the grass-roots up."[65] Yet because this was a scathing attack against the government, several Kingston publishers refused to print it "for fear of political victimization." This pained Jacques Garvey "to the point of tears"; yet she persisted, including having a limited edition mimeographed for the public.[66]

Jacques Garvey had experienced many disappointments in her political life, and she believed that eventually these emotions and frustrations had registered in her body. She had "reached a point after all of these years," Rupert Lewis remembered, where she described her body as being "like asbestos" and just as "inflammable." The last two weeks of her life were "wrecked with excruating pain" as a result of cancer. On 25 July 1973 she died from the disease, which she had with characteristic vividness "connected to the personal impact of the twists and turns of the black liberation struggle, in particular its setbacks, on her life."[67]

CONCLUSION

It is difficult to situate the life and work of an activist like Amy Jacques Garvey. At first blush, one remembers how she interpreted the regional politics of Jamaica, the Jim Crow divides of America, or the international contexts of diasporic citizens. However, after tracing her geographic movements throughout the world, one sees not only the making of a black radical subject, but also the making of a diasporic consciousness that was just as fluid as her sojourning body. In this biography, I have studied her published writings, her private correspondence, and the historical context to reconstruct and represent an Amy Jacques Garvey who reflects her person—a woman who embraced her own thoughts, acknowledged the worthiness of her ideas, and massaged her rhetoric into an impressive canon of Pan-African discourse.

To most observers, Jacques Garvey entered the political landscape through her husband's legacy. Similar to the work of most politically active wives of famous men, her influence on Garveyism has seldom been examined for its own merit or celebrated for its contribution to progressive politics. In fact, it is surprising how many Garvey scholars have failed to grasp Jacques Garvey's crucial role in shaping the ideological framework of Garveyism—a strain of black nationalism and the basis of Pan-Africanism.

Jacques Garvey was not merely an emissary for the cofounder, Marcus Garvey, but labored daily to keep Garveyite ideas in the forefront of black nationalist and Pan-African conversations well after his demise. This dedication was no easy feat considering the "haters" of black people in general and Marcus Garvey in particular. She defended attacks against Garvey the man and Garveyism the ideology by rebutting critiques at every turn. The fact that Garveyism is so pronounced today is due primarily to the life-long work of Amy Jacques Garvey. Her efforts resonate in the Rastafarian movement, the Nation of Islam, the Moorish Science Temple, and a variety of political sects that all pay homage to Garveyism.

Moreover, it is because of Jacques Garvey's scholarship that we know so much about Garvey himself. As a popular cultural phenomenon, Marcus Garvey (second only to Malcolm X) is a hip-hop icon, and his 1920s slogan, "One God, One Aim, One Destiny," continues to resonate throughout the African diaspora, largely due to Jacques Garvey's passionate preservation of his image. Not without ego, she understood that her work, which kept Garvey at the center of Garveyism, was also an investment in her own historical importance and immortality. By constantly involving Garvey, one of the most controversial and influential personalities of the twentieth century, in Pan-African discussions, Jacques Garvey positioned herself as an influential strategist of progressive political ideas. Initially, her writings replicated her husband's every utterance. But it was not long before she penned her own thoughts, which deviated—at times, considerably—from Garvey's. Differences aside, she rightfully claimed ownership of his intellectual production, making it clearly her political property. This stance was important because it gave her a certain omnipotent authority over his rhetoric. No one, in her opinion, could interpret, analyze, or unpack the meaning of his words better than she. This point, whether real or imagined, meant that Jacques Garvey saw herself as the most knowledgeable Garveyite, the person who could move Garveyism to new heights.

Always forward-looking in her work, and determined to generate an intellectual interest in the black world, Jacques Garvey explored the cross-fertilization of Pan-African ideas in her writings. She viewed Africa and the diaspora as a dialectical equation: if Africans on the continent were exploited, then their condition reflected on their "family" scattered throughout the far corners of the globe. To produce a strong, unified Africa, an Africa that all people of African descent could not only call home but also seal with a legal nationality, Jacques Garvey believed that a redemptive philosophy was essential.

She argued that an informed constituency invested in the motherland could liberate Africa from the clutches of Europeans. Determined to educate the mind and the soul for action, whether it was through the African Study Circle or coalescing forces to produce the *Memorandum Correlative of Africa, the West Indies, and the Americas*, Jacques Garvey believed that the sharing of ideas—theorizing—was an important form of activism that would not only inspire a collective political movement but also stimulate a genuine fellowship of love among black people.

Using repetition and long explanations to unravel the political, economic, cultural, and social features of the Universal Negro Improvement Association (UNIA) program, Jacques Garvey simultaneously unleashed an arsenal against racism, colonialism, and imperialism. A rigorous thinker who enjoyed serious dialogue and debate, her ideological reservoir expanded with each succeeding decade. Bold and aggressive, she continued the tradition of black radical thought by claiming wholeheartedly that people of African descent were entitled to the material resources necessary to ensure a good life.

Amy Jacques Garvey's lifelong commitment to the Pan-African struggle illustrates how one actually becomes a black radical and the steadfast determination it takes to remain committed to dynamic political ideas. She often worked in isolation and had few close friends, but her desire to see a free Africa, a place that its diasporic family could call home, fueled her intellectual attachment to progressive politics. Reflecting on her accomplishments, she wrote, "I only regret that I have one life to give, but rest assured it has been, it is, and will be a full life, for the ancestral Home and my people everywhere."[1] Jacques Garvey's legacy is recorded in her prolific editorials, essays, pamphlets, and books—written words pregnant with multiple meanings; it is just as eclectic as the diaspora of black people whom she loved so dearly.

NOTES

Abbreviations

AJG
  Amy Jacques Garvey

AJG Papers
  Amy Jacques Garvey Papers, Fisk University Special Collections, Nashville, Tenn.

Du Bois Papers
  W. E. B. Du Bois Papers, Microfilm Collections, Manuscripts and Archives, Sterling Library, Yale University, New Haven, Conn.

FRUS
  U.S. Department of State, *Foreign Relations of the United States*

Garvey/UNIA Papers
  Marcus Garvey and the Universal Negro Improvement Association Papers, 7 vols., ed. Robert A. Hill (Los Angeles: University of California Press, 1983–86, 1989–90).

MG
  Marcus Garvey

MGC
  Marcus Garvey Collection, FBI Reading Room, Washington, D.C.

NA
  National Archives

UNIA Papers
  Universal Negro Improvement Association Papers, 1921–86, Western Reserve Historical Society, Cleveland, Ohio

Introduction

1. J. A. G., "10 Minutes with Mrs. Marcus Garvey," *Negro World*, 17 March 1923, 6; copy in box 12, file 1, AJG Papers.

2. AJG, "The Role of Women in Liberation Struggles," *Massachusetts Review* (Winter–Spring 1972): 109–12.

3. E. U. Essien-Udom and AJG, eds., *More Philosophy and Opinions of Marcus Garvey* (Great Britain: Frank Cass, 1977), 247.

4. Rupert Lewis, "Amy Jacques Garvey: A Political Portrait," *Jamaica Daily News*, 29 July 1973.

Chapter One

1. Rupert Lewis and Maureen Warner-Lewis, "Amy Jacques Garvey," *Jamaica Journal* 20 (1987): 39; H. P. Jacobs, *A Short History of Kingston: Vol. I, 1692–1871* (Kingston, Jamaica: Ministry of Education, 1976), 54.

2. "Amy Euphemia Jacques was born 31/12/1895 in Kingston." Ms. J. Brown for C.E.O. Registrar General & Deputy Keeper of the Records, Registrar General's Department, Jamaica, W.I., to author, 4 October 2001.

3. Jacobs, *Short History of Kingston*, 30; E. M. Bacon and E. Aaron, *The New Jamaica* (New York: Walbridge and Co., 1890), reprinted in *Working Miracles: Women's Lives in the English-Speaking Caribbean*, ed. Olive Senior (Mona, Jamaica: Institute Social and Economic Research, 1991), 108.

4. Kingston began as a parish in 1693; it became a city in 1801 and finally the island's capital in 1872. The Common Council Proceedings (1803–15) listed an unidentified mayor as early as 1808. Frank Cundall wrote, "John Jacques, the mayor, was one of Kingston's three representatives." Cundall, *Historic Jamaica* (London: Institute of Jamaica, 1915), 103.

5. For example, in 1864, out of a population of close to 440,000, only 1,903 persons were eligible to vote for members of the Jamaican House of Assembly. See Johnston, *The Negro in the New World*, 255.

6. Ibid., 255–56.

7. Edward Brathwaite, *The Development of Creole Society in Jamaica, 1770–1820* (Oxford: Clarendon Press, 1971), 59.

8. Lewis and Warner-Lewis, "Amy Jacques Garvey," 39; Hon. W. Fawcett, "Tobacco in Jamaica," *West Indian Bulletin* (1907): 227.

9. Lewis and Warner-Lewis, "Amy Jacques Garvey," 48, 40; George Samuel Jacques, "Last Will and Testament," Spanish Town Archives, 3 August 1913; Jacobs, *Short History of Kingston*, 35.

10. AJG stated that her father had "illegitimate children, but in those days they didn't count." Quoted in Ida Lewis, "Mrs. Marcus Garvey Talks with Ida Lewis," *Encore*, May 1973, 68. In 1906 the percentage of "illegitimate births" was 65 out of every 100. Johnston, *The Negro in the New World*, 275.

11. B. W. Higman, *Slave Population of the British Caribbean, 1807–1834* (Baltimore: Johns Hopkins University Press, 1984), 19. Higman states that the Cayman Islands was the only place in the British Caribbean where color distinctions were not recorded. Some records simply state distinctions between black and colored, but in others more detailed gradations are noted.

12. Arnold A. Sio, "Race, Color, and Miscegenation: The Free Colored of Jamaica and Barbados," *Caribbean Studies* 16 (April 1976): 8.

13. Higman, *Slave Population of the British Caribbean*, 109.

14. H. G. DeLisser, *Twentieth Century Jamaica* (Kingston, Jamaica: Jamaican Times, 1913), 53.

15. Lewis and Warner-Lewis, "Amy Jacques Garvey," 40.

16. Irma Watkins-Owens, *Blood Relations: Caribbean Immigrants and the Harlem Community, 1900–1930* (Bloomington: University of Indiana Press, 1996), 13.

17. DeLisser, *Twentieth Century Jamaica*, 52.

18. Ida Lewis, "Mrs. Marcus Garvey Talks with Ida Lewis," *Encore*, May 1973, 68.

19. AJG, "The Role of Women in Liberation Struggles," *Massachusetts Review* (Winter–Spring 1971): 110. Parents as agents in their offspring's educational development was nothing new. In the eighteenth and nineteenth centuries, middle- and upper-class children often obtained formal schooling at home from their parents or paid tutors. Moreover, highly educated women usually came from families, and especially had fathers, who supported girls' education. See Nancy Wallace, *Better Than School: One Family's Declaration of Independence* (New York: Larson, 1983), 28. Significantly, newspapers were considered a luxury for the average working-class Jamaican. See "Charles S. Shirley to the Gleaner," in *Garvey/UNIA Papers*, 1:47–48.

20. Millicent Whyte, *A Short History of Education in Jamaica* (London: Hodder and Stoughton, 1977), 51–52.

21. Wolmers School, Kingston, *Wolmers Bicentenary Souvenir, 1729–1929* (Kingston, Jamaica: Committee, 1929) (quotation). Wolmers began when a Kingston goldsmith left in his will £2,360 for the founding of a free school. Clinton Black, *The Story of Jamaica: From Prehistory to the Present* (London: Collins, 1965), 187. Ethlin Jacques died as a young adult; she is noted as deceased in the *Wolmers Bicentenary Souvenir*.

22. It was not until 1920 that the British government introduced a grant-in-aid scheme for secondary schools. At this time, 42 percent of Jamaican women were working on banana plantations, struggling primarily due to their lack of a formal education. See Joan French and Honor Ford Smith, *Women, Work, and Organization in Jamaica, 1900–1944* (Mona, Jamaica: Sistern Research Institute of Social Science, 1986), 44; Johnston, *The Negro in the New World*, 270.

23. Marlene Hamilton, *Wolmers Alumni Association of the U.S.A.: Wolmers, 1729–1979* (Souvenir Programma, 1979), 17–25 (quotations, p. 23). Jamaicans commonly associated with individuals of the same class. See DeLisser, *Twentieth Century Jamaica*, 51.

24. Etienne Balibar and Immanuel Wallerstein, *Race, Nation, Class: Ambiguous Identities* (London: Verso, 1991), 94.

25. Stuart Hall, "Minimal Selves," in *Black British Cultural Studies: A Reader*, ed. Houston A. Baker, Manthia Diawara, and Ruth H. Lindeborg (Chicago: University of Chicago Press, 1996), 116.

26. Joyce Bennett Justus, "Women's Roles in West Indian Society," in *The Black Woman Cross-Culturally*, ed. Filomina Steady (Cambridge, Mass: Schenkman,

1981), 437 (first quotation); Ida Lewis, "Mrs. Marcus Garvey Talks with Ida Lewis," 68 (second quotation). Amy's sister, Ida Repole, also referred to their mother as "quiet and soft." Mrs. Ida Repole, interview by author, Kingston, Jamaica, 15 November 1990.

27. Justus, "Women's Role in West Indian Society," 436.

28. Terry Smith, "Amy Jacques Garvey: Portrait of a Courageous Woman," *Jamaican Housewife*, Winter 1964, 23.

29. Ida Lewis, "Mrs. Marcus Garvey Talks with Ida Lewis," 68.

30. AJG, *Garvey and Garveyism* (London: Collier-Macmillan, Ltd., 1970), 112–13 (first quotation); Ida Lewis, "Mrs. Marcus Garvey Talks with Ida Lewis," 68.

31. George Samuel Jacques, "Last Will and Testament," 1–2. These properties included "Jacques Villa on Long Mountain Road, 35 Weldman St., a Bryand Loss Same, 5 Rumbus Lane, and a piece of land on the S.E. corner of Bre St. and Black St. in Brown L——."

32. Ibid., 3–4.

33. Lewis and Warner-Lewis, "Amy Jacques Garvey"; Nicholas J. White, "Malaria," in *Manson's Tropical Disease*, ed. Gordon Cook (London: WB Saunders Co., Ltd. 1996), 1088; Simeon Margolis, ed., *Johns Hopkins Symptoms and Remedies* (New York: Rebus, Random House, 1995), 521; Mark F. Boyd, "Historical Introduction to the Symposium on Malaria," in *Human Malaria*, ed. Forest Ray Moulton (Washington, D.C.: American Association for Advancement of Science, 1941), 14, 17; Mrs. Ida Repole, interview by author, Kingston, Jamaica, 16 November 1990; William Bispham, *Malaria: Its Diagnosis, Treatment, and Prophylaxis* (Baltimore: Wm and Wilkins Co., 1944), 70 ("sudden collapse"); Paul Russel, *Malaria: Basic Principles Briefly Stated* (Oxford: Scientific Publishers, 1952), 33; Bernard Nocht and Martin Mayer, *Malaria: A Handbook of Treatment, Parasitology, and Prevention* (London: John Bale Medical Publishers, 1937), 5 (last quotation). In the southern United States, primarily the coastal regions, malaria was still evident but not epidemic.

34. AJG, *Garvey and Garveyism*, 113.

35. Watkins-Owen, *Blood Relations*, 23 (first quotation), 22 (second quotation); AJG, *Garvey and Garveyism*, 113 (last quotation).

36. Index of Passenger Manifests, "States Immigration Officer at Port of Arrival" (26 April 1917), line 2, NA—Northeast Region. Rupert Lewis and Maureen Warner-Lewis ("Amy Jacques Garvey," 39) state that AJG left Jamaica to "stay with a paternal cousin" in New York.

37. AJG, *Garvey and Garveyism*, 113, 53.

Chapter Two

1. Calvin B. Holden, "The Causes and Composition of West Indian Immigration to New York City, 1900–1952," *Afro-Americans in New York Life and History* 2 (January 1987): 2–27.

2. AJG, *Garvey and Garveyism* (London: Collier-Macmillan, Ltd., 1970), 113.

3. AJG listed her occupation as "typist" on the immigration records at Ellis Island.

4. Terry Smith, "Amy Jacques Garvey: Portrait of a Courageous Woman," *Jamaican Housewife*, Winter 1964, 24; *Garvey/UNIA Papers*, 2:168; Beverly Reed, "Amy Jacques Garvey: Black, Beautiful, and Free," *Ebony*, June 1971, 48; AJG, *Garvey and Garveyism*, 113.

5. Cheryl Harris, "Finding Sojourner's Truth: Race, Gender, and the Institution of Property," *Cardoza Law Review* 18 (November 1996): 317.

6. Eighty-two percent of immigrants came from the English-speaking Caribbean. See Irma Watkins-Owen, *Blood Relations: Caribbean Immigrants and the Harlem Community, 1900–1930* (Bloomington: University of Indiana Press, 1996), 4. After 1924 Congress set quotas to curtail immigration. See Holden, "Causes and Composition of West Indian Immigration," 7–27; David Hellwig, "Black Meets Black: Afro-American Reactions to West Indian Immigrants in the 1920s," *South Atlantic Quarterly* 77 (1978): 233; Thomas Sowell, ed., *Essays on Data on American Ethnic Groups* (Washington, D.C.: Urban Institute, 1978), 41–49.

7. Ira De A. Reid, *The Negro Immigrant: His Background, Characteristics, and Social Adjustment, 1899–1937* (ca. 1939; reprint, New York: Arno Press, 1969), 235, app. A, table III, an adapted report by the Commission of Immigration and the Secretary of Labor, U.S. Department of Labor, 1899–1937.

8. Watkins-Owen, *Blood Relations*, 19.

9. Carole Marks, *Farewell—We're Good and Gone: The Great Black Migration* (Bloomington: Indiana University Press, 1989).

10. Reid, *Negro Immigrant*, 122.

11. Mrs. Ida Repole, interview by author, Mona, Jamaica, 15 November 1990; Watkins-Owen, *Blood Relations*, 45.

12. U.S. Department of Commerce, Bureau of Foreign and Domestic Commerce, *Statistical Abstract of the United States, 1919* (Washington, D.C.: GPO, 1920), 822–23; Jacqueline Jones, *Labor of Love, Labor of Sorrow: Black Women, Work, and the Family, from Slavery to the Present* (New York: Vintage Books, 1985), 164; Paule Marshall, "Black Immigrant Women in Brown Girl, Brownstones," in *Female Immigrants to the United States: Caribbean, Latin America, and African Experiences*, ed. Delores M. Mortimer and Roy S. Bryce-Laporte (Washington, D.C.: Smithsonian Institution, RIIES Occasional Papers No. 2, 1981), 6; Tera Hunter, *To Joy My Freedom: Southern Black Women's Lives and Labors after the Civil War* (Cambridge: Harvard University Press, 1997).

13. Terry Smith, "Amy Jacques Garvey."

14. Joyce Toney, "The Perpetuation of a Culture of Migration: West Indian American Ties with Home, 1900–1979," *Afro-Americans in New York Life and Culture* 13 (January 1989): 53.

15. Watkins-Owen, *Blood Relations*, 155 (first quotation); Carol Boyce Davies,

Black Women Writing and Identity: Migration of the Subject (New York: Routledge, 1994), 20.

16. Marshall, "Black Immigrant Women in Brown Girl," 8.

17. Ibid., 8–9.

18. Watkins-Owens, *Blood Relations*, 155.

19. "The Case against Marcus Garvey Is Making History," *Negro World*, 16 June 1923, 8; J. A. Rogers, *World's Great Men of Color* (New York: J. A. Rogers, 1947), 2:602.

20. AJG, *Garvey and Garveyism*, 39, 41.

21. Lionel M. Yard, *Biography of Amy Ashwood Garvey, 1897–1969: Co-Founder of the UNIA* (Washington D.C.: Associated Publisher, 1990), 16, 14.

22. *Garvey/UNIA Papers*, 1:162.

23. Ibid., 69, 100.

24. "Marcus Garvey to T. A. McCormack," in ibid., 193.

25. "Active Members Wanted for the Universal Negro Improvement Association of Jamaica," *Daily Chronicle*, November 1915, reprinted in ibid., 168.

26. Yard, *Amy Ashwood Garvey*, 68–69.

27. Ibid., 33; Tony Martin, *Race First: The Ideological and Organizational Struggles of Marcus Garvey and the Universal Negro Improvement Association* (Westport, Conn.: Greenwood Press, 1976), 7, 23 (quotation); *Garvey/UNIA Papers*, 1:cxiii, 2:76; Watkins-Owen, *Blood Relations*, 113.

28. Yard, *Amy Ashwood Garvey*, 70.

29. Winston James, *Holding Aloft the Banner of Ethiopia: Caribbean Radicalism in Early Twentieth-Century America* (London: Verso Press, 1998), 134–35.

30. Rev. George A. Weston, a former vice president of the UNIA's New York Division, concurs with Ashwood's story. Weston, however, found himself in sharp conflict with AJG. In March 1926 he was publicly ousted from the organization on charges of rebellion at Liberty Hall. See Elton C. Fax, *Garvey: The Story of a Pioneer Black Nationalist* (New York: Dodd, Mead, 1972), 110. For the feud between AJG and Weston, see *Garvey/UNIA Papers*, 6:364, 395, 433, 453.

31. Yard, *Amy Ashwood Garvey*, 82; Tony Martin, "Amy Ashwood Garvey: Wife No. 1," *Jamaica Journal* 30 (August–October 1987): 33; *Garvey/UNIA Papers*, 2:636.

32. Paul Mitchell, ed., *Race Riots in Black and White* (Englewood Cliffs, N.J.: Prentice-Hall, 1970); Peter H. Rossi, ed., *Ghetto Revolts* (New Brunswick, N.J.: Aldine Publishing Co., 1973); Craig Wyn Wade, *The Fiery Cross: The Ku Klux Klan in America* (New York: Simon and Schuster, 1987), 151; *Garvey/UNIA Papers*, 1:lxi.

33. U.S. Department of Commerce, Bureau of the Census, *Fourteenth Census of the United States Taken in the Year 1920: Volume 2, Population, Reports by States, New York*. Washington, D.C.: GPO, 1923. This record confirms that Jacques was a lodger in their home.

34. Ibid.

35. Amy Ashwood Garvey Collection MS 1977B, box 7, "Marcus Garvey Chapter II," 21, National Library of Jamaica, Kingston.

36. AJG, *Garvey and Garveyism*, 43.

37. AJG, ed., *The Philosophy and Opinions of Marcus Garvey; Or, Africa for the Africans* (Dover, Mass.: Majority Press, 1986), 124.

38. Paul Gilroy, *The Black Atlantic: Modernity and Double Consciousness* (Cambridge: Harvard University Press, 1993), 26.

39. Honor Ford Smith, "Women and the Garvey Movement in Jamaica," in *Garvey: His Work and Impact*, ed. Rupert Lewis and Patrick Bryan (Mona, Jamaica: Institute of Social and Economic Research, 1988), 77.

40. *Marcus Garvey v. Amy Ashwood Garvey*, Supreme Court of New York County, no. 24028, NNHR, 15 July 1920.; *Garvey/UNIA Papers*, 2:408 n. 2; AJG, *Garvey and Garveyism*, 43.

41. "The Case against Marcus Garvey Is Making History," *Negro World*, 16 June 1923, 8; William Seraille, "Henrietta Vinton Davis and the Garvey Movement," *Afro-Americans in New York Life and History* (July 1983): 7–24; Reports of FBI Agents Mortimer J. Davis and James Amos, 6 March 1922, book 1, MGC; AJG, *Garvey and Garveyism*, 197.

42. Martin, *Race First*, 334 n. 7.

43. AJG, *Philosophy and Opinions of Marcus Garvey*, 2:87.

44. AJG, *Garvey and Garveyism*, 43.

45. See Mary Helen Washington's introduction to Anna Julia Cooper, *A Voice from the South* (New York: Oxford University Press, 1988), xxxvi.

46. Martin, "Wife No. 1," 32–33.

47. E. Frances White, "Africa on My Mind: Gender, Counter Discourse, and African-American Nationalism," *Journal of Women's History* 2 (Spring 1990): 93.

48. *Garvey/UNIA Papers*, 2:641 (first quotation), 638 (last quotation); Martin, "Wife No. 1," 33 (second quotation).

49. *Garvey/UNIA Papers*, 3:724.

50. Davies, *Black Women Writing*, 17; Gilroy, *Black Atlantic*, 34; Horace Campbell, "Garveyism, Pan-Africanism, and African Liberation in the Twentieth Century," in *Garvey: His Work and Impact*, ed. Rupert Lewis and Patrick Bryan (Mona, Jamaica: Institute of Social and Economic Research, 1988), 172; Julian F. Jaffee, *Crusade against Radicalism: New York during the Red Scare, 1914–1924* (Port Washington: Kennikat Press, 1972); Theodore Kornweibel, ed., *Federal Surveillance of Afro Americans, 1917–1925: The First World War, the Red Scare, the Garvey Movement* (Frederick, Md.: University Publications of America, 1986).

51. Kenneth O'Reilly, *Racial Matters: The FBI's Secret File on Black America, 1960–1972* (New York: Free Press, 1989).

52. *Garvey/UNIA Papers*, 2:638, 641.

53. Martin, "Wife No. 1," 33; W. E. B. Du Bois, "Marcus Garvey," *Crisis*, December 1920, 60.

54. *Garvey/UNIA Papers*, 3:237–38.

55. Martin, *Race First*, 184–85; *Garvey/UNIA Papers*, 3:723 n. 1.

56. Marlene D. Beckman, "The White Slave Traffic Act: The Historical Impact of a Criminal Law Policy on Women," *Georgetown Law Journal* 72 (1984): 1112 n. 3.

57. Ibid., 1124, 1111–12, 1128.

58. Ibid., 1115 (quotation); Deborah Gray White, *Ar'n't I a Woman* (New York: Norton, 1985).

59. *Garvey/UNIA Papers*, 3:716, 721, 728–29.

60. Cyril Briggs, editorial, *Crusader*, November 1921, 13. Also, the aims of the African Blood Brotherhood were to "cement into one great universal brotherhood all persons possessing in any degree the glorious heritage of African blood. To work for a free Africa and the immediate protection and ultimate liberation of Negroes everywhere. To secure absolute race equality—political, economic, and social; and to see that there is an equal application of the laws where ever Negroes have to live and work. To develop commercial enterprises among Negroes in various parts of the world. To gain for Negro labor the full reward of its toil and prevent capitalist exploitation and oppression of the workers of the race." *Crusader*, December 1921, 1322.

61. Ueda Reed, "West Indians," *Harvard Encyclopedia of American Ethnic Groups*, ed. Stephan Thernstrom (Cambridge: Harvard University Press, 1980), 1020–27 (quotation, p. 1025).

62. Decree of Divorce granted on 15 June 1922, box 4, file 7, AJG Papers.

63. Report of FBI Agent Andrew Battle, 1 August 1922, book 2, MGC.

64. AJG, *Garvey and Garveyism*, 88–89.

65. Fax, *Garvey*, 160.

66. *Amy Garvey v. Marcus Garvey*, Action for Absolute Divorce, 24 August 1922, New York State Supreme Court Case file, New York County Clerk Index 31291/1922 (quotation); Report of FBI Agent Mortimer J. Davis, 31 March, 24 April 1923, book 3, MGC.

67. Stephanie Shaw, *What a Woman Ought to Be and to Do: Black Professional Women Workers during the Jim Crow Era* (Chicago: University of Chicago Press, 1996), 41–67.

68. Winston James, *Holding Aloft the Banner of Ethiopia*, 96.

69. AJG, *Garvey and Garveyism*, 39.

70. Joy James, *Transcending the Talented Tenth: Black Leaders and American Intellectuals* (New York: Routledge, 1997), 46.

71. Shaw, *What a Woman Ought to Be and to Do*, 41–67.

Chapter Three

1. Tony Martin, *Race First: The Ideological and Organizational Struggles of Marcus Garvey and the Universal Negro Improvement Association* (Westport, Conn.: Greenwood Press, 1976), 14–16; Cheryl Louise Townsend Gilkes interview with

"Audley (Queen Mother) Moore," in *The Black Women's Oral History Project*, ed. Ruth Edmonds Hill (London: Meckler, 1991), 8:120–23.

2. Martin, *Race First*, 930 (first quotation), 925 (second and third quotations); *Garvey/UNIA Papers*, 4:989.

3. *Garvey/UNIA Papers*, 4:934–42 (first quotation, p. 1037); Evelyn Brooks Higginbotham, *Righteous Discontent: The Women's Movement in the Black Baptist Church, 1880–1920* (Cambridge: Harvard University Press, 1993), 196.

4. *Garvey/UNIA Papers*, 4:934–41 (quotations, p. 936).

5. Ida B. Wells-Barnett, *Crusade for Justice: The Autobiography of Ida B. Wells* (Chicago: University of Chicago Press, 1972); *Garvey/UNIA Papers*, 4:936.

6. Ula Y. Taylor, "As-Salaam Alaikum, My Sister: The Honorable Elijah Muhammad and the Women Who Followed Him," *Race & Society* 1 (1998): 177–96.

7. The NAACP and the National Urban League did not have separate leadership positions designated exclusively for women.

8. *Garvey/UNIA Papers*, 4:1037.

9. Barbara Bair, "True Women, Real Men: Gender, Ideology, and Social Roles in the Garvey Movement," in *Gender Domains: Rethinking Public and Private in Women's History*, ed. Dorothy O. Helly and Susan M. Reverby (Ithaca, N.Y.: Cornell University Press, 1992), 155.

10. George L. Mosse, *Nationalism and Sexuality: Respectability and Abnormal Sexuality in Modern Europe* (New York: Howard Fertig, 1985), 19–20.

11. *Garvey/UNIA Papers*, 4:788.

12. Ibid., 1038.

13. Carole Boyce Davies, *Black Women, Writing, and Identity: Migrations of the Subject* (New York: Routledge, 1994); E. Frances White, "Africa on My Mind: Gender, Counter Discourse, and African American Nationalism," *Journal of Women's History* 2 (1990): 86.

14. AJG, ed., *The Philosophy and Opinions of Marcus Garvey; Or, Africa for the Africans* (Dover, Mass: Majority Press, 1986), 1:preface. Randall Burkett has argued that the language in Garvey's August 1921 speech, for example, was "altered by Mrs. Garvey so that the familiar passage from Psalms 68:31 is substituted in place of some of Garvey's more rhapsodical passages concerning Jesus." He adds that "numerous other changes from the *Negro World* versions have been made in this and many of the speeches published in *Philosophy and Opinions*." It is understandable why Burkett offered this conclusion. His analysis centered on comparing a speech printed in the *Negro World* with a reprint in *Philosophy and Opinions*. Substantial changes are indeed evident but not because Jacques was a copious editor. Garvey gave an inordinate number of speeches, and Burkett mistakenly compared two entirely different ones that Garvey had given days apart. Several phrases in both texts are the same, and Garvey even gave an explanation for the identical phrasing by introducing a section of his second speech with, "I said some nights ago." Considering the fact that Burkett analyzed dissimilar texts, it is no wonder that

he found that Jacques Garvey had made numerous changes in her husband's speeches. See Burkett, *Black Redemption: Churchmen Speak for the Garvey Movement* (Philadelphia: Temple University Press, 1978), 185 n. 11.

15. AJG, *Philosophy and Opinions of Marcus Garvey*, 1:preface.

16. *Garvey/UNIA Papers*, 4:324.

17. Ibid., 1:xciv.

18. Martin, *Race First*, 152–53; Judith Stein, *The World of Marcus Garvey: Race and Class in Modern Society* (Baton Rouge: Louisiana State University Press, 1986), 70–71.

19. Stein, *World of Marcus Garvey*, 93.

20. W. E .B. Du Bois, "Marcus Garvey," *Crisis*, January 1921, 112–15. See also Stein, *World of Marcus Garvey*, 84.

21. Cyril V. Briggs, "Lessons in Tactics: For the Liberation Movement," *Crusader*, November 1921, 15; Stein, *World of Marcus Garvey*, 74.

22. "Report of UNIA Meeting," *Negro World*, 17 July 1920, reprinted in *Garvey/UNIA Papers*, 2:410–11.

23. "J. E. Hoover to John B. Cunningham," 10 August 1922, reprinted in *Garvey/UNIA Papers*, 4:841.

24. *Garvey/UNIA Papers*, 5:374; J. A. Rogers, *World's Great Men of Color* (New York: J. A. Rogers, 1947), 2:605; Reports of FBI Agents James E. Amos and Mortimer J. Davis, 6 March 1922, and FBI Agent James E. Amos, 15 March 1922, book 2, MGC.

25. "Garvey Wins Fight to Have His Wife Testify at Trial," *Negro World*, 6 June 1923, "Object to Garvey's Wife as Witness!," *The Times*, 7 June 1923, and "Garvey Wins Fight to Have His Wife Testify at Trial," *Negro World*, 6 June 1923, copies in box 8, file 2, Newspaper Clippings, AJG Papers.

26. "Garvey Plays a Queen in Court," *Sun and Globe*, 6 June 1923, copy in box 8, file 2, Newspaper Clippings, AJG Papers ("much younger than Garvey"); "Garvey Wins Fight to Have His Wife Testify at Trial," *Negro World*, 6 June 1923, copy in box 8, file 2 (Garvey "opened no mail"); "Object to Garvey's Wife as Witness!," *The Times*, 7 June 1923, copy in box 8, file 2; "The Case against Marcus Garvey Is Making History," *Negro World*, 16 June 1923, 8 ("appeared extremely nervous," "broke down").

27. *Garvey/UNIA Papers*, 5:375.

28. "Wife of UNIA Leader Advocate of Calm Counsel—I Am Here to Tell You to BE Calm and Quiet in All Your Words and Actions," *Pittsburgh American*, 20 July 1923; *Hotel Talter*, 12 August 1923, copy in box 13, file 1, Scrapbook, AJG Papers.

29. David Cronon, *Black Moses: The Story of Marcus Garvey and the Universal Negro Improvement Association* (1955; reprint, Madison: University of Wisconsin Press, 1969), 100.

30. AJG, *Garvey and Garveyism*, 41, 38. For the impact of the Black Star Line on the UNIA, see Stein, *The World of Marcus Garvey*.

31. Joy James, *Transcending the Talented Tenth: Black Leaders and American Intellectuals* (New York: Routledge, 1997), 46 ("feminine gentility"); Terry Smith, "Amy Jacques Garvey: Portrait of a Courageous Woman," *Jamaican Housewife*, Winter 1964, 24 ("fear and sorrow").

32. "Garvey's Wife Hits Detention [of] Provisional President of African Republic Imprisoned for Political Reasons, She Declares," *Commercial Fortune Cincinnati*, 21 May 1923; copy in box 8, file 1, MG Memorial Collection, Fisk University Special Collections, Nashville, Tenn. (first quotation); *Garvey/UNIA Papers*, 5:700 (second quotation); AJG, *Garvey and Garveyism*, 121 (last quotation).

33. Report of FBI Agent James W. Dillion, 11 September 1923, book 5, MGC.

34. *Garvey/UNIA Papers*, 5:453 (Garvey); George McGuire, "Out of the Tombs," *Negro Churchman* 1 (September–October 1923): 11.

35. *Garvey/UNIA Papers*, 5:453; George Mosse, *The Image of Man: The Creation of Modern Masculinity* (New York: Oxford University Press, 1996), 149.

36. Michael Kimmel, *Manhood in America: A Cultural History* (New York: Free Press, 1996), 7.

37. AJG, *Garvey and Garveyism*, 129.

38. Ibid., 130.

39. "Mrs. Amy Jacques Garvey Writes of Her Interesting Experiences," *Negro World*, 17 November 1923, 2.

40. Quoted in Theodore G. Vincent, *Voices of a Black Nation: Political Journalism in the Harlem Renaissance* (San Francisco: Ramparts Press, 1973), 16.

41. "Mrs. Amy Jacques Garvey Writes of Her Interesting Experiences," *Negro World*, 27 October 1923, 2; Kathleen M. Blee, *Women of the Klan: Racism and Gender in the 1920s* (Berkeley: University of California Press, 1991), 30, 94, 146–47 (quotation).

42. AJG, "The Value of Propaganda," *Negro World*, 6 March 1927; AJG, *Philosophy and Opinions of Marcus Garvey*, 1:98.

43. "Mrs. Amy Jacques Garvey Writes of Her Interesting Experiences," *Negro World*, 10 November 1923, 5; "Mrs. Amy Jacques Garvey Writes of Her Interesting Experiences," *Negro World*, 17 November 1923, 2.

44. Miriam Brody, *Manly Writing: Gender, Rhetoric, and the Rise of Composition* (Carbondale: Southern Illinois University Press, 1993), 62.

45. "Mrs. Amy Jacques Garvey Writes of Her Interesting Experiences," *Negro World*, 17 November 1923, 7.

46. Glenda Elizabeth Gilmore, *Gender and Jim Crow: Women and the Politics of White Supremacy in North Carolina, 1896–1920* (Chapel Hill: University of North Carolina Press, 1996), xxii.

47. "Mrs. Amy Jacques Garvey Writes of Her Interesting Experiences," *Negro World*, 3 November 1923, 2.

48. "Mrs. Amy Jacques Garvey Writes of Her Interesting Experiences," *Negro World*, 27 October 1923, 2.

49. Carol Mattingly, "Woman-Tempered Rhetoric: Public Presentation and the WCTU," *Rhetoric Review* 14 (Fall 1995): 51; AJG, "Leaving Beautiful California for the Wild South on a Trip across the Continent," *Negro World*, 2.

50. AJG, *Garvey and Garveyism*, 131.

51. *Garvey/UNIA Papers*, 5:700 (Garvey); "Mrs. Amy Jacques Garvey Writes of Her Interesting Experiences," *Negro World*, 3 November 1923, 2.

52. McGuire, "Out of the Tombs"; Martha H. Verbrugge, *Able-Bodied Womanhood: Personal Health and Social Change in Nineteenth-Century Boston* (New York: Oxford University Press, 1988), 107.

53. *New York Age*, 25 March 1921.

54. "Mrs. Amy Jacques Garvey Writes of Her Interesting Experiences," *Negro World*, 3 November 1923, 2.

55. Verbrugge, *Able-Bodied Womanhood*, 106.

56. AJG, *Garvey and Garveyism*, 162.

57. Ibid., 166.

58. Higginbotham, *Righteous Discontent*, 147.

59. AJG, *Garvey and Garveyism*, 164.

60. Ibid.

61. Ibid., 165.

62. Ibid.

63. Report of Agent James E. Amos, 26 October 1926, Re: MG, New York file 36/60, NA—Suitland, Md.

64. H. C. Heckman, Administrative Assistant to Warden John W. Snook, 13 November 1926, and O. H. Luhring to Postmaster General, 30 November 1926, in Re: MG, New York file 36, NA—Suitland, Md.; Snook to Heckman, Assistant to Superintendent of Prisons, Department of Justice, 16 November 1926, and Harry S. New, Postmaster General, to Attorney General, 23 December 1926, ibid.

65. Report of Agent James E. Amos, 26 October 1926, in Re: MG, New York file 36, NA—Suitland, Md.

66. MG to Hon. J. W. Snook, Warden, 15 November 1926, ibid.

67. AJG, "Petition for Naturalization," 6 July 1926, U.S. Department of Labor, New York City.

68. AJG, *Garvey and Garveyism*, 167.

69. *Garvey/UNIA Papers*, 5:361.

70. Gypsey Da Silva, "The Copy Editor and the Author," in *Editors and Editing: What Writers Need to Know about What Editors Do*, ed. Gerald Gross (New York: Grove Press, 1993).

71. AJG, *Garvey and Garveyism*, 168. For other statements regarding AJG's poor health and MG's attitude toward her complaints, see *Garvey/UNIA Papers*, 6:265, 274, 350, 417, 425–26.

72. Honor Ford Smith, "Women and the Garvey Movement in Jamaica," in

Garvey: His Work and Impact, ed. Rupert Lewis and Patrick Bryan (Mona, Jamaica: Institute of Social and Economic Research, 1988), 78.

Chapter Four

1. Penny A. Weiss, "Feminist Reflections on Community," in *Feminism and Community*, ed. Penny A. Weiss and Marilyn Friedman (Philadelphia: Temple University Press, 1995), 3.

2. J. A. G., "10 Minutes with Mrs. Garvey," *Negro World*, 17 March 1923, 6, copy in box 12, file 1, AJG Papers.

3. Quoted in "Mrs. Garvey Confined to Her Home," *Negro World*, 29 November 1924, 8. The *Negro World*, established in January 1918 and published in Harlem, was the UNIA's most effective weekly propaganda newspaper.

4. AJG, "Away with Lip Service," *Negro World*, 6 February 1926, 7; Margaret Ward, *Unmanageable Revolutionaries: Women and Irish Nationalism* (London: Pluto Press, 1983), 2.

5. "Look Out for Mud," *Negro World*, 14 July 1923.

6. "Mrs. Garvey Replies to the Negro World—Defends Herself against References to Her Being Helpless," *Negro World*, 21 July 1923. Following this reply, no other articles about AJG's leadership role in the UNIA appeared in the *Negro World*.

7. AJG, "Talk to Yourself If You Must Talk," *Negro World*, 23 January 1926, 7.

8. *Garvey/UNIA Papers*, 6:365.

9. Ibid.

10. Ibid., 368.

11. AJG, "Away with Lip Service."

12. AJG, "God Give Us Men!," *Negro World*, 2 January 1926, 7.

13. AJG, "Women as Leaders Nationally and Racially," *Negro World*, 24 October 1925, 7; AJG, "Send in Your Articles for This Page," *Negro World*, 6 February 1926, 7.

14. *Chicago Defender*, 23 September 1916, 15 July 1916; *New York Age*, 5 January 1918 ("Wedding Invitations"), 26 January 1918 ("For Stout Figure").

15. AJG, "Our Page Is Three Years Old," *Negro World*, 12 February 1927, 7; AJG, "Send in Your Articles for This Page," *Negro World*, 6 February 1926, 7; AJG, "Have a Heart," *Negro World*, 7 June 1924.

16. W. E. B. Du Bois, *The Education of Black People: Ten Critiques, 1906–1960* (Amherst: University of Massachusetts Press, 1973), 32; AJG, "Have a Heart."

17. Benedict Anderson, *Imagined Communities: Reflections on the Origins and Spread of Nationalism* (London: Verso, 1983), 16.

18. AJG, "Can Ghandhi's Fasting Unite Moslems and Hundus?," *Negro World*, 4 October 1924, 6.

19. Eleanor Hinton Hoytt, "International Council of Women of the Darker Races: Historical Notes," *Sage* 3 (Fall 1986): 54.

20. AJG, "Enslave the Mind and You Enslave the Body," *Negro World*, 20 June 1925, 7.

21. Ibid.

22. James D. Anderson, *The Education of Blacks in the South, 1860–1935* (Chapel Hill: University of North Carolina Press, 1988), 28.

23. AJG, "Black Women's Resolve for 1926," *Negro World*, 9 January 1926, 7.

24. AJG, "Women's Function in Life," *Negro World*, 12 December 1925; AJG, "Lifting Up Filipino Women," *Negro World*, 22 November 1924, 8; AJG, "Have Scientific Achievements of Negroes Benefitted Our Race?" *Negro World*, 8 November 1924, 10; AJG, "Going to Africa?," *Negro World*, 16 April 1927, 7.

25. AJG, "No Sex in Brains and Ability," *Negro World*, 27 December 1924, 8.

26. Anna Julia Cooper, *A Voice from the South* (New York: Oxford University Press, 1988), 78–79.

27. Evelyn Brooks Higginbotham, *Righteous Discontent: The Women's Movement in the Black Baptist Church, 1880–1920* (Cambridge: Harvard University Press, 1993), 28.

28. Cooper, *Voice from the South*, 172.

29. Kevin K. Gaines, *Uplifting the Race: Black Leadership, Politics, and Culture in the Twentieth Century* (Chapel Hill: University of North Carolina Press, 1996), 133.

30. AJG, "Women's Function in Life."

31. AJG, "No Sex in Brains and Ability."

32. AJG, "Will the Entrance of Woman in Politics Affect Home Life?," *Negro World*, 14 June 1924, 12.

33. AJG, "Woman as Man's Helper," *Negro World*, 28 February 1925.

34. AJG, "The Joy of Living," *Negro World*, 21 June 1924, 12.

35. Jean Bethke Elshtain, "Feminism, Family, and Community," in *Feminism and Community*, ed. Penny A. Weiss and Marilyn Friedman (Philadelphia: Temple University Press, 1995), 260; Deborah Gray White, *Too Heavy a Load: Black Women in Defense of Themselves* (New York: Norton, 1999), 44. See Paula Giddings, *When and Where I Enter: The Impact of Black Women on Race and Sex in America* (New York: Morrow, 1984).

36. AJG, "Duties of Parents to Children," *Negro World*, 9 May 1925. The black women's club movement between the 1890s and 1920s encompassed a wide variety of activities, from offering protection to young women from exploitative employers to bourgeoisie teas. For more on the black club movement, see Dorothy Salem, *To Better Our World: Black Women in Organized Reform, 1890–1920* (Brooklyn, N.Y.: Carlson Publishers, 1990); Mildred I. Thompson, *Ida B. Wells-Barnett: An Exploration Study of an American Black Woman, 1893–1930* (Brooklyn, N.Y.: Carlson Publishers, 1990); and Beverly Washington Jones, *Quest for Equality: The Life and Writings of Mary Eliza Church Terrell, 1883–1954* (Brooklyn, N.Y.: Carlson Publishers, 1990).

37. "Universal African Black Cross Nurses," *Negro World*, 2 August 1924.

38. AJG, "Women as Cannon Fodder," *Negro World,* 9 February 1924, 10.

39. "The Obligations of Motherhood—Mothers Are Examples for Children and Should Be Guarded in Behavior and Speech," *Negro World,* 29 March 1924.

40. Pierce and Williams, "And Your Prayers Shall Be Answered."

41. Reprints came from a variety of newspapers and magazines including the *Chicago Tribune, New York Evening Post, New York American, Daily Worker, New Republic,* and *Survey Graphic.*

42. "Five Essential Qualities in a Negro Woman," *Negro World,* 2 August 1924.

43. "Politics Purified by Women's Entry," *Negro World,* 14 June 1924.

44. "Women Legislate for Better Living Conditions," *Negro World,* 14 June 1924.

45. "Will Women Neglect Race Propagation for Public Life?," *Negro World,* 14 June 1924.

46. "Our Women Getting into the Larger Life," *Negro World,* 14 June 1924.

47. "Women in the Home—Twentieth-Century Freedom for Women Is World Slogan," 9 February 1924.

48. Ibid.; "Girls Should Be Taught to Keep House Properly," *Negro World,* 19 April 1924.

49. Paulette Pierce and Brackette F. Williams, "And Your Prayers Shall Be Answered through the Womb of a Woman," in *Women Out of Place: The Gender of Agency and the Race of Nationality,* ed. Brackette F. Williams (New York: Routledge, 1996), 187.

50. "What Makes a Good Wife?," *Negro World,* 16 August 1923.

51. "The Ideal Wife," *Negro World,* 15 April 1924.

52. Hazel V. Carby, *Race Men* (Cambridge: Harvard University Press, 1998), 20.

53. AJG, "Listen Women!," *Negro World,* 9 April 1927.

54. Deborah Gray White, "The Cost of Club Work, the Price of Black Feminism," in *Invisible Women: New Essays on American Activism,* ed. Nancy Hewitt and Suzanne Lebsock (Urbana: University of Illinois Press, 1993), 253; AJG, "The Negro Race Needs Trained Men," *Negro World,* 3 July 1926.

55. AJG, "Listen Women!."

56. AJG, "Are Negro Women More Easily Satisfied than White Women?," *Negro World,* 9 May 1925; AJG, "Listen Women!."

57. Hazel V. Carby, " 'It Jus Be's Dat Way Sometime': The Sexual Politics of Women's Blues," *Radical America* 20, no. 4 (1986): 9–22 (quotations, p. 20).

58. AJG, "The Negro Race Needs Trained Men."

59. Anne Witte Garland, *Women Activists Challenging the Abuse of Power* (New York: Feminist Press, 1988), xvi–xvii.

60. AJG, "Women as Leaders Nationally and Racially," *Negro World,* 24 October 1925; AJG, "Are Negro Women More Easily Satisfied Than White Women?"; AJG, "Listen Women!."

61. Deborah Gray White, "The Cost of Club Work," 254; "Black Women's Part in Race Leadership," *Negro World,* 19 April 1924.

62. Deborah Gary White, "The Cost of Club Work," 254; Gerda Lerner, *Black Women in White America* (New York: Vintage Books, 1992), 341.

63. AJG, "Do Negro Women Want to Express Themselves?," *Negro World*, 11 April 1925 (first quotation); AJG, "The Busy Have No Time for Tears," *Negro World*, 18 June 1927.

64. Carol Boyce Davies, *Black Women Writing and Identity: Migrations of the Subject* (New York: Routledge, 1994), 50.

65. Of course, there is no single, monolithic form of patriarchy, but common factors include male control over female labor power, sexist ideology, and a gender hierarchy in which men are authoritarian and aggressive.

66. Stephanie Shaw, *What a Woman Ought to Be: Professional Black Women during the Jim Crow Era* (Chicago: University of Chicago Press, 1996), 119.

67. Ibid.; Elsa Barkley Brown, "Mothers in Mind," in *Double Stitch: Black Women Write about Mothers and Daughters*, ed. Patricia-Bell Scott et al. (New York: Harper Perennial, 1991), 86–89 (quotation, p. 87).

68. Cynthia Enloe, *Bananas, Beaches, and Bases: Making Feminist Sense of International Politics* (Los Angeles: Pandora Press, 1989), 61, 42, 62.

69. See, e.g., Lois A. West, ed., *Feminist Nationalism* (New York: Routledge, 1997); Andrew Parker, Mary Russo, Doris Sommer, Patricia Yaeger, eds., *Nationalisms and Sexualities* (New York: Routledge, 1992); Margaret Ward, *Unmanageable Revolutionaries: Women and Irish Nationalism* (London: Pluto Press, 1983); and Paula Gilbert Lewis, ed., *Traditionalism, Nationalism, and Feminism: Women Writers of Quebec* (Westport, Conn.: Greenwood Press, 1985).

70. Partha Chatterjee, *The Nation and Its Fragments: Colonial and Postcolonial Histories* (Princeton, N.J.: Princeton University Press, 1993), 148.

71. AJG, *Garvey and Garveyism*, 188.

72. *Garvey/UNIA Papers*, 7:45.

73. AJG, *Garvey and Garveyism*, 190.

Chapter Five

1. Carl Stone, "Race and Economic Power in Jamaica," in *Garvey: His Work and Impact*, ed. Rupert Lewis and Patrick Bryan (Mona, Jamaica: Institute of Social and Economic Research, 1988), 248–49. By the end of 1930 only 1.5 percent of blacks had access to a postsecondary education.

2. Rupert Lewis, "Garvey's Perspective on Jamaica," in *Garvey: His Work and Impact*, ed. Rupert Lewis and Patrick Bryan (Mona, Jamaica: Institute of Social and Economic Research, 1988), 236 (quotation), and *Marcus Garvey: Anti-Colonial Champion* (Trenton, N.J.: African World Press, 1988), 200.

3. "Liberty Hall Meeting," *Negro World*, 28 March 1925, 3.

4. See Ralph Ellison, *Shadow and Acts* (New York: Vintage Books, 1972); Hazel V. Carby, *Reconstructing Womanhood: The Emergence of the Afro-American Woman Novelist* (New York: Oxford University Press, 1987); and Karen Sanchez Eppier,

Touching Liberty: Abolition, Feminism, and the Politics of the Body (Berkeley: University of California Press, 1993).

5. *Garvey/UNIA Papers*, 7:43.

6. AJG, *Garvey and Garveyism*, 190.

7. Ibid.

8. Rupert Lewis, *Anti-Colonial Champion*, 199.

9. AJG, *Garvey and Garveyism*, 190; J. A. Rogers, "Marcus Garvey Interviewed by Negro Journalist Discusses Difficulties Facing the Race," *Negro World*, 6 October 1928.

10. AJG, *Garvey and Garveyism*, 191.

11. Hakim Adi, *West Africans in Britain, 1900–1960: Nationalism, Pan-Africanism, and Communism* (London: Lawrence and Wishart, 1998), 3.

12. Edmund Cronon, *Black Moses: The Story of Marcus Garvey and the Universal Negro Improvement Association* (1955; reprint, Madison: University of Wisconsin Press, 1968), 145–46 (press report); AJG, *Garvey and Garveyism*, 191–92; Hakim Adi, *West Africans in Britain*, 46 (Solanke).

13. AJG, *Garvey and Garveyism*, 192.

14. Ibid.

15. Charles V. Hamilton, "Pan-Africanism and the Black Struggle in the U.S.," in *Pan-Africanism*, ed. Robert Chrisman and Nathan Hare (New York: Bobbs-Merrill, 1974), 146.

16. AJG, "What Has the League of Nations Accomplished?," *Negro World*, 3 October 1925, 7; AJG, "Premier Painleve Flies to Africa," *Negro World*, 20 June 1925, 4.

17. MG, "Hon. Marcus Garvey, Writing from France, Discusses Treatment Accorded Negroes There and in Other Countries of the World," *Negro World*, 11 August 1928, 1; "Garvey in Paris Speaks to Famed Club de Faubourg," *Negro World*, 27 October 1928.

18. MG, "United Race for 1924, Wish of Head of Great Organization," *Negro World*, 5 January 1924, 1; MG, "Writing from France," 1; Tyler Stovall, *Paris Noir: African Americans in the City of Lights* (New York: Houghton Mifflin, 1996), 25–81.

19. AJG, *Garvey and Garveyism*, 193.

20. Phillipe Dewitte, *Les Mouvements Nègres en France, 1919–1930* (Paris: Editions L'Harmattan, 1985), 172. I am grateful to Douglas Palacios for this citation.

21. AJG, *Garvey and Garveyism*, 193; MG, "German Thoroughness Impressed Garvey," *Negro World*, 25 August 1928, 1.

22. AJG, "What Germany Wants," *Negro World*, 8 September 1928.

23. Michael Burleigh and Wolfgang Wipperman, *The Racial State: Germany, 1933–1945* (Cambridge: Cambridge University Press, 1991), 44–73; Jeffrey Herf, *Reactionary Modernism: Technology, Culture, and Politics in Weimar and the Third Reich* (Cambridge: Cambridge University Press, 1984).

24. Tony Martin, *Race First: The Ideological and Organizational Struggles of*

Marcus Garvey and the Universal Negro Improvement Association (Westport, Conn.: Greenwood Press, 1976), 59.

25. "Garvey and Mussolini," *Negro World*, 5 November 1927, 4; J. A. Rogers, *World's Great Men of Color* (New York: J. A. Rogers, 1947), 602, 610.

26. AJG, "Experiments in Government," *Negro World*, 24 September 1927, 4.

27. Francine M. King, "Marcus Garvey's View of Fascism as It Relates to the Black Struggle for Equal Rights: An Analysis of Commentaries from the Black Man, 1935–1939," *Proceedings and Papers of the Georgia Association of Historians* 10 (1989): 28, 30.

28. Carol Aisha Blackshire-Belay, "Historical Revelations: The International Scope of African Germans Today and Beyond," in *The African-German Experience: Critical Essays*, ed. Blackshire-Belay (London: Praeger, 1996), 110–11.

29. Eva Aldred Brooks, "A Pure, Healthy, Unified Race, Plea of Women: Miscegenation Destroys Race Pride—Produces Weak Off-Spring," *Negro World*, 23 May 1925, 7.

30. William S. McFreely, *Frederick Douglass* (New York: Norton, 1991), 327; Claude McKay, *A Long Way from Home* (New York: Arno Press, 1969), 239; George Padmore, ed., *History of the Pan-African Congress* (London: Hammersmith Bookshop, Ltd., 1947), 36 (Armattoe).

31. "Liberty Hall Meeting," *Negro World*, 28 March 1925, 3; AJG, "British Negroes in England Rated as Aliens, Why?," *Negro World*, 30 January 1926, 7.

32. "Mrs. Garvey Delivers Ringing Message to White Women of London at Great Meeting: Tells of Insults and Suffering," *Negro World*, 22 September 1928.

33. Ibid.; "The Greatest Negro Woman of Our Race," *Negro World*, 3 November 1928, 3.

34. "Marcus Garvey Tells English People Some Striking Truths . . . ," *Negro World*, 29 September 1928, 2.

35. "Full Text of U.N.I.A. Petition to League of Nation," *Negro World*, 27 October 1928 (second petition); Petition of the UNIA African Communities League to the League of Nations, Geneva, Switzerland (first petition), and Lewis W. Haskell, American Consul, to Hon. Joseph C. Gres, American Minister, 18 September 1922, both in MG Decimal File 800.4016/19, NA—Suitland, Md.

36. MG, "Great Drive for Freedom Planned," *Negro World*, 3 November 1928, 1; AJG, *Garvey and Garveyism*, 193.

37. "The Greatest Negro Woman of Our Race," 3; AJG, *Garvey and Garveyism*, 194 (the schedule "allowed no rest"); "Philadelphia Pays Fine Tribute to Mrs. Garvey Back from Europe," *Negro World*, 10 November 1928.

38. "Mrs. AJG on Visit to New York City Gets Uproarious Welcome," *Negro World*, 10 November 1928.

39. "Philadelphia Pays Fine Tribute to Mrs. Garvey."

40. AJG, *Garvey and Garveyism*, 195.

41. See *Garvey/UNIA Papers*, 2:xxxix; AJG, *Garvey and Garveyism*, 195; and

Cronon, *Black Moses*, 150. Walter Rodney has brilliantly shown how Liberians were deceived by Firestone and the role of the United States in the underdevelopment of Africa. Walter Rodney, *How Europe Underdeveloped Africa* (London: Bogle-L'Ouverture Pub., 1972).

42. MG, "Garvey Linking Hoover and Firestone in Sinister Liberians Rubber Project Urges Negroes to Vote for Smith," *Negro World*, 1 September 1928; MG, "Every Negro with a Ballot Must Vote for Alfred Smith," *Negro World*, 20 October 1928; "Canada and Garvey," *Negro World*, 17 November 1928; "Article in the Montreal Gazette," 1 November 1928, reprinted in *Garvey/UNIA Papers*, 7:228.

43. Mopsie [AJG] to Popsie [MG], 29 October 1928, box 4, file 2, AJG Papers; AJG, *Garvey and Garveyism*, 195.

44. AJG, *Garvey and Garveyism*, 195; "Mrs. Amy Jacques Garvey at Bermuda," *Negro World*, 1 December 1928, n.p.

45. "Mrs. Amy Jacques Garvey at Bermuda," n.p.

46. Joy James, *Transcending the Talented Tenth: Black Leaders and American Intellectuals* (New York: Routledge, 1997), 184; AJG, "Wanted-Missionaries for Africa," *Negro World*, 21 February 1925, 7 (last quotation).

47. Partha Chatterjee, *The Nation and Its Fragments: Colonial and Postcolonial Histories* (Princeton, N.J.: Princeton University Press, 1993), 6.

48. "Mrs. Amy Jacques Garvey at Bermuda," n.p.; "Mrs. A. J. Garvey in Interview Tells Cincinnati Commercial Tribune Her Husband Was Imprisoned for Political Reasons," *Negro World*, 30 May 1925, 7.

49. AJG, *Garvey and Garveyism*, 191.

50. *Negro World* 4, 25 May, 1 June 1929, n.p.; *Garvey/UNIA Papers*, 7:316.

51. *Garvey/UNIA Papers*, 7:417 n. 1; AJG, *Garvey and Garveyism*, 196.

52. Marcus Garvey served as managing editor for the *Negro World* from 1918 until he split from the UNIA New York Division in the early 1930s. No issues of the newspaper have been found after October 17, 1933. *Blackman* began as a daily newspaper but by 1930 was published weekly; by February 1931 it ceased publication. See Robert A. Hill and Barbara Bair, eds., *Marcus Garvey Life and Lessons: A Centennial Companion to the Marcus Garvey and UNIA Papers* (Los Angeles: University of California Press, 1987), 362, 413–14. Many articles and announcements in *Blackman* focused on issues relevant to women—e.g., "A Mother's Prayer," 15 April 1929; "The Black Woman," 20 April 1929; "Woman's Progress through the Ages," 22 April 1929; "Insulting Negro Womanhood," 17 May 1929; "Women Who Do a Man's Work Should Get a Man's Pay," 22 June 1929; "Women and Modern Life," 13 June 1929; "Birth Control," 6 August 1929; "A Night for Women, Come Listen to Their Views," 7 August 1929; "Madame MLT DeMena Speaks," 22 February 1930; and "U.S. Garveyites Hear Lady Davis," 24 January 1931. The incomplete microfilm reels of *Blackman* published during 1929–February 1931 are available at the Institute of Jamaica, Kingston.

53. For instance, within a two-week period AJG's five editorials in *Blackman*

were entitled "Make Opportunities out of Misfortunes" (6 May 1929), "He That Endureth to the End" (8 May 1929), "Women and World Peace" (11 May 1929), "Experiments in Government" (15 May 1929), and "They Conquer Who They Believe They Can" (20 May 1929). She had published four of these articles in the *Negro World* with the same title and slight modifications: "He That Endureth to the End" (17 January 1925), "Women and World Peace" (31 January 1925), "Experiment in Government" (September 1927), and "They Conquer Who They Believe They Can" (26 September 1925).

54. AJG, "Poverty Is Slavery," *Blackman*, 22 June 1929, 4; R. Palme Dutt, *Fascism and Social Revolution* (New York: International Publishers, 1934), 235, 240. AJG published an editorial entitled "Poverty Is Slavery" in the *Negro World* on 21 August 1926 with an abridged text.

55. AJG, "Some Fallacies about Children," *Blackman*, 29 August 1929.

56. Rupert Lewis, *Anti-Colonial Champion*, 220.

57. *Garvey/UNIA Papers*, 7:318 nn. 2–3, 315.

58. Ibid., xl–xli, 292.

59. Ibid., 328–29.

60. Rupert Lewis, *Anti-Colonial Champion*, 209.

61. *Garvey/UNIA Papers*, 7:xxxix, 341, 346–47.

62. Rupert Lewis, *Anti-Colonial Champion*, 223; AJG, *Garvey and Garveyism*, 209–10. Their home was not actually mortgaged until 1934.

63. Rupert Lewis, *Anti-Colonial Champion*, 226.

64. *Garvey/UNIA Papers*, 7:339 n. 1.

Chapter Six

1. There is evidence that women used birth control methods throughout the United States in the early twentieth century. In addition, female activists are often cited for their efforts to delay motherhood and deliberately space the birth of their babies. See John D. Emilo and Estelle B. Freeman, *Intimate Matters: A History of Sexuality in America* (New York: Harper and Row, 1988).

2. Recent studies have documented that the conventional attitude among Caribbean women is to view a childless woman as a "mule" and "beyond the pale of society." In addition, a common belief that took root in the early twentieth century was that a childless woman would have poor health and be subject to "numerous disorders ranging from headaches to madness." Mother Brown, who was born in Jamaica in 1861, recalled that she was "advised by her doctor that marriage and childbearing was the cure" for her severe headaches. Finally, in the 1920s and 1930s psychoanalytic theorists argued that "normal" women desired children, and those who elected not to be mothers were rejecting femininity. Olive Senior, *Working Miracles: Women's Lives in the English-Speaking Caribbean* (Mona, Jamaica: Institute of Social and Economic Research, 1991), 68; Erna Brodber, "Afro-Jamaican Women at the Turn of the Century," *Social and Economic Studies* 35 (1986): 35. See also

Madeline Kerr, *Personality and Conflict in Jamaica* (Liverpool, U.K.: University Press, 1952), 25, and Evelyn Nakano Glenn, Grace Chang, and Linda Rennie Forcey, *Mothering: Ideology, Experience, and Agency* (New York: Routledge, 1994), 9.

3. AJG, *Garvey and Garveyism*, 219, 210–11.

4. Ibid., 211, 218.

5. Ibid., 218–19.

6. W. R. Garside, *British Unemployment, 1919–1939: A Study in Public Policy* (Cambridge: Cambridge University Press, 1990), 198; Thomas Holt, *The Problem of Freedom: Race, Labor, and Politics in Jamaica and Britain, 1832–1938* (Baltimore: Johns Hopkins University Press, 1992), 358–65.

7. G. E. Cumper, ed., *The Economy of the West Indies* (Kingston, Jamaica: Institute of Social and Economic Research, 1960), 9, 178.

8. Gisela Eisner, *Jamaica, 1830–1930: A Study in Economic Growth* (London: Manchester University Press, 1961), xviii, 325. Households also spent 13.9 percent on rent, 12.9 percent on other consumer goods, 12.1 percent on clothing, 9.6 percent on personal services, and 2.1 percent on passenger transport.

9. Kerr, *Personality and Conflict in Jamaica*, 118–19 (Anglican Church); "Christening of Marcus Garvey Jr. Tuesday," *Blackman*, 8 November 1930, 1; AJG, *Garvey and Garveyism*, 219.

10. U.S. Congress, House, Committee on Immigration and Nationalization, H. Rept. 898, 2 pts., 71st Cong., 2d sess., 1930.

11. *Garvey/UNIA Papers*, 7:552–53.

12. Holt, *Problem of Freedom*, 372, 374.

13. *Garvey/UNIA Papers*, 7:421, 422 n. 4; Ngugi Thiong'o, "Language, Writing, and Politics," Oxford Lecture Series, University of California, Berkeley, 12 November 1996.

14. AJG, *Garvey and Garveyism*, 196–97.

15. Economic theory may provide the best scholarly analysis of AJG's response to her husband's behavior. Since MG was the patriarchal head, she expected him to reduce his own consumption and his contributions to other family members. Gary S. Becker, "A Theory of Social Interactions," *Journal of Political Economy* 82 (1974): 1077, 1076.

16. Brodber, "Afro-Jamaican Women at the Turn of the Century," 48 n. 29.

17. Alec Waugh, *Love and the Caribbean: Tales, Characters, and Scenes of the West Indies* (New York: Farrar, Straus and Cudahy, 1958), 131; AJG, *Garvey and Garveyism*, 196.

18. George W. Roberts and Sonja A. Sinclair, *Women in Jamaica: Patterns of Reproduction and Family* (New York: KTO Press, 1978), 150–51.

19. AJG, *Garvey and Garveyism*, 219.

20. I viewed the *Blackman* newspaper on microfilm at the Institute of Jamaica for the period 30 March 1929–24 January 1931. The film may be incomplete, but it is a good representation of the newspaper as a whole.

21. I viewed the *New Jamaican* for the period July–9 September 1932. This newspaper did not have a woman's page, but it did contain articles on women's issues: e.g., "Employment of Children" (26 May 1933), "Birth Control Clinics" (6 July 1933), and "Sterilization of the Unfit" (2 August 1933). Due to a landlord debt, the *New Jamaican* ceased publication on 15 September 1933.

22. *Garvey/UNIA Papers*, 7:537 ("racially dead"); AJG, *Garvey and Garveyism*, 220.

23. Nancy Etcoff has scientifically established that beauty can be a source of "women's power," and Camille Paglia points out that supreme moments throughout the history of civilization, such as "Ancient Egypt, Classical Athens or Renaissance Florence, were always accompanied by the worship of beauty." Although AJG's attractiveness may not have had "power," it had inspired MG to take notice of her as well as project on her other pleasing attributes. It seems that human beings are more deeply "wired" for visual attraction than the capacity to assess positive qualities through other means; many contemporary studies have shown that it is not unusual for people from various cultures to assume that aesthetically beautiful people somehow also possess a wider range of attractive personality traits. Karen Springen, "Eyes of the Beholders," *Newsweek*, 3 June 1996, 68 (Etcoff, Paglia); Laura C. Longo and Richard D. Ashmore, "The Looks-Personality Relationship: Global Self-Orientations as Shared Precursors of Subjective Physical Attractiveness and Self-Ascribed Traits," *Journal of Applied Social Psychology* (1 March 1995): 371–99; and Michael R. Cunningham, Alan R. Roberts, Anita P. Barbee, Perrie B. Druen, and Cheng-Huan Wu, "Their Ideas of Beauty Are, on the Whole, the Same as Ours: Consistency and Variability in the Cross-Cultural Perception of Female Physical Attractiveness," *Journal of Personality and Social Psychology* (February 1995): 261–80.

24. AJG, *Garvey and Garveyism*, 222 ("over a year's taxes"); *Garvey/UNIA Papers*, 7:lxxvi. Julius Caesar (Roman statesman and general) and Winston Churchill (British statesman and later prime minister) were powerful leaders who faced their share of controversy. Caesar was both a defender of the people's rights and an ambitious demagogue who used vicious tactics to force his way to power. Churchill was undoubtedly one of the greatest public figures of the twentieth century, a bold military leader who was willing to use any measure to maintain Britain as a great imperial power. But Churchill was extremely conservative, and his role in the Boer War indicates that he was definitely anti-African. See Robert Rhodes James, *Churchill: A Study in Failure, 1900–1939* (New York: World, 1970); Henry Pelling, *Winston Churchill* (New York: Dutton, 1974); Lily Ross Taylor, *Party Politics in the Age of Caesar* (Berkeley: University of California Press, 1961); and AJG, *Garvey and Garveyism*, 222.

25. AJG, *Garvey and Garveyism*, 222–23.

26. Mrs. Ida Repole, interview by author, Kingston, Jamaica, 17 November 1990.

27. Kerr, *Personality and Conflict in Jamaica*, 1.

28. AJG, *Garvey and Garveyism*, 223.

29. Evelyn Nakano Glenn, "Social Constructions of Mothering: A Thematic Overview," in *Mothering: Ideology, Experience, and Agency*, ed. Evelyn Nakano Glenn, Grace Chang, and Linda Rennie Forcey (New York: Routledge, 1994), 22–23.

30. The *Black Man* was published for one year in Jamaica. When Garvey moved to London in 1935, he took the magazine with him. The *Black Man* was more a quarterly magazine, and a total of twenty-four issues appeared over five and a half years. The publication ceased in 1939 due to financial difficulties. For reprints of the magazine, see MG, *The Black Man: A Monthly Magazine of Negro Thought and Opinion* (New York: Kraus Thomson Organized, Ltd., 1975). The introduction, written by Robert Hill, provides an excellent chronological discussion placing the political emphasis of the magazine in historical context.

31. Joan French and Honor Ford Smith, *Women, Work, and Organization in Jamaica, 1900–1944* (Jamaica: Sistern Research and Institute of Social Science, 1986), 216.

32. For a detailed discussion of the variety of activities of these women, see ibid., 216–26.

33. Ibid., vi–vii, 170.

34. Jill Watts, *Shout the Victory: The History of Father Divine and the Peace Mission Movement, 1879–1942* (Los Angeles: University of California Press, 1989), 332–39; Mark Naison, *Communists in Harlem during the Depression* (New York: Grove Press, 1983); *Garvey/UNIA Papers*, 7:xlvi.

35. *Garvey/UNIA Papers*, 7:xlvi.

36. AJG, *Garvey and Garveyism*, 231–32.

Chapter Seven

1. Edna Brodber, "Afro-Jamaican Women at the Turn of the Century," *Social and Economic Studies* 35 (1986): 35; Evelyne Huber Stephens and John D. Stephens, *Democratic Socialism in Jamaica: The Political Movement and Social Transformation in Dependent Capitalism* (London: Macmillan, 1986), 13; Samuel J. Hurwitz and Edith F. Hurwitz, *Jamaica: A Historical Portrait* (New York: Praeger, 1971), 194.

2. AJG, *Garvey and Garveyism*, 231, 236.

3. Ibid., 236.

4. Robert S. McElvaine, ed., *Down and Out in the Great Depression: Letters from the Forgotten Man* (Chapel Hill: University of North Carolina Press, 1983), 53–65.

5. AJG, "Listen Women!," *Negro World*, 9 April 1927.

6. *Garvey/UNIA Papers*, 7:742.

7. Sudhanshu Handa, "The Determinants of Female Headship in Jamaica: Results from a Structural Model," *Economic Development and Cultural Change* 44 (June 1996): 811.

8. Lee Gang and Joseph Hraba, "Economic Reform in the Czech Republic:

Economic Strain, Depression, Hostility, and the Difference in Coping Strategies," *Sociological Inquiry* (Winter 1994): 103–13.

9. AJG, *Garvey and Garveyism*, 70.

10. *Garvey/UNIA Papers*, 7:743.

11. AJG, *Garvey and Garveyism*, 236.

12. *Garvey/UNIA Papers*, 7:742 (quotation); Dad [MG] to Mopsie [AJG], May 23 [1937], box 4, file 2, AJG Papers; AJG, *Garvey and Garveyism*, 236. AJG wrote on an envelope (in box 4, file 2) that she left Jamaica with their children on 8 June 1937. For a reprint, see *Garvey/UNIA Papers*, 7:742.

13. AJG, *Garvey and Garveyism*, 314, 232.

14. Ibid., 244.

15. *Garvey/UNIA Papers*, 7:745.

16. Ibid., 816.

17. AJG, *Garvey and Garveyism*, 316, 245.

18. Ibid., 245–46.

19. Ibid., 246, 241.

20. Ibid., 248.

21. Ibid.

22. Ibid.

23. Ibid.

24. Ibid., 249.

25. Thomas Holt, *The Problem of Freedom: Race, Labor, and Politics in Jamaica and Britain, 1832–1938* (Baltimore: Johns Hopkins Press, 1992), 376, 375.

26. Stephens and Stephens, *Democratic Socialism in Jamaica*, 14; Ken Post, *Arise Ye Starvelings: The Jamaican Labour Rebellion of 1938 and Its Aftermath* (London: Martinus Nijhoff, 1978), 276–82.

27. Wendell Bell, *Jamaican Leaders: Political Attitudes in a New Nation* (Berkeley: University of California Press, 1964), 16; Post, *Arise Ye Starvelings*, dedication page.

28. AJG, *Garvey and Garveyism*, 249.

29. Ibid., 249–50.

30. Ibid., 251.

31. Ibid., 242, 251.

32. MG sent letters addressed to each boy with identical messages: Dad to Chubbie [Julius] and Dad to Junior [Marcus], 8 December 1938, box 4, file 3, AJG Papers; letter to Julius reprinted in *Garvey/UNIA Papers*, 7:900.

33. AJG, *Garvey and Garveyism*, 252.

34. AJG to Ethel Collins, 7 August 1944, box 1, file 4, AJG Papers; AJG, *Garvey and Garveyism*, 287.

35. Both handwritten letters from Junior and Julius to MG, 11 January 1939, are in box 4, file 3, AJG Papers.

36. *Garvey/UNIA Papers*, 7:928, 905, 902.

37. There are thirty-six surviving letters written by MG, or typed by his secretary with his signature, to Junior and Julius between 8 December 1938 and 1 June 1940 in box 4, file 3, AJG Papers.

38. AJG to Ethel Collins, 7 August 1944; AJG, *Garvey and Garveyism*, 251.

39. Joan French and Honor Ford Smith, *Women, Work, and Organization in Jamaica, 1900–1944* (Mona, Jamaica: Sistern Research Institute of Social Science, 1986), 63.

40. *Garvey/UNIA Papers*, 7:xlvii.

41. AJG, *Garvey and Garveyism*, 261.

42. *Garvey/UNIA Papers*, 7:939; Daisy Whyte to AJG, 9 June 1940, and a post office telegram to AJG, 11 June 1940, both in box 4, file 6, AJG Papers.

43. "First Message to the Negroes of the World from Atlanta Prison," 10 February 1925, in AJG, ed., *The Philosophy and Opinions of Marcus Garvey; Or, Africa for the Africans* (Dover, Mass: Majority Press, 1986), 2:238.

44. *Garvey/UNIA Papers*, 7:932, 950.

Chapter Eight

1. Paul C. Rosenblatt, R. Patricia Walsh, and Douglas A. Jackson, *Grief and Mourning in Cross-Cultural Perspective* (New Haven, Conn.: HRAF Press, 1976), 8. The fact that she was not living with MG at the time of his death had to influence her reaction to it. Rosenblatt argues that "the more roles a deceased person occupied and the more important these roles were, the more disruptive the death will be to organizations and groups of which the deceased was a member." The first stage of widowhood, Joan M. Rawlins points out in her study on Jamaican women, is usually marked by a lack of companionship that leaves a void in their lives and foments a consequent loneliness. How widows cope with loneliness depends "to a great extent on whether there were young children in the home," concludes Sakinah Salahu-Din in her contemporary study on African American widows. AJG did not record feeling lonely, most likely because her children were present. Nor did she share other feelings produced by death such as anxiety, depression, fear, confusion, rage, and helplessness. As a proud person, AJG elected to grieve privately. Ibid.; Sakinah N. Salahu-Din, "A Comparison of Coping Strategies of African American and Caucasian Widows," *Omega: Journal of Death and Dying* 33 (1996): 114; Virginia Montero Seplowin and Egilde Seravalli, "A Historical Perspective on Bereavement," in *Loss, Grief, and Bereavement*, ed. Otto S. Margolis (New York: Praeger, 1985), 47.

2. Juan L. Turner, "Personal Reflections of the African American Experience," in *Ethnic Variations in Dying, Death, and Grief*, 201; Richard A. Kalish and David K. Reynolds, *Death and Ethnicity: A Psychocultural Study* (Los Angeles: University of Southern California Press, 1967), 31.

3. Hosea L. Perry, "Mourning and Funeral Customs of African Americans," in *Ethnic Variations in Dying, Death, and Grief*, 63; "Elaborate Memorial Service Is

Held for Marcus Garvey Here," *New York Age*, 27 July 1940, 1; *Garvey/UNIA Papers*, 7:951.

4. Ethel Collins to AJG, 28 June 1940, box 4, file 6, AJG Papers; *Garvey/UNIA Papers*, 7:955 (UNIA commissioners). For an example of a letter sent by AJG to UNIA divisions, see AJG to Thomas I. Clarke, Secretary Guachapali, Division Canal Zone, 9 August 1940, box 1, file 4, AJG Papers.

5. AJG, "Opening Message to the UNIA," box 4, file 6, ibid., reprinted in *Garvey/UNIA Papers*, 7:952.

6. *Garvey/UNIA Papers*, 7:953; "Address of Hon. Marcus Garvey Delivered at Trinity Auditorium, Los Angeles, California, Monday Evening, June the 5th, 1922," book 2, MGC.

7. *Garvey/UNIA Papers*, 7:953.

8. Ibid., 957, n. 1.

9. Ibid., 6:365–66.

10. AJG to N. H. Grissom, Commissioner, Wisconsin UNIA, 1 May 1945, box 2, file 2, AJG Papers.

11. James Stewart to AJG, 19 June 1942, box 4, file 6, ibid.

12. N. H. Grissom, Commissioner, Wisconsin UNIA, to AJG, 8 May [1945], box 2, file 2, ibid.

13. AJG to Grissom, 1 May 1945; E. M. Collins to AJG, 19 October 1942, box 1, file 1, AJG Papers.

14. AJG to B. Gibbons, President of the Garvey Club, 6 March 1945, box 1, file 12, ibid.

15. See stationary letterhead, AJG to Mr. A. Balfour Linton, Editor, *The African*, 3 July 1944, box 1, file 1, ibid.

16. AJG to Mr. B. Gibbons, 20 April 1944, box 1, file 12, ibid.

17. J. Bowlby, "Processes of Mourning," *International Journal Psychoanalysis* 42 (1961): 317–40; Marcia Kraft Goin, R. W. Burgoyne, and John M. Goin, "Timeless Attachment to a Dead Relative," *American Journal Psychiatry* 136 (July 1979): 988–89; AJG to Mr. B. Gibbons, 17 March 1944, box 1, file 12, and copy of the African Study Circle of the World circular letter, box 10, file 5, AJG Papers.

18. AJG to Mr. Geo. Covington, 2 May 1946, box 1, file 5, ibid. (first quotation); AJG to B. Gibbons, 20 April 1944, box 1, file 12, ibid. (second quotation); AJG to Mr. Nnamdi Azikiwe, 14 April 1944, box 1, file 2, ibid. (third quotation); AJG to Mr. Wyalt Dougherty, 17 January 1945, box 1, file 7, ibid.

19. AJG to Mr. Blades, 14 August 1944, box 1, file 3, ibid.

20. AJG to A. Philip Randolph, President of the Brotherhood of Sleeping Porters, 11 February 1944, box 3, file 1, ibid.

21. "Statement Issued to the Press by President Roosevelt," 14 August [1941], in *FRUS, Diplomatic Papers: General and the Soviet Union, 1941* (Washington, D.C.: GPO, 1958), 1:368; Franklin D. Roosevelt and Winston S. Churchill, "The Atlanta Charter," in *Yearbook of the United Nations, 1946–1947* (New York: Department of

Public Information, United Nations, 1947), 2; Francis Loewenheim, Harold Langley, and Manfred Jonas, eds., *Roosevelt and Churchill: Their Secret Wartime Correspondence* (New York: Saturday Review Press, 1975), 71 n. 1.

22. "The Declaration by United Nations," in *Yearbook of the United Nations, 1946–1947*, 1; "The Minister in Egypt (Kirk) to the Secretary of State," 9 June 1942, in *FRUS, Diplomatic Papers: The Near East and Africa, 1942* (Washington, D.C.: GPO, 1963), 4:105; James W. Ford, *The Negro People and the New World Situation* (New York: Workers Library Publications, 1941), 15.

23. Rochelle Chadakoff, ed., *Eleanor Roosevelt's My Day: Her Acclaimed Columns, 1936–1945* (New York: Pharos Books, 1989), 334; "Issues Dealt with by Mrs. Roosevelt in Press Conference," *Daily Gleaner*, 9 March 1944, 4; AJG to Adam Clayton Powell Jr., 13 March 1944, box 2, file 13, AJG Papers.

24. "Statement Issued to the Press by President Roosevelt," 16 December 1942, in *FRUS, Diplomatic Papers: Europe, 1942* (Washington, D.C.: GPO, 1962), 483; Chadakoff, *Eleanor Roosevelt's My Day*, 266 (radio message).

25. "Churchill to Roosevelt," 22 September 1942, in Loewenheim, Langley, and Jonas, *Roosevelt and Churchill*, 255, 54.

26. Eric Larrabee, *Commander in Chief: Franklin Delano Roosevelt, His Lieutenants, and Their War* (New York: Harper and Row Pub, 1987), 625.

27. Neil Hickney and Ed Edwin, *Adam Clayton Powell and the Politics of Race* (New York: Fleet Publishing Corp., 1965), 76; Adam Clayton Powell Jr., *Adam by Adam* (New York: Dail Press, 1971), 68; Charles V. Hamilton, *Adam Clayton Powell, Jr.: The Political Biography of an American Dilemma* (New York: Maxwell Macmillan International, 1992), 124, 141.

28. Adam Clayton Powell Jr. to AJG, 14 February 1944, box 2, file 13, AJG Papers.

29. AJG to Adam Clayton Powell Jr., 13 March 1944, ibid.

30. Ibid.; AJG to Mr. Nnamdi Azikiwe, 14 April 1944, box 1, file 2, ibid.

31. AJG to Mr. Nnamdi Azikiwe, 14 April 1944, box 1, file 2, ibid.

32. AJG to Adam Clayton Powell Jr., 13 March 1944; Claudia Jones, *Jim-Crow in Uniform* (New York: New Age Publishers, 1940), 7.

33. Keith E. Byerman, *Seizing the Word: History, Art, and Self in the Work of W. E. B. Du Bois* (Athens: University of Georgia Press, 1994), 90; Claudia Jones, *Jim-Crow in Uniform*, 7; "The Atlantic Charter and British West Africa, Memorandum on Post-War Reconstruction of the Colonies and Protectorates of British West Africa," August 1943, AJG Papers. See also "The National Council of Nigeria and the Cameroons Memorandum on the New Constitution for Nigeria," 27 March 1945, in box 13, file 6.

34. AJG to W. E. B. Du Bois, 31 January 1944, reel 56, frame 104, and Du Bois to AJG, 9 February 1944, reel 56, frame 107, Du Bois Papers.

35. AJG to Mr. B. Gibbons, 4 July, 16 May 1944, box 1, file 12, AJG Papers. A copy of the *Memorandum Correlative of Africa, West Indies, and the Americas* is in box 13, file 7.

36. AJG, *Memorandum Correlative*, 1.

37. AJG to Mr. A. Alladin, 1 June 1947, box 1, file 2, AJG Papers.

38. Roi Ottley, *New World a-Coming* (New York: Literary Classics, Inc., 1943), 343; AJG, *Memorandum Correlative*, 12; W. E. B. Du Bois, *Color and Democracy: Colonies and Peace* (New York: Harcourt, Brace, 1945), 17.

39. AJG to W. E. B. Du Bois, 24 April 1944, reel 56, frame 111, Du Bois Papers; Stokely Carmichael and Charles Hamilton, *Black Power: The Politics of Liberation in America* (New York: Vintage, 1967), 36–37; Du Bois, "The Name 'Negro,'" *Crisis*, March 1928.

40. Ruth W. Grant and Marion Orr, "Language, Race, and Politics: From 'Black' to 'African American,'" *Politics & Society* 24 (June 1996): 138, 140, 139.

41. At the bottom of "Garvey's African Communities League" stationary, AJG stenciled, "PS. Please send me any Newspapers, Magazines, or Books about Africa, Africans, people of African descent (commonly called Negroes)."

42. Paul Gilroy, *The Black Atlantic: Modernity and Double Consciousness* (Cambridge: Harvard University Press, 1993), 112.

43. AJG to Mrs. Allman, 6 November 1946, box 1, file 2, AJG Papers.

44. AJG to Mr. B. Gibbons, 7 May 1944, box 1, file 12, ibid.

45. AJG to Mr. James Blades, 14 August 1944, box 1, file 3, and AJG to Mr. B. Gibbons, 7 May, 20 June 1944, box 1, file 12, ibid.

46. AJG to Mr. Azikiwe, 24 October 1944, box 1, file 2, ibid.

47. MG, "The American Negro," *Black Man*, November 1938; Tony Martin, *Race First: The Ideological and Organizational Struggles of Marcus Garvey and the Universal Negro Improvement Association* (Westport, Conn.: Greenwood Press, 1976), 348–50; Ethel Wolfskill Hedlin, "Earnest Cox and Colonization: A White Racist's Response to Black Repatriation, 1923–1966" (Ph.D. diss., Duke University, 1974), iii.

48. AJG to Mr. Gibbons, 20 June 1944, box 1, file 12, Earnest S. Cox to AJG, 18 December 1947, box 1, file 5 (Bilbo), and James A. Blades to AJG, 7 August 1944, box 1, file 3, all in AJG Papers.

49. AJG to Mr. Brown, 31 October 1947, box 1, file 1, and N. H. Grissom to AJG, 20 June 1945, box 2, file 2, AJG Papers. For the relationship between Earnest Cox and MG, see Hedlin, "Earnest Cox and Colonization."

50. AJG to Mr. James A. Blades, 14 August 1944, box 1, file 3, AJG Papers.

51. Mr. B. Gibbons, President Garvey Club, to AJG, 13 November 1944, and AJG to Brother Gibbons, 23 November 1944, box 1, file 12, ibid.

52. AJG to W. E. B. Du Bois, 4 April 1944, reel 56, frame 108, Du Bois Papers; AJG to Du Bois, 4 April 1944, box 1, file 8, AJG Papers; Du Bois, "A Lunatic or a Traitor," *Crisis*, May 1924, 8–9, reprinted in *The Seventh Son: The Thought and Writings of W. E. B. Du Bois*, ed. Julius Lester (New York: Random House, 1971), 2:184–85.

53. Lester, *Seventh Son*, 2:734; Gerald Horne, *Black and Red: W. E. B. Du Bois and the Afro-American Response to the Cold War, 1944–1963* (New York: State University Press, 1986), 42, 113.

54. W. E. B. Du Bois to AJG, 9 February 1944, reel 56, frame 107, Du Bois Papers.

55. Lester, *Seventh Son*, 729; W. E. B. Du Bois to Miss Allison Burroughs, 7 January 1946, reel 58, frame 644, Du Bois Papers.

56. AJG to W. E. B. Du Bois, 4 April 1944, box 1, file 8, AJG Papers.

57. AJG to Adam Clayton Powell, 13 March 1944, box 2, file 13, ibid.; Walter White, *A Man Called White: The Autobiography of Walter White* (New York: Viking, 1948), 295; Horne, *Black and Red*, 36.

58. AJG to Adam Clayton Powell, 13 March 1944; Rupert Lewis, "Amy Jacques Garvey: A Political Portrait," *Jamaican Daily News*, 29 July 1973.

59. Horne, *Black and Red*, 36; W. E. B. Du Bois to Chairman of Liberian and Haitian Delegation, 29 April 1945, reel 58, frames 51–52, Du Bois Papers. Only four nations from the African continent were represented at the session: Ethiopia, Liberia, Egypt, and South Africa.

60. Leland M. Goodrich, *The United Nations in a Changing World* (New York: Columbia University Press, 1974), 179–201 (chap. 9, "The Passing of Colonialism").

61. AJG to Mrs. Allman, 6 November 1946, and Allman to AJG, 12 November 1946, box 1, file 2, AJG Papers; Mr. Guillermo Belt to AJG, 13 July 1945, box 1, file 3, ibid.

Chapter Nine

1. W. E. B. Du Bois to AJG, 8 April 1944, reel 56, frame 110, Du Bois Papers.

2. AJG to W. E. B. Du Bois, 24 April 1944, reel 56, frame 111, ibid.

3. George Padmore, ed., *History of the Pan-African Congress* (London: Hammersmith Bookshop, Ltd., 1947), 17–18.

4. W. E. B. Du Bois to AJG, 8 April 1944, reel 56, frame 110, enclosure, and George Padmore to Du Bois, 17 August 1945, reel 57, frame 1040, Du Bois Papers.

5. AJG to Mr. Gibbons, 5 April 1944, box 1, file 12, AJG Papers.

6. AJG to W. E. B. Du Bois, 24 April 1944, reel 56, frames 111–12.

7. Nnamdi Azikiwe, *My Odyssey: An Autobiography* (New York: Praeger, 1970), 162; I. F. Nicolson, *The Administration of Nigeria, 1900 to 1960: Men, Methods, and Myths* (Oxford: Clarendon Press, 1969), 252; Sir James Robertson, *Transition in Africa: From Direct Rule to Independence* (New York: Harper and Row, 1974), 189 ("variable character"); AJG to W. E. B. Du Bois, 26 April 1944, reel 56, frame 113, Du Bois Papers.

8. AJG to W. E. B. Du Bois, 24 April 1944, reel 56, frame 111, Du Bois Papers; Gerald Horne, *Black and Red: W. E. B. Du Bois and the Afro-American Response to*

the Cold War, 1944–1963 (New York: State University Press, 1986), 37 (harmless "nuisance").

9. AJG to W. E. B. Du Bois, 26 April 1944, reel 56, frame 113, Du Bois Paper; Mary Hawkesworth, "Confounding Gender," *Signs* 22 (Spring 1997): 654; Joan Scott, "Gender: A Useful Category of Historical Analysis," *American Historical Review* 91 (December 1986): 1063.

10. George Padmore to AJG, 9 July 1945, box 2, file 2, and AJG to Brother Gibbons, 28 July, 17 September 1945, box 1, file 12, AJG Papers; Padmore, *History of the Pan-African Congress*, 72.

11. AJG to Mr. Padmore, 28 July 1945, box 2, file 2, AJG Papers.

12. Joan French and Honor Ford Smith, *Women, Work, and Organization in Jamaica, 1900–1944* (Mona, Jamaica: Sistern Research Institute of Social Science, 1986), 237–39.

13. Robert Hill and Barbara Bair, eds., *Marcus Garvey Life and Lessons: A Centennial Companion to the Marcus Garvey and UNIA Papers* (Berkeley: University of California Press, 1987), 378; AJG to Mr. Domingo, 28 July 1945, box 1, file 7, AJG Papers.

14. AJG to Mr. Padmore, 28 July 1945.

15. AJG, interview by Dabu Gizenga, 10 January 1973, Kwame Nkrumah Collection 128-1–128-2, Moorland Spingard Library, Howard University, Washington, D.C.; Amy Ashwood Garvey to W. E. B. Du Bois, 8 September 1924, reel 13, frame 744, Du Bois Papers.

16. AJG to W. E. B. Du Bois, 4, 24 April 1944, box 1, file 8, AJG Papers.

17. B. Gibbons to AJG, 4 June 1946, box 1, file 13, ibid.

18. AJG to Editor, *Amsterdam News*, 4 April 1944, box 1, file 2, ibid.; C. B. Powell, Editor, *Amsterdam News*, to AJG, 12 April 1944, box 1, file 1, ibid.

19. N. H. Grissom to AJG, 9 April 1947, box 2, file 2, ibid.; Tony Martin, "Amy Ashwood Garvey, Wife No. 1," *Jamaica Journal* 30 (August–October 1987): 35–36.

20. Audre Lorde, *Sister Outsider: Essays and Speeches* (Freedom, Calif.: Crossing Press, 1984), 169; AJG to Mr. Azikiwe, 28 November 1944, box 1, file 2, AJG Papers.

21. Martin, "Wife No. 1," 33.

22. Padmore, *History of the Pan-African Congress*, 52. Miss Alma La Badie, representing the UNIA, was the only other female voice recorded in the proceedings. La Badie also elaborated on the problems of Jamaican women, connecting the "high illegitimate birth rate" to the fact that "women have little means of livelihood, and, therefore, get into difficulties."

23. Lorde, *Sister Outsider*, 167.

24. Padmore, *History of the Pan-African Congress*, 4; AJG interview, Kwame Nkrumah Collection, 128-1–128-2.

25. AJG to Mr. Azikiwe, 28 November 1945, box 1, file 32, AJG Papers.

26. AJG to W. E. B. Du Bois, 24 April 1944, reel 56, frame 111, Du Bois Papers.

Chapter Ten

1. AJG, "Be Prepared," *The African*, May 1946, 12.

2. Rupert Lewis, *Marcus Garvey: Anti-Colonial Champion* (Trenton, N.J.: African World Press, 1988); AJG, "The Coming Era: Africans View of a World under Demolition and Reconstruction," *The African*, August 1944, 5; Wang Qinmei, "Africa Contributes to World War II Victory," *Beijing Review 38* (15 June 1995): 20.

3. AJG, "Be Prepared"; AJG, "The Coming Era."

4. AJG, "Where Are My Children?," *The African*, June 1946, 11.

5. Paul Bartrop, "From Lisbon to Jamaica: A Study of British Refugee Rescue during the Second World War," *Immigrants & Minorities* (1994): 48–64; "Hitler Conveniently Avoided Congratulating Jesse Owens," *Chicago Defender*, 8 August 1936; "Hitler Won't Shake Hands," *Afro-American*, 8 August 1936; James R. Hooker, *Black Revolutionary: George Padmore's Path from Communism to Pan-Africanism* (New York: Praeger, 1967), 55; "Hitler Wants Part of Africa from Britain: British Cabinet Pondering over Consideration of New Issue," *Chicago Defender*, 5 November 1938; "Africans in Demonstration against Nazi Germany," *Chicago Defender*, 5 November 1938.

6. Mercer Cook, "The Negro Knows Fascism," *Free World*, November 1942, 147–50.

7. Gerald Horne, *Black Liberation/Red Scare: Ben Davis and the Communist Party* (Newark, N.J.: University of Delaware Press, 1994), 81; "Britain Has Its Hitlers: English Color Bar Stirs Deep Hatred of Colonials," *Afro-American*, 26 November 1938.

8. Cook, "The Negro Knows Fascism," 148.

9. Hooker, *Black Revolutionary*, 59.

10. Rita Headrick, "African Soldiers in World War II," *Armed Forces and Society* (1978): 505, 503.

11. AJG, "Garveyism as a Philosophy of Life," *West African Pilot*, 26 April 1945.

12. AJG, "Where Are My Children?"

13. AJG, "Africans at Home and Abroad," *West African Pilot*, 28 September 1945.

14. AJG, "Garveyism as a Philosophy of Life."

15. Harold Preece, "Africa Awakes," *Crisis*, December 1945; Nnamdi Azikiwe, "Address Delivered at the Inauguration of the African Continental Bank, September 1, 1948," in *Colonial Rule in Africa: Readings from Primary Sources*, ed. Bruce Fetter (Madison: University of Wisconsin Press, 1979), 114 (quotations).

16. AJG to Mr. Azikiwe, 28 November 1945, box 1, file 2, AJG Papers.

17. AJG, "China Milks Africa in the Caribbean," *West African Pilot*, 28 December 1945.

18. Ibid.

19. Layle Silbert, "We Export Race Prejudice to China," *Crisis*, July 1948, 208.

20. Natasha B. Barnes, "Face of the Nation: Race, Nationalism, and Identities

in Jamaican Beauty Pageants," *Massachusetts Review* (Autumn–Winter 1994): 483; Rex M. Nettleford, *Mirror, Mirror: Identity, Race, and Protest in Jamaica* (Jamaica: William Collins and Sangster, 1970), 13.

21. AJG also offered editorial suggestions to Nnamdi Azikiwe's *West African Pilot* and *West African Opinion*.

22. The AJG Papers, box 1, file 1, contain numerous handwritten notes calculating the funds received by agents. For other money exchanges for *The African*, see AJG to Mrs. Iris Davis, Hannah Town, Kingston, 12 March 1947, and Davis to AJG, 3 October 1947, box 1, file 7, AJG Papers.

23. J. L. Brown to AJG, 20 March 1947, box 1, file 1, AJG Papers.

24. Ridley Lewis to AJG, 4 April 1945, and AJG to Lewis, 19 April 1945, ibid.

25. AJG to Mr. James L. Brown, 6, 26 September 1944, ibid.

26. AJG to Mr. Ridley Lewis, 9 April 1946, and AJG to Mr. James Brown, 21 November 1946, ibid.

27. "African Study Circle of the World" circular letter, *The African*, November–December 1944.

28. Molefi Kete Asante, *Kemet, Afrocentricity, and Knowledge* (Trenton, N.J.: African World Press, 1990).

29. AJG to Mr. Wyatt Dougherty, Secretary of Union of People of African Descent, American Section Black International, 17 January 1945, box 1, file 7 (first quotation), and AJG to Mr. Wright, Attention Mr. Gibbons, 17 March 1944, box 1, file 12, AJG Papers.

30. AJG to Mr. Wm. Douglas, Secretary of UNIA, Panama, June 20 1944, box 1, file 7, ibid.

31. Harrison Ross Steeves, *Learned Societies and English Literary Scholarship: In Great Britain and the United States* (New York: AMS Press, 1970), xiv.

32. "African Study Circle of the World," advertisement, *The African*, November–December 1944.

33. AJG to Mr. Gibbons, 20 April 1944, box 1, file 12, AJG Papers.

34. Mary Kelley, *Private Woman, Public Stage: Literary Domesticity in Nineteenth-Century America* (New York: Oxford University Press, 1984); Frances B. Cogan, *All-American Girl: The Ideal of Real Womanhood in Mid-Nineteenth-Century America* (Athens: University of Georgia Press, 1989), 67 (quotation).

35. Anne Meis Knupfer, *Toward a Tender Humanity and a Nobler Womanhood* (New York: New York University Press, 1996), 114; Carolyn Cooper, "Race and the Cultural Politics of Self-Representation: A View from the University of the West Indies," *Research in African Languages* 27 (Winter 1996): 100; Dorothy B. Porter, "The Organized Educational Activities of Negro Literary Societies, 1828–1846," *Journal of Negro Education* (October 1936): 569.

36. Cooper, "Race and the Cultural Politics of Self-Representation."

37. AJG suggested these books for the first series: Selwyn Jones, *South of the Congo*; Nagley Farson, *Behind God's Back*; J. A. Rogers, *Sex and Race in the Old*

World, Sex and Race in the New World, and *One Hundred Amazing Facts about the Negro;* Melville Herskowitz, *The Myth of the Negro Past;* W. E. B. Du Bois, *Black Folk;* Donald Pierson, *Negroes in Brazil;* Xavier Hebert, *Capricornia (Australia);* Paul Laurence Dunbar, *The Complete Poems;* Denis Saurat, *Watch Over Africa;* and Bronze Booklet, *Negro Art Past and Present*—located at the Crisis Book Shop in New York. AJG informed Nnamdi Azikiwe that she was going to "include your two books, 'Renascent Africa' and the other on Liberian Politics, for our Circle second series of readings and discussions." AJG to Azikiwe, 24 October 1944, box 1, file 1, AJG Papers.

38. Donald Pierson, *Negroes in Brazil: A Study of Race Contact at Bahia* (Carbondale: Southern Illinois University Press, 1967), 46, 50; Negley Farson, *Behind God's Back* (New York: Harcourt, Brace, 1941), 471.

39. Asante, *Kemet, Afrocentricity, and Knowledge.*

40. J. A. Rogers, *Sex and Race: Negro-Caucasian Mixing in All Ages and All Lands* (St. Petersburg, Fla.: Helga M. Rogers, 1968), 1; "African Study Circle of the World," advertisement, *The African,* November–December 1944.

41. Peggy R. Sabatier, " 'Elite' Education in French West Africa: The Era of Limits, 1903–1945," *International Journal of African Historical Studies* 11 (1978): 256.

42. Fay Gadsden, "The African Press in Kenya, 1945–1952," *Journal of African History* 21 (1980): 516 (first quotation); Daiziel Fuller, Secretary of African Study Circle, Auxiliary of the Guachapali Division, #244, to AJG, 21 December 1947, box 1, file 10, AJG Papers.

43. John Egerton, "The Pre-Brown South," *Virginia Quarterly Review* 70 (Autumn 1994): 604; Robert A. Dentler, "School Desegregation since Gunnar Myrdal's American Dilemma," in *The Education of African Americans,* ed. Charlie V. Willie, Antonie M. Garibaldi, and Wornie L. Reed (New York: Auburn House, 1991), 29 (quotation).

44. Joseph Woolcock, "Class Conflict and Class Reproduction: An Historical Analysis of the Jamaican Educational Reforms of 1957 and 1962," *Social and Economic Studies* 33 (1984): 52. There had been so much resistance to opening up secondary schools to the masses of black Jamaicans that even though the Common Entrance Examination was formally adopted in 1943, it was not implemented until 1957.

45. AJG to Mr. Gibbons, 20 June 1944, box 1, file 12, AJG Papers.

46. AJG to Mr. J. L. Brown, Circulation Manager for *The African,* 1 May 1944, and AJG to Mr. A. Balfour Linton, 4 July 1944, box 1, file 1, ibid.

47. Miss Irene Ford, Cleveland, Ohio, to AJG, 18 January 1945, box 1, file 7, ibid.; Daiziel Fuller to AJG, 21 December 1947.

48. Stuart Hall, "Negotiating Caribbean Identities," *New Left Review* (January– February 1995): 11.

49. Paul Gilroy, *The Black Atlantic: Modernity and Double Consciousness* (Cambridge: Harvard University Press, 1993), 199.

Chapter Eleven

1. W. E. B. Du Bois, *Dusk of Dawn* (New York: Kraus Thomson Organization, Ltd., 1975), 303; David Levering Lewis Collection, "Voices from the Renaissance Transcripts," box 1, file 2, Schomburg Library Special Collections Unit, New York; Sanford Pinsker, "The Black Intellectuals' Common Fate and Uncommon Problems," *Virginia Quarterly Review* (Spring 1994): 235.

2. Wendell Bell, *Jamaican Leaders: Political Attitudes in a New Nation* (Berkeley: University of California Press, 1964), 8; AJG to Mr. Haynes, 4 June 1946, box 3, file 4, AJG Papers.

3. R. W. Thompson, *Black Caribbean* (London: Macdonald and Co., 1946), 211; Carol Mae Morrissey, "Ol' Time Tram and the Tramway Era 1876–1948," *Jamaica Journal* 6 (November 1983): 12–21.

4. The location of election meetings was listed daily in the *Daily Gleaner* along with the proposed speakers.

5. AJG to Mr. W. Y. Reurtado, A.M.I.C.E., Director of Public Works Department, 5 November 1947, box 5, file 8, AJG Papers. The department replied that the "matter was receiving consideration by the government," 3 January 1948, box 5, file 2.

6. "P.N.P. Holds Big Meeting at Halfway Tree," *Daily Gleaner*, 13 November 1944, 9.

7. AJG to Mr. Andronicus Jacobs, 12 December 1944, box 2, file 5, and AJG to Editor, *Daily Gleaner*, 23 March 1944, box 31, file 13, AJG Papers.

8. Ken Post, *Arise Ye Starvelings: The Jamaican Labour Rebellion of 1938 and Its Aftermath* (London: Martinus Nijhoff, 1978), 423; C. Paul Bradley, "Mass Parties in Jamaica: Structure and Organization," *Social and Economic Studies* 9 (December 1960): 393.

9. This political power block was so well financed that it eliminated the possibility for a formidable third party, despite the efforts of conservative planters who formed the Jamaican Democratic Party for "free enterprise." Ironically, this was the only party that put forth a Charter for Women. See "Charter for Women," *Daily Gleaner*, 14 November 1944, 5.

10. AJG to Mr. Mitchell, Colon, 24 October 1947, box 2, file 9, AJG Papers; "Large Crowd Cheer Dr. Fagan at Meeting," *Daily Gleaner*, 25 November 1944, 13; Frank Hill, *Bustamante and His Letters* (Kingston, Jamaica: Kingston Publishing Ltd., 1976), 34.

11. Diane Austin, *Urban Life in Kingston, Jamaica: The Culture and Class Ideology of Two Neighborhoods* (New York: Cordon and Breach Science Publishers, 1984), 13 ("two sides of the same coin"); T. R. Makonnen, Editor, *Pan-Africa*, to AJG, 18 February 1947, box 5, file 2, AJG Papers.

12. Aggrey Brown, *Color, Class, and Politics in Jamaica* (New Brunswick, N.J.: Transaction Books, 1979), 111; a series of editorials and commentary in the *Daily Gleaner*, November 1944.

13. Post, *Arise Ye Starvelings*, 453.

14. Carl Stone, *Class, Race, and Political Behavior in Urban Jamaica* (Mona, Jamaica: Institute of Social and Economic Research, 1973).

15. Morris E. Parkin, "P.N.P. and Bustamante," *Daily Gleaner*, 6 November 1944, 6.

16. Linnette Vassell, "Women of the Masses: Daphne Campbell and 'Left' Politics in Jamaica in the 1950s," in *Engendering History: Caribbean Women in Historical Perspective*, eds. Verene Shepherd, Bridget Brereton, and Barbara Bailey (New York: St. Martin's Press, 1995), 322.

17. AJG to Mr. Brown, Editor, *The African*, 11 December 1944, and AJG to Mr. Azikiwe, 30 November 1944, box 1, file 1, AJG Papers. The following year she sent Azikiwe a news clipping on the Jamaican elections. AJG to Mr. Azikiwe, 10 April 1945, box 1, file 2, ibid.

18. Aggrey Brown, *Color, Class, and Politics in Jamaica*, 116; Bell, *Jamaican Leaders*, 19.

19. Cornel West, "Marxist Theory and the Specificity of Afro-American Oppression," in *Marxism and the Interpretation of Culture*, ed. C. Nelson and L. Grossbert (Urbana: University of Illinois Press, 1988), 276.

20. E. M. Collins to AJG, 19 October 1942, and AJG to Mrs. Carmen Cordoza, Executive Secretary of the UNIA, 26 February 1945, box 1, file 5, AJG to Brother Gibbons, 28 July 1945, box 1, file 3; AJG to Mr. Nnamdi Azikiwe, 14 April 1944, box 31, file 2; AJG to Mr. Dougherty, 14 November 1945, box 1, file 7—all in AJG Papers.

21. AJG to Sylvester Uguru, Lagos, Nigeria, 18 December 1944, box 3, file 8, ibid.

22. James Stewart, President General, to Mrs. Beulah McDonald, New Orleans, La. Division, 5 June 1941, roll 1, folder 3, UNIA Papers; Box 3, file 2, AJG Papers.

23. James Stewart to Thomas Clarke, Ancon Division, Canal Zone, 9 September 1941, roll #1, folder 4, and Executive Council minutes, Roll 6, folder 42, UNIA Papers.

24. "Have You Forgotten Them?," *New Negro World* 1 (December 1942), in roll 15, folder 92, and James Stewart to Steve Braithwait, Glace Bay, Nova Scotia, 5 June 1941, roll 1, folder 3, UNIA Papers.

25. *New York Age*, 6, 13, 20 July 1946; "Garvey Returns," *New York Age*, 13 July 1946; "Mrs. Garvey Gets Warm Greeting from Friend," *New York Amsterdam News*, 3 August 1946, 8.

26. AJG to Mr. A. L. Crawford, 28 May 1946, box 1, file 6, AJG Papers.

27. AJG to Mr. T. R. Mackonen, 8 December 1946, box 2, file 8, AJG Papers; AJG to Mr. A. L. Crawford, 28 May 1946.

28. "UNIA Convenes Aug 4th," *New York Age*, 20 July 1946; "30-Day Convention Opens in Harlem," *New York Times*, 5 August 1946, 22.

29. AJG to Mr. Clark, 30 September 1949, box 31, file 4, AJG Papers; "Mrs. Garvey Speaks," *New York Age*, 7 September 1946; Mr. Berry Byl[?] to AJG, 25 August 1946, box 1, file 3, AJG Papers; Winston James, *Holding Aloft the Banner of*

Ethiopia: Caribbean Radicalism in the Early Twentieth-Century America (London: Verso Press, 1998), 3; "Mrs Garvey Speaks."

30. AJG, "Wartime Neglect of U.S. Children Blamed for Delinquency," *Daily Gleaner*, 19 October 1946; Karen Anderson, *Wartime Women: Sex Roles, Family Relations, and the Status of Women during World War II* (Westport, Conn.: Greenwood Press, 1981), 95–96; Walter A. Lunden, *Statistics on Delinquents and Delinquency* (Springfield, Ill.: Charles C. Thomas, Publishers, 1964), 167–68; Sheldon Glueck and Eleanor Glueck, *Family Environment and Delinquency* (Boston: Houghton Mifflin, 1962), 109–12.

31. AJG, "Wartime Neglect of U.S. Children Blamed for Delinquency"; Karen Anderson, *Wartime Women*, 96 ("so-called commando gangs").

32. A. W. Burke, "A Cross Cultural Study of Delinquency among West Indian Boys," *International Journal of Social Psychiatry* 26 (1980): 81; Austin, *Urban Life in Kingston, Jamaica*, 53.

33. Guy Standing, *Unemployment and Female Labour: A Study of Labour Supply in Kingston, Jamaica* (New York: St. Martin's Press, 1981), 88, 93–95.

34. AJG to Mr. Grissom, 7 October 1948, box 2, file 2; B. Gibbons to AJG, 29 August 1945, box 1, file 12; AJG to Miss Ethel Collins, 7 August 1944, box 1, file 4; AJG to Mr. Gibbons, 20 April 1944, box 1, file 12—all in AJG Papers.

35. AJG to Miss Ethel Collins, 7 August 1944 ("the highest marks"); AJG to Mr. W. H. Douglass, 26 December 1944, box 3, file 7; AJG to Mr. Booth, 17 January 1945, box 1, file 3; AJG to Headmaster, [Wolmers], 8 September 1947, box 5, file 5—all in AJG Papers.

36. "Passes University Exams," *New York Age*, 22 June 1946, 5; AJG to Mr. Anderson, 31 October 1947, box 1, file 1, AJG Papers; Nancy Foner, *Status and Power in Rural Jamaica: A Study of Educational and Political Change* (New York: Teachers College Press, 1973), 61.

37. AJG to Mr. L. Booth, 17 January 1945, box 1, file 3 ("keep him nourished"), and AJG to Nnamdi Azikiwe, 5 February 1945, box 1, file 1 ("taste for good acting"), AJG Papers; Julius Garvey, *Essence* 17 (November 1986): 63; AJG to Mr. James L. Brown, 6 September 1944, box 31, file 1, AJG Papers (last quotation).

38. AJG to Mr. Alladin, 1 June 1947, box 1, file 1, ibid.

39. Mark Figueroa, "The Formation and Framework of Middle Strata Leadership in Jamaica: The Crisis of the Seventies and Beyond," *Caribbean Studies: Puerto Rico* 21 (1988): 46.

40. Patrick S. Washburn, *A Question of Sedition: The Federal Government's Investigation of the Black Press during World War II* (New York: Oxford University Press, 1986), 5 (post office examiner); Walter White, *A Rising Wind* (1945; Westport, Conn.: reprint, Negro University Press, 1971), 144.

41. AJG to Mr. Fishel, 1 September 1965, MG UNIA Collection, State Historical Society of Wisconsin; Gerald Horne, *Black and Red: W. E. B. Du Bois and the Afro-*

American Response to the Cold War, 1944–1963 (New York: State University Press, 1986), 66–67.

42. Manning Marable, *Race, Reform, and Rebellion: The Second Reconstruction* (Jackson: University of Mississippi Press, 1991), 21 (first quotation); Brenda Gayle Plummer, *Rising Wind: Black Americans and U.S. Foreign Affairs, 1935–1960* (Chapel Hill: University of North Carolina Press, 1996), 194.

43. Penny M. Von Eschen, *Race against Empire: Black Americans and Anti-colonialism, 1937–1957* (Ithaca, N.Y.: Cornell University Press, 1997), 145.

44. Ibid., 146.

45. E. L. Pierre, an agent for the *African Opinion* magazine, was informed by the publishers to send the $6.06 he collected from sales to AJG. Pierre to AJG, 15 May 1950, box 2, file 11, AJG Papers. Mr. Alladin sent AJG a check for $12.00 for sales of *The African*. Alladin to AJG, 19 May 1950, box 1, file 2, ibid.

46. J. L. Brown, Editor, *African Opinion*, to AJG, 31 March 1951, box 1, file 1, ibid.

47. AJG to *Daily Gleaner*, 20, 26 July, 10 August 1952, 27 July 1957; AJG to J. Johnson, Editor, *Ebony*, 18 July 1952—all in box 1, file 9, AJG Papers; AJG to Mr. Boronme, 14 March 1953, AJG to George Shepperson, 11 September 1952, and AJG to Samuel A. Hayes, 15 May 1950, box 1, file 3, AJG Papers.

48. AJG to David Cronon, 28 Marcus 1955, box 10, file 6, AJG Papers.

49. Ibid.

50. Ibid.

51. J. L. Brown to AJG, 25 August 1950, and AJG to Mr. M. Taylor, 21 July 1956, box 5, file 3; Jean Blackwell to AJG, 16 April, 29 July, 9 September 1952, box 3, file 2—all in AJG Papers.

52. AJG to Mrs. Taylor, Secretary General, UNIA, 9 September 1957, box 3, file 4, and William Sherrill to AJG, 21 September 1957, box 33, file 4, AJG Papers.

53. AJG to William Sherrill, 24 September 1957, box 33, file 4, ibid.

54. George Padmore to AJG, 3 October 1950, box 33, file 11, ibid.

55. *Daily Gleaner*, 8 November 1956.

56. "Division News Kingston," *Garvey's Voice*, August 1957, in Western Historical Reserve Society, Cleveland, Ohio.

Chapter Twelve

1. Walter Rodney, *How Europe Underdeveloped Africa* (Washington, D.C.: Howard University Press, 1982), 277–78; Hakim Adi, *West Africans in Britain, 1900–1960: Nationalism, Pan-Africanism, and Communism* (London: Lawrence and Wishart, 1998), 186, 160–70.

2. [AJG], "Unite as One People, One Race with One Destiny," *Evening News*, 29 November 1960, 5 ("Africa shall be free"); AJG, "Destiny Being Fulfilled," manuscript, box 5, file 13, AJG Papers.

3. "Notables to Witness Zik's Ceremony," *West African Pilot*, 15 November 1960; "Zik's Inauguration as Gov-Gen to Be Filmed," *West African Pilot*, 9 November 1960, 1; "Botsio Attends Swearing In of Azikiwe," *Ghanaian Times*, 16 November 1960. AJG had also been invited to attend Kwame Nkrumah's inauguration celebration in 1957 but did not have the plane fare. See AJG to Kwame Nkrumah, Prime Minister, 18 February 1957, box 2, file 10, AJG Papers.

4. *Respect for Human Dignity: An Inaugural Address Delivered by His Excellency Dr. Nnamdi Azikiwe: Governor-General and Commander-in-Chief*, 16 November 1960, 2, 5, in University of Ghana Balme Library, Accra, Ghana; "Garvey Suggests Extracts from Zik's Speech Should Be Taught to School Children," *West African Pilot*, 25 November 1960.

5. "She Flies in at Osagyefo's Invitation," *Ghanaian Times*, 25 November 1960, 5; "Garvey Suggests Extracts from Zik's Speech Should Be Taught to School Children"; "Mrs. Garvey for Ghana Tomorrow," *Daily Express Lagos, Nigeria*, 22 November 1960; "Garvey's Wife in Ghana," *Ghanaian Times*, 24 November 1960.

6. St. Clair Drake, "Diaspora Studies and Pan-Africanism," in *Global Dimensions of the African Diaspora*, ed. Joseph E. Harris (Washington, D.C.: Howard University Press, 1982), 361–62; James E. Turner, "Historical Dialectics of Black Nationalist Movements in America," *Western Journal of Black Studies* 1 (September 1977): 165.

7. St. Clair Drake, "Diaspora Studies and Pan-Africanism," 350; Leslie Alexander Lacy, "The Rise and Fall of the Proper Negro," in *A Stranger in the Village: Two Centuries of African-American Travel Writing*, ed. Farah J. Griffin and Cheryl J. Fisher (Boston: Beacon Press, 1998), 158; Richard Wright, *Black Power: A Record of Reactions in a Land of Pathos* (New York: Harper and Brothers, 1954), 57.

8. Kwame Nkrumah, *The Autobiography* (London: Panaf Books, 1957), 37; "Black Star Line: Now a Ghanaian Enterprise," *Ghanaian Times*, 26 July 1960, 1; Michael W. Williams, "Marcus Garvey and Kwame Nkrumah: A Case of Ideological Assimilation, Advancement, and Refinement," *Western Journal of Black Studies* 7 (1983): 94.

9. Jean Blackwell to AJG, 18 March 1957, Schomburg Center for Research in Black Culture Collection, New York, N.Y.; "She Flies in at Osagyefo's Invitation"; AJG, "Destiny Being Fulfilled," unpublished essay, box 5, file 13, AJG Papers.

10. "Mrs. Garvey for Ghana Tomorrow"; Basil Davidson, *Black Star: A View of the Life and Times of Kwame Nkrumah* (Boulder, Colo.: Westview Press, 1989), 2; "A Visit to Bureau," *Daily Graphic Ghana*, 25 November 1960; *Ghana Institute of Languages Admission Guide*, 2, in possession of author.

11. *Ghana Institute of Languages Admission Guide*, 2. Ghana made some important educational gains under Nkrumah's leadership. By 1964, the number of students receiving primary schooling was almost seven times greater than it had been in 1950; the number of children in middle school was four times higher, and

secondary school attendance was ten times greater. See Davidson, *Black Star*, 160. Unfortunately, this educational model would be contested by elites who understood education as a way to guarantee their privileges. One participant in the coup that overthrew Nkrumah in 1966 claimed that the action was justified because "Nkrumah's rule had planted havoc . . . in the field of education [by] a crippling or lowering of educational standards." Although it is true that the quality of education failed to keep abreast with the expansion of schools, criticism of its "quantity at the expense of quality," Davidson argues, was merely "another angle of discontent, essentially a political angle" (160–61).

12. "Dr. Nkrumah Is Osagyefo for the World—Mrs. Garvey," *Ghanaian Times*, 5 December 1960, 5–6; C. L. R. James, *Nkrumah and the Ghana Revolution* (Westport, Conn.: Lawrence Hill and Co., 1977), 106, 119; Kent Worchester, "C. L. R. James and the Development of a Pan-African Problematic," *Journal of Caribbean History* 27 (1993): 70.

13. AJG to Mrs. Evelyn Amarteifio, Secretary, Federation of Women, 26 January 1958, box 1, file 1, AJG Papers.

14. Kwame Nkrumah, "Appeal to National Workers, on 2nd April, 1962," in *The Eleventh Party Congress*, Kwame Nkrumah, 29 July 1962; Davidson, *Black Star*, 176; [AJG], "Unite as One People, One Race with One Destiny," 5.

15. David N. Gibbs, *The Political Economy of Third World Intervention: Mines, Money, and U.S. Policy in the Congo Crisis* (Chicago: University of Chicago Press, 1991), 99.

16. Prof. St. Clair Drake, "Why Nkrumah Supports Patrice Lumumba," *New Ashanti Times*, 26 November 1960, 7; W. Scott Thompson, *Ghana's Foreign Policy, 1957–1966: Diplomacy, Ideology, and the New State* (Princeton, N.J.: Princeton University Press, 1969), 129, 131; [AJG], "Unite as One People, One Race with One Destiny," 5.

17. AJG, "Destiny Being Fulfilled," unpublished essay, box 5, file 13, AJG Papers; Clayton Eshleman and Annette Smith, ed., *Aimé Césaire: The Collected Poetry* (Berkeley: University of California Press, 1983), 77.

18. AJG, "Destiny Being Fulfilled."

19. Ibid.

20. Vernon McKay, *Africa in World Politics* (New York: Harper and Row, 1963), 402–3 (quotation, 403); "Southern Hospitality," *Crisis*, February 1961, 100.

21. AJG, "New Africa and the West Indies," box 14, file 1, AJG Papers. There is no evidence that this essay was published, but AJG did receive one letter, dated 1 June 1961, from the Bureau of Ghana Languages indicating that her article with the same title was well received. See letter in box 1, file 3, ibid.

22. See, e.g., Gerald Horne, *Black and Red: W. E. B. Du Bois and the Afro-American Response to the Cold War, 1944–1963* (New York: State University of New York Press, 1986); Penny Von Eschen, *Race against Empire: Black Americans*

and Anticolonialism, 1937–1957 (Ithaca, N.Y.: Cornell University Press, 1997); and Brenda Gayle Plummer, *Rising Wind: Black Americans and U.S. Foreign Affairs, 1935–1960* (Chapel Hill: University of North Carolina Press, 1996).

23. AJG to Mr. Bennett, 6 May 1960, box 5, file 2, AJG Papers; Von Eschen, *Race against Empire*, 56; David Watts, *The West Indies: Patterns of Development, Culture, and Environmental Change since 1942* (London: Cambridge University Press, 1987), 522.

24. Gordon K. Lewis, *The Growth of the Modern West Indies* (New York: Monthly Review Press, 1968), 186; AJG, response to George Hopewell's article, "New Africa and the West Indies: Who Leads?," *Daily Gleaner*, 11 June 1961, box 1, file 14, AJG Papers.

25. G. E. Cumper, ed., *The Economy of the West Indies* (Kingston, Jamaica: Institute of Social and Economic Research, 1960), 181; AJG, handwritten notes on a speech by Harold Macmillan, Conservative British prime minister, in Cape Town, 3 February 1961, box 2, file 8, AJG Papers.

26. A. Lynn Bolles, *Sister Jamaica: A Study of Women, Work, and Households in Kingston* (New York: University Press of America, 1996), 27; Gordon K. Lewis, *Growth of the Modern West Indies*, 186 ("heroes in colonial garb"); AJG to Michael Manley, Prime Minister of Jamaica, 6 April 1973, box 5, file 2, AJG Papers.

27. Anthony Payne, *Politics in Jamaica* (New York: St. Martin's Press, 1994), 20.

28. Trevor Munroe, "From Marxist Study Groups to the Proletarian Vanguard," *World Marxist Review 23* (November 1980): 29; Payne, *Politics in Jamaica*, 20; AJG to Michael Manley, Prime Minister of Jamaica, 6 April 1973.

29. AJG to Michael Manley, 6 April 1973.

30. William Sherrill to AJG, 28 December 1957, and AJG to William Sherrill, 24 September 1957, box 3, file 4, AJG Papers; Jeannette Smith-Irvin, *Marcus Garvey's Footsoldiers of the Universal Negro Improvement Association* (Trenton, N.J.: African World Press, 1989), 85; AJG to T. A. McKay, 3 May 1957, box 5, file 2, AJG Papers.

31. William Sherrill to AJG, 7 January 1958, box 3, file 4, AJG Papers.

32. AJG, statement dated December 1962, box 5, file 13, and AJG to Ndugu Cecil Elombe Brath, Director, AJASS, 20 May 1970, box 2, file 2, ibid.

33. *Daily Gleaner*, 28 August 1963, announced that the book had been published.

34. Lerone Bennett Jr., "The Ghost of Marcus Garvey: Interviews with Crusader's Two Wives," *Ebony*, March 1960, 54.

35. The following names and organizations were featured on the circular letter in support of *Garvey and Garveyism*: Vivian Durham, London journalist; Jaja Nwokocha, Nigerian journalist; E. L. Allen, Minister of Education, Jamaica; H. P. Jacobs, *Daily Gleaner*; Henry Gorden, New York City; and *New Day* magazine. A copy of the letter is located in MG UNIA Collection, State Historical Society of Wisconsin.

36. AJG to Ndugu Cecil Elombe Brath, 29 May 1970, box 2, file 3, and AJG to Dr. Norman Hodges, 29 May 1970, box 3, file 2 AJG Papers.

37. B. A. Barker to L. A. Thoywell-Henry, 31 January 1946, and B. Gibbons to George Padmore, 23 February 1946, box 4, file 9, ibid.

38. Bennett, "The Ghost of Marcus Garvey," 54.

39. Ibid., 58, 54; Rupert Lewis, interview by author, Los Angeles, Calif., 18 February 1998.

40. AJG to Mr. Bennett, 6 May 1960, box 5, file 2, AJG Papers.

41. Lionel M. Yard, *Biography of Amy Ashwood Garvey, 1897–1969: Co-Founder of the UNIA* (Washington, D.C.: Associated Publisher, 1990), 208.

42. AJG to Hon. Alexander Bustamante, 21 October 1965, box 4, file 11, AJG Papers.

43. Rupert Lewis interview, 18 February 1998; AJG to Hon. Alexander Bustamante, 21 October 1965.

44. Gordon K. Lewis, *Growth of the Modern West Indies*, 176; W. A. Domingo, "Garvey," *Public Opinion*, 9 October 1964; W. A. Domingo, "Evaluating Garvey," *Daily Gleaner*, 12 October 1964; V. L. Arnett, "Garvey," *Public Opinion*, 30 October 1964; AJG, *Public Opinion*, 23, 28 October 1964; AJG, "Garvey's Activities for Jamaicans," *Daily Gleaner*, 7, 9 November 1964.

45. "Son, 3 Govt. Ministers Look at His Face," *Daily Gleaner*, 12 November 1964.

46. AJG, "The Re-Interment of the Body of Marcus Garvey in Jamaica West Indies," box 4, file 11, AJG Papers.

47. Stokely Carmichael and Charles V. Hamilton, *Black Power: The Politics of Liberation in America* (New York: Vintage Books, 1967), 53; AJG, *Garvey and Garveyism* (London: Collier-Macmillan, Ltd., 1970), 312.

48. AJG to Dr. Fishel, 15 August 1966, box 1, file 4, AJG Papers; Akinsola Akiwowo, "Racialism and Shifts in the Mental Orientation of Black People in West Africa and the Americas, 1856 to 1956," *Phylon* 31 (1970): 264; Turner, "Historical Dialectics of Black Nationalist Movements in America," 173; AJG, *Garvey and Garveyism*, 307.

49. "Garvey First to Give Negroes Sense of Dignity-King," *Daily Gleaner*, 23 June 1965; AJG, *Garvey and Garveyism*, 308.

50. AJG, *Garvey and Garveyism*, 313, 309, 312, 307. AJG reprinted the pamphlet, *Black Power in America* (Kingston, Jamaica: Amy Jacques Garvey, 1968), in the epilogue of *Garvey and Garveyism* (1970 ed.).

51. See AJG, "Is Religion a Spent Force?," *Daily Gleaner*, 19 January 1969; AJG, "Is Materialism Crushing Truth?," *Public Opinion*, 11 April 1969; AJG, "A Widow's Portrait of Marcus Mosiah Garvey," *Negro Digest*, May 1969; AJG, "Economic Straight Jacket of Black Jamaicans" (1970), box 5, file 1, "American Blunders in Asia and Africa" (1970), box 5, file 11, and "Does the Mind of Mankind Determine the Trend of Civilization?" (1969), box 14, file 1, all in AJG Papers.

52. Robert Hill to AJG, 21 May 1970, box 2, file 3, AJG Papers.

53. AJG to Dr. Kenneth Clarke, 9 May 1970, ibid.

54. Ibid.; AJG to Dr. Kenneth Clarke, 19 May 1970, box 2, file 2, AJG Papers. I was unable to locate AJG's reply in which she stated her "stand and opinion on certain aspects of this matter."

55. AJG received telephone calls from Joy Elliott of Washington, D.C., Benton Arnowits of Macmillan/Collier Books, Shirley Hunter, John Henrik Clark, Robert Hill, and Dr. Vincent Harding. AJG to Dr. Kenneth Clarke, 9 May 1970, box 2, file 3, AJG Papers.

56. "Papers Found in Harlem Were Not Lost," *Daily Gleaner,* 10 July 1970.

57. AJG to Dr. Vincent Harding, 7 September 1970, box 3, file 1, and AJG to Ndugo Cecil Elombe Brath, 20 May 1970, box 32, file 3, AJG Papers. Rupert Lewis confirmed that she still experienced some financial hardship in the last years of her life. Rupert Lewis interview, 18 February 1998.

58. AJG to Ndugu Cecil Elombe Brath, 20 May 1970.

59. Smith-Irvine, *Marcus Garvey's Footsoldiers,* 85.

60. See Theodore G. Vincent, *Black Power in the Garvey Movement* (San Francisco: Ramparts Press, 1971); John Henrik Clarke, *Marcus Garvey and the Vision of Africa* (New York: Random House, 1974); Gordon K. Lewis, *Growth of the Modern West Indies.*

61. See Ida B. Wells-Barnett with Alfred Duster, ed., *Crusade for Justice: The Autobiography of Ida B. Wells* (Chicago: University of Chicago Press, 1970), 365, 374, 382, 395, 414.

62. John A. Aarons, "Recognizing Excellence: The Musgrave Medals of the Institute of Jamaica," *Jamaica Journal 22* (May–June 1989): 19–23; "Musgrave Medals Presented to Seven," *Daily Gleaner,* 8 May 1971; Newsletter of the College of Arts, Science, and Technology (CAST), 19 June 1970, box 5, file 8, AJG Papers.

63. AJG to Hon. Michael Manley, Prime Minister of Jamaica, 6 April 1973, box 5, file 4, AJG Papers.

64. AJG, *Why Mrs. Garvey Refused the $6,800 Pension* (Mona, Jamaica: Student Union, UWI, 1973). This pamphlet is located in the Special Collections Unit of the University of West Indies (UWI), Jamaica.

65. Ibid.

66. Rupert Lewis, "AJG: A Political Portrait," *Jamaican Daily News,* 29 July 1973.

67. Ibid.

Conclusion
1. AJG to Nnamdi Azikiwe, 24 October 1944, box 1, file 2, AJG Papers.

SELECTED BIBLIOGRAPHY

Archives

Accra, Ghana
  Ghana Balme Library
Cleveland, Ohio
  Western Reserve Historical Society
    Universal Negro Improvement Association Papers, 1921–86
Kingston, Jamaica
  National Library of Jamaica
    Amy Ashwood Garvey Collection MS 1977B
Madison, Wisconsin
  State Historical Society of Wisconsin
Mona, Jamaica
  University of West Indies
    Special Collections Unit
Nashville, Tennessee
  Fisk University Special Collections
    Amy Jacques Garvey Papers
    Marcus Garvey Memorial Collection
New Haven, Connecticut
  Sterling Library, Yale University
    Microfilm Collections, Manuscripts and Archives
      W. E. B. Du Bois Papers
New York, New York
  Schomburg Center Special Collections Unit
    David Levering Lewis Collection, "Voices from the Renaissance Transcripts"
Spanish Town, Jamaica
  Spanish Town Archives
Suitland, Maryland
  National Archives
    Marcus Garvey Decimal File 800.4016/19

Washington, D.C.
    Federal Bureau of Investigation Reading Room
        Marcus Garvey Collection, 6 books
    National Archives—Northeast Region
        Index of Passenger Manifests
            Naturalization Petitions

Pamphlets

Garvey, Amy Jacques. *Black Power in America*. Kingston, Jamaica: Amy Jacques
    Garvey, 1968.
——. *Memorandum Correlative of Africa, the West Indies, and the Americas*.
    Kingston, Jamaica, May 1944.
——. *Why Mrs. Garvey Refused the $6,800 Pension*. Mona, Jamaica: Student
    Union, UWI, 1973.
Ghana Institute of Languages Admission Guide. Accra, n.d.
Hamilton, Marlene. *Wolmers Alumni Association of the U.S.A.: Wolmers, 1729–
    1979*. Souvenir Program, 1979.
*Respect for Human Dignity: An Inaugural Address Delivered by His Excellence Dr.
    Nnamdi Azikiwe: Governor-General and Commander-in-Chief*. University of
    Ghana Balme Library, Accra, Ghana, 16 November 1960.
Wolmers School, Kingston. *Wolmers Bicentenary Souvenir, 1729–1929*. Kingston,
    Jamaica: Committee, 1929.

Reports, Proceedings, and Court Records

Marcus Garvey v. Amy Ashwood Garvey, Supreme Court of New York County,
    no. 24028, NNHR, 15 July 1920.
Mortimer, Delores M., and Roy S. Bryce-Laporte, eds. *Female Immigrants to the
    United States: Caribbean, Latin America, and African Experiences*. Washington,
    D.C.: Smithsonian Institution, RIIES Occasional Papers No. 2, 1981.
Proceedings and Papers of the Georgia Association of Historians 10 (1989).
U.S. Congress. House. Committee on Immigration and Nationalization. Report.
    71st Cong., 2d sess., 1930. H. Doc. 898, 2 pts.
U.S. Department of Commerce. Bureau of Foreign and Domestic Commerce.
    Statistical Abstract of the United States, 1919. Washington, D.C.: GPO, 1920.
——. Bureau of the Census. *Fourteenth Census of the United States Taken in the
    Year 1920, Volume 2: Population, Reports by States, New York*. Washington,
    D.C.: GPO, 1923.
U.S. Department of State. *Foreign Relations of the United States, 1941*. Vol. 1,
    Diplomatic Papers: General and the Soviet Union. Washington, D.C.: GPO,
    1958.
——. *Foreign Relations of the United States, 1942*. Vol. 2, *Europe*. Washington,
    D.C.: GPO, 1962.

———. *Foreign Relations of the United States, 1942.* Vol. 4, *The Near East and Africa.* Washington, D.C.: GPO, 1963.

Yearbook of the United Nations, 1946–1947. New York: Department of Public Information, United Nations, 1947.

Interviews

Rupert Lewis. Interview by author. Los Angeles, 1998.

Mrs. Ida Repole. Interview by author. Kingston and Mona, Jamaica, November 1990.

Newspapers and Journals

The African
Afro-American
Amsterdam News
Blackman
Black Man: A Monthly Magazine of Negro Thought and Opinion
Crisis
Crusader
Daily Gleaner
Ghanian Times
Jamaican Daily News
Negro World
New Ashanti Times
New Jamaican
New York Age
New York Times
Public Opinion
The Times
West African Opinion
West African Pilot

Books

Adi, Hakim. *West Africans in Britain, 1900–1960: Nationalism, Pan-Africanism, and Communism.* London: Lawrence and Wishart, 1998.

Anderson, Benedict. *Imagined Communities: Reflections on the Origins and Spread of Nationalism.* London: Verso, 1983.

Anderson, James D. *The Education of Blacks in the South, 1860–1935.* Chapel Hill: University of North Carolina Press, 1988.

Anderson, Karen. *Wartime Women: Sex Roles, Family Relations, and the Status of Women during World War II.* Westport, Conn.: Greenwood Press, 1981.

Asante, Molefi Kete. *Kemet, Afrocentricity, and Knowledge.* Trenton, N.J.: African World Press, 1990.

Austin, Diane. *Urban Life in Kingston, Jamaica: The Culture and Class Ideology of Two Neighborhoods.* New York: Cordon and Breach Science Publishers, 1984.

Azikiwe, Nnamdi. *My Odyssey: An Autobiography.* New York: Praeger, 1970.

Baker, Houston A., Manthia Diawara, and Ruth H. Lindeborg, eds. *Black British Cultural Studies: A Reader.* Chicago: University of Chicago Press, 1996.

Balibar, Etienne, and Immanuel Wallerstein. *Race, Nation, Class: Ambiguous Identities.* London: Verso, 1991.

Barnett, Ida B. Wells. *Crusade for Justice: The Autobiography of Ida B. Wells.* Chicago: University of Chicago Press, 1970.

Belay, Carol Aisha Blackshire, ed. *The African-German Experience: Critical Essays.* London: Praeger, 1996.

Bell, Wendell. *Jamaican Leaders: Political Attitudes in a New Nation.* Berkeley: University of California Press, 1964.

Bispham, William. *Malaria: Its Diagnosis, Treatment, and Prophylaxis.* Baltimore: Wm and Wilkins Co., 1944.

Black, Clinton. *The Story of Jamaica: From Prehistory to the Present.* London: Collins, 1965.

Blee, Kathleen. *Women of the Klan: Racism and Gender in the 1920s.* Berkeley: University of California Press, 1991.

Bolles, Lynn A. *Sister Jamaica: A Study of Women, Work, and Households in Kingston.* New York: University Press of America, 1996.

Brathwaite, Edward. *The Development of Creole Society in Jamaica, 1770–1820.* Oxford: Clarendon Press, 1971.

Brody, Miriam. *Manly Writing: Gender, Rhetoric, and the Rise of Composition.* Carbondale: Southern Illinois Press, 1993.

Brown, Aggrey. *Color, Class, and Politics in Jamaica.* New Brunswick, N.J.: Transaction Books, 1979.

Burkett, Randall K. *Garveyism as a Religious Movement: The Institutionalization of a Black Civil Religion.* Metuchen, N.J.: Scarecrow Press, 1978.

Burleigh, Michael, and Wolfgang Wipperman. *The Racial State: Germany, 1933–1945.* Cambridge: Cambridge University Press, 1991.

Byerman, Keith E. *Seizing the Word: History, Art, and Self in the Work of W. E. B. Du Bois.* Athens: University of Georgia Press, 1994.

Carby, Hazel V. *Reconstructing Womanhood: The Emergence of the Afro-American Woman Novelist.* New York: Oxford University Press, 1987.

Carmichael, Stokely, and Charles Hamilton. *Black Power: The Politics of Liberation in America.* New York: Vintage Books, 1967.

Chadakoff, Rochelle, ed. *Eleanor Roosevelt's My Day: Her Acclaimed Columns, 1936–1945.* New York: Pharos Books, 1989.

Chatterjee, Partha. *The Nation and Its Fragments: Colonial and Postcolonial Histories.* Princeton, N.J.: Princeton University Press, 1993.

Chrisman, Robert, and Nathan Hare, eds. *Pan-Africanism*. New York: Bobbs-Merrill, 1974.

Clarke, John Henrik. *Marcus Garvey and the Vision of Africa*. New York: Random House, 1974.

Cogan, Frances B. *All-American Girl: The Ideal of Real Womanhood in Mid-Nineteenth-Century America*. Athens: University of Georgia Press, 1989.

Cook, Gordon, ed. *Manson's Tropical Disease*. London: W. B. Saunders Co., Ltd., 1996.

Cooper, Anna Julia. *A Voice from the South*. New York: Oxford University Press, 1988.

Cronon, David. *Black Moses: The Story of Marcus Garvey and the Universal Negro Improvement Association*. Madison: University of Wisconsin Press, 1969.

Cumper, G. E., ed. *The Economy of the West Indies*. Kingston, Jamaica: Institute of Social and Economic Research, 1960.

Cundall, Frank. *Historic Jamaica*. London: Institute of Jamaica, 1915.

Davidson, Basil. *Black Star: A View of the Life and Times of Kwame Nkrumah*. Boulder, Colo.: Westview Press, 1989.

Davies, Carole Boyce. *Black Women, Writing, and Identity: Migrations of the Subject*. New York: Routledge, 1994.

DeLisser, H. G. *Twentieth Century Jamaica*. Kingston: Jamaican Times, 1913.

Dewitte, Phillipe. *Les Mouvements Negres en France, 1919–1930*. Paris: Editions L' Harmattan, 1985.

Du Bois, W. E. B. *Color and Democracy: Colonies and Peace*. New York: Harcourt, Brace, 1945.

——. *Dusk of Dawn*. New York: Kraus Thomson Organization, Ltd., 1975.

——. *The Education of Black People: Ten Critiques, 1906–1960*. Amherst: University of Massachusetts Press, 1973.

Dutt, R. Palme. *Fascism and Social Revolution*. New York: International Publishers, 1934.

Eisner, Gisela. *Jamaica, 1830–1930: A Study in Economic Growth*. London: Manchester University Press, 1961.

Ellison, Ralph. *Shadow and Acts*. New York: Vintage Books, 1972.

Emilo, John D., and Estelle B. Freeman. *Intimate Matters: A History of Sexuality in America*. New York: Harper and Row, 1988.

Enloe, Cynthia. *Bananas, Beaches, and Bases: Making Feminist Sense of International Politics*. Los Angeles: Pandora Press, 1989.

Eppier, Karen Sanchez. *Touching Liberty: Abolition, Feminism, and the Politics of the Body*. Berkeley: University of California Press, 1993.

Eshleman, Clayton, and Annette Smith, eds. *Aimé Césaire: The Collected Poetry*. Berkeley: University of California Press, 1983.

Essien-Udom, E. U., and Amy Jacques Garvey, eds. *More Philosophy and Opinions of Marcus Garvey*. Great Britain: Frank Cass, 1977.

Farson, Negley. *Behind God's Back*. New York: Harcourt, Brace, 1941.

Fax, Elton C. *Garvey: The Story of a Pioneer Black Nationalist*. New York: Dodd, Mead, 1972.

Fetter, Bruce, ed. *Colonial Rule in Africa: Readings from Primary Sources*. Madison: University of Wisconsin Press, 1979.

Foner, Nancy. *Status and Power in Rural Jamaica: A Study of Educational and Political Change*. New York: Teachers College Press, 1973.

Ford, James W. *The Negro People and the New World Situation*. New York: Workers Library Publications, 1941.

French, Joan, and Honor Ford-Smith. *Women, Work, and Organization in Jamaica, 1900–1944*. Mona, Jamaica: Sistern Research Institute of Social Science, 1986.

Gaines, Kevin K. *Uplifting the Race: Black Leadership, Politics, and Culture in the Twentieth Century*. Chapel Hill: University of North Carolina Press, 1996.

Garland, Anne Witte. *Women Activists Challenging the Abuse of Power*. New York: Feminist Press, 1988.

Garside, W. R. *British Unemployment, 1919–1939: A Study in Public Policy*. Cambridge: Cambridge University Press, 1990.

Gibbs, David N. *The Political Economy of Third World Intervention: Mines, Money, and U.S. Policy in the Congo Crisis*. Chicago: University of Chicago, 1991.

Gilmore, Glenda Elizabeth. *Gender and Jim Crow: Women and the Politics of White Supremacy in North Carolina, 1896–1920*. Chapel Hill: University of North Carolina Press, 1996.

Gilroy, Paul. *The Black Atlantic: Modernity and Double Consciousness*. Cambridge: Harvard University Press, 1993.

Glenn, Evelyn Nakano, Grace Chang, and Linda Rennie Forcey. *Mothering: Ideology, Experience, and Agency*. New York: Routledge, 1994.

Glueck, Sheldon, and Eleanor Glueck. *Family Environment and Delinquency*. Boston: Houghton Mifflin, 1962.

Goodrich, Leland M. *The United Nations in a Changing World*. New York: Columbia University Press, 1974.

Gordon, Lewis K. *The Growth of the Modern West Indies*. New York: Monthly Review Press, 1968.

Griffin, Farah J., and Cheryl J. Fisher, eds. *A Stranger in the Village: Two Centuries of African-American Traveling Writing*. Boston: Beacon Press, 1998.

Gross, Gerald, ed. *Editors and Editing: What Writers Need to Know about What Editors Do*. New York: Grove Press, 1993.

Harris, Joseph E., ed. *Global Dimensions of the African Diaspora*. Washington, D.C.: Howard University Press, 1982.

Helly, Dorothy O., and Susan M. Reverby, eds. *Gender Domains: Rethinking Public and Private in Women's History*. Ithaca, N.Y.: Cornell University Press, 1992.

Herf, Jeffrey. *Reactionary Modernism: Technology, Culture, and Politics in Weimar and the Third Reich.* Cambridge: Cambridge University Press, 1984.

Hewitt, Nancy, and Suzanne Lebsock, eds. *Invisible Women: New Essays on American Activism.* Urbana: University of Illinois Press, 1993.

Hickney, Neil, and Ed Edwin. *Adam Clayton Powell and the Politics of Race.* New York: Fleet Publishing Corp., 1965.

Higginbotham, Evelyn Brooks. *Righteous Discontent: The Women's Movement in the Black Baptist Church, 1880–1920.* Cambridge: Harvard University Press, 1993.

Higman, B. W. *Slave Population of the British Caribbean, 1807–1834.* Baltimore: Johns Hopkins University Press, 1984.

Hill, Frank. *Bustamante and His Letters.* Kingston, Jamaica: Kingston Publishing, Ltd., 1976.

Hill, Robert A., ed. *Marcus Garvey and the Universal Negro Improvement Association Papers.* 7 vols. Los Angeles: University of California Press, 1983–86, 1989–90.

Hill, Robert, and Barbara Bair, eds. *Marcus Garvey: Life and Lessons: A Centennial Companion to the Marcus Garvey and UNIA Papers.* Los Angeles: University of California Press, 1987.

Holt, Thomas. *The Problem of Freedom: Race, Labor, and Politics in Jamaica and Britain, 1832–1938.* Baltimore: Johns Hopkins University Press, 1992.

Hooker, James R. *Black Revolutionary: George Padmore's Path from Communism to Pan-Africanism.* New York: Praeger, 1967.

Horne, Gerald. *Black and Red: W. E. B. Du Bois and the Afro-American Response to the Cold War, 1944–1963.* New York: State University of New York Press, 1986.

——. *Black Liberation/Red Scare: Ben Davis and the Communist Party.* Newark, N.J.: University of Delaware Press, 1994.

Hunter, Tera. *To Joy My Freedom: Southern Black Women's Lives and Labors after the Civil War.* Cambridge: Harvard University Press, 1997.

Hurwitz, Samuel J., and Edith F. Hurwitz, *Jamaica: A Historical Portrait.* New York: Praeger, 1971.

Irish, Donald, Kathleen Lundquist, and Vivian Nelson, eds. *Ethnic Variations in Dying, Death, and Grief: Diversity in Universality.* London: Taylor and Francis, 1993.

Irvin-Smith, Jeannette. *Marcus Garvey's Footsoldiers of the Universal Negro Improvement Association.* Trenton, N.J.: African World Press, 1989.

Jacobs, H. P. *A Short History of Kingston: Vol. 1, 1692–1871.* Kingston, Jamaica: Ministry of Education, 1976.

Jacques Garvey, Amy. *Garvey and Garveyism.* Memoir. London: Collier-Macmillan, Ltd., 1963, 1970.

——, ed. *The Philosophy and Opinions of Marcus Garvey; Or, Africa for the Africans.* 1923, 1925. Reprint, Dover, Mass.: Majority Press, 1986.

Jaffee, Julian F. *Crusade against Radicalism: New York during the Red Scare, 1914–1924.* Port Washington, N.Y.: Kennikat Press, 1972.

James, C. L. R. *Nkrumah and the Ghana Revolution.* Westport, Conn.: Lawrence Hill and Co., 1977.

James, Joy. *Transcending the Talented Tenth: Black Leaders and American Intellectuals.* New York: Routledge, 1997.

James, Winston. *Holding Aloft the Banner of Ethopia: Caribbean Radicalism in Early Twentieth-Century America.* London: Verso Press, 1998.

Johnston, Sir Harry S. *The Negro in the New World.* New York: Macmillan, 1910.

Jones, Beverly Washington. *Quest for Equality: The Life and Writings of Mary Eliza Church Terrell, 1883–1954.* Brooklyn, N.Y.: Carlson Publishers, 1990.

Jones, Claudia. *Jim-Crow in Uniform.* New York: New Age Publishers, 1940.

Jones, Jacqueline. *Labor of Love, Labor of Sorrow: Black Women, Work, and the Family, from Slavery to the Present.* New York: Vintage Books, 1985.

Kalish, Richard A., and David K. Reynolds. *Death and Ethnicity: A Psychocultural Study.* Los Angeles: University of Southern California Press, 1967.

Kelley, Mary. *Private Woman, Public Stage: Literary Domesticity in Nineteenth-Century America.* New York: Oxford University Press, 1984.

Kerr, Madeline. *Personality and Conflict in Jamaica.* Liverpool, U.K.: University Press, 1952.

Kimmel, Michael. *Manhood in America: A Cultural History.* New York: Free Press, 1996.

Knupfer, Anne Meis. *Toward a Tender Humanity and a Nobler Womanhood.* New York: New York University Press, 1996.

Kornweibel, Theodore, ed. *Federal Surveillance of Afro Americans, 1917–1925: The First World War, the Red Scare, the Garvey Movement.* Frederick, Md.: University Publications of America, 1986.

Larrabee, Eric. *Commander in Chief: Franklin Delano Roosevelt, His Lieutenants, and Their War.* New York: Harper and Row, 1987.

Lester, Julius, ed. *The Seventh Son: The Thought and Writings of W. E. B. Du Bois.* 2 vols. New York: Random House, 1971.

Lewis, Paula Gilbert, ed. *Traditionalism, Nationalism, and Feminism: Women Writers of Quebec.* Westport, Conn.: Greenwood Press, 1985.

Lewis, Rupert. *Marcus Garvey: Anti-Colonial Champion.* Trenton, N.J.: African World Press, 1988.

Lewis, Rupert, and Patrick Bryan, eds. *Garvey: His Work and Impact.* Mona, Jamaica: Institute of Social and Economic Research, 1988.

Loewenheim, Francis, Harold Langley, and Manfred Jonas, eds. *Roosevelt and Churchill: Their Secret Wartime Correspondence.* New York: Saturday Review Press, 1975.

Lorde, Audre. *Sister Outsider: Essays and Speeches.* Freedom, Calif.: Crossing Press, 1984.

Lunden, Walter A. *Statistics on Delinquents and Delinquency.* Springfield, Ill.: Charles C. Thomas, Publishers, 1964.

Marable, Manning. *Race, Reform, and Rebellion: The Second Reconstruction.* Jackson: University of Mississippi Press, 1991.

Margolis, Otto S., ed. *Loss, Grief, and Bereavement.* New York: Praeger, 1985.

Margolis, Simeon, ed. *Johns Hopkins Symptoms and Remedies.* New York: Rebus, Random House, 1995.

Marks, Carole. *Farewell—We're Good and Gone: The Great Black Migration.* Bloomington: Indiana University Press, 1989.

Martin, Tony. *Race First: The Ideological and Organizational Struggles of Marcus Garvey and the Universal Negro Improvement Association.* Westport, Conn.: Greenwood Press, 1976.

McElvaine, Robert S., ed. *Down and Out in the Great Depression: Letters from the Forgotten Man.* Chapel Hill: University of North Carolina Press, 1983.

McFreely, William S. *Frederick Douglass.* New York: Norton, 1991.

McKay, Claude. *A Long Way from Home.* New York: Arno Press, 1969.

McKay, Vernon. *Africa in World Politics.* New York: Harper and Row, 1963.

Mitchell, Paul, ed. *Race Riots in Black and White.* Englewood Cliffs, N.J.: Prentice-Hall, 1970.

Mosse, George L. *The Image of Man: The Creation of Modern Masculinity.* New York: Oxford University Press, 1996.

———. *Nationalism and Sexuality: Respectability and Abnormal Sexuality in Modern Europe.* New York: Howard Fertig, 1985.

Moulton, Forest Ray, ed. *Human Malaria.* Washington, D.C.: American Association for Advancement of Science, 1941.

Naison, Mark. *Communists in Harlem during the Depression.* New York: Grove Press, 1983.

Nelson, C., and L. Grossbert, eds. *Marxism and the Interpretation of Culture.* Urbana: University of Illinois Press, 1988.

Nettleford, Rex M. *Mirror, Mirror: Identity, Race, and Protest in Jamaica.* Jamaica: William Collins and Sangster, 1970.

Nicolson, I. F. *The Administration of Nigeria, 1900 to 1960: Men, Methods, and Myths.* Oxford: Clarendon Press, 1969.

Nkrumah, Kwame. *The Autobiography.* London: Panaf Books, 1957.

Nocht, Bernard, and Martin Mayer. *Malaria: A Handbook of Treatment, Parasitology, and Prevention.* London: John Bale Medical Publishers, 1937.

O'Reilly, Kenneth. *Racial Matters: The FBI's Secret File on Black America, 1960–1972.* New York: Free Press, 1989.

Ottley, Roi. *New World a-Coming.* New York: Literary Classics, Inc., 1943.

Padmore, George, ed. *History of the Pan-African Congress.* London: Hammersmith Bookstore, Ltd., 1947.

Parker, Andrew, Mary Russo, Doris Sommer, and Patricia Yeager, eds. *Nationalism and Sexualities*. New York: Routledge, 1992.

Payne, Anthony. *Politics in Jamaica*. New York: St. Martin's Press, 1994.

Pierson, Donald. *Negroes in Brazil: A Study of Race Contact at Bahia*. Carbondale: Southern Illinois University Press, 1967.

Plummer, Brenda Gayle. *Rising Wind: Black Americans and U.S. Foreign Affairs, 1935–1960*. Chapel Hill: University of North Carolina Press, 1996.

Post, Ken. *Arise Ye Starvelings: The Jamaican Labour Rebellion of 1938 and Its Aftermath*. London: Martinus Nijhoff, 1978.

Powell, Adam Clayton, Jr. *Adam by Adam*. New York: Dail Press, 1971.

Reid, Ira De A. *The Negro Immigrant: His Background, Characteristics, and Social Adjustment, 1899–1937*. Ca. 1939. Reprint, New York: Arno Press, 1969.

Roberts, George W., and Sonja A. Sinclair. *Women in Jamaica: Patterns of Reproduction and Family*. New York: KTO Press, 1978.

Robertson, Sir James. *Transition in Africa: From Direct Rule to Independence*. New York: Harper and Row, 1974.

Rodney, Walter. *How Europe Underdeveloped Africa*. London: Bogle-L'Ouverture Pub., 1972.

Rogers, J. A. *Sex and Race*. Vol. 1, *Negro-Caucasian Mixing in All Ages and All Lands*. St. Petersburg, Fla.: Helga M. Rogers, 1968.

——. *World's Great Men of Color*. Vol. 2. New York: J. A. Rogers, 1947.

Rossi, Peter H., ed. *Ghetto Revolts*. New Brunswick, N.J.: Aldine, 1973.

Russel, Paul. *Malaria: Basic Principles Briefly Stated*. Oxford: Scientific Publishers, 1952.

Salem, Dorothy. *To Better Our World: Black Women in Organized Reform, 1890–1920*. Brooklyn, N.Y.: Carlson Publishers, 1990.

Senior, Olive. *Working Miracles: Women's Lives in the English-Speaking Caribbean*. Mona, Jamaica: Institute of Social and Economic Research, 1991.

Shaw, Stephanie. *What a Woman Ought to Be and to Do: Black Professional Women Workers during the Jim Crow Era*. Chicago: University of Chicago Press, 1996.

Shepherd, Verene, Bridget Brereton, and Barbara Bailey, eds. *Engendering History: Caribbean Women in Historical Perspective*. New York: St. Martin's Press, 1995.

Sowell, Thomas, ed. *Essays on Data on American Ethnic Groups*. Washington, D.C.: Urban Institute, 1978.

Standing, Guy. *Unemployment and Female Labour: A Study of Labour Supply in Kingston, Jamaica*. New York: St. Martin's Press, 1981.

Steady, Filomina, ed. *The Black Woman Cross-Culturally*. Cambridge, Mass.: Schenkman, 1981.

Steeves, Harrison Ross. *Learned Societies and English Literary Scholarship: In Great Britain and the United States*. New York: AMS Press, 1970.

Stein, Judith. *The World of Marcus Garvey: Race and Class in Modern Society*. Baton Rouge: Louisiana State University Press, 1986.

Stephens, Evelyne Huber, and John D. Stephens. *Democratic Socialism in Jamaica: The Political Movement and Social Transformation in Dependent Capitalism.* London: Macmillan, 1986.

Stone, Carl. *Class, Race, and Political Behavior in Urban Jamaica.* Mona, Jamaica: Institute of Social and Economic Research, 1973.

Stovall, Tyler. *Paris Noir: African Americans in the City of Lights.* New York: Houghton Mifflin, 1996.

Thompson, Mildred I. *Ida B. Wells-Barnett: An Exploration Study of an American Black Woman, 1893–1930.* Brooklyn, N.Y.: Carlson, Publishers, 1990.

Thompson, R. W. *Black Caribbean.* London: Macdonald and Co., 1946.

Thompson, Scott W. *Ghana's Foreign Policy, 1957–1966: Diplomacy, Ideology, and the New State.* Princeton, N.J.: Princeton University Press, 1969.

Verbrugge, Martha H. *Able-Bodied Womanhood: Personal Health and Social Change in Nineteenth-Century Boston.* New York: Oxford University Press, 1988.

Vincent, Theodore G. *Black Power and the Garvey Movement.* San Francisco: Ramparts Press, 1971.

——. *Voices of a Black Nation: Political Journalism in the Harlem Renaissance.* San Francisco: Ramparts Press, 1973.

Von Eschen, Penny M. *Race against Empire: Black Americans and Anticolonialism, 1937–1957.* Ithaca, N.Y.: Cornell University Press, 1997.

Wade, Craig Wyn. *The Fiery Cross: The Ku Klux Klan in America.* New York: Simon and Schuster, 1987.

Wallace, Nancy. *Better Than School: One Family's Declaration of Independence.* New York: Larson, 1983.

Ward, Margaret. *Unmanageable Revolutionaries: Women and Irish Nationalism.* London: Pluto Press, 1983.

Washburn, Patrick S. *A Question of Sedition: The Federal Government's Investigation of the Black Press during World War II.* New York: Oxford University Press, 1986.

Watkins-Owen, Irma. *Blood Relations: Caribbean Immigrants and the Harlem Community, 1900–1930.* Bloomington: University of Indiana Press, 1996.

Watts, David. *The West Indies: Patterns of Development, Culture, and Environmental Change since 1942.* London: Cambridge University Press, 1987.

Watts, Jill. *Shout the Victory: The History of Father Divine and the Peace Mission Movement, 1879–1942.* Los Angeles: University of California Press, 1989.

Waugh, Alec. *Love and the Caribbean: Tales, Character, and Scenes of the West Indies.* New York: Farrar, Straus and Cudahy, 1958.

Weiss, Penny A., and Marilyn Friedman, eds. *Feminism and Community.* Philadelphia: Temple University Press, 1995.

West, Lois A., ed. *Feminist Nationalism.* New York: Routledge, 1997.

White, Deborah Gray. *Ar'n't I a Woman.* New York: Norton, 1985.

——. *Too Heavy a Load: Black Women in Defense of Themselves.* New York: Norton, 1999.

White, Walter. *A Man Called White: The Autobiography of Walter White.* New York: Viking, 1948.

——. *A Rising Wind.* 1945. Reprint, Westport, Conn.: Negro University Press, 1971.

Whyte, Millicent. *A Short History of Education in Jamaica.* London: Hodder and Stoughton, 1977.

Williams, Brackette F., ed. *Women out of Place: The Gender of Agency and the Race of Nationality.* New York: Routledge, 1996.

Wright, Richard. *Black Power: A Record of Reactions in a Land of Pathos.* New York: Harper and Brothers, 1954.

Yard, Lionel M. *Biography of Amy Ashwood Garvey, 1897–1969: Co-Founder of the UNIA.* Washington, D.C.: Associated Publisher, 1990.

Articles and Dissertations

Aarons, John A. "Recognizing Excellence: The Musgrave Medals of the Institute of Jamaica." *Jamaica Journal* 22 (May–June 1989): 19–23.

Barnes, Natasha B. "Face of the Nation: Race, Nationalism, and Identities in Jamaican Beauty Pageants." *Massachusetts Review* (Autumn–Winter 1994): 471–92.

Bartrop, Paul. "From Lisbon to Jamaica: A Study of British Refugee Rescue during the Second World War." *Immigrants & Minorities* (1994): 48–64.

Becker, Gary S. "A Theory of Social Interactions." *Journal of Political Economy* 82 (1974): 1063–93.

Beckman, Marlene D. "The White Slave Traffic Act: The Historical Impact of a Criminal Law Policy on Women." *Georgetown Law Journal* 72 (1984): 1111–42.

Bennett, Lerone, Jr. "The Ghost of Marcus Garvey: Interviews with Crusader's Two Wives." *Ebony*, March 1960, 54.

Bowlby, J. "Processes of Mourning." *International Journal of Psychoanalysis* 42 (1961): 317–40.

Bradley, C. Paul. "Mass Parties in Jamaica: Structure and Organization." *Social and Economic Studies* 9 (December 1960): 375–416.

Brodber, Erna. "Afro-Jamaican Women at the Turn of the Century." *Social and Economic Studies* 35 (September 1986): 23–50.

Burke, A. W. "A Cross Cultural Study of Delinquency among West Indian Boys." *International Journal of Social Psychiatry* 26 (1980): 81–87.

Cook, Mercer. "The Negro Knows Fascism." *Free World*, November 1942, 147–50.

Cooper, Carolyn. "Race and the Cultural Politics of Self-Representation: A View from the University of the West Indies." *Research in African Literatures* 27 (Winter 1996): 97–106.

Cunningham, Michael R., Alan R. Roberts, Anita P. Barbee, Perrie B. Druen, and Cheng-Huan Wu. "Their Ideas of Beauty Are, on the Whole, the Same as Ours: Consistency and Variability in the Cross-Cultural Perception of Female Physical Attractiveness." *Journal of Personality and Social Psychology* (February 1995): 261–80.

Egerton, John. "The Pre-Brown South." *Virginia Quarterly Review* 70 (Autumn 1994): 603–23.

Fawcett, Hon. W. "Tobacco in Jamaica." *West Indian Bulletin* (1907): 209–28.

Figueroa, Mark. "The Formation and Framework of Middle Strata Leadership in Jamaica: The Crisis of the Seventies and Beyond." *Caribbean Studies: Puerto Rico* 21 (1988): 44–66.

Gadsden, Fay. "The African Press in Kenya, 1945–1952." *Journal of African History* 21 (1980): 515–35.

Gang, Lee, and Joseph Hraba. "Economic Reform in the Czech Republic: Economic Strain, Depression, Hostility, and the Difference in Coping Strategies." *Sociological Inquiry* (Winter 1994): 103–13.

Goin, Marcia Kraft, R. W. Burgoyne, and John M. Goin. "Timeless Attachment to a Dead Relative." *American Journal Psychiatry* 136 (July 1979): 988–89.

Grant, Ruth W., and Marion Orr. "Language, Race, and Politics: From 'Black' to 'African American.'" *Politics and Society* 24 (June 1996): 137–52.

Hall, Stuart. "Negotiating Caribbean Identities." *New Left Review* n. 209 (January–February 1995): 3–14.

Handa, Sudhanshu. "The Determinants of Female Headship in Jamaica: Results from a Structural Model." *Economic Development and Cultural Change* 44 (June 1996): 793–815.

Harris, Cheryl. "Finding Sojourner's Truth: Race, Gender, and the Institution of Property." *Cardozo Law Review* 18 (November 1996): 309–409.

Headrick, Rita. "African Soldiers in World War II." *Armed Forces and Society* (1978): 501–26.

Hedlin, Ethel Wolfskill. "Earnest Cox and Colonization: A White Racist's Response to Black Repatriation, 1923–1966." Ph.D. diss., Duke University, 1974.

Hellwig, David. "Black Meets Black: Afro-American Reactions to West Indian Immigrants in the 1920s." *South Atlantic Quarterly* 77 (1978): 206–24.

Holden, Calvin B. "The Causes and Composition of West Indian Immigration to New York City, 1900–1952." *Afro-Americans in New York Life and History* 2 (January 1987): 2–27.

Hoytt, Eleanor Hinton. "International Council of Women of the Darker Races: Historical Notes." *Sage* 3 (Fall 1986): 54–55.

Jacques Garvey, Amy. "The Role of Women in Liberation Struggles." *Massachusetts Review* (Winter–Spring 1972): 109–12.

Lewis, Ida. "Mrs. Marcus Garvey Talks with Ida Lewis." *Encore*, May 1973, 68.

Lewis, Rupert. "Amy Jacques Garvey: A Political Portrait." *Jamaica Daily News*, 29 July 1973.

Lewis, Rupert, and Maureen Warner-Lewis. "Amy Jacques Garvey." *Jamaica Journal* 20 (August–October 1987): 39–43.

Longo, Laura C., and Richard D. Ashmore. "The Looks-Personality Relationship: Global Self-Orientations as Shared Precursors of Subjective Physical Attractiveness and Self-Ascribed Traits." *Journal of Applied Social Psychology* (March 1995): 371–99.

Martin, Tony. "Amy Ashwood Garvey: Wife No. 1." *Jamaica Journal* 30 (August–October 1987): 32–36.

——. "Discovering African Roots: Amy Ashwood Garvey's Pan-Africanist Journey." *Comparative Studies of South Asia, Africa, and the Middle East* 17, no. 1 (1997): 118–26.

Mattingly, Carol. "Woman-Tempered Rhetoric: Public Presentation and the WCTU." *Rhetoric Review* 14 (Fall 1995): 44–61.

Morrissey, Carol Mae. "Ol' Time Tram and the Tramway Era, 1876–1948." *Jamaica Journal* 16 (November 1983): 12–21.

Munroe, Trevor, "From Marxist Study Groups to the Proletarian Vanguard." *World Marxist Review* 23 (November 1980): 28–32.

Pinsker, Thomson. "The Black Intellectuals' Common Fate and Uncommon Problems." *Virginia Quarterly Review* (Spring 1994): 220–38.

Porter, Dorothy B. "The Organized Educational Activities of Negro Literary Societies, 1828–1846." *Journal of Negro Education* (October 1936): 555–76.

Qinmei, Wang. "Africa Contributes to World War II Victory." *Beijing Review* 38 (15 June 1995): 19–20.

Reed, Beverly. "Amy Jacques Garvey: Black, Beautiful, and Free." *Ebony*, June 1971.

Sabatier, Peggy R. " 'Elite' Education in French West Africa: The Era of Limits, 1903–1945." *International Journal of African Historical Studies* 11 (1978): 247–66.

Salahu-Din, Sakinah N. "A Comparison of Coping Strategies of African American and Caucasian Widows." *Omega: Journal of Death and Dying* 33 (1996): 103–20.

Scott, Joan. "Gender: A Useful Category of Historical Analysis." *American Historical Review* 91 (December 1986): 1053–75.

Seraille, William. "Henrietta Vinton Davis and the Garvey Movement." *Afro-Americans in New York Life and History* 7 (July 1983): 7–24.

Sio, Arnold A. "Race, Color, and Miscegenation: The Free Colored of Jamaica and Barbados." *Caribbean Studies* 16 (April 1976): 5–21.

Smith, Terry. "Amy Jacques Garvey: Portrait of a Courageous Woman." *Jamaican Housewife*, Winter 1964, 23.

Springen, Karen. "Eyes of the Beholders." *Newsweek*, 3 June 1996, 68.

Taylor, Ula Y. "As-Salaam Alaikum, My Sister: The Honorable Elijah Muhammad and the Women Who Followed Him." *Race & Society* 1 (1998): 177–96.

Toney, Joyce. "The Perpetuation of a Culture of Migration: West Indian American Ties with Home, 1900–1979." *Afro-Americans in New York Life and History* 13 (January 1989): 39–55.

Turner, James E. "Historical Dialectics of Black Nationalist Movements in America." *Western Journal of Black Studies* 1 (September 1977): 164–83.

White, E. Frances. "Africa on My Mind: Gender, Counter Discourse, and African American Nationalism." *Journal of Women's History* 2 (1990): 73–97.

Williams, Michael W. "Marcus Garvey and Kwame Nkrumah: A Case of Ideological Assimilation, Advancement, and Refinement." *Western Journal of Black Studies* 7 (1983): 94–102.

Woolcock, Joseph. "Class Conflict and Class Reproduction: An Historical Analysis of the Jamaican Educational Reforms of 1957 and 1962." *Social and Economic Studies* 33 (December 1984): 51–99.

Worchester, Kent. "C. L. R. James and the Development of a Pan-African Problematic." *Journal of Caribbean History* 27 (1993): 54–80.

INDEX

Note: "Amy Jacques Garvey" is abbreviated "AJG" throughout the index.

GENDER & AMERICAN CULTURE